Visual Basic Controls

Control	Control Name	Control	Control Name
Pointer	Pointer	Data	Data
Text Box	Text Box	Data-Bound Combo	Data-Bound Combo
Check Box	Check Box	3D Check Box	3D Check Box
List Box	List Box	3D Panel	3D Panel
Timer	Timer	Tabbed Property List	Tabbed Property List
File List Box	File List Box	Image List	Image List
Image	Image	Label	Label
Data-Bound List	Data-Bound List	Command Button	Command Button
Spin Button	Spin Button	Combo Box	Combo Box
3D Command Button	3D Command Button	Vertical Scroll Bar	Vertical Scroll Bar
3D Group Push Button	3D Group Push Button	Directory List Box	Directory List Box
Grid	Grid	Line	Line
Picture Box	Picture Box	OLE	OLE
Frame	Frame	Common Dialog	Common Dialog
Option Button	Option Button	3D Frame	3D Frame
Horizontal Scroll Bar	Horizontal Scroll Bar	3D Option Button	3D Option Button
Drive List Box	Drive List Box	Data-Bound Grid	Data-Bound Grid
Shape	Shape	Communications	Communications

Basic Operators

Operator	Type	Description
^	Arithmetic	Raise a number to a power
*	Arithmetic	
/	Arithmetic	
\	Arithmetic	
+	Arithmetic	Sums two numbers
-	Arithmetic	Difference between two numbers
MOD	Arithmetic	Remainder of division of two numbers
&	Concatenation	Combine two strings
+	Concatenation	Combine two strings (not recommended)
AND	Logical	Conjunction of two expressions
NOT	Logical	Negation of an expression
EQV	Logical	Equivalence of two expressions
OR	Logical	Disjunction of two expressions
IMP	Logical	Implication of two expressions
XOR	Logical	Exclusion of two expressions
<	Comparison	Less than
<=	Comparison	Less than or equal to
>	Comparison	Greater than
>=	Comparison	Greater than or equal to
=	Comparison	Equal
<>	Comparison	Not equal to
IS	Comparison	Compare two object references
LIKE	Comparison	Compare two strings

Visual Basic File Extensions

Extension	Description
VBP	Project file
FRM	Form file
FRX	Binary data file
CLS	Class module
BAS	Standard module
VBX	VB extension file
OCX	OLE custom control file
RES	Resource file
EXE	Executable file

Essential Visual Basic 4

Mark Steven Heyman

SAMS
PUBLISHING

201 West 103rd Street
Indianapolis, IN 46290

This book is dedicated to the memory of my mother, Helen Heyman; and to Grace, whose love and constancy keep me online.

Copyright © 1995 by Sams Publishing

FIRST EDITION

International Standard Book Number: 0-672-30771-5

Library of Congress Catalog Card Number: 95-74774

98 97 96 95   4 3 2 1

Interpretation of the printing code: the rightmost double-digit number is the year of the book's printing; the rightmost single-digit, the number of the book's printing. For example, a printing code of 95-1 shows that the first printing of the book occurred in 1995.

Composed in AGaramond and MCPdigital by Macmillan Computer Publishing

Printed in the United States of America

Trademarks

Publisher and President *Richard K. Swadley*

Acquisitions Manager *Greg Weigand*

Development Manager *Dean Miller*

Managing Editor *Cindy Morrow*

Marketing Manager *Gregg Bushyeager*

Assistant Marketing Manager *Michelle Miner*

Acquisitions Editor
Bradley L. Jones

Development Editor
Anthony Amico

Production Editor
Anne Owen

Technical Reviewer
Alfonso Hermida

Editorial Coordinator
Bill Whitmer

Technical Edit Coordinator
Lynette Quinn

Formatter
Frank Sinclair

Editorial Assistant
Sharon Cox

Cover Designer
Jay Corpus

Book Designer
Alyssa Yesh

Production Team Supervisor
Brad Chinn

Page Layout
Carol Bowers, Terrie Deemer, Steph Mineart, Casey Price, Angelina Ward

Proofreading
Michael Brumitt, Mike Dietsch, Mike Henry, Kevin Laseau, Nancy Price, Brian-Kent Proffitt, SA Springer, Tim Taylor

Indexer
Charlotte Clapp

Overview

Contents

Acknowledgments

The author wishes to thank all the folks at Sams for the opportunity to write this book, and for their individual skills and professionalism in making it a reality. Special thanks are due to Brad Jones, acquisitions editor, who actually hit the cybernetic bricks in search of an author. Many thanks also to Tony Amico, development editor; Anne Owen, production editor; and Alfonso Hermida, technical editor. Their sharp eyes and thoughts were invaluable in keeping the author safe from his own occasionally blundering fingers and tied tongue.

About the Author

Mark Steven Heyman is the owner and founder of InfoPro Consulting Services, a computer consulting and training firm which has specialized in DOS and Windows database systems in Los Angeles, San Francisco, and Seattle for more than 13 years.

Mark lives under the volcano, in the woods and shadow of Mount Rainier in the state of Washington. He may be contacted via CompuServe (ID 76460,1705), the Internet (infopro@compumedia.com), or by FAX at (360) 893-2235.

Introduction

This book is for programmers, beginning or experienced, who want to develop Windows applications using Visual Basic 4.0. The idea here is to provide a no-nonsense approach to Windows programming, with plenty of here's-how examples, and without a great deal of lofty theory. In short, this book's approach is the programmer's approach: just show me how, and let me do it.

If this is your first stab at Windows programming, you'll find that the code you'll develop here is different from the monolithic, linear, continuous programs you might be used to. This is because Windows programs are *object-oriented* and *event-driven*, which means that your code will often be divided into snippets (blocks), attached to this button or that icon, to handle specific events, such as a keypress or mouse click. Also, this book may be unlike other programming books you've read in that much of what it covers has to do with using Visual Basic to "visually design" your software by actually "drawing" objects on your forms (windows). Therefore, you'll spend some time looking at and fiddling with windows on the screen, seeing what makes them tick.

Visual Basic provides an impressive array of programming resources, and this book is going to show you how to make the most of them. As mentioned, the focus here will be on *doing*, rather than *theorizing*; but a little theory will be necessary to get the ball rolling. You must be comfortable with a few important concepts involved in Visual Basic—concepts like objects, events, forms, controls, properties, methods, functions, and procedures. Therefore, the first section of the book will concentrate on these ideas, but there will be plenty of "doing" as well.

From then on, the book will be heavily task-oriented. As you'll see, many of the chapters are written to cover one or two specific types of Visual Basic controls—buttons, check boxes, list boxes, or menus, for example—including their related properties and methods. In this way, you'll develop your Visual Basic programming skills as you develop your windows—piece by piece—continually adding more functionality to your applications. This learning process will allow you to handle, methodically and gradually, any programming nuances and complexities that might arise.

What's New in VB 4.0?

Visual Basic 4.0 has many new features and improvements over its predecessor, the most obvious and welcome being the capability to create 32-bit Windows applications. Here are just a few of the many enhancements covered in this book:

■ A new Project File Extension helps to distinguish Visual Basic project files from source files used by other development tools; the file extension for Visual Basic project files has changed from .MAK to .VBP.

■ The Line Continuation character (_) allows one logical line of code to be split over two or more physical lines.

- New Appearance Property on 32-bit forms and controls, allowing for either a flat or 3D look.
- New Toolbar buttons for the Object Browser, Project Window, and Lock Controls features.
- The Object Browser, which presents a hierarchical display of all the classes, properties, and methods available to your application from Visual Basic and other OLE components (Chapter 13).
- Improved Setup Toolkit and Setup Wizard (Chapter 18).
- Most controls have a `MouseIcon` property which provides a custom icon that is used when the `MousePointer` property is set to 99 (Chapters 19 and 20).
- New Data-Bound Controls, including the new DBList, DBCombo, and DBGrid controls (Chapters 24–27).
- Improved Debug Window (Chapters 32–33).
- New OLE Automation Objects allow you to borrow the functionality of other applications by controlling their objects from within your Visual Basic program (Chapter 38).
- The API Text Viewer, which allows you to easily locate and paste cumbersome API function declarations directly into your applications (Chapter 39).

What You'll Need

To get the most out of this book, some programming experience, with a knowledge of Basic, is desirable. However, the programming here is not generally advanced, and new Basic concepts and constructions are explained as required. If you have trouble with Chapters 1–3, you might want to become more familiar with Basic before continuing.

You'll need at least Windows 3.1 or Windows for WorkGroups if you're going to use the 16-bit version of Visual Basic, and be limited to the development of 16-bit programs. You must have Windows 95 or Windows NT 3.51, with at least eight megabytes of memory if you intend to take advantage of the full power of Visual Basic 4.0 and to be able to create both 16-bit and 32-bit applications.

That's all you need to get going. It's time to turn to Chapter 1 for a brief discussion of objects, events and why they represent important concepts in Windows programming.

PART I

The Visual Basic Language and Visual Environment

Windows Programming: Why Objects and Events?

You live in a world of events. In the morning, you slap the snooze alarm, open the refrigerator, and twist the cap off a bottle of orange juice. Later, you click your car door handle, turn the ignition key, shift into drive, then press the accelerator. You seldom think about how the clock radio works, how the fridge keeps things cold, or how gasoline translates magically into power. Nothing is more natural, or more transparent, to you than the relationship of objects and the events you generate when interacting with them. A program written for a *Graphical User Interface (GUI)* such as Microsoft Windows should be just as familiar and natural to use.

In this chapter, you'll be introduced to the concepts behind *Object-Oriented, Event-Driven programming (OOED)*. You'll learn why such a design philosophy is important in the development of user-friendly, commercially viable applications. Finally, you'll use Visual Basic 4.0 and the OOED philosophy to create a very simple program.

What Are Programming Objects and Events?

What

A typical Windows application presents one or more screens full of objects with which the user will interact in order to determine the flow of the program. In the simplest, visual sense, programming objects are your application's forms and the controls you draw on them. Examine the Visual Basic Toolbox, and you'll see a number of tools for creating a wide variety of objects. There are tools for drawing push buttons, list boxes, drop-down combos, check boxes, radio buttons, scroll bars, and more. Each of these objects exhibits its own predefined behavior. When clicked, a push button "pushes in and pops out"; as the user types, a text box receives and displays each keystroke.

In order to produce a nontrivial program, however, you must *augment* or *override* this limited behavior. You do so by writing custom code and attaching it to the target object's significant event. For example, a command button's `Click` event might contain the single Visual Basic statement `End`. When this button is clicked, the code associated with its `Click` event fires off, so, in this case, the program ends.

Programming objects and events are closely related, just as objects and events are in real life. Events occur as a result of user action or program code, or they can be triggered by the system. Most objects will respond to a number of user-generated events, including mouse clicks or double-clicks, keypresses, or dragging and dropping. In addition, objects may recognize system occurrences, including timer and load events, the former firing off at specified intervals, the latter occurring when an object, such as a form, is first loaded into memory.

Why Objects and Events

Remember that most Windows applications, as well as other programs employing a Graphical User Interface, consist of one or more screensful of objects—menus, buttons, drop-down lists, edit boxes—all dormant until the user instigates an event in the form of a keypress, a mouse-click, a finger-touch, or a voice command. Once the event occurs, the user expects each object to behave in a reliable (and predictable) manner—a menu selection opens a dialog box, a series of keystrokes are captured and displayed in a text control, and a mouse-click on an OK button closes the dialog box so that processing may resume.

It is this requirement of reliability and predictability that makes Object-Oriented, Event-Driven programming perfect for the development of Windows applications. Visual Basic provides a development environment in which working with such objects and events becomes a straightforward and, more important, a well-structured process.

The steps in this process are as follows:

- Create and name a new form.
- Draw and name the objects to be displayed on that form.
- Attach to significant objects whatever code will be executed in response to user or system-generated events.

A Simple Object-Oriented, Event-Driven Program

To see the Object-Oriented, Event-Driven model in action, you'll create a simple "Hello, World!" Windows application using Visual Basic 4.0. The application will consist of three visible objects—a form and two command buttons—as seen in Figure 1.1.

How

Figure 1.1.
A simple Windows application—"Hello, World!".

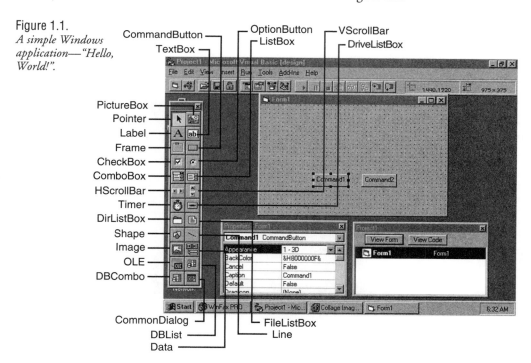

To create this application, start Visual Basic. You should see a new, blank form, named Form1 by default; if not, create it by pressing the New Form button, located at the extreme left of the horizontal Toolbar found near the top of the screen. You may also see the Project and Properties windows, as well as the Visual Basic Toolbox. If any of these windows are not visible, open them by selecting the proper item from the View drop-down menu. Once the windows are open, you may arrange them in any manner you like.

You're now ready to begin the visual implementation of your new application. Complete the following steps:

1. In the Visual Basic Toolbox, click the Command Button tool. (Notice the "Tool Tips" as you pass the mouse pointer over each button.)

2. On your new form, Form1, draw a command button by moving your mouse with the left button depressed. Release the left button once you've achieved the desired size and shape. For now, you'll accept the button's default Name and Caption, Command1.

3. In the same way, draw and size a second button, Command2.

4. To add code to Command1's Click event, double-click it. This will open a new window into which you will type the following Visual Basic statement:

```
Cls
```

5. Close the code window by double-clicking the Control icon in the upper-left corner.

6. Double-click the second button, Command2, and enter the following code, as in Figure 1.2:

```
Print "Hello, World!"
```

Figure 1.2.
The code window for a button's Click *event.*

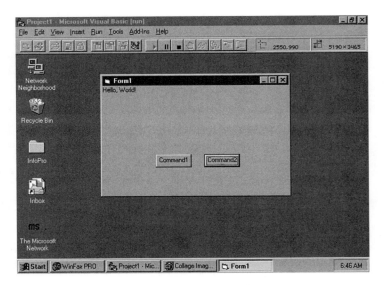

You may now test your new program by clicking the Start button on the Visual Basic Toolbar near the top of the screen, or by pressing F5. At run time, each click of the button labeled Command2 prints the phrase "Hello, World!" on your application's one and only form. Click Command1, and the form is cleared of text. You may stop your test and return to Design mode by closing your program's main form (double-click the Control icon in the upper-left corner), or by clicking the End button on the Toolbar.

> **Tip** It's probably a good idea to run your mouse pointer along the Toolbar at the top of the screen, and make a note of each button's name. Visual Basic supplies Tool Tips for each button to assist with identification.

Of course, in anything other than the most trivial application, a certain amount of thought goes into the program's design phase before the first line of code is written, before the first object is drawn, and before the first form is even created. Here, and throughout this book, in order to focus on instruction and demonstration, you will skip the design phase. In commercial application development—and even in small-scale projects for home and personal use—a thorough study and design phase will save you, the programmer, a world of woe.

Essential Summary

In this introductory chapter, you've learned that there's a close correlation between how you interact with objects in the real world and how you might manipulate objects in any program employing a Graphical User Interface such as Windows. In Windows applications, objects such as buttons, lists, and text boxes are presented to the user so that he or she may control the program by instigating events, usually in the form of keystrokes or mouse-clicks.

What

Because users expect their computer programs to behave in a reliable and predictable fashion, it is important to understand how Object-Oriented, Event-Driven programming will contribute to your program's well-structured and modular format.

Why

By visually creating a single form and by writing a single line of code, you have completed a functioning program that, although trivial, demonstrates all the elements of good OOED design. You created and named your significant objects, then attached code to a relevant control, the push button, so that a mouse-click event to that button would perform the desired function—in this case, printing the phrase "Hello, World!".

How

Forms, Controls, Properties, and Methods

In the previous chapter, you learned that forms and controls such as command buttons comprise the visual aspect of a Windows application. They create the graphical interface with which the user interacts in order to manipulate the program. However, there's a lot more to forms, controls, and other programming objects.

In this chapter, you'll see how the functionality and appearance of programming objects may be greatly enhanced by modifying their properties at design time. You'll come to understand the difference between *properties*, which determine an object's characteristics, and *methods*, which are procedures or functions that impart some action to an object.

Finally, you'll write a program that uses *dot notation* to read and set an object's properties, as well as execute specific methods, at run time.

What Are Properties and Methods?

In this section, you'll examine the differences between properties and methods, and see how and when each should come into play.

Properties

What

Real world objects are loaded with properties. Your sweater is a certain color, a certain size and weight, and made from a specific material with its own particular texture. In fact, a strong philosophical argument can be made that an inanimate object is really nothing more than the sum of its properties. It should come as no surprise, then, that programming objects are defined by their own set of properties, as well.

Strictly speaking, a *property* is a named attribute of a programming object. Properties define object characteristics—such as size, color, screen location—or sometimes the way in which an object behaves, whether or not a text box accepts multiple lines, for example, or if a particular menu item is currently enabled.

Methods

What

Your cat is an object, though some might resent such a cold classification. Still, his properties include long black hair and golden eyes; he's 20 inches long and weighs 7 pounds—but that's not *all* he is. A complete definition of your cat must encompass more than what he looks like. It must include an itemization of what he *does*.

Therefore, your cat's *methods* might be move, purr, sleep, play, eat, and breathe. A computer program simulating your cat's behavior might contain lines resembling the following pseudocode:

```
Cat.Play     'Has that rubber mouse again...
Cat.Eat      'Requires sustenance...
Cat.Purr     'Contented...so..
Cat.Sleep
```

Similarly, in objected-oriented programming, a *method* is a connected or built-in procedure, a block of code that can be invoked to impart some action to a particular object. Unlike other procedures or functions in the Visual Basic language, methods require an object to give them a context. There is, for example, a Move method associated with most objects. In Visual Basic the word *Move*, by itself, has no meaning. On the other hand, the statement

```
imgLightBulb.Move 720,1440
```

performs a very precise action indeed. (There'll be much more on this method later, in Chapter 21, but let's kill the suspense. This statement would move an image control containing a picture of, say, a light bulb, to a location approximately 1/2 inch from the left border and 1 inch from the top of the active window.) In short, while properties tend to *describe* an object, methods allow an object to *do* something. Properties are data; methods are code. In the grammar of object-oriented programming, objects are nouns, properties are adjectives, and methods are verbs.

Properties and Dot Notation

You may have noticed the use of dot notation in the code samples seen earlier. In code, you refer to both properties and methods by using the dot (.) operator. The syntax for setting an object's property is:

```
Object.Property = Setting
```

For example, suppose that you have a form named frmMyForm. You might want to store the current setting of frmMyForm's background color property, then change it to a different color. Examine the following Visual Basic statements:

```
lOldColor = frmMyForm.BackColor        'Read Current Color
frmMyForm.BackColor = QBColor(BLUE)    'Set New Color
```

Here, lOldColor is a variable (more on Visual Basic variables in Chapter 3). You use the dot operator to read the form's current color and store it to lOldColor, in case you want to put things back the way you found them. The second line of code changes, or *sets*, the form's background color to blue. To change back to the original color, you would use the following:

```
frmMyForm.BackColor = lOldColor
```

Methods and Dot Notation

Calling, or executing, an object's methods is similar to setting an object's properties in that both make use of the dot operator. Unlike properties, however, methods may require additional information in the form of arguments. Here's the general syntax for calling an object's methods:

```
Object.Method Arg1,Arg2...ArgN
```

For example, assume that you have a Picture control called picEarth. As part of an animation sequence, you might decide to move picEarth to the upper-left corner of the current form. To do so, you would call picEarth's Move method, which requires two arguments specifying the horizontal and vertical coordinates of the new location. Since you're sending your picture to the upper-left corner, these coordinates would be 0,0 (more on animation techniques and screen positioning in Chapters 21 and 22). Here's the call:

```
picEarth.Move 0,0        'Send to upper left of current window
```

Why Work with Properties and Methods?

By manipulating objects, by setting properties and by calling methods at run time, you may control discrete portions of your program without interfering with the rest of the application.

Furthermore, object-property-method techniques make applications development easier by providing tools more closely suited to the way people think about the world. By employing such techniques, you may efficiently model the complexity of real-world systems or the simplicity of a home checkbook program.

How to Set Properties and Execute Methods

An object's properties may be set at design time; that is, at the time you draw or modify your forms. Properties set at design time are in effect when your application is first executed. They remain in effect until the application ends, unless changed programmatically by you or by the user's actions. You might change the picture displayed in an Image control, for example, or the user might drag a form to a different location, thereby changing the form's Top and Left properties.

Unlike properties, methods may be executed only at run time, or under special circumstances during a debugging session (more on the Visual Basic Debugger in Chapters 32 and 33). In the following section, you will visually implement (draw) a new form containing two command buttons whose Name and Caption properties will be set at design time. At run time, clicking the first button will change the form's background color property. When clicked, the second button will call the form's Circle method, thereby drawing a circle.

Examining Properties in Design Mode

You are in Design mode when Visual Basic is first started. The design environment, or desktop, usually consists of a Project window listing all the files associated with the current project. The Toolbox may be seen, as well, often displayed on the left side of the desktop. The Properties window becomes available as soon as a form is opened for original design or editing. To see the Properties window, press F4 or select Properties from the **V**iew drop-down menu. The contents of the Properties window change according to which object is currently selected. You may select different objects by clicking them (notice the "handles," the tiny black rectangles at the center of each horizontal and vertical border) or by pressing the Tab key to cycle through all objects on the current form. In either case, the properties associated with the selected object are listed in the Properties window, allowing you to scroll through them, read them, and change them as necessary.

Naming Your Objects

A good habit to get into is to set the Name property of all your application's significant objects—those objects whose properties and methods you expect to make use of in code. Change them from the generic enumerated, Form1, Command1, Command2, offered by Visual

Basic, to something more meaningful. It's conventional to use a three-letter, lowercase prefix when naming your significant objects (see Table 2.1). You'll know immediately which object is referenced by cmdOK or frmMain, while Command5 or Form7 will have you guessing.

Table 2.1. Visual Basic object naming conventions.

Visual Basic Object	Prefix	Example
Form	frm	frmStartUp
Command Button	cmd, btn	cmdExit, btnHelp
Label	lbl	lblOptions
Text Box	txt	txtHello
Scroll Bars: Horizontal, Vertical	hsb, vsb	hsbRate, vsbTime
Menu	mnu	mnuMain
Option Button	opt	optPrinter
Check Box	chk	chkSound
List Box	lst	lstColors
Combo Box	cbo	cboEmployees
Frame	fra	fraOptions
Picture Box	pic	picMouse
Image	img	imgLightBulb
Panel	pnl	pnlStatus
Shape	shp	shpOval
Line	lin	linDiagonal
Timer	tmr	tmrAnimate
Data Control	dtc	dtcTelephone
Grid Control	grd	grdDisplay

Now start Visual Basic if you haven't done so already. If Visual Basic is already running, and if the form you created in Chapter 1 is still on the screen, select **N**ew Project from the **F**ile menu (you don't need to save any changes). Create a new form or click Form1 if it's present. If the Properties window is not visible, press F4 to see it. Arrange the windows on your "desktop" any way you like, then complete the following steps:

1. While holding the Ctrl key, click the Command Button tool in the Toolbox. This will keep the tool selected so that you may draw several buttons without having to "dip" repeatedly into the Toolbox.
2. Draw two buttons on your form.

3. Click anywhere on the form to make sure it's selected. Then activate the Properties window by clicking it. You may now scroll through a list of the form's properties.

4. Notice that you may jump between the Properties window and the form by pressing Alt+F6. While on the form, you may press the Tab key to jump from button to button (from object to object), or press Esc to select the form itself. The Properties window always displays a list of the currently selected object's properties.

While in the Properties window, you may change many properties by simply typing over the old setting. Some properties are set by selecting from an associated drop-down list.

Both buttons and forms have Caption properties. A form's Caption is displayed in the title bar of the form. A command button's Caption appears on the button itself. Again, *all* significant objects should be given meaningful names. You should get in the habit of changing an object's default Name property soon after you draw it.

Captions Are Not the Same as Names

A Caption is used to identify an object to the user. Names are used to identify an object in code; that is, to the *programmer!*

Keeping in mind the preceding steps and referring to Table 2.2, you will be able to set the properties of your test program's significant objects. Do so now.

Table 2.2. Design-time settings—Property/Method Test program.

Visual Basic Object	Property	Design-Time Setting
Form	Name	frmTest
	Caption	Property/Method Test
Command Button	Name	cmdSwitch
	Caption	Switch Color
Command Button	Name	cmdCircle
	Caption	Draw Circle

At this point, your form should look something like Figure 2.1.

Figure 2.1.
*The Property/Method
Test form.*

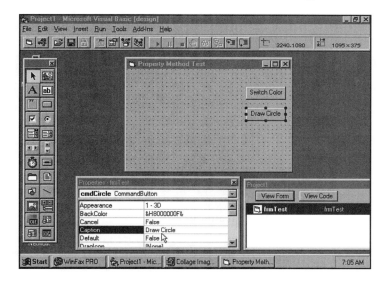

Setting Properties at Run Time

In order to manipulate properties at run time, it is necessary to write some code. You want the command button, cmdSwitch, to change frmTest's background color. To do so, double-click it. This will open a code window for the button's Click event. As in Figure 2.2, between the `Private Sub` and `End Sub` statements (kindly provided by Visual Basic), enter the following code:

```
Static TheColor                           'Declare a variable
TheColor = TheColor + 1                    'Bump it...
TheColor = IIf(TheColor < 15, TheColor, 1) 'Make sure it's not too high...
frmTest.BackColor = QBColor(TheColor)      'Change form's BackColor.
```

For now, don't worry about the references to variables and colors. You'll get plenty of practice with these later. What's important at this point is that in the last line, you're changing the form's BackColor property, in code dynamically, at run time. When the program is running, the form's color will change each time you click the button captioned "Switch Colors." You can test this now. Click the Start button, or press F5. When you're finished testing, stop your program by double-clicking its window's Control icon in the upper-left corner.

Figure 2.2.
Code window for the
Switch Color button's
Click event.

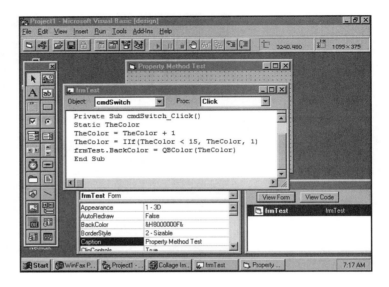

Executing Methods at Run Time

At this point, you might be inclined to close cmdSwitch's code window to reduce screen clutter. You could then double-click your second command button, cmdCircle, in order to enter the call to the form object's Circle method. It's not necessary to close the code window while switching between a form's objects. Just select whatever object you're interested in from the drop-down list labeled "Object." Select cmdCircle from this list, and you'll be transported to the code window for cmdCircle's Click event.

In this code window, enter the following single line, a call to the forms Circle method:

```
frmTest.Circle (1400, 1400), Rnd * 1400
```

The Circle method requires two arguments, a pair of numbers locating the center of the circle, and a second argument (in this case, randomly generated) specifying the circle's radius. (There'll be more about Circle and other graphical methods in Chapters 19 and 20.)

Your program is ready for testing.

Essential Summary

In this chapter, you've learned how the appearance and functionality of your program's forms and controls may be enhanced by manipulation of their properties and methods. You saw that properties specify the defining characteristics of an object—a form's size, position, and color, for example—and that they may be read and set at both design time and run time. An object's methods are called to impart some action to the object, to make it *do* something, such as move around the screen. Methods, unlike properties, must be called at run time, or under special debugging conditions.

Manipulation of an object's properties and methods makes it easy to control individual portions of your program. Setting properties and calling methods allows you to create computerized objects which more closely correlate to the ways in which people think about and interact with the real world.

Why

You examined and set some of the properties possessed by forms and command buttons by scrolling through the Properties window at design time. By creating a simple program, you explored the run time relationship of objects to properties and methods. A click of one button caused the form's background color (a property) to change. Clicking your program's second button called the form's Circle method, causing a circle of random radius to be drawn.

How

Variable Types, Declarations, and Scope

In this chapter, you'll learn what variables are, as well as how to declare and use them in your programs. You'll be introduced to the many variable types provided by Visual Basic, and you'll see how to define your own custom variable types as needed. You'll come to understand the concept of *scope* as it relates to variables and where they are declared. Finally, you'll write a simple program to create and manipulate several variables of different types, thereby reinforcing the concepts covered in this chapter.

What Are Variables?

What A *variable* is a named, temporary storage location residing in memory. A variable is capable of containing a certain type of data that can be modified during program execution. A program may use many variables, each with a unique name that identifies it within its own level of scope (more on scope later in this chapter).

In Visual Basic, variable names must be limited to 255 characters, must begin with an alpha character (so that the compiler doesn't assume that it's a numeric value), and cannot contain an embedded period. Also, variable names cannot be Visual Basic reserved words, such as Sub or Function.

The data types available for variables in Visual Basic are shown in Table 3.1, along with their storage sizes, type-declaration suffixes, and ranges of acceptable values.

Table 3.1. Visual Basic data types.

Data Type	Suffix	Storage Size	Range
Byte	None	1 Byte	0 – 255
Boolean	None	2 Bytes	True or False
Integer	%	2 Bytes	–32,768 to 32,767
Long (Integer)	&	4 Bytes	–2,147,483,648 to 2,147,483,647
Single (Precision)	!	4 Bytes	–3.40E38 to 3.40E38
Double (Precision)	#	8 Bytes	–1.80E308 to 1.80E308
Currency	@	8 Bytes	–9.22E14 to 9.22E14
Date	None	8 Bytes	Jan 1, 100 – Dec 31, 9999
Object	None	4 Bytes	Any Object Reference
String	$	1 Byte/Character	Approximate Max 65,500 Bytes
Variant	None	As Appropriate	Determined by Type
User-Defined	None	As Required	Determined by Element Type

Variable Declaration and Type Conventions

If you're familiar with older flavors of Basic, the Currency and Variant data types may be new to you. Although originally designed to hold currency values, the Currency type is attractive for other reasons, as well. It may be used to store numbers with 15-place accuracy to the left of the decimal point, with 4 fixed places to the right.

The explicit Byte, Boolean, Date, and Object types are newly available in Visual Basic 4.0. Bytes are used to store small positive integers less than or equal to 255. Boolean variables may contain one of only two possible values, and may be read or set by using Visual Basic's reserved keywords True or False. Variables declared as Date may be assigned values by setting them to any recognizable literal date. Literal dates must be enclosed within number sign characters (#); for example, #December 15, 1993# or #17 Aug 52#.

Object variables are often used to refer to OLE automation objects within an application (more on OLE in Chapter 38). A variable declared as an Object may be assigned a value by using the Visual Basic Set statement. This variable may then be used to manipulate any object produced by your application.

The Variant Data Type

The Variant data type is the default for Visual Basic; it is the data type that all variables become if they are not explicitly declared as some other type using the Dim or Static statements as described later in this chapter. The Variant is a special data type that can contain numeric, string, or date data as well as the special values Empty and Null. Don't confuse Empty with Null. Empty is a value that indicates a variable has not been initialized. It is equal to 0 (in a numeric context) or zero-length (in a string context). Null is a value that indicates that a variable intentionally contains no valid data.

Always use the Variant data type when the data could contain date information, an Empty, or a Null. You may also use the Variant data type in place of any fundamental data type to work with data in a more flexible way. For example, if the contents of a Variant variable are digits, they may be either the string representation of the digits or their actual value, depending on the context.

Implicit and Explicit Declarations

You can indicate to Visual Basic that you want to use a certain name as a variable name in two ways. As with other Basic compilers, you may append a type-declaration character to a variable name when you first use it. This suffix, as indicated in Table 3.1, *implicitly* declares the new variable's data type. For example, you can indicate to Visual Basic that a variable called EmpAge is an integer by adding a % character to the end of it, like this:

```
EmpAge% = 42          'Implicit variable declaration
```

If this is the first time that the compiler sees the variable, this becomes an implicit declaration. If the last character is not a special type-declaration character—%, &, !, #, @, or $—then the default type is Variant.

The other, and more proper, way to identify your variables is to use the Dim statement to specifically declare them at the beginning of a procedure, as in the following:

```
Dim MyInt As Integer
Dim MyDouble As Double
Dim MyString,YourString As String
Dim My_Fixed_String As String * 10
```

Pay special attention to the last two lines. The next-to-last line declares two variables at once; the first is a Variant (not explicitly typed), and the second is a String which may vary in length anywhere from 0 to approximately 65,535 characters. The last line declares a fixed-length string variable with room enough for exactly 10 characters.

In Visual Basic, there are several places to put such declarations. Where a variable is declared determines its *scope,* which refers to the portion of the program to which the variable is visible. If a variable is *out of scope* to a certain part of the program, that part may not interact with the variable in any way. The variable, for all intents and purposes, is *invisible.*

Establishing a Variable's Scope

As mentioned earlier, a variable's scope refers to the areas of your program to which the variable is visible. There are four different levels of scope, corresponding to the four different places (and ways) you may declare variables: procedure level, static variables within procedures, form level, and standard module level.

The first place to declare variables, either implicitly or with the Dim statement, is at the *procedure level.* There are two kinds of procedures in Visual Basic: Sub procedures and Function procedures (you'll learn all about these in Chapter 6). Variables declared in procedures are *local* to that procedure. Accessible only by the procedures in which they are declared, local variables have the lowest visibility and the narrowest scope.

An important thing to remember about local variables is that they do not outlive the procedure in which they are defined. When a procedure terminates, all its local variables are removed from memory, which is good from a resource conservation standpoint. This means, however, that a procedure's local variables are *reinitialized* each time the procedure is called. In other words, you must not expect a local variable to retain its value between procedure calls.

Note Static Variables

It is possible to make local variables permanent by declaring them with the keyword Static in place of Dim. Visual Basic will never reinitialize a static variable, allowing it to maintain its value through repeated calls to the procedure in which it's declared. However, static variables should be used sparingly to maximize available memory. Also, making a variable static in no way affects its scope. It will still be visible only to the procedure in which it is declared.

The next two places to declare variables are at the *form module level* and the *code module level.* If you declare a form level variable, it will be available to every procedure in that form. In this way, you are able to share information between procedures. The same goes for code modules, which are discussed in detail in Chapter 6. Briefly, code modules are created by selecting the Module item from Visual Basic's Insert menu (or by clicking the Module button on the Toolbar); code modules are used to hold your application's general, non-event-related sub procedures and functions, as well as its *global* variables and *constants.*

The way to declare a variable at either module level is to place it in the declarations part of the general object, which is accessible through the Code window (see Figure 3.1).

Figure 3.1.
A Form module's declaration section.

The final, and broadest, level of scope is at the *global level*. Every sub procedure and function, every line of code in your application, has access to global variables. To identify a global variable, declare it by using the Global keyword in the general/declarations section of a code module. Here's how you declare three global variables of different types:

```
'Declared In The General/Declarations Section Of A Code Module
Global AppName As String
Global DollarCost As Currency
Global HighTemp As Double
```

User-Defined Data Types

In addition to Visual Basic's own data types, you are able to define and use your own custom data types, as well. User-defined types can contain one or more elements of any fundamental data type listed in Table 3.1. You define your own data types in the General/Declarations section of a code module, using the Type and End Type keywords. This is the only place you can define your own data types, which makes sense because your data types must be visible to all regions of your application, as are Visual Basic's. Here's how a custom data type's definition would look:

```
Type EmpType    ' Create user-defined type.
ID As Long
Name As String * 15
Wage As Currency
End Type
```

You would then declare a variable of this type as you would any other. You may use the Dim, Static, and Global keywords (within their proper contexts) to establish the persistency and scope of the variable. You would initialize and manipulate the elements of your new variable by using dot notation, like so:

```
Dim Employee As EmpType
Employee.ID = 1234
Employee.Name = "Sam Roberts"
Employee.Wage = 15.26
```

Why Variables Are Indispensable

Why
The power and flexibility added to your computer programs by a judicious and well-informed use of variables is beyond dispute and cannot be overestimated. In fact, any but the most trivial programs will make thoughtful use of a wide variety of variables, spanning the spectrum of available types. Custom data types are useful in database programs where it's helpful to conceive of several different data elements as a single entity, an employee record, for example, or a customer invoice. In general, establishing variables of the proper type and scope will ensure the most efficient use of memory in your programs.

How to Use Variables in Your Programs

How
In this section, you'll create a program consisting of a single form containing three buttons representing two of Visual Basic's available data types, and a custom type to be defined by you. As each button is clicked, the name, contents, and visibility of a variable of that type will be displayed on the program's form. You'll declare variables at all four levels of scope, as well as create and employ your own custom data type.

Start Visual Basic, if it's not already running. If Visual Basic is already running with Chapter 2's exercise still on the screen, select **N**ew Project from the **F**ile menu to start fresh. Draw three command buttons on your new form. Stack them vertically along the form's right border, as seen in Figure 3.2. Refer to Table 3.2 in drawing and naming your objects, and setting their properties.

Table 3.2. Design-time settings—Variable Exploration program.

Visual Basic Object	Property	Design-Time Setting
Form	Name	frmVariables
	Caption	Variable Exploration Program
Command Button	Name	cmdInteger
	Caption	Integer
Command Button	Name	cmdDouble

Visual Basic Object	Property	Design-Time Setting
	Caption	Double
Command Button	Name	cmdCustom
	Caption	Custom

Figure 3.2.
*The Variable
Exploration program.*

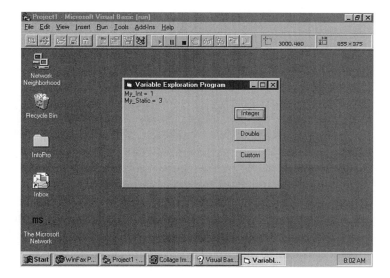

Using Local Variables

You'll create two variables, both local to cmdInteger's Click procedure. The first variable, My_Int, will be declared using the Dim statement and will therefore be reinitialized to 0 each time the procedure is called. The other variable, My_Static, will maintain its value through repeated calls to cmdInteger_Click. Neither variable will be visible outside the button's Click procedure, as you'll see.

Double-click the button captioned "Integer" to open its code window. Notice the Object and Proc drop-down lists showing cmdInteger and Click, respectively. Now enter the following code between the Private Sub and End Sub statements:

```
Dim My_Int As Integer        'Local, non-Static
Static My_Static As Integer  'Local, Static

My_Int = My_Int + 1          'Bump 'em
My_Static = My_Static +1

Cls                          'Clear the form
Print "My_Int  = "; My_Int   'Print 'em out...
Print "My_Static = ";My_Static
```

Form Level Variables

To declare a form level variable, select (General) from the Object drop-down list. This will take you to the form module's General Declarations section. If the words "Option Explicit" appear here, comment them out by placing an apostrophe (single quote) at the beginning of the line. On the first available line, enter the following:

```
Dim My_Double As Double            'Visible To Entire Form
```

Now go to the Object drop-down list and select cmdDouble. Check the Proc drop-down to make sure you're in the button's Click procedure, then enter these lines:

```
My_Double = 123.45                 'Give it a value...

Cls
Print "My_Double = ";My_Double         'You'll see this fine....
Print "My_Static = ";My_Static; "Sorry, out of scope..."        'But not this.
Print "Company = ";Customer.Company   'You'll see this once it's initialized
```

After entering these lines, close the form's code window.

Tip **Option Explicit**

The words "Option Explicit" will appear by default in any module's general declarations section if the Visual Basic environment has been configured to enforce mandatory variable declaration. When this option is in effect, the compiler will balk at any undeclared variable, which can save a lot of debugging time. Otherwise, undeclared variables are allowed and will default to the Variant type.

To automatically include, or exclude, the Option Explicit line in your project's modules, select **O**ptions from the **T**ools menu, then select the Environment tab from the Visual Basic Options dialog box, and check the Require Variable Declaration check box.

Module Level Variables

This project will require a code module for defining your custom data type and declaring a global variable of that type. Select **M**odule from the **I**nsert menu to see a code window into Module1.bas, the default name and extension for the first code module added to a project. Check the Object and Proc drop-down lists to make sure (general) and (declarations) are selected. Define your new data type as follows:

```
Type CustType              ' Create user-defined type.
ID As Long
Company As String
Contact As String * 15
Phone As String * 8
End Type
```

```
Global Customer As CustType        'You now have a global variable named
                                   'Customer of type CustType

Dim My_Mod As String               'String variable visible in this module only
```

You may now close the code module window and return to your project's form, still in Design mode.

Finishing Up and Testing

You must now attach code to your program's last button, cmdCustom. To do so, open a code window for cmdCustom by double-clicking it. Here's the code for setting and displaying the values of your global variable, Customer, of type CustType:

```
Customer.ID = 5678
Customer.Company = "Big Ideas, Inc."
Customer.Contact = "Sam Jones"
Customer.Phone = "555-1212"

Cls
Print "ID: "; Customer.ID
Print "Company: "; Customer.Company
Print "Contact: "; Customer.Contact
Print "Phone: "; Customer.Phone
```

Close the code window and run your program. Notice that each click of the Integer button displays an increasing value for the static variable, while the non-static variable is always 1 (refer to Figure 3.2).

Clicking the Double button displays a value for My_Double, but My_Static is empty; it's not visible from this procedure. At first, Customer.Company appears empty also, but this is because the elements of the Customer variable, which is global in scope, have not been assigned any values. Click the Custom button, note the output, then click Double again. You'll see that the contents of Customer.Company are properly displayed.

Essential Summary

You've learned that variables are named storage locations residing in memory. A variable is capable of containing a certain type of data that can be modified during program execution. You've seen that how and where variables are declared determines their data type and visibility. A program may use many variables of different types, each with a unique name that identifies it within its own level of scope.

What

It's important to understand the best way to declare and use variables in any computer application. A well-informed use of properly scoped variables will add power and flexibility to your programs, as well as ensure the most efficient use of system memory.

Why

How

In this chapter, you have seen how to declare variables using the Dim, Static, and Global key words. You've learned how to declare variables at four different levels of scope: local, form module, code module, and global. You've written a program employing a few of the seven data types provided by Visual Basic. You've also used the Type...End Type construct to define your own custom data type.

Simple I/O with *MsgBox()* and *InputBox()*

Almost any computer program will be able to get textual information from the user and process it, often outputting it to the screen or printer. Visual Basic's built-in InputBox() and MsgBox() functions, and the MsgBox procedure, allow for simple input/output (I/O) operations using predefined dialog boxes that you can customize with a selection of icons and response button combinations. In this chapter, you will explore all aspects of these useful functions and procedures.

What Are *InputBox()*, *MsgBox()*, and *MsgBox*?

Although functions and procedures are discussed in detail in Chapter 6, a word here is appropriate. Both functions and procedures are comprised of code, either internal to Visual Basic or defined by you, which performs a discrete programming task. Both might or might not accept arguments. The difference, simply stated, is that a function returns a value, and procedures do not. This is reflected in the syntax used in calling them. You may often identify functions by their use of parentheses and an equal sign for capturing the return value to a variable. Procedures, on the other hand, are called without parentheses or equal signs, as you will see later in this chapter.

The *InputBox()* Function

The InputBox() function displays a prompt in a dialog box, waits for the user to input text or choose a button, then returns the contents of the text box. The value returned by the function is either a Variant or a String, depending on which variation in syntax is used.

```
RetVal = InputBox(prompt ,title, default, xpos, ypos,helpfile,context )
➡'Returns Variant
```

or

```
RetVal$ = InputBox$(prompt ,title, default, xpos, ypos,helpfile,context )
➡'Returns String
```

Only the first argument, prompt, is required. It should be a descriptive string expression prompting the user for input; it's displayed adjacent to the text box into which the user will type. If prompt will consist of more than one line, be sure to include a carriage return, CHR(13), and linefeed, CHR(10), between each line (you may use the predefined constant vbCrlf to achieve the same effect). The second argument, title, is a string displayed in the title bar of the dialog box. If you omit title, nothing is placed in the title bar.

If you'd like a string displayed in the text box, to be accepted as the default response if no other input is provided, include it as the default argument. If you omit default, the text box is displayed empty.

The third and fourth arguments, xpos and ypos, are numeric expressions specifying, in twips, the horizontal and vertical distance of the upper-left corner of the dialog box from the upper-left corner of the screen. If you omit xpos, you must also omit ypos. If both are omitted, the dialog box is centered horizontally, approximately one third of the way down the screen. If you omit either title or default or both but want to include xpos and ypos, you must still include the commas that separate the arguments.

In both InputBox() and MsgBox(), the last two arguments, helpfile (a string) and context (an integer), are used to provide context-sensitive help. (Appendix B covers the creation and implementation of Windows-style on-line Help.) When both helpfile and context are provided, the user can press F1 to view the Help topic created for the corresponding dialog box.

If the user chooses the OK button or presses Enter, the InputBox() function returns whatever is in the text box. If the user enters no text or chooses the Cancel button, the function returns a zero-length string ("").

The *MsgBox* Procedure and *MsgBox()* Function

Both the MsgBox procedure and MsgBox() function display a message in a dialog box and wait for the user to choose a button. The MsgBox() function returns an integer value indicating which button the user has chosen; the MsgBox procedure does not. You use the procedure when you want to display a message and don't care how the dialog box containing it is closed.

The MsgBox() function syntax is:

```
RetVal% = MsgBox(msg,type,title,helpfile,context)
```

The MsgBox procedure syntax is:

```
MsgBox msg ,type,title,helpfile,context
```

msg is a string expression displayed as the message in the dialog box. The third argument, title, is a string expression which appears in the dialog box's title bar. The type argument is a numeric expression that is the *sum* of values specifying the number and type of buttons to display, the icon to use, the identity of the default button, and the dialog box's modality (you'll see several examples of combined type arguments throughout this book). Table 4.1 illustrates the values used and the meaning of each group of values:

Table 4.1. MsgBox Type configuration values.

Value	*Meaning*	*Suggested Symbolic Constant*
0	Display OK button only	vbOKOnly
1	Display OK and Cancel buttons	vbOKCancel
2	Display Abort, Retry, and Ignore buttons	vbAbortRetryIgnore
3	Display Yes, No, and Cancel buttons	vbYesNoCancel
4	Display Yes and No buttons	vbYesNo
5	Display Retry and Cancel buttons	vbRetryCancel
16	Display Critical Icon	vbCritical
32	Display Question Mark	vbQuestion
48	Display Exclamation Point	vbExclamation
64	Display Information Icon	vbInformation
0	First button is default	vbDefaultButton1
256	Second button is default	vbDefaultButton2
512	Third button is default	vbDefaultButton3
0	Application Modal	vbApplicationModal
4096	System Modal	vbSystemModal

The first group of values describes the number and type of buttons displayed in the dialog box; the second group determines the icon style; the third group sets the default button; and the fourth group establishes the modality of the message box. When adding numbers to create a final value for the type argument, use only one number from each group. If omitted, the default value for type is 0.

In both the function and procedure versions, the msg argument is required, while type and title are optional. If you decide to leave out type but include title, however, you must include the commas as placeholders.

Note Application versus System Modal

If a dialog box is Application Modal, the default setting, the user must respond to the box before continuing work in the current application. With a System Modal box, all applications are suspended until the user responds to the dialog box.

The value returned by the MsgBox() function indicates which button has been selected, as shown in Table 4.2:

Table 4.2. MsgBox() return values.

Value	Meaning	Suggested Symbolic Constant
1	OK button selected	vbOK
2	Cancel button selected	vbCancel
3	Abort button selected	vbAbort
4	Retry button selected	vbRetry
5	Ignore button selected	vbIgnore
6	Yes button selected	vbYes
7	No button selected	vbNo

Tip Symbolic Constants

It's strongly recommended that you use symbolic constants whenever possible; they provide better code documentation and readability. In code, vbIgnore is easily understood, where the raw number 5 is not. All message box definitions, as well as many other useful constants, are built into Visual Basic. These more meaningful, symbolic names can therefore be used in all your form and code modules.

Why Use *InputBox()* and *MsgBox()*?

The InputBox() and MsgBox() functions provide a way to handle simple input/output tasks. Although you'll often want to create your own custom dialog boxes in order to more closely control the way your application receives and displays user input, these two elements of the Visual Basic language will be very useful in handling common I/O tasks such as displaying error and help messages, as well as About boxes, which are frequently used to present an application's name, authors, and copyright information.

How to Use *InputBox()* and *MsgBox()* Functions

To learn how to work with the InputBox() and MsgBox() functions, you'll create a new program consisting of a single form and two command buttons. To begin, start Visual Basic, or, if it's already running, select New Project from the File menu. (Again, it's not necessary to save your form from the previous chapter, but if you'd like to, feel free to do so.)

With a fresh Form1 on the screen, refer to Table 4.3 in drawing and naming the visual components of your new program.

Table 4.3. Design-time settings—Message Box exercise.

Visual Basic Object	Property	Design-Time Setting
Form	Name	frmMessage
	Caption	Message Box Exercise
Command Button	Name	cmdGet
	Caption	Get Name
Command Button	Name	cmdShow
	Caption	Show Name

In the following exercise, you'll define a form-level variable and two constants to be used in your dialog boxes. Here's a listing of what should appear in the form's general declarations section:

```
Dim sName As String                    'Must Be visible to both buttons

'InputBox/Message Box Titles
Const IB_TITLE = "Input Box Demonstration"
Const MB_TITLE = "Current Value Of sName"
```

A Word about Constants

Oddly enough, a *constant* may be thought of as a variable whose value never changes, remaining the same throughout the life of the program. As mentioned, the use of constants will greatly increase the readability of your code. Like variables, a constant's scope is determined by where it is declared. A constant may be local, form-level, module-level, or global. In the code lines in the preceding section, you're using the Const keyword to establish two constants at the form level. By convention, the names of constants should be in uppercase letters, making them easy to spot. You're also declaring one form-level variable, sName, which will be used to receive input from InputBox() and to display output with MsgBox().

Tip **Variable Prefixes**

Programmers often name their variables using a short, lowercase, prefix to identify its type, i for integer, s for String, 1 for Long, and so on. (Do not confuse these with the data type *suffixes* to be used for implicit variable declaration.) In fact, there's a kind of standard variable prefix list, called *Hungarian Notation*, after the nationality of the Microsoft programmer who thought of it. Although Hungarian Notation was invented to be used in Windows programming with C, you'll see a Visual Basic adaptation of it throughout this book.

Using *InputBox()*

In this application, when the user clicks the "Get Name" button, an input box will appear, prompting for a name. You'll display the box in two different locations by changing the X and Y positions between calls. Finally, you'll check the input to make sure something was entered, displaying an error message only if the input box is left blank, or the user presses Cancel. Note the use of the MsgBox procedure at this point, since you don't care how the user closes the box.

Here's the code, with annotation, to be entered into cmdGet's Click procedure:

```
Dim sPrompt As String                   'Local variable...
Static iXPos As Integer, iYPos As Integer  'Value maintained between calls...

sPrompt = "Enter Your Name: "           'Set the prompt...

iXPos = IIf(iXPos > 0, 0, 1440)         'Change window location...
iYPos = IIf(iYPos > 0, 0, 1440)         'IIF() Covered next chapter...

sName = InputBox$(sPrompt, IB_TITLE, , iXPos, iYPos)   'Display box, get input

If sName = "" Then                      'If nothing entered, show error message
MsgBox "No Value Entered!", vbCritical, "Error Condition"
End If
```

In the call to InputBox(), fourth line from the end, notice the extra comma after your constant IB_TITLE. Although you're not passing a *default* argument, the comma is required to hold its place. Notice also the use of Visual Basic's built-in constant, vbCritical, in the call to MsgBox. If you're not sure what's going on with the IIF() function in the preceding lines, suffice it to say that they're responsible for alternating the input box's position with each call to cmdGet Click. There'll be much more information about the IIF() function, as well as other forms of decision-making, branching, and looping, in the next chapter.

Feel free to run and test your program. Compare your screen output to Figure 4.1. Notice that the position of the InputBox changes each time you click cmdGet. If you fail to type something into the InputBox, or press the Cancel button, an appropriate message is displayed.

Figure 4.1.
*The InputBox()
window.*

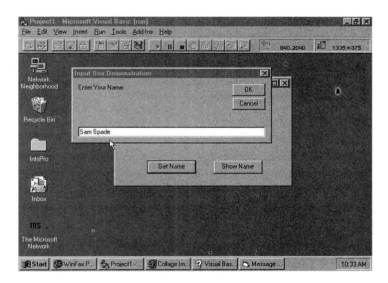

Using *MsgBox()*

Now you'll add code to the cmdShow button's Click event. The cmdShow button makes use of both the MsgBox() function and the MsgBox procedure (or statement). When this button is clicked, the current value of sName is displayed in a dialog box containing a question mark icon and three buttons: Yes, No, and Cancel. Because this box is displayed using the MsgBox() function (rather than the procedure), you'll be able to identify which of the three buttons was pressed by checking the return value. A message indicating the selected button is then displayed using the MsgBox procedure.

Enter the following lines into cmdShow's Click procedure:

```
Dim sMsg As String                          'Declare vars...
Dim iType As Integer, iRetVal As Integer

iType = vbYesNoCancel + vbQuestion              ' Set  type...

iRetVal = MsgBox("You Entered " & sName, iType, MB_TITLE)    'Display it, Get
➡button
```

```
If iRetVal = vbYes Then                           'Check against constants...
sMsg = "You Pressed YES!"                          ' And set message
➥accordingly...
ElseIf iRetVal = vbNo Then
sMsg = "You Pressed NO!"
ElseIf iRetVal = vbCancel Then
sMsg = "You Pressed Cancel!"
End If

MsgBox sMsg, vbInformation, "MsgBox Procedure"        'Display Button
```

Notice in the call to the MsgBox() function (the fourth line of code), that the first argument, rather than a single variable, is a valid string expression. In this case it's a concatenation of a literal string and a string variable, using the time-honored BASIC ampersand operator (&). In the more modern versions of the language, such as Visual Basic, you could have used a plus operator (+), as well. Based on the data types of the operands, the compiler is smart enough to know whether you're adding numbers or concatenating strings.

Again, in the If...ElseIf...EndIf construct above, there's an intimation of the sort of decision-making techniques you'll encounter in Chapter 5. Still, you'll probably get a feel for what's going on here: you're just deciding which of three possible messages to display in the call to MsgBox on the last line.

It's time to run the program. See Figure 4.2 for comparison.

Figure 4.2.
The complete Message
Box program.

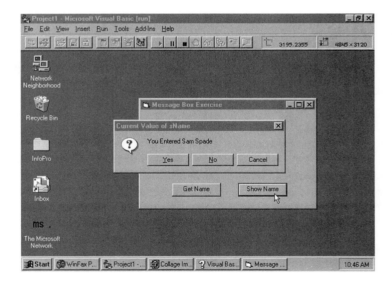

Essential Summary

In this chapter, you took a pretty exhaustive look at Visual Basic's InputBox() and MsgBox() functions. You learned that InputBox() is used to display a dialog box, including a prompt and title, into which the user may enter textual information, such as a name or account number. This information is then returned to the calling procedure for processing. In a similar way, the MsgBox() function is used to display information. The MsgBox() function accepts arguments that specify the box's message and title, and determine the type of buttons and icons to be displayed. By examining the function's return value, you may discover which button was pressed in closing the dialog box.

What

The InputBox() and MsgBox() functions provide a simple way to handle straightforward tasks involving screen input and output. Although limited, these two functions may be very useful in handling common I/O routines, such as displaying error messages or instructions.

Why

By using specific numeric codes or, better, symbolic constants of your own or those provided by Visual Basic, you were able to customize the appearance of MsgBox()'s dialog box. Such customization might include the addition of special icons and button sets.

How

Decision Making: Branching and Looping

A program unable to alter its flow in response to changing conditions, either internal or external, would be powerless. Imagine a banking system unable to detect when a depositor's account balance dropped below zero; or a video game that could not decide in which direction a joy stick had been pushed. How about a label-printing program that couldn't tell when it reached the end of your mailing list? In fact, computer programming is hardly anything *other* than decision-making. You receive your input, monitor your internal conditions, *decide* what to do about them, then do it. In this chapter, you'll examine most of the decision-making tools available to you in Visual Basic.

What Are Decision-Making Constructs?

What

Visual Basic's *decision-making constructs* fall into two broad categories familiar to all computer programmers: *branching* and *looping*. Branching devices like If...Then and Select Case cause the program to strike off in one direction when a particular condition is encountered, sometimes never to look back. Looping constructs such as Do...Loop and While...Wend are used to repeat a certain limited block of instructions until a specified condition becomes True or False.

Branching with *If...EndIf*

Remember the powerless banking program from this chapter's introduction? A simple bit of conditional branching would allow it to print an "Account Overdrawn" message under the appropriate circumstances. Here's a snippet of pseudocode which, if properly implemented, would do the trick:

```
If CurrentBalance - CheckAmount < 0 Then
   Print OverDrawn Message
Else
   CurrentBalance = CurrentBalance - CheckAmount
EndIf
```

It's possible, but messy and unnecessary, to nest If...EndIf constructs. Instead, you should use the If...ElseIf...EndIf construct or, when evaluating situations in which there are several possible actions, the Select Case construct, which is discussed later in this chapter.

Here's an example of If...ElseIf...EndIf from the preceding chapter:

```
If iRetVal = vbYes Then                    'Check against constants...
   sMsg = "You Pressed YES!"               ' And set message accordingly...
   ElseIf iRetVal = vbNo Then
      sMsg = "You Pressed NO!"
      ElseIf iRetVal = vbCancel Then
         sMsg = "You Pressed Cancel!"
End If
```

This code snippet makes a decision based on three mutually exclusive values—vbYes, vbNo, vbCancel—for the variable, iRetVal. This particular example suggests a subtle weakness. What should be done if *none* of the three values applies? Although it's possible, through careful coding, to guarantee that iRetVal's value is one of the three, there may be times when it's not desirable to do so. In such a case, a final Else clause, prior to the EndIf, would be appropriate.

Sometimes it's possible to condense the If...Then...Else...EndIf construct into a single line of code. This is accomplished with the IIF() (immediate if) function. Being a function, IIF() returns a value that must be stored to a variable. You saw an example of IIF() in the preceding chapter. Take another look:

```
TheColor = IIF(TheColor < 15, TheColor, 1)        'Make sure it's not too high...
```

This function requires three arguments, the *condition* to check, what to return if the condition is true, and what to return if it's false. Therefore, in this example, the value of TheColor stays the same, unless it's 15 or more, in which case it's set to 1.

Select Case...End Select

When you need to execute one of several groups of statements depending on the value of a string or numeric expression, the Select Case...End Select construct is best. For example, suppose that you wanted to check a person's age in order to assign them to a particular category. You might do so in the following way:

```
Select Case iAge
   Case 5                              'Exactly 5....
   sCategory = "Five Year Old"

   Case 13 To 19                       'Between 13 and 19, inclusive
   sCategory = "Teenager"

   Case 20 To 35,50,60 To 65           'Two ranges, one exact match
   sCategory = "Special Adult"

   Case Is >65                         'Over 65
sCategory = "Senior"

   Case Else
   sCategory = "Everybody Else"
End Select
```

Notice that it's possible to check for a range of values by using To. Comparison operators such as > and < are also acceptable. You may place several target values or ranges within a single Case by separating them with commas. There may also be a Case Else clause preceding the statement or statements to be executed if none of the prior Case conditions are met.

Looping Constructs

There are several looping constructs available in Visual Basic. The While...Wend construct repeatedly executes one or more statements as long as a given condition is True. Here's the syntax:

```
While condition
     [statements]
Wend
```

Here condition is a numeric or string expression that evaluates to True or False. If condition is True, all statements are executed until the Wend keyword is encountered. At that point, control returns to the While statement, and condition is evaluated again. If condition is still True, the process is repeated; if it's not True, execution resumes with the statement following Wend.

The Do...Loop construct provides a more structured and flexible way to perform looping. It repeats a block of code while a condition is True or until a condition becomes True. It also provides a way to exit the loop at any time. Here's how you might use the Do...Loop construct to print a list of customers in your database:

```
Do  Until  dsCustomers.EOF          'Till End Of File...
   Print dsCustomers("Name")        'Print name...
   dsCustomers.MoveNext              'Next, please...
Loop
```

You could also use this equally valid syntax (this time you'll exit the loop when you encounter the first California customer):

```
Do
If dsCustomers("State") = "CA" Then
    Exit Do
    Else
    Print dsCustomers("Name")
EndIf
Customers.MoveNext
Loop Until Customers.EOF
```

The Exit Do can only be used within a Do...Loop control structure to provide an alternate way to quit the loop. Any number of Exit Do statements may be placed anywhere in the Do...Loop. Often used with the evaluation of some condition, as in the If...Then in the preceding code, Exit Do transfers control to the statement immediately following the loop.

The For...Next statement repeats a group of statements a specified number of times. This looping construct creates a counter variable, specifying its starting and ending values. Here's how you could use it to list your first ten customers:

```
For iCounter = 1 To 10
Print dsCustomers("Name")
dsCustomers.MoveNext
Next
```

You may also specify the Step interval, the amount the counter is changed each time through the loop. If not specified, step defaults to 1. Using a Step interval, you could easily print a column of numbers depicting a gradient of 5 percent:

```
For iPercent = 0 To 100 Step 5
Print iPercent & "%"
Next
```

Once the loop starts and all statements in the loop have been executed, the step interval is added to the counter. At this point, either the statements in the loop execute again (if counter has not reached its "To" limit), or the loop is exited and execution continues with the statement following Next.

As with the Do...Loop, it's possible to prematurely terminate a For...Next loop. The Exit For statement provides an alternate way to exit, and any number of such statements may be placed in the loop. Like Exit Do, the Exit For is often used with the evaluation of some If...Then conditional and transfers control to the statement immediately following Next.

Why Make Decisions?

In life, you need to be able to alter your actions (or imagine you do) in the face of changing circumstances. If the weather looks like rain, you grab an umbrella. If traffic is backed up on the interstate, you take a back road...or stay home. If 25 guests are coming to dinner, you'll want to set 25 places at the table, which involves a decision *and* a considerable amount of repetitive activity.

Computer languages, too, must be able to perform different sets of actions, sometimes repeatedly, as dictated by internal or external circumstances. For example, in a Personnel Management System, if an employee has been with the company for one year, that employee is given a raise. If the employee's age falls within certain predetermined ranges, that employee is entitled to a specific kind of medical coverage. While printing mailing labels, the system should stop once the end of the employee table has been reached. Adequate knowledge of the decision-making and looping constructs available to you in Visual Basic will enable you to write programs whose flow and outcome change in a prescribed and, therefore, controlled manner.

How to Make Decisions

As you've seen, Visual Basic comes with a number of excellent decision-making constructs. In this section, you'll write a program that makes use of three of them. You'll create a form with four buttons—one to enter your age using the `InputBox()` function and three to process that information using `Select Case`, `Do Until`, and `For...Next`.

To begin, create a new form with the visual elements listed in Table 5.1:

Table 5.1. Design-time settings—Decision-Making exercise.

Visual Basic Object	Property	Design-Time Setting
Form	Name	frmDecision
	Caption	Decision Making Exercise
Command Button	Name	cmdGetAge
	Caption	Enter Age
Command Button	Name	cmdSelect
	Caption	Select Case
Command Button	Name	cmdDo
	Caption	Do Until
Command Button	Name	cmdFor
	Caption	For...Next

You'll need a variant variable, `vAge` (in case it's left null or empty), which should be visible throughout the form. Open the form's General Declarations section and declare it there. Then you'll prompt the user for `vAge`'s value by entering the following in `cmdGetAge`'s code window:

```
vAge = InputBox("What Is Your Age?","Decision Program Input")

If vAge ="" Then                         'Check it...
   MsgBox "You Didn't Enter A Value!",vbCritical,"Error!"
EndIf
```

Using *Select Case*

When the Select Case button is pushed, your program will display one of four messages, depending on the current value of vAge. Add the following code to cmdSelect's Click event:

```
Dim sMsg As String                           'Local variable for message

Select Case vAge                             'Branch on value of iAge
   Case Is < 13
   sMsg = "You're just a kid."

   Case Between 13 And 19
   sMsg = "You're a teenager."

   Case 20 To 39
   sMsg = "You're a mature adult."

   Case Else
   sMsg= "You're over the hill."

End Select

sMsg = vAge & " years old!"  &  Chr(13) & sMsg     'Break line with CR
MsgBox sMsg,vbInformation,"Select Case Example"    'Display message
```

> **Note** Visual Basic's Chr(*charcode*) function returns a character corresponding to the numeric character code passed to it. In the preceding code, notice the use of Chr(13), the carriage return character, to split your message into two lines. A Chr(10), line feed, would have had the same effect. (As mentioned in the previous chapter, you may use the constant vbCrlf when you need both the carriage return and line feed characters.)

Go ahead and test at this point. You'll be able to enter an age (or get an error message if you don't). With an age of 42, (yes, I'm over the hill), clicking the Select Case button should produce output similar to Figure 5.1.

In the next section, you'll add code to cmdDo's Click event.

Figure 5.1.
*Decision Making
program: Select Case.*

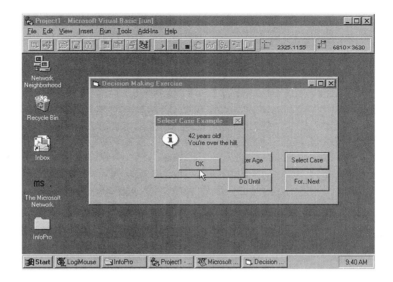

Using *Do Until*

By using a `Do...Until` loop, your program will print a descending list of ages, starting at the current value of `vAge` and stopping at zero. Actually, the lowest value in the visible list may be determined by the size of your form, as you'll see. Open the code window for `cmdDo`'s `Click` event and add the following:

```
Cls                                 'Clear the form...
Do Until vAge < 0                   'Keep printing until....
   Print CStr(vAge) + " Years old...and counting down..."
   vAge = vAge - 1                       'Decrement vAge...
Loop
```

Notice that the use of Visual Basic's conversion function `CStr()`. `CStr()` takes a single argument and returns a String type equivalent. Remember that `vAge` is a Variant variable which, at this point, contains a number. In order to create the Print string, you need to "add," or concatenate, two string expressions. You're using the + operator, rather than the ampersand (&) (which would have *coerced* `vAge` to the proper type), so `vAge` must first be converted. If you don't convert `vAge`, a "Type Mismatch" error will occur at runtime.

Obviously, in any kind of looping structure, you'll want to be sure to provide a way out of the loop. In the preceding code sample, this is done by decreasing the value of `vAge` with each iteration, thereby ensuring that `vAge` will eventually slip below zero. Once `vAge` is less than zero, program control "drops through" to the first line after the `Loop` statement.

> **Caution** If you fail to provide a way out of a Loop construct, your program will endlessly repeat the loop's statements, a condition known as an *infinite loop*. Should you encounter such a condition during testing, you may stop the program by pressing Ctrl+Break.

Using *For...Next*

In this section, you'll add code to cmdFor's Click event, setting up a For...Next loop that will display an odd-numbered list starting with 1 and ending with (or near) the current value of vAge. You'll include only odd numbers in your list by providing a Step value of 2. Here's the code:

```
Cls                                          'Clear the form...
For iCounter = 1 To vAge Step 2
  Print "Line " & iCounter & "...and stepping 2"    'Use iCounter for line number...
Next
```

Notice that here you're using an ampersand (&) for string concatenation, so it's not necessary to convert vAge before "adding" it to the printed string.

That's it for the Decision Making program. During testing, you may notice that, once cmdDo has been clicked, clicking cmdFor appears to do nothing other than clear the form. If you investigate by pressing the Select Case button, you'll see that vAge has a value of –1! This is because your Do...Until loop *decreases* vAge until it's less than 0; that is, until it's equal to –1, at which point you drop through the loop. Now remember, vAge is a form-level variable which may be accessed by any object on the form; therefore, when you click cmdFor, after cmdDo, your For...Next loop is *never entered* because the loop's starting value is already higher than the ending value. To print a list using cmdFor, you'll need to click the Enter Age button again, inputting a value greater than zero.

Here's some screen output from a possible session with your new program. The age entered was 25. The For...Next button was pressed to print the list you see in Figure 5.2.

Figure 5.2.
Decision Making program: For...Next *loop.*

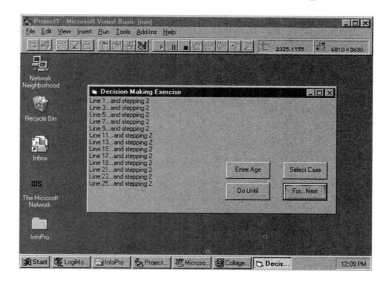

Essential Summary

In this chapter, you were introduced to most of Visual Basic's decision-making constructs. You learned that simple branching may be accomplished by using the If...Else...EndIf construct and the immediate IIF() function. You saw that the Select Case statement provides more decision-making power in cases where an expression must be tested for a large number of values. In addition, you learned about three different looping constructs—While loops, Do loops, and For loops—which allow for the repetition of a statement (or statements) while a certain a condition is True, until it becomes True, or for a specified number of times.

What

Computer languages must be able to perform different sets of actions, sometimes repeatedly, in response to changing circumstances. A thorough understanding of the decision-making and looping constructs available to you in Visual Basic will enable you to write programs whose flow and outcome changes in a prescribed, predictable, and therefore controlled manner.

Why

By creating a small program that asked for a single numeric value and stored it to a variable, you were able to put to work three powerful decision-making constructs. You used the Select Case construct to test the variable against a wide range of values, displaying one of four corresponding messages accordingly. You created a Do...Until loop that printed a list of numbers descending from the variable's input value to 0. Finally, you used a For...Next loop and Step increment to put up a list of all the odd numbers between 0 and the variable's current value.

How

Modules and Procedures

In Visual Basic 4.0, there are three kinds of modules: *Form modules*, *Code modules*, and *Class modules*. All three kinds may contain procedures that can be shared at various levels of scope throughout your application. All the code you've written so far, except for the global variables declared in Chapter 3, has been stored in modules associated with a particular *Form*. That is, when you write code to respond to a button's Click event, you're creating an *event procedure* (as opposed to a *general procedure*), and that code becomes part of the form on which the button resides. Unless you remove the Private keyword from the event procedure's header, this code will not be visible outside the form.

Class modules contain the formal definition of a class to be instantiated as an OLE automation object. Although there's an overview of OLE (Object Linking and Embedding) in Chapter 38, a detailed look at the subject is beyond the scope of this book. Suffice it to say that a class acts as the template from which an object is created at run time. The class defines the properties of the object, as well as the methods used to control the object's behavior.

In this chapter, you'll create a new form and a single Code module containing the general procedures (a Sub procedure and two functions) needed to receive a word or phrase, encrypt and display it, then decrypt it. In the process, you'll learn the difference between sub procedures and functions, as well as be introduced to several more built-in Visual Basic statements and functions.

What Are Modules, Sub Procedures, and Function Procedures?

What

Strictly speaking, a *Code module* contains public code—declarations, sub procedures, and functions—that can be shared among all modules in a project. In later versions of Visual Basic, a code module is referred to as a *Standard module* (as opposed to a Class or Form module).

General versus Event Procedures

A *general procedure* tells your application how to perform a specific task. Once you've defined the procedure, it must be explicitly *invoked*, or called, by your application. On the other hand, an *event procedure* remains idle until called upon to respond to events caused by the user (a mouse click) or triggered by the system (a timer or load event). You can place a general procedure in a form module, code module, or class module.

Sub Procedures

Any *procedure* is a named sequence of statements executed as a unit. For example, Function and Sub are types of procedures. A *Sub procedure* (hereafter referred to simply as a *procedure*) is a unit of code that performs a specific task within a program but returns no explicit value. A Sub procedure begins with a Sub statement and ends with an End Sub statement, as you've seen in many of the procedures associated with particular events, such as a button's Click event.

Visual Basic has many built-in procedures (or statements), some of which you've already used (MsgBox and Print). See Table 6.1 for a small sample of other procedures offered by Visual Basic.

Table 6.1. A few other useful Visual Basic procedures.

Procedure	Description	Usage Example
FileCopy	Copies a disk file	FileCopy "Bozo.Cln","Chuckles.Cln"
Name	Renames a file	Name "OldName.Old" As "NewName.New"
Kill	Deletes a file	Kill "DeadFile.Ded"
Beep	Sounds a beep	Beep
Date	Sets system date	Date #January 27, 1994#

You're not limited to the procedures provided by Visual Basic. Often you'll want to define your own specialized routines for performing actions unique to your current application. For example, you might find it necessary to regularly delete several different files from your application's disk environment. Rather than make repeated calls to the `Kill` procedure, you could open a code module and define your own procedure, as follows:

```
Sub DiskCleanUp ()                          'Definition header...
Kill "*.Dat"
Kill "*.Txt"
Kill "JustOne.Tmp"
Beep
MsgBox "Disk Is Clean!",vbInformation,"Procedure Complete!"
End Sub
```

Notice that your new procedure, `DiskCleanUp`, "rings" the computer's bell and displays a message upon completion. Now you may call all the statements in `DiskCleanUp` from anywhere in your application, simply by including its name as a statement in your code:

```
DiskCleanUp                      'Calls your new procedure
```

Notice also that you do not use parentheses when calling a procedure, although they appear in the procedures declaration header. This particular *programmer-defined procedure (PDP)* requires no arguments, but it's possible to pass additional information to your procedures. If a procedure is to accept arguments, the arguments must be specified in the procedure's header. Here's a PDP that takes two integer arguments and sets a global variable equal to their product:

```
Sub Multiply(iFirst As Integer, iSecond As Integer)        'Definition header...
iGlobalVar = iFirst * iSecond
End Sub
```

Notice that the parameters of this procedure's header specify the incoming variable names and types. If the words "As Integer" had been omitted, the arguments would have come in as variants. Here's how a call to this procedure might look in code:

```
Dim iThis As Integer,iThat As Integer
iThis = 3
iThat = 4
Multiply iThis,iThat                         'Here's the call...
```

Again, when passing arguments to a procedure, you do not enclose them in parentheses. Simply type the name of the procedure, type a space, then type a comma-delimited list of arguments, if required.

Note Although the words *argument* and *parameter* are often used interchangeably, there is a difference between the two. Arguments are the variables or literals passed to a procedure or function. Parameters are the comma delimited, name/type specifiers that appear between the parentheses of a function's (or procedure's) definition header.

Function Procedures

A *Function procedure* (or just *function*) is a procedure that performs a specific task within a Visual Basic program and *returns a value*. Also, since a function returns a value, it is, in a sense, *equal* to the value it returns. Therefore, the function itself may be used as part of a more complex expression. A function is defined in a module, beginning with a Function statement and ending with an End Function statement. Here, in Table 6.2, are a few useful Visual Basic functions:

Table 6.2. A few useful Visual Basic functions.

Function	Description	Usage Example	Return Value
Len()	Returns length of string	iLen = Len("Bozo")	iLen = 4
Mid()	Returns part of a string	Mid("Bozo",1,2)	sStr = "Bo"
Chr()	Returns character from code	sChar = Chr(65)	sChar = "A"
Asc()	Returns code from character	iCode=Asc("A")	iCode = 65
UCase()	Coverts to uppercase	sUp=UCase("bozo")	sUp = "BOZO"
LCase()	Converts to lowercase	sLow=LCase("BOZO")	sLow = "bozo"
InStr()	Returns position of substring	sSub=InStr ("Bozo","z")	sSub = 3

These predefined string functions are often useful, but, again, you may create your own programmer-defined functions (PDFs) to augment Visual Basic's built-in offerings. For example, you might find it necessary to convert a phrase of several words to a proper noun title so that "the world is an oyster" becomes "The World Is An Oyster." To do this, you could create a function called, say, Title(). It might look something like this:

```
Function Title(sInString As String) As String
Dim sOutString As String
Dim iSpace As Integer

sInString = Trim(LCase(sInString)) + " "

iSpace = InStr(sInString, " ")
```

```
While iSpace > 0
sOutString = sOutString + UCase(Mid(sInString, 1, 1)) + Mid(sInString, 2, iSpace -
➡1)
sInString = LTrim(Mid(sInString, iSpace + 1))
iSpace = InStr(sInString, " ")
Wend

Title = sOutString
End Function
```

For now, don't worry about exactly how this function works. Most of the work is done inside the `While...Wend` loop, where `sInString` is parsed into separate capitalized words. Notice that the function's body falls between the `Function` header and `End Function` footer. The header specifies the name of the function. Inside the parentheses are the names and types of the expected arguments, if any, and outside the parentheses is the data type of the return value, if any. The return value of a function is set by assigning it to the function's name, as in the line before the footer (see preceding code listing).

To call this function, you might use the following expression:

```
stile = Title(sPhrase)                    'Use variable to receive return value
```

Functions are always called in this manner. Even if a function expects no arguments, you must still provide the empty parentheses. Since all functions return a value, you must provide a variable to "catch" it, or you must include the function in a more complex expression. Here's an example:

```
Dim sFavBook As String
sFavBook = "the french lieutenant's woman"
Print "My favorite book is "+ Title(sFavBook)
```

Why Work with Functions and Procedures?

Programmer-defined functions and procedures enable you to create your own custom routines to meet the needs of your particular application and to avoid the awkward and unnecessary repetition of code. You may boost the power and versatility of your procedures by including any of Visual Basic's built-in statements and functions, as well as routines previously defined by you or by others.

A thoughtful use of custom procedures and functions can help divide a complex application into more manageable units of code. By writing your own form-level procedures and functions, you may share code among all the controls on a form. By adding your own procedures to a standard module, you may share your code among all the forms in your application.

How to Work with Functions and Procedures

How In this section, you'll create and save a new project called EVB_BOOK to which, during the course of this book, you will add a code module and many forms. Follow these steps to begin your Encryption/Decryption program:

1. Select New Project from the File menu.

2. Change Form1's name to frmEncrypt.

3. Open a new code module by selecting Module from Visual Basic's Insert menu or by clicking the Module tool on the Toolbar, the second button from the left. In the modules code window, declare a global variable, sPhrase, by typing **Global sPhrase As String**.

4. As with other significant objects in your application, it's best to give your new module a meaningful name. Change the Name property of the new module to EVB_CODE.

5. Save your project by selecting Save Project As... from Visual Basic's File menu. At this point, you'll be asked if you want to save the module and form, as well. You should do so. Save the project as EVB_BOOK.

Compare your screen to Figure 6.1.

Figure 6.1.
*Creating a new
Code module.*

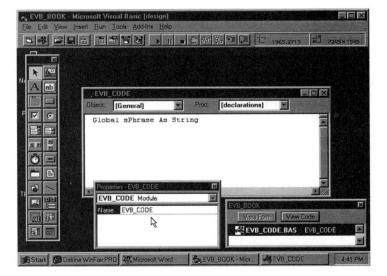

Creating New Procedures

Now that your project contains a standard code module, you may write your new functions and procedures. Select or open your module's code window. Notice that the Object drop-down list contains the word (General) and the Proc list contains (Declarations). As you've seen, it is in this General Declarations section of your module that you would declare any module-level, or global, variables and constants. It is here, too, that you may begin the definition of your new module's procedures and functions.

You'll create a new procedure called GetPhrase(), which you'll call to get the user to enter a word or phrase for encryption. You may create a new procedure by selecting Procedure from Visual Basic's Insert menu, then selecting Function or Procedure and setting the scope as Public or Private. There's an easier way, however. On the last line of the General Declarations section, type **Sub** followed by a space and the name of your procedure. Visual Basic will open a code window containing a Sub...End Sub template.

In your code module window, below the variable declaration, type **Sub GetPhrase**, then press the Enter key. Between the Sub and End Sub statements, add the call to InputBox() you see here:

```
Sub GetPhrase()
sPhrase = InputBox$("Please Enter Phrase: ", "Phrase To Be Encrypted")
End Sub
```

Now you'll be able to call the GetPhrase() procedure from anywhere in your application, thereby getting a value for the global variable sPhrase. In the following section, you'll create the Encrypt() and Decrypt() functions for your application.

Creating New Functions

The process of creating a function is very similar to that of sub procedures. The differences are that you use the Function statement rather than Sub and that you must set up a return value. You could go back to your module's General Declarations section to define your function, but this is not necessary. You may begin the Encrypt() function by typing **Function Encrypt** on any blank line in your module. Do so now, then fill in the required parameter information, as well as the body of the function. Here's the annotated listing:

```
Function Encrypt(sInPhrase As String) As String   'Header...
Dim iLen As Integer                               'Need some vars...
Dim sOut As String, sCurrent As String, sNew As String

iLen = Len(sInPhrase)                             'Measure the string...

For x = 1 To iLen                                 'For each letter...
    sCur = Mid$(sInPhrase, x, 1)                  'Pull it out...
    sNew = Chr$(Asc(sCur) + 1)                    'Bump it...
    sOut = sOut & sNew                            'Add to out string...
    Next
Encrypt = sOut                                    'Set return value...
End Function
```

As you may have determined on your own, this function employs a less-than-mission-critical encryption algorithm. In fact, all you're doing is bumping each letter of the phrase by one ASCII value so that "HAL" becomes "IBM", for example (for those hard-core *2001* fans out there).

> **Tip** Strictly speaking, it's not possible to define new procedures or functions within other procedures or functions. However, when you type **Function** or **Sub**, Visual Basic 4.0 is smart enough to know what you want and opens a new code window accordingly. This allows you to jump quickly to new functions and procedures as you need to create them. Also remember to use the Object and Proc drop-down lists to efficiently navigate between the code elements of your module.

Your application's Decrypt() function is really just a copy of the Encrypt() function with a couple of small changes. In fact, one way to create it would be to type **Function Decrypt** and press Enter (to get the Decrypt() function template), then copy the body of Encrypt() into it. The changes you'll make are highlighted in the following listing:

```
Function Decrypt(sInPhrase As String) As String     'Different name...
Dim iLen As Integer
Dim sOut As String, sCurrent As String, sNew As String

iLen = Len(sInPhrase)

For x = 1 To iLen
    sCur = Mid$(sInPhrase, x, 1)
    sNew = Chr$(Asc(sCur) - 1)                      'Minus, not plus...
    sOut = sOut & sNew
    Next
Decrypt = sOut                                      'Decrypt, not Encrypt...
End Function
```

> **Tip** Copying code is OK, but there's a better, more efficient way of handling your program's encryption and decryption. Since the two functions are so similar, why not create a single function called, say, CryptIt(), which takes two arguments rather than one? The first argument would still be the incoming phrase, but the second argument, say, iWhich, would be an integer equal to 1 or −1, depending on whether you were encrypting or decrypting. The header of this function would be Function CryptIt(sInPhrase,iWhich) As String. Then, in the body, rather than +1 or −1, you'd have +iWhich.

Calling Your Functions and Procedures

All that remains is to create your application's form, from which you'll call your custom procedure and functions. The form will contain three buttons, one to get the phrase to be encrypted, one to encrypt and display it, and one to display the decrypted phrase. Open or select frmEncrpyt, and complete visual implementation according to Table 6.3:

Table 6.3. Design-time settings—Procedure/Function program.

Visual Basic Object	Property	Design-Time Setting
Form	Name	frmEncrypt
	Caption	Procedure/Function Exercise
Command Button	Name	cmdGet
	Caption	Get Phrase
Command Button	Name	cmdEncrypt
	Caption	Encrypt It
Command Button	Name	cmdDecrypt
	Caption	Decrypt It

Once the form is ready, it's time to add code to the buttons. Since your custom procedures are written and ready to use, safely stored and accessible in your code module, your buttons' Click events will contain just a few simple lines. Open the appropriate code window and add them.

```
Private Sub cmdGet_Click()
GetPhrase                               'Call GetPhrase
End Sub

Private Sub cmdEncrypt_Click()
Dim sEncrpyted As String
sEncrypted = Encrypt(sPhrase)           'Call Encrypt()
MsgBox sEncrypted, vbExclamation, "Phrase Encrypted!"
End Sub

Private Sub cmdDecrypt_Click()
Dim sDecrypted As String
sDecrypted = Decrypt(Encrypt(sPhrase))     'Call both in same expression
MsgBox sDecrypted, vbExclamation, "Phrase Decrypted!"
End Sub
```

Once this code is added to the appropriate buttons, you'll be ready to test. Clicking cmdGet will call GetPhrase to display an InputBox in which the user will enter a phrase to be encrypted. The other two buttons will display the phrase, alternately encrypted and decrypted. See Figures 6.2 and 6.3 for examples of possible output.

Figure 6.2.
Encryption in action.

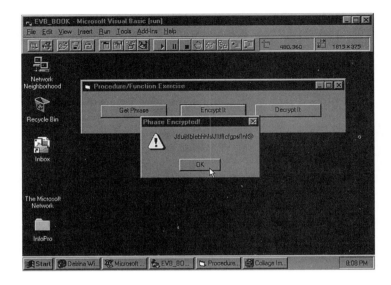

Figure 6.3
The phrase decrypted.

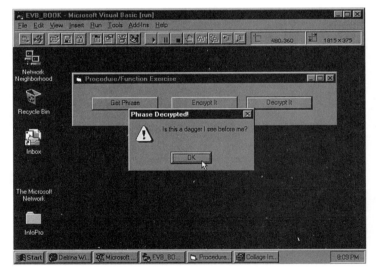

Essential Summary

In this chapter, you learned the difference between sub procedures and functions, and how to create them. You saw that both procedures and functions perform specific tasks in your application, but that procedures do not return values and that functions do. In addition, you were introduced to many new Visual Basic statements and string functions and saw how they might be used to enhance your own custom routines.

Custom functions and procedures allow you to create your own special routines to meet the demands of your particular application. They contribute to your application's overall modularity and reduce the amount of repetitive code. You are able to enhance the power and flexibility of your own procedures by including any of Visual Basic's predefined statements and functions.

Why

By creating a new project containing a form and code module, you were able to declare and call a custom procedure, GetPhrase, as well as two programmer-defined functions, Encrypt() and Decrypt(). You saw how and why procedures are called, as opposed to functions. You saw that functions are always called with parentheses as part of an expression, and that procedures are invoked simply by calling their names with, or without, a comma-delimited list of arguments.

How

PART II

Exploring the Toolbox Controls

Command Buttons, Text Boxes, and Labels

In this chapter, you will expand your understanding of command buttons and are introduced to two new controls, TextBox and Label, and most of their associated properties. In the process of exploring these new controls and properties, you'll create a fully functional Password Entry form that may be incorporated into any application.

What Are Command Buttons?

What You've already created several *command buttons* in the previous chapters. Generally speaking, you use a CommandButton control to begin, interrupt, or end a particular process. When clicked or otherwise selected, a command button appears pushed in and, therefore, is sometimes called a push button.

To display text on a CommandButton control, you must set its Caption property. Any ampersand (&) appearing in the text of the Caption property causes the character following the ampersand to become an Alt access key. That character will appear underlined in the caption and may be used in conjunction with the Alt key for quick keyboard access.

A user will often choose a command button by clicking it or tabbing to it and pressing Enter. If a button's Default property is set to True, the user may select it by pressing Enter at any time, regardless of which control currently has the focus. To allow the user to choose the button by pressing Esc, set the button's Cancel property to True. See Table 7.1 for a summary of commonly used command button properties.

Table 7.1. Common command button properties.

Property	Description	Settings Examples
Appearance	Selects 3-D or flat appearance	1=3-D, 0=Flat
Cancel	Allows selection with Esc	True, False
Caption	String to be displayed on button	Literal or string expression
Default	Allows selection with Enter	True, False
Font	Set font type, style, size	MS Sans Serif, Bold, 12

What Are Labels?

What

A *label* is a graphical control you use to display text that a user can't edit directly. However, you can write code that changes the text displayed as a label in response to events at run time. For example, if your application takes a few minutes to loop through a database table, you can use a label to display a message such as Processing...Remain Calm.... In addition, labels are often used to identify another control, such as a text box, that doesn't have its own Caption property.

If you want the label to properly display multiple lines of varying lengths, you may set the AutoSize and WordWrap properties to True. Table 7.2 summarizes other frequently used Label control properties.

Table 7.2. Other commonly used Label properties.

Property	Description	Settings Examples
Alignment	Aligns caption within border	0=Left Justify, 2=Center
Appearance	Selects 3-D or flat appearance	1=3-D, 0=Flat

Property	Description	Settings Examples
BorderStyle	Determines type of border	0=None, 1=Fixed Single
Caption	String to be displayed	Literal or string expression
Font	Set font type, style, size	MS Sans Serif, Bold, 12

What Are Text Boxes?

A *TextBox* control—sometimes called an edit field, edit box, or edit control—is used to display information entered by you at design time, by the user at run time, or programmatically assigned to the control in code. The displayed text may be accessed by setting, or reading, the control's Text property. This may be done directly at design time or by using dot notation in code. For example, you may store the current contents of a text box to a variable, then set it to something different. Here's a snippet that would do just that, assuming that you have a text box named txtMyBox:

```
Dim sOldText,sNewText As String
sNewText = "New Text"
sOldText = txtMyBox.Text                 'Read current text
txtMyBox.Text = sNewText                 'Set new text
```

> **Tip** Since the essence of a TextBox control is its Text property, you may read or set the text displayed in the edit area by referring directly to the control's Name. In the last line in the preceding code, for example, you could have omitted the reference to the Text property and simply written **txtMyBox = sNewText.**

If you need to display multiple lines of text, you must set the MultiLine property to True. If a multiline text box doesn't have a horizontal scroll bar, text will wrap automatically, even when the text box is resized. To customize the scroll bar combination on a text box, you may set the ScrollBars property to Horizontal, Vertical, Both, or None.

As long as the MultiLine property is True, you can use the Alignment property to adjust the text to the left, right, or center of the edit area. If the MultiLine property is False, setting the Alignment property has no effect. The text is left-aligned by default. Here, in Table 7.3, is a list of other TextBox properties.

Table 7.3. Other useful TextBox properties.

Property	Description	Settings Examples
Appearance	Selects 3-D or flat appearance	1=3-D, 0=Flat
BorderStyle	Determines type of border	0=None, 1=Fixed Single
Font	Set font type, style, size	MS Sans Serif, Bold, 12
PasswordChar	Hides text with a single character	Might use * or #, for example
SelStart	Start position for selecting text	Run Time Only
SelLength	Set length of selected text	Run Time Only
Tag	Stores additional information	Any string expression

The SelStart and SelLength properties are available at run time only, so you won't see them listed in your text box's Properties window. They're used to select, or highlight, all or part of the text displayed in the edit area. You'll work with these properties later in this chapter when you create your Password Entry program.

The Tag property is not unique to a TextBox control. In fact, it's available to almost any control, as well as form objects and menu objects. The Tag property is useful for storing any extra data needed by your program. For example, you can use this property to assign an identification string to an object without affecting any of its other property settings or causing unexpected side effects. In your Password Program, you'll use the Tag property to store your system's password at design time.

Why Use Command Buttons, Text Boxes, and Labels?

It would be difficult, if not impossible, to find a useful Windows application that did not make generous use of these three controls. One way to overcome the limitations of Visual Basic's InputBox() and MsgBox() functions is to design your own dialog boxes for getting user input and displaying output. Any such dialog boxes would be likely to contain one or more labels, text boxes, and Command buttons.

If you require another example of the usefulness of these controls, think of a simple database application. When field data is viewed through a form, it's usually stored (or attached) to multiple TextBox controls, which in turn are identified by labels. The same form is likely to contain at least a few, and probably several, command buttons for navigating through the database records, as well as for inserting and deleting records as required.

Using Command Buttons, Text Boxes, and Labels

In this section, you'll create a Password Input form employing command buttons, text boxes and labels. You'll manipulate many of these controls' properties at both design time and run time, as well as attach code to significant push button events to make your Password form fully functional.

How

First, open your EVB_BOOK project, if it's not still on the screen from the last chapter. If frmEncrypt is still open, close it by double-clicking the icon in its upper-left corner. Then create a new form by selecting **F**orm from the **I**nsert menu, or by clicking the Form button at the extreme left of the toolbar.

Referring to Figure 7.1, draw the following objects and set their properties according to Table 7.4.

Figure 7.1.
Design view: the
Password program.

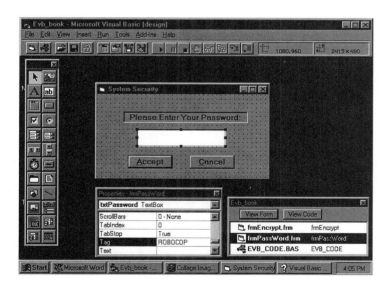

Table 7.4. Design-time settings—Password program.

Visual Basic Object	Property	Design-Time Setting
Form	Name	frmPassword
	Caption	System Security
Label	Name	lblPassword
	Caption	Please Enter Your Password:
	Alignment	2 - Center
	BorderStyle	1 - Fixed Single
	FontSize	10
	FontStyle	Bold
Text Box	Name	txtPassword
	FontSize	14
	FontStyle	Regular
		Password Char*
	Tag	ROBOCOP
Command Button	Name	cmdAccept
	Caption	&Accept
	Default	True
Command Button	Name	cmdCancel
	Caption	&Cancel
	Cancel	True

Now that you're ready to create a second form in the current project, you'll want to make sure that this form is the project's startup form. If you ran your program now, you might be surprised to see frmEncrypt show up, even though you've been working on the Password form. To change the project's startup form, you'll need to select Options from the Visual Basic Tools menu, then click on the Project tab. From the Startup Form drop-down list, select frmPassword. During the design phase, you may want to repeat this process for every new form you add to your application.

You'll see from Table 7.4, as well as from Figure 7.1, that your program's password will be "ROBOCOP," which has been stored in txtPassword's Tag property. For security, you'll use an asterisk as the text box's password character.

> **Caution** Many Control properties have a way of interacting with one another in somewhat surprising ways. For example, a text box's PasswordChar setting will have no effect if the MultiLine property is set to True. Similarly, the MultiLine property *must* be True if you want to set the Alignment property to anything other than Left-Align. For this reason, it's wise to keep track of the properties you're changing and to test frequently to be sure specific property combinations produce the desired effect.

Notice how the label's BorderStyle setting creates a kind of sunken 3-D effect. Notice also the use of ampersands in the command button captions, allowing for Alt key access. The cmdAccept button's Default property is set to True so that it may be activated at any time by pressing the Enter key. Similarly, cmdCancel's Cancel property is set to True, allowing Esc key access.

Adding Code to the Buttons

All the code for your Password program is contained in the two buttons' Click event procedures. In fact, except for a single End statement in cmdCancel (which, not surprisingly, causes the program to end), all the code action occurs when cmdAccept is clicked or otherwise selected. Here are the two listings:

```
Private Sub cmdCancel_Click()             'Select Cancel...
End                                        'And the program ends...
End Sub

Private Sub cmdAccept_Click()
Static iTries                              'To count the tries...
If UCase(txtPassword) = txtPassword.Tag Then    'If match....
MsgBox "You're In!", vbExclamation, "Access Granted!"   'Access granted
Else                                       'If wrong...
iTries = iTries + 1                        'Bump iTries
If iTries = 3 Then                         'If three tries...You're out!
MsgBox "Sorry...Too Many Attempts", vbCritical, "Access Denied!"
End
Else                                       'Otherwise, try again...
MsgBox "Press OK And Try Again", vbInformation, "Incorrect Password!"
txtPassword.SelStart = 0                   'Highlight the
txtPassword.SelLength = Len(txtPassword) 'last entry...
End If
End If
txtPassword.SetFocus
End Sub
```

This code warrants a little discussion. First, notice that you're setting up a Static variable, iTries, to keep track of password entry attempts. If the user can't get the right password in three attempts, you'll display a critical error message and end the program. If they are able to enter the proper password (which is stored, remember, in the text box's Tag property), a friendlier, "Access Granted" message is displayed.

After the first two unsuccessful attempts, you'll want the user to be able to enter another word without having to delete or backspace through the incorrect one. You perform this kind of service by selecting (or highlighting) the previous entry so that the user may simply type over it. This is where the SelStart and SelLength properties come in. The text box's SelStart property is set to 0 (the first character in the incorrect password); then, using SelLength, the rest of the word is selected. The last line before End Sub calls a method, SetFocus, which ensures that the txtPassword control will be ready to receive the next keystrokes.

Note To incorporate this Password form into a larger application, that is, to use it as a startup form through which the user must gain access, a little tweaking is necessary. Rather than put up a congratulatory message when the proper password is entered, you'll want to close the password dialog box and display the application's main interface form. Assuming your application has a main form named frmMain, this could be accomplished with these two statements, shown on a single line:

```
frmMain.Show : frmPassword.Hide.
```

That's it for the Password program. Go ahead and test. Refer to Figure 7.2 for output from a sample session.

Figure 7.2.
A sample session with
the Password program.

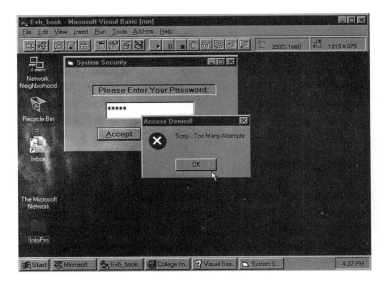

Essential Summary

In this chapter, you added to your understanding of command buttons, which you use to begin, interrupt, or end a particular procedure. You were introduced to two new controls, text boxes and labels, and had a chance to use many of their associated properties. You saw that labels are usually used to display read-only information to the user, while text boxes are best for both showing and editing data.

What

By using command buttons, text boxes, and labels, you may design your own forms and dialog boxes for getting input and displaying output. In fact, any useful Windows application is likely to contain at least a few, and probably several, of these controls. Their functionality and appearance may be greatly enhanced through a well-conceived, and well-implemented, interaction of associated properties.

Why

You put to use your study of command buttons, text boxes, and labels by creating a Password Input form composed of two command buttons, a text box, and one label. You adjusted several of these control's common properties at design time, as well as read and manipulated them at run time. The final result, after adding code to your form's Accept and Cancel buttons, was a fully functional Password Input form that might be integrated into any application.

How

Option Buttons, Check Boxes, and Frames

In designing Windows applications, it is often necessary to create forms and dialog boxes that present the user with a number of choices—some of which may be displayed as a group of mutually exclusive options, while others may be categorized in a way that allows for one or more options to be in effect at once. For example, in a game program, you may want the user to select a level of play from a list of three choices, such as Beginner, Intermediate, or Advanced. On the other hand, the game's environment settings may include Color, Sound, Modem, and Mouse, any or all of which may be enabled at one time.

By using option buttons, check boxes, and frames (and by writing a little code), you'll be able to quickly implement such forms and functionality. In this chapter, you'll explore these controls and their associated properties, and you'll put them to use in a simple OptionButton/CheckBox program.

What Are Option Buttons?

What An *OptionButton control* displays an option that can be turned on or off, with the button's Value property set to True or False, accordingly. Usually, option buttons are displayed in a framed group, comprising a mutually exclusive list of options. You group OptionButton controls by drawing them inside a container, such as a frame, picture box, or form. To group OptionButton controls in a frame or picture box, draw the frame or picture box first, and then draw the OptionButton controls inside. All OptionButton controls within the same container act as a single group; that is, only one at a time may be *on*, and the entire group may be moved or deleted at design time by dragging or deleting the container.

> **Caution** You *must* draw the controls within the container (usually a frame) to assure their mutual exclusivity and to create a valid containership hierarchy. Drawing the controls outside the frame and dragging them in, copying them within the frame, or drawing the frame around existing controls will not produce the desired results.

You may display a text identifier next to the option button by setting its Caption property. To determine the state of the button, selected or not selected, you must read its Value property, which will be set to True or False, accordingly. The following snippet might be used to check the current setting of a button called optLevel:

```
If optLevel.Value = True Then
    MsgBox "Button Selected!"
Else
    MsgBox "Button Not Selected!"
EndIf
```

> **Tip** Since an option button's default property is Value, and since it's not even necessary to use the word True in evaluating a Boolean expression, the first line in the preceding code snippet could have been shortened to `If optLevel Then`. You'll see this type of shorthand throughout this book.

While option buttons and check boxes may appear to function similarly, there is an important difference: When a user selects an option button, the other OptionButton controls in the same group are automatically unavailable. In contrast, any number of CheckBox controls can be selected at once.

What Are Check Boxes?

 A *CheckBox control* displays a check when selected; the check disappears when the box is cleared. Use this control to give the user a True/False, Yes/No, or On/Off option. You can organize check boxes into groups, thereby displaying multiple choices from which the user can select one or more.

As with option buttons, you may display text next to the check box by setting the Caption property. Use the Value property to determine the state of the control: 1 = Checked, 0 = Cleared, and 2 = Unavailable (disabled, meaning grayed out or dimmed). Here's a Select Case snippet that would determine the state of a check box called chkSound:

```
Select Case chkSound
    Case 0
    Msg ="Not Checked!"

    Case 1
    Msg="Checked!"

    Case 2
    Msg="Not Available!"

End Select
MsgBox Msg
```

What Are Frames?

A *frame* provides an attractive way of grouping related controls. In any Windows application, you're likely to see groups of option buttons and check boxes enclosed by, or *contained by*, a frame. You can also use a frame to subdivide a form in other ways; for example, to separate groups of related text boxes bound to fields in a database table.

Again, to group controls, first draw the Frame control, and then draw the controls inside the frame. This enables you to move the frame and the controls it contains together. If you draw a control outside the frame and then try to move it inside, the control will be on top of the frame, and you'll have to move the frame and controls separately. To select multiple controls in a frame, hold down the Ctrl key while using the mouse to draw a box around them, or hold the Shift key and click each control you want to include in the selection.

What

Why Option Buttons and Check Boxes?

In Windows programming, it is often necessary to design dialog boxes that present to the user a variety of options, some of which may be displayed as a mutually exclusive group, while others are classified in a manner allowing for one or more options to take effect at once.

A thorough understanding of the relationship between frames, option buttons, and check boxes, as well as their associated properties and events, will greatly enhance your ability to design visually and functionally concise Windows forms and dialog boxes.

Why

How to Use Option Buttons, Check Boxes, and Frames

In this section, you'll create a new form similar to the one depicted in Figure 8.1. To begin, start Visual Basic and open your EVB_BOOK project. If the last chapter's form is still on the screen, close it and create a new form to be named frmFrames. Give this form a caption of Frames, OptionButtons and CheckBoxes, then save it, accepting the default file name. Using Figure 8.1 and Table 8.1 as references, complete the visual implementation of your new form.

Figure 8.1.
Design view:
OptionButton/
CheckBox program.

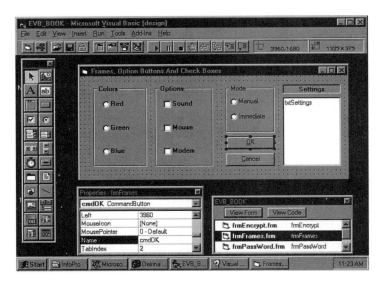

Table 8.1. Names and special settings—OptionButton/CheckBox program.

Visual Basic Object	Property	Design-Time Setting
Text Box	Name	txtSettings
	MultiLine	True
Frame	Name	fraColors
	Caption	Colors (bold font)
Frame	Name	fraOption
	Caption	Options (bold font)
Frame	Name	fraMode
	Caption	Mode (bold font)
Option Button	Name	optRed
	Caption	Red (bold font)
Option Button	Name	optGreen
	Caption	Green (bold font)
Option Button	Name	optBlue
	Caption	Blue (bold font)

Visual Basic Object	Property	Design-Time Setting
Check Box	Name	chkSound
	Caption	Sound (bold)
Check Box	Name	chkMouse
	Caption	Mouse (bold)
Check Box	Name	chkModem
	Caption	Modem (bold)
Option Button	Name	optManual
	Caption	Manual
Option Button	Name	optImmediate
	Caption	Immediate

Program Overview

As you can see, this form contains two groups of option buttons. One group presents a choice of three colors to be used as the form's background. The other OptionButton group, Mode, displays the two modes in which the program operates, Manual and Immediate.

You'll notice also a group of three check boxes that displays a list of user-selectable "Options," including Sound, Mouse, and Modem. The MultiLine text box, txtSettings, will be used to display a list of the program's current settings as determined by the user's interaction with the form's check boxes and buttons.

When running in Manual mode, you'll have to click the OK button before the new settings will take effect and be displayed in the text box. In Immediate mode, the selected settings will take effect *immediately* upon clicking one of the Color option buttons or one of the Option check boxes.

Adding Code

To add this functionality to your program, you'll need to write a little code. Remember, although the following snippets may comprise a long listing, a judicious use of your editor's cut, copy, and paste features will save a lot of time and typing.

The first step is to declare some useful constants, as it's easier to remember what is meant by CHECKED or RED than by the raw numbers, 1 or 4. Because you want these constants to be global in scope, you'll add them to your code module's general declarations section. Open the module EVB_CODE by double-clicking it in the Project window.

> **Note** The code module, or standard module, EVB_CODE was created in Chapter 6 of this book. If it's not in your current project, you may create it now by selecting **Module** from Visual Basic's **Insert** menu, or by clicking the Module button, second from the left on Visual Basic's toolbar. Remember to save it as EVB_CODE rather than as the default MODULE1.

Here's what EVB_CODE's general declarations section should contain:

```
'Global Variables...              'May already be here...
Global sPhrase As String

'Add the following Global constants...
Global Const CHECKED = 1          'For check boxes

Global Const RED = 4
Global Const GREEN = 2            'QBColor Constants
Global Const BLUE = 1
```

You'll also want a couple of *form level variables*, that is, variables that will be visible throughout the form. Close your code module by double-clicking its icon in the upper-left corner, then select, or open, your new form named frmFrames. Locate the form's general declarations section by selecting (General) from the Object drop-down list, and (Declarations) from the Proc list. Enter the following lines:

```
'Form level variables...
Dim bImmediate As Boolean         'For tracking mode...
Dim CRLF As String                'For creating multi-line strings...
```

A good place to assign initial values to form level variables is in the form's Load event. The variable CRLF will contain a string made up of a carriage return and line feed character which, when concatenated with other strings, will produce the desired multi-line effect. Open a code window for the form's Load event and add the following line between the Private Sub and End Sub statements:

```
Private Sub Form_Load()
CRLF = Chr$(13) + Chr$(10)
End Sub
```

Now, most of your program's code is contained in the OK button's Click event. Use the drop-down lists to locate cmdOK's Click procedure. Although it requires a few lines, all that happens here is a "polling" of the various option buttons and check boxes, in order to determine their current values. As the settings are determined, a multi-line string, sSettings, is built to reflect them. Then the Visual Basic function QBColor() is used to change the form's background color; and finally, the settings string is displayed in the text box named txtSettings. Here's the documented listing:

```
Private Sub cmdOK_Click()
Dim sSettings As String, sColor As String      'For current settings

                                               'Poll check boxes...
```

```
If chkSound = CHECKED Then              'Add sound status to sSettings
sSettings = sSettings & "Sound Is On"
Else
sSettings = sSettings & "Sound Is Off"
End If

If chkMouse = CHECKED Then              'Add mouse status...
sSettings = sSettings & CRLF & "Mouse Is Enabled"
Else
sSettings = sSettings & CRLF & "Mouse Is Disabled"
End If

If chkModem = CHECKED Then              'Add modem status...
sSettings = sSettings & CRLF & "Modem Is On"
Else
sSettings = sSettings & CRLF & "Modem Is Off"
End If

                                        'Poll Color Options...
If optRed Then
sColor = "Color Is Red"                 'Set color string...
BackColor = QBColor(RED)                 'Change to red...

ElseIf optGreen Then
sColor = "Color Is Green"               'Set string...
BackColor = QBColor(GREEN)              'Change to green...

ElseIf optBlue Then
sColor = "Color Is Blue"                'Set string...
BackColor = QBColor(BLUE)               'Change to blue...
End If

sSettings = sSettings & CRLF & sColor   'Add color to sSettings...
txtSettings = sSettings                 'Display the list...
End Sub
```

Notice that the check boxes had to be evaluated separately, using three different If...Else...EndIf constructs. This is because it's possible for any, all, or none of them to be checked. In contrast, the option buttons could be polled by using a single If...ElseIf...EndIf device, since only one color button at a time may be selected.

As a new color option is selected, you change your form's background by setting it's BackColor property. An easy way to manipulate colors in Visual Basic is to use the QBColor() function, which requires a single integer argument between 0 and 15. In this program, you have constants representing the colors RED, GREEN, and BLUE, which you send to QBColor(). (You'll learn more about QBColor(), and the other Visual Basic color function RGB(), in Chapters 19 and 20.)

At this point, your program will work fine, as long as you click the OK button to display your selected settings. Now it's time to implement the Manual and Immediate mode option buttons. When Immediate mode is selected, any change to the Color option buttons, or to the Options check boxes, should result *immediately* in a change of colors and/or an updated list of current settings. One way to make this happen is to set the value of bImmediate, the form level Boolean variable, to True when optImmediate is clicked on, and False otherwise. In this way, all your form's controls may check bImmediate's value to determine the current mode. When the user clicks optImmediate or optManual, you'll set bImmediate's value accordingly. Here's a listing of the appropriate `Click` event procedures:

```
Private Sub optImmediate_Click()
bImmediate = optImmediate            'Set 'em equal
End Sub

Private Sub optManual_Click()
bImmediate = Not optManual           'Set 'em opposite
End Sub
```

All that remains is to add a single three-line If...Then construct to each of the color button's and check box's `Click` events. If bImmediate is True, and one of these buttons or boxes is clicked, you want the program to act as if the OK button was clicked, as well. That is, you want the color changed and the list of settings refreshed immediately. You "press" a command button from code by setting its Value property to True. Copy the following three lines into each color button's and each check box's `Click` event. Remember to place them between the Private Sub and End Sub statements:

```
If bImmediate Then
cmdOK = True            ;"Press" OK...
End If
```

> **Note** If you're thinking you could have not bothered with bImmediate at all and just checked the value of optImmediate directly...you're right. But then you wouldn't have had this perfect opportunity to declare and use your first Boolean variable. Besides, in a more ambitious program, you would find many other uses for bImmediate as a form level variable.

Finally, add the statement End to your Cancel button's `Click` event, and you'll be ready to test. Figure 8.2 shows output from a sample session.

Figure 8.2.
A sample session with the
CheckBox program.

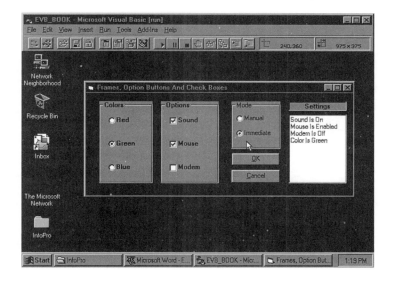

Essential Summary

In this chapter, you became familiar with three important, and closely related, Visual Basic controls: option buttons, check boxes, and frames. You learned that frames are often used as containers for both option buttons and check boxes, providing an attractive and convenient way of grouping related buttons or check boxes. In the case of option buttons, a frame ensures the desired mutual exclusivity of choices, while a group of check boxes allows for one or more, or none, of the choices to be in effect.

What

A thorough understanding of the interaction between option buttons, check boxes, and frames, as well as a clear idea of their related properties and events, will greatly improve your ability to design forms and dialog boxes that are both visually appealing and functionally efficient.

Why

You put to use your new understanding of option buttons, check boxes, and frames by adding a new form to your EVB_BOOK project. This form contained two groups of option buttons and a group of check boxes, as well as a multi-line text box to display user-selected settings. You added code that polled the form's check boxes and option buttons, and displayed an appropriate list of settings. You allowed your program to function in either a Manual or Immediate mode, depending on the user's mode selection.

How

List Boxes and Drop-Down Combinations

In this chapter, you'll learn how to use two new powerful Visual Basic controls: list boxes and combo boxes. In the process, you'll be introduced to several new properties and methods, and to special multi-dimensional variables called *arrays*. You'll also work with the KeyPress event procedure, as well as Visual Basic's UBound() function.

What Are List Boxes?

What A *list box* displays a list of items from which the user can select one or more items. If the number of items exceeds the number that can be displayed, a scroll bar is automatically added to the ListBox control. The list box's Click or DoubleClick events are usually used to process the selection. For example, upon double-clicking an item in a list called lstMyList, the following snippet would display the user's selection in a text box named txtChoice:

```
Private Sub lstMyList_DblClick()
txtChoice = lstMyList
End Sub
```

Refer to Figure 9.1 to see how this might look on the screen.

Figure 9.1.
*Displaying a list box
selection.*

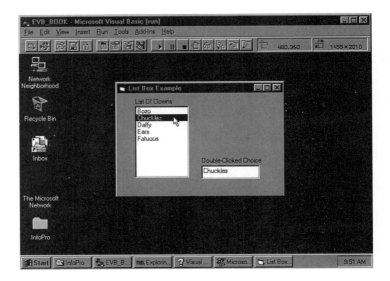

A list's ListCount property returns the number of items in the list, while the ListIndex property is used to track the currently selected item. If no item is selected, the ListIndex is set to −1. The first item in the list has a ListIndex of 0, while the last item's ListIndex is always set to one less than ListCount.

A ListBox control's MultiSelect property returns (at run time) or sets (at design time) a value indicating whether or not a user can make multiple selections, and how the multiple selections can be made. In order to select more than one item from a list, the ListBox control's MultiSelect property must be set to 1 or 2. Here's a summary description of possible MultiSelect settings:

Setting	Description
0	No multiple selection allowed. (Default setting).
1	Simple multiple selection. A mouse click or pressing the spacebar selects or deselects an item in the list. You may use the arrow keys to move focus from one item to another.
2	Extended multiple selection. Pressing Shift and clicking the mouse, or pressing Shift and one of the arrow keys, extends the selection from the previously selected item to the current item. Pressing Ctrl and clicking the mouse selects or deselects an item in the list, which may be used for multi-selecting noncontiguous items.

In programs where multiple selection is allowed, additional code is required to determine which items in the list have been selected. This is done by using a loop to iterate through the items in the list, checking each one's Selected property to see if it's True. Such a snippet might look something like this:

```
iSize = lstClowns.ListCount - 1
For X = 0 To iSize
    If lstClowns.Selected(X) = True Then
        MsgBox lstClowns.List(X)
    End If
Next
```

What Are Combo Boxes?

The difference between *combo boxes* and list boxes is that a ComboBox control *combines* the features of a TextBox control and a ListBox control. If the user does not want to select one of the choices offered, he or she may enter information in the text box portion of the control.

What

A combo box comes in three different styles, as determined by its Style Property setting. This property returns or sets a value indicating the type of ComboBox control and the behavior of its list box portion. ComboBox Style settings are summarized here.

Setting	Description
0	Dropdown Combo—Includes a drop-down list and a text box. The user can select from the list or type in the text box. (Default setting).
1	Simple Combo—Includes a text box and a list that doesn't drop down. The size of a Simple ComboBox includes both the edit and list portions. By default, a Simple ComboBox is sized so that none of the list is displayed. You may display more of the list by enlarging the box at design time, or increasing the Height property at run time.
2	Dropdown List—This style is not really a ComboBox at all. It only allows selection from the drop-down list, as the TextBox portion is unavailable to the user.

By setting the Style to 0 (Dropdown Combo) or 1 (Simple Combo) you give the user a list of choices. Either style enables the user to enter an alternative choice in the text box. On a form where space is at a premium, Setting 0 is best because the list portion closes when the user selects an item.

Common List Properties and Methods

List boxes and combo boxes have most of their properties and methods in common. They are summarized in Table 9.1.

Table 9.1. Useful List properties and methods.

Property	Description	Usage Example
ListCount	Number of list items	iItems = lstMyList.ListCount −1
ListIndex	Numeric index of current item	lstMyList.ListIndex = 3
List	With index, returns list item	sSixthItem = lstMyList.List(5)
Selected	True if item is selected	If lstMyList.Selected(3) Then...
Sorted	List auto-sorted if True	lstMyList.Sorted = True

Method	Description	Usage Example
AddItem	Adds string item to list	lstMyList. AddItem "Jones, Sam"
Clear	Removes all items from list	lstMyList.Clear
RemoveItem	Removes single item from list	lstMyList.RemoveItem 5

Please notice an important difference between the way in which the AddItem and RemoveItem methods work. Both require a single argument, but AddIem expects a string expression, while RemoveItem requires a numeric index. You'll put all of these properties and methods to work, later in this chapter.

Why Use List Boxes and Combo Boxes?

As a Windows programmer, you'll discover a variety of uses for both list boxes and combo boxes. There's almost always a need to display information in a list format from which the user must make a choice or, sometimes, be permitted to enter his or her own new textual information. ListBox and ComboBox controls offer a wide variety of list properties and methods that may be used to greatly simplify the process of adding such functionality to your programs.

How to Use List Boxes and Combo Boxes

In this section, you'll add a new form, frmLists, to your EVB_BOOK project. This form will include a combo box and two list boxes that will be used to explore all the properties and methods discussed earlier in this chapter. Add the form now, and don't forget to change your project's StartUp form accordingly. Refer to Figure 9.2 and Table 9.2 in completing visual implementation of your form.

Figure 9.2.
Design mode: the List Box program.

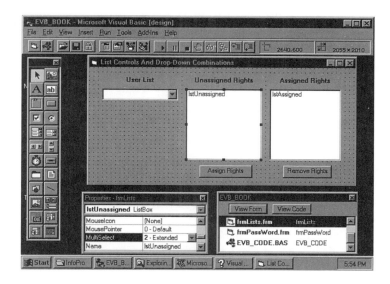

Table 9.3. Design-time settings—List Box program.

Visual Basic Object	Property	Design-Time Setting
Form	Name	frmLists
	Caption	List Controls And Dropdown Combinations
Combo Box	Name	cboUsers
	Style	0 - Dropdown Combo
	Sorted	True
List Box	Name	lstUnAssigned
	MultiSelect	True
List Box	Name	lstAssigned
	MultiSelect	True
Command Button	Name	cmdAssign
	Caption	Assign Rights
Command Button	Name	cmdRemove
	Caption	Remove Rights

Program Overview

This program presents a form similar to one that might be used by a system administrator while assigning network rights to individual users. You'll be able to select a user from a drop-down combo box, or add a new user to the list. You'll assign or remove rights one at a time by double-clicking them in the appropriate list. In addition, you'll be able to select several rights at once, employing the multi-select techniques discussed in the section "What Are List Boxes?"; you then assign or remove them by clicking the appropriate command button.

Note This program will provide no way to save or retrieve the user and rights information to and from disk, which obviously limits it's usefulness. Be patient because you'll see how to handle disk I/O in Chapters 20 and 36.

Using Arrays

So far you've worked only with regular variables, each having its own unique name. But it's often convenient to use *multi-dimensional* variables, called arrays, which may contain a set of sequentially indexed elements having the same intrinsic data type. In this way, an element of an array called Clowns may be initialized and referenced in the following manner:

```
Dim saClowns(3) As String        'Declare size and type

saClowns(1) = "Bozo"             'Assign values...
saClowns(2) = "Chuckles"
saClowns(3) = "Daffy"
```

Notice that the array is declared, or dimensioned, by using parentheses enclosing the number of elements. (The conventional prefix *sa* stands for *string array*). Since each element of an array has a unique identifying index number, it's easy to iterate through them by using a simple counter loop. Here's how you could print a list of clowns:

```
For iIndex = 0 To 2
Print saClowns(iIndex)
Next
```

Adding Code to the ListBox Program

In the ListBox/ComboBox program, you'll dimension and initialize two arrays: one for populating the user list and one for maintaining a list of network rights. Locate the General Declarations section of your new form and add the following lines:

```
Dim saUsers(5) As String
Dim saRights(8) As String
```

You'll need to give values to these arrays by adding the following lines to your form's Load event procedure (a form's Load event is always a good place to initialize form level variables).

```
Private Sub Form_Load()
saUsers(0) = "Adams, John"
saUsers(1) = "Baker, Sally"
saUsers(2) = "Collins, David"
saUsers(3) = "Dobbs, Jerry"
saUsers(4) = "Edwards, Brian"

saRights(0) = "Create"
saRights(1) = "Open"
saRights(2) = "Read"
saRights(3) = "Write"
saRights(4) = "Delete"
saRights(5) = "Parental"
saRights(6) = "Encrypt"
saRights(7) = "Decrypt"
LoadUsers
LoadRights
End Sub
```

You probably noticed the calls to LoadUsers and LoadRights in the preceding lines. These are two Sub procedures, to be defined by you. In the general declarations section, locate a blank line and type **Sub LoadUsers**. Press Enter to open a new code window. Here's what **LoadUsers** should look like:

```
Sub LoadUsers()                         'Loop to populate users list...
For iCount = 0 To UBound(saUsers) - 1
   cboUsers.AddItem saUsers(iCount)
Next
cboUsers.ListIndex = 0                  'Select the first item...
End Sub
```

Here you're using Visual Basic's UBound() function to determine the number of elements in your array. You subtract 1 to determine your loop maximum because the first index in an array is always 0.

Now create the LoadRights procedure in a similar manner. Here's the listing:

```
Sub LoadRights()                   'To populate rights list...
lstAssigned.Clear                  'First empty them...
lstUnassigned.Clear
For iCount = 0 To UBound(saRights) - 1        'Then loop
   lstUnassigned.AddItem saRights(iCount)
Next
End Sub
```

To prevent duplication, you'll empty the rights lists each time you call LoadRights. You'll need to call LoadRights every time you select a new user, so cboUsers' Click event should contain the call, like so:

```
Private Sub cboUsers_Click()
LoadRights
End Sub
```

In this program, the actual assignment or removal of rights occurs when the user clicks the Assign Rights or Remove Rights buttons. The processes of assigning or removing rights are very similar. In both cases, you'll loop through the list to determine which, and how many, rights are selected. Then you'll add those rights to the appropriate list and use a `While...Wend` loop to remove them from the current one. This produces the effect of the selected rights "jumping" from one list box to the other. Here's what cmdAssign's `Click` event procedure should look like:

```
Private Sub cmdAssign_Click()
Dim iSize, iSelected As Integer                 'Vars for loop and selected items...

iSize = lstUnassigned.ListCount - 1          'Get loop max...

For X = 0 To iSize
If lstUnassigned.Selected(X) = True Then      'If selected...
    lstAssigned.AddItem lstUnassigned.List(X) 'Add to Assigned list...
    iSelected = iSelected + 1                 'Keep track of number selected...
End If
Next

iCur = 0
While iSelected > 0                           'Now find selected items
If lstUnassigned.Selected(iCur) = True Then
    lstUnassigned.RemoveItem iCur             'And remove them from current list
    iSelected = iSelected - 1                 'Don't forget to decrement iSelected
Else
    iCur = iCur + 1                           'Not selected?  Move to next item..
End If
Wend
End Sub
```

The Remove Rights button's `Click` event will contain nearly identical code, so there's no need to list it here. You can simply copy the preceding lines into cmdRemove's `Click` event and change all instances of "Assigned" to "UnAssigned," and vice versa.

Now, you'll also want to be able to assign or remove rights one at a time, by double-clicking. It's simple to add this extra functionality just by "pressing" (or calling) cmdAssign or cmdRemove from within code attach to each list box's `DblClick` event. Here's the listing:

```
Private Sub lstAssigned_DblClick()
cmdRemove = True
End Sub

Private Sub lstUnassigned_DblClick()
cmdAssign = True
End Sub
```

Finally, you'll want to be able to type a new user's name into the TextBox portion of cboUsers and have the chance to add it to the user list. This will be accomplished by using the combo box's `KeyPress` event to monitor incoming characters, in order to *trap* the Enter key (ASCII 13). Here's the annotated listing, with explanation to follow:

```
Private Sub cboUsers_KeyPress(KeyAscii As Integer)
If KeyAscii = 13 Then                          'If ENTER is pressed...
    If cboUsers.ListIndex = -1 Then            'And entry is not in list...

    If MsgBox("Want To Add " & cboUsers & "?", vbYesNo + vbQuestion, _
```

```
        "No Such User!") = vbYes Then         'Put up a message...

        cboUsers.AddItem cboUsers             'And add if yes...
        End If

    End If
End If
End Sub
```

You'll notice something different about the KeyPress() event procedure's header: you are passed an integer variable, KeyAscii, corresponding to the key that triggered the event. The only keypress you're interested in is the Enter key. When that comes in, if the text box contains an entry not found in the list (ListIndex = -1), you'll display a dialog box asking if the name should be added.

Tip Finally, in Visual Basic 4.0, there is a *line continuation character*—a space followed by an underscore (_)—which allows a logical line of code to be typed on two or more physical lines. You see an example of this in the call to MsgBox in the preceding listing. Note that the line-continuation character can't be used to continue a line of code within a string expression.

It's now time to compile and thoroughly test all the features of your new program.

Essential Summary

In this chapter, you became familiar with two new Visual Basic controls: list boxes and combo boxes. You saw that these controls have many properties and methods in common, and you learned how to manipulate them in order to best meet your program requirements. You saw how to create and initialize special, indexed variables called arrays; and you had a chance to explore Visual Basic's KeyPress event procedure.

What

In Windows programming, there's almost always a need to display information in a list format from which the user may make a choice or, sometimes, enter his or her own new information. ListBox and ComboBox controls offer a wide variety of list properties and methods which may be used to greatly simplify the process of adding such functionality to your programs.

Why

You added to your EVB_BOOK project a new form containing a drop-down combo box and two list boxes. You set list box properties, called list box methods, and added your own code to produce a program to simulate a System Administrator's rights management screen. With this program, you are able to select a user from the cboUsers drop-down list; you can also add new users as required. You may add or remove rights one at a time by double-clicking them, or several at a time by multi-selecting and pressing the appropriate button.

How

Scroll Bars and Spinners

In this chapter, you'll learn how to create and manipulate vertical and horizontal scroll bars by working with the VScrollBar and HScrollBar controls. You'll also be introduced to a *third-party control* (or *OCX*), the SpinButton, which you'll add to Visual Basic's Toolbox. You'll use these controls to create a new form that will serve as a Loan Payment Calculator and, in the process, become familiar with three new Visual Basic functions: Pmt(), for calculating payments on fixed annuities; Format(), which is used to format string output; and the conversion function CDbl(), which converts other data types to type Double.

What Are Scroll Bars?

What Vertical and horizontal scroll bars are familiar to all Windows program users. You've already manipulated many of Visual Basic's own scroll bars, for example, while *scrolling* through the Properties or Project windows. *Scroll bars* provide a visually attractive and intuitive way to navigate through a long list of options, or other large amounts of information, such as a word processing document. Because of their gauge-like appearance, scroll bars are sometimes used as analog indicators of position or progress. They may be used as input devices, as well, where the user may visually adjust a quantity setting such as speed, temperature, or volume, for example.

Both types of scroll bars are comprised of three separate areas which may be clicked, or dragged, in order to change the scroll bar's Value property. These areas are the arrows at the ends, the scroll box or *thumb*, and the body of the bar itself, on either side of the thumb (see Figure 10.1).

Figure 10.1.
The parts of a scroll bar.

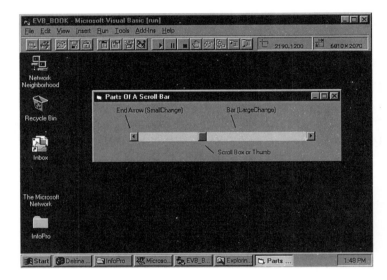

When you're using a scroll bar as an indicator of quantity or speed, or as an input device, you set the bar's Max and Min properties to establish the appropriate range of values.

To specify the amount of change to report in a scroll bar, use the LargeChange property for clicking in the bar itself and the SmallChange property for clicking the arrows at the ends of the scroll bar. The scroll bar's value increases or decreases with each click, according to the amounts set for the LargeChange and SmallChange properties. You can position the *thumb* at run time by setting the bar's value between 0 and 32,767, inclusive.

Scroll Bar Events

Whenever a scroll bar is clicked, its Change event procedure is executed. This is where you'd place code to display the bar's current value, for example, or to perform a dependent calculation. When a scroll bar's thumb is dragged, the Scroll event fires off, followed by the Change event when the thumb is released. This is where you'd add code to see or use the bar's value as it "scrolls" higher or lower.

The SpinButton Control

A *SpinButton* is a spinner control you can use with another control, such as a label or text box, to increment and decrement numbers. You may orient a spinner either horizontally or vertically by setting its SpinOrientation property. Like a scroll bar, you can use a spinner to scroll back and forth through a range of values or a list of items. Unlike a scroll bar, a spinner contains no body or thumb and, therefore, is more compact in appearance but could not be used as an analog gauge of time or position.

The SpinButton control has many properties for adjusting its appearance and behavior. You may change its colors, border thickness, and shadow, as well as its 3-D look. You may increase or decrease the amount of time between spin events (while the user holds down the mouse) by setting the Delay property.

Spinner Events

At run time, when the user clicks the up (or right) arrow of the spin button, SpinUp events are generated repeatedly until the mouse is released. Similarly, when the user clicks the down (or left) arrow, SpinDown events are generated. When using this control, you write code for the SpinUp and SpinDown events that increments or decrements the desired values. If you change the value or contents of a control in response to a Spin event, you must also call that control's Refresh method to insure that the updated value is displayed.

> **Note** When you create and distribute applications that use the spin button control, you should install the file SPIN32.OCX in the customer's WINDOWS \SYSTEM subdirectory. The Setup Wizard included with Visual Basic (and discussed in Chapter 18) provides tools to help you write setup programs that install your applications correctly.

Why Use Scroll Bars?

Scroll bars are an attractive and convenient way to provide navigation through a long list of items or a large amount of information. They can also provide an analog representation of a current position to indicate your location in a long document, for example, or the passing of time. Scroll bars are often used as input devices or indicators of speed, temperature, or other quantities. For example, they may be used to control the volume of a computer game, or to create custom colors by mixing different amounts of red, blue, and green.

How to Use Scroll Bars

How

In this section, you'll add a new form to your EVB_BOOK project. Do so now, naming it frmScrollBars. Again, don't forget to change the name of your startup form by selecting **Op**tions from the **T**ools menu, clicking the Project tab, and selecting your new form from the startup form drop-down list.

Before you can draw a spin button on your form, you'll have to add it to Visual Basic's default Toolbox. The SpinButton control is a custom control developed by a third party (that is, not Microsoft) and distributed with Visual Basic. To add it to your Toolbox, follow these steps:

1. Open Visual Basic's **T**ools menu and select **C**ustom Controls.
2. Scroll through the list of available controls to locate the Outrider SpinButton control. Click the check box to select it.
3. Click the OK button to add the control to your Toolbox.

Now it's time to complete the visual implementation of your Payment Calculator program. Refer to Figure 10.2 and Table 10.1.

Figure 10.2.
Design mode: the
Payment Calculator.

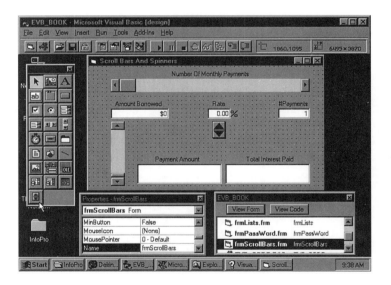

Table 10.1. Design-time settings—Payment Calculator program.

Visual Basic Object	Property	Design-Time Setting
Form	Name	frmScrollBars
	Caption	Scroll Bars And Spinners
Text Boxes	Name	txtBorrowed
	Name	txtRate

Visual Basic Object	Property	Design-Time Setting
	Name	txtPayments
	MultiLine	True
	Alignment	Right Justify
Text Boxes	Name	txtPayment
	Name	txtInterest
	FontSize/Style	18 Bold
	ForeColor	Payment Blue, Interest
Red		
	MultiLine	True
	Alignment	Right Justify
SpinControl	Name	spnRate
	BorderThickness	1
	ShadowThickness	1
	TDThicknness	1
	Delay	125
HScrollBar	Name	hsbPayments
	Min	1
	Max	120
	SmallChange	1
	LargeChange	12
	Value	1
VScrollBar	Name	vsbBorrowed
	Min	30000
	Max	0
	SmallChange	100
	LargeChange	3000
	Value	0

Program Overview

This program serves as a fully functional, though somewhat limited, Loan Payment Calculator. The user may set the loan amount and number of monthly payments by adjusting the vertical and horizontal scroll bars, respectively. The annual interest rate is selected with the spnRate control, by spinning it up or down. Any change to these controls causes immediate recomputation and display of the corresponding monthly payment, as well as the total interest paid over the life of the loan.

Adding Code

The first step in adding code to your new form is to create a form level sub procedure called `CalcPayment`. This procedure will perform the main thrust of the program, which is to compute the monthly payment and total interest, and display them in the appropriate text boxes. Since this procedure will be called when either vsbBorrowed or hsbPayments is changed or scrolled, you'll use it to display the loan amount and number of payments, as well. Open a code window for the General Declarations section of your form. Find a blank line and enter **Sub CalcPayment**. Here's what the procedure should contain:

```
Sub CalcPayment()
Dim dblPayment As Double, dblInterest As Double
txtBorrowed = "$" + CStr(vsbBorrowed)      'Display amount borrowed
txtPayments = hsbPayments                  '...And number of payments..

'***Compute payment/interest....
dblPayment = Pmt(CDbl(txtRate) / 100 / 12, hsbPayments, -vsbBorrowed)
dblInterest = (dblPayment * hsbPayments) - vsbBorrowed

'***Display payment/interest
txtPayment =  Format(dblPayment, "Currency")
txtInterest = Format(dblInterest, "Currency")

'***Refresh controls...Necessary when using Spinners...
txtPayment.Refresh
txtInterest.Refresh
End Sub
```

The *Pmt()* Function

A discussion of the `Pmt()` function is in order. The `Pmt()` function computes and returns the payment for an annuity based on periodic, constant installments and a constant interest rate. An annuity is a series of constant cash payments made over a period of time, such as a home mortgage or a monthly savings plan. The `Pmt()` function expects a minimum of three arguments. Here's the syntax:

```
RetVal = Pmt(rate, nper, pv)
```

The first argument *rate* is the interest rate per period. For example, if you get a boat loan at an annual percentage rate of 7 percent and make monthly payments, the rate per period is 0.07 divided by 12. In your program, this value is determined by the current setting of txtRate, which must be converted to a Double type and then divided by 100 (to get the percent equivalent), then divided again by 12 to arrive at the monthly (or periodic) rate of interest.

The function's second required argument, *nper*, is the total number of payment periods in the life of the annuity, in this example, a loan. Therefore, if you make monthly payments on a three-year loan, there will be a total of 3 X 12 (or 36) payment periods. In your program, this value is always equal to the current setting of the payments scroll bar, hsbPayments.

The last argument required by Pmt() is *pv*, the loan's present value; that is, what the value of a series of payments to be paid in the future is worth *now*. For example, when you borrow money to buy your boat, the loan amount is the present value to *the lender* of the monthly car payments you will make (that's why the present value to you is negative).

The *Format()* Function

You'll often want a specific expression to be displayed in a particular manner. For example, a value of type Double equal to 33.30, if left to its own devices, would be displayed as 33.3. Likewise, a value of 16.766 would be displayed that way, even though you'd prefer only two decimal places. Visual Basic's Format() function formats an expression according to instructions contained in a valid named or programmer-defined format expression.

In your program, you're using Visual Basic's predefined format expression Currency to ensure that the payment amount and interest are displayed in a currency format with a dollar sign, at least one digit to the left and two digits to the right of the decimal point. Here's a list of a few other predefined numeric format names:

Named Format	Description
General Number	Display number as is, with no thousands separators.
Currency	Display number with thousands separator, if appropriate; display two digits to the right of the decimal separator.
Fixed	Display at least one digit to the right and two digits to the left of decimal separator.
Standard	Display number with thousands separator, at least one digit to the left and two digits to the right of the decimal separator.
Percent	Display number multiplied by 100 with a percent sign (%) appended to the right; always display two digits to the right of the decimal separator.
Scientific	Use standard scientific notation.

Your program uses a spin button to set the loan's annual interest rate. The SpinUp event will bump the interest rate by a quarter percent. You'll need to add the following code to spnRate's SpinUp procedure:

```
Private Sub spnRate_SpinUp()
txtRate = Format(CStr(CDbl(txtRate) + 0.25), "Fixed")    'Set the rate....
```

The SpinDown event decrements the interest rate, but never below 0%. Here's the listing:

```
Private Sub spnRate_SpinDown()
Dim dblRate As Double
dblRate = CDbl(txtRate)                    'Convert to type Double...
If dblRate > 0 Then                        'If  more than 0...
txtRate = Format(CStr(dblRate - 0.25), "Fixed")        '...decrement....
Else
txtRate = "0.00"                           'Otherwise, zero..
End If

txtRate.Refresh                            'Spin event must refresh...
CalcPayment                                'Call...
End Sub
```

Notice the use of the Fixed format expression in displaying the interest rate. Also notice that it's necessary to check the numeric value of txtRate before decrementing, to make sure it doesn't drop below 0%. Remember that Spin events will not automatically update controls displaying the spinner's value; therefore, you need to do this by invoking the appropriate Refresh method.

The last coding step is to make sure that CalcPayment is called whenever either scroll bar is changed, whether by clicking or scrolling. Make sure the scroll bar's Change and Scroll event procedures should look like the following:

```
Private Sub hsbPayments_Change()
CalcPayment
End Sub

Private Sub hsbPayments_Scroll()
CalcPayment
End Sub

Private Sub vsbBorrowed_Change()
CalcPayment
End Sub

Private Sub vsbBorrowed_Scroll()
CalcPayment
End Sub
```

Your Payment Calculator program is ready for testing. Figure 10.3 shows the screen output from a sample session.

Figure 10.3.
The Payment Calculator
in action.

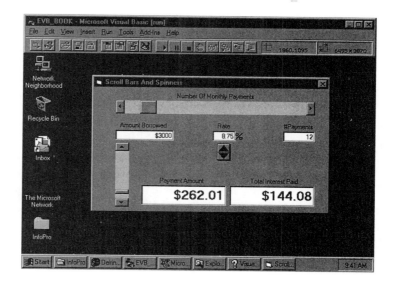

Essential Summary

In this chapter, you learned how to create and manipulate vertical and horizontal scroll bars by working with the VScrollBar and HScrollBar controls. You were introduced to a third-party control, the SpinButton, which you added to Visual Basic's Toolbox by using the Custom Controls dialog box. In addition, you saw how and when to use three new Visual Basic functions: CDbl(), Pmt(), and Format().

What

Because it is often necessary to provide your user's with a convenient, visual way of moving through a long list of items or quantities, a command of scroll bars, spin buttons, and their associated properties and methods is a powerful addition to your repertoire of Visual Basic skills. Scroll bars are often used as input devices or indicators of progress or other quantities, while spin buttons provide a similar functionality but consume less space and, therefore, less program overhead.

Why

You put your new skills to use by creating a Payment Calculator program, which consisted of a horizontal and vertical scroll bar for setting the loan amount and number of payments. The program also employed a spin button for regulating the annual rate of interest in increments, or decrements, of one quarter percent. The final result was to calculate and display the loan's monthly payment, and total interest, by using Visual Basic's powerful Pmt() and Format() functions.

How

Image Controls and Drag/Drop Events

It's time to relax a little and explore some of the more entertaining aspects of programming with Visual Basic. In this chapter, you'll see how to display images—bitmaps, metafiles, and icons—by using the PictureBox and Image controls, seeing the advantages and disadvantages of each. You'll learn how to use Drag/Drop methods and events to provide your users with the ability to relocate items on the screen, allowing them to customize the way the program looks and feels. In the process, you'll get a chance to work with many new properties, as well as the Shape and Line controls found in Visual Basic's Toolbox. You'll also get your first look at Visual Basic's MouseMove event, the Move method, and the LoadPicture() function.

What Are Image/PictureBox Controls?

What
Picture boxes and image controls are the two most commonly used ways to display graphics in Visual Basic. Image controls are often preferable to PictureBox controls because they repaint faster and use up fewer system resources. One other important advantage is that graphics placed in an image may be freely resized, by setting the control's Stretch property to True. However, image controls support only a small subset of the PictureBox properties, events, and methods. They are not designed to accept drawn graphics and may not be used as containers for other controls.

Picture boxes, on the other hand, have more than 40 different properties, many of them relating to the active drawing of graphics at run time. If a graphic loaded from a file is too big for the picture box, it will be cropped, unless the AutoSize property is set to True. This will make the picture box fit snugly around whatever graphics file you place in it, allowing neither white space nor cropping.

> **Note** Graphics are divided into two categories. The first is composed of pre-existing graphics files—such as bitmaps, icons, and metafiles—which are imported by way of a control's Picture property or the LoadPicture() function. The second graphics category consists of designs drawn while your program is running by using the Line, Circle, and PSet methods (covered in Chapters 19 and 20).

Basically, there are two ways to import a graphic from disk into a picture box or image control. At design time, you may click the control's Picture property, then click the ellipsis (...) to open a Load Picture dialog box, from which you may browse your system for the desired file (see Figure 11.1).

You may also load graphics files at run time by using Visual Basic's LoadPicture() function. Assuming that you have an image control called imgMoney, here's how you would use it to display an icon called dollars.ico:

```
imgMoney.Picture = LoadPicture("c:\vb40\icons\dollars.ico")
```

To load a picture, the LoadPicture() function expects a string expression equating to the name of the graphics file to be loaded. You must include a fully qualified path if the file is not contained in the current directory. Similarly, graphics may be cleared from picture boxes and image controls by setting the Picture property to LoadPicture() with no argument.

Following is a list describing the four types of graphics files that may be imported into an image or picture box control:

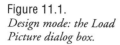

Figure 11.1.
*Design mode: the Load
Picture dialog box.*

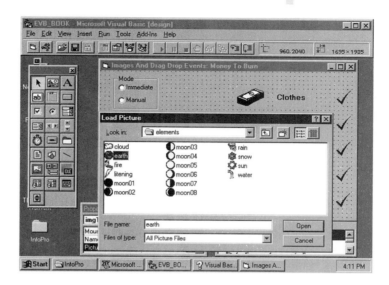

File Type	Description
Bitmap	An image represented by pixels and stored as a collection of bits in which each bit corresponds to one pixel. On color systems, more than one bit corresponds to each pixel. A bitmap usually has a .BMP filename extension.
Icon	Essentially, an icon file is a bitmap with a maximum size of 32×32 pixels. Icons have an .ICO filename extension and may be thought of as a graphical representation of an object or concept. In Windows, icons are often used to represent minimized applications.
Metafile	A file that stores an image as a collection of graphical objects (lines, circles, polygons) rather than pixels. Metafiles preserve an image more accurately than bitmaps when the image is resized. There are two types of metafiles, standard and enhanced, the first having a .WMF extension, and the second having the extension .EMF.
RLE	Files that employ run-length-encoding, a special graphics compression technique.

Dragging and Dropping

In Windows programs, *dragging* means relocating something on the screen by moving the mouse pointer over it, pressing and holding the mouse button, and then moving the mouse to slide the object around the screen. When the mouse button is released, a DragDrop event occurs. The *drop* triggers whatever code is stored in the DragDrop procedure of the control onto which the object was dropped. If the object is not over a control when dropped, it falls onto the form itself. If no code has been written to handle the drop, the object remains at the location at which it was picked up.

> **Caution** Dropping an object somewhere new onscreen does not automatically move it to that location. In order for an object to actually move, you must set its Left and Top properties to the current X and Y screen coordinates, or use the object's Move method, as you'll see later in this section.

You can call an object's Drag method to instigate, or terminate, a Drag event regardless of what the user is doing. In fact, this rather odd but interesting method is the only way in Visual Basic to immediately cancel a drag operation in progress. It also provides extra functionality for the truly indolent. As you'll see, a clever combination of the Drag method and the DragOver event (discussed later in this section) will allow the user to drag items around the screen without holding the mouse button down at all.

Not surprisingly, an object's DragOver event fires off whenever an item is dragged over it or is moved within the object's boundaries. The DragOver event makes it possible for objects to recognize when their space has been invaded, if you will, and to take some action accordingly. You'll put this method to use in the program you'll write later in this chapter, where a trash bin will demand food whenever an object is dragged near it.

There are two drag-related properties: DragMode and DragIcon. If an object is to be draggable (without you writing code involving the Drag method), you must set its DragMode property to 1, Automatic. The DragIcon property determines how the mouse pointer (or cursor) looks while a drag operation is in progress. In this chapter's example program, the mouse pointer becomes a magnet, "pulling" the dragged object around the screen.

Why Use Images and Drag/Drop Events?

If you want to include graphics in your program, whether they're created at run time or loaded from disk, you need to become familiar with Image and PictureBox controls. A tasteful use of graphics—icons, toolbars, drawings, and other images—always adds a touch of professionalism to any program.

By using Drag/Drop methods and events, you can allow your users to customize the way your program looks by changing the location of various items onscreen. Other uses include copying files or records, deleting, appending, and so on, by "physically" lifting one thing onto another. For example, you might allow the user to drop an icon representing a file onto a bitmap of a trash can, thereby triggering a procedure that removes the file from disk. Or you could have a calendar program where meetings or phone calls are scheduled by dropping a handshake or telephone icon onto a particular date.

How to Use Images and Drag/Drop Methods

In this section, you'll create a new form, frmDragDrop, saving it as part of the EVB_BOOK project and establishing it as the project's startup form. You know how to do this by now, so go ahead. (See the preceding chapter for a refresher.) Bearing in mind that many of this form's controls will (at first) be invisible at run time, complete the visual implementation by referring to Figure 11.2 and Tables 11.1 and 11.2. Here's how the form looks at design time.

Figure 11.2.
Design mode: the Drag Drop program.

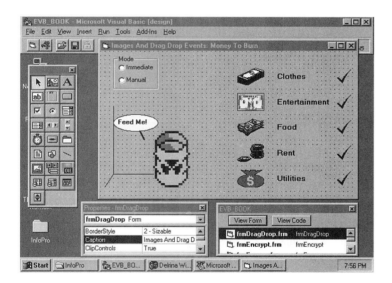

The following two tables describe your program's significant objects:

Table 11.1. Design-time settings—the Drag Drop program.

Visual Basic Object	Property	Design-Time Setting
Form	Name	frmDragDrop
	Caption	Images And DragDrop Events: Money To Burn
OptionButtons	Name	optImmediate
	Name	optManual

continues

Table 11.1. continued

Visual Basic Object	Property	Design-Time Setting
Label	Name	lblFeed
	Caption	"Feed Me!"
	BackStyle	0 - Transparent
	Visible	False
Shape	Name	shpFeed
	BackColor	Light Yellow
	BackStyle	Opaque
	Shape	2 - Oval
	Visible	False
Line	Name	linFeed
	BorderWidth	2
	Visible	False

Caution The icons and metafiles used in this program come with Visual Basic. The paths to these files assume that Visual Basic has been installed in the VB40 directory of the C: drive. You may need to adjust them to match the Visual Basic directory on your system.

Table 11.2. Design-time settings—Image/Picture controls.

Visual Basic Object	Property	Design-Time Setting
Picture Boxes	Name	picClothes
	Picture	\vb40\metafile\business\monystk2.wmf
	Name	picEnt
	Picture	\vb40\metafile\business\dollar.wmf
	Name	picFood
	Picture	\vb40\metafile\business\money.wmf
	Name	picRent
	Picture	\vb40\metafile\business\coins.wmf
	Name	picUtils
	Picture	\vb40\metafile\business\moneybag.wmf

Visual Basic Object	Property	Design Time Setting
Image Controls	Name	imgCheckClothes
	Picture	\vb40\icons\misc\checkmrk.ico
	Name	imgCheckEnt
	Picture	(same)
	Name	imgCheckFood
	Picture	(same)
	Name	imgCheckRent
	Picture	(same)
	Name	imgCheckUtils
	Picture	(same)
	Name	imgTrash
	Picture	\vb40\icons\computer\trash02a.ico

In this program, you'll use both picture boxes and image controls, even though image controls could have been used for all the money pictures, as well. This will give you a chance to compare the two for performance. You'll see that picture boxes take noticeably longer to load and display their graphics. Generally speaking, if all you want to do is show a picture, the image control is best. On the other hand, if your program involves more elaborate graphics and run time drawings, or if it needs pictures that can also act as containers, then the picture box is the way to go.

To create the effect of a talking trash bin, you use Visual Basic's Shape and Line controls to draw a cartoon balloon containing a label captioned "Feed Me!". This balloon is invisible at run time, unless a money bundle is dragged near it, as you'll see. A Shape control allows you to easily draw and size many standard shapes. You do so by setting the control's Shape property, then dragging the rectangular outline to the desired size. Here's a description of Shape property settings:

Setting	Description
0	Rectangle, the default
1	Square
2	Oval
3	Circle
4	Rounded Rectangle
5	Rounded Square

You add the balloon's line toward the trash can by using the Line control. With this, you can draw vertical, horizontal, or diagonal lines of different widths and styles. (Examine the

BorderStyle and BorderWidth properties). The Line control is perfect for drawing the "corner" in which your hungry trash bin resides.

All the imgCheck controls should have no borders, and their Visible properties will be set to False at design time, so they'll show up only when necessary as the program runs. The trash bin's image control should have its Stretch property set to True, which will allow you to adjust the size of the bin.

The picture controls, containing the bundles of money, have BackColors set to the same color as the form. Their appearance is Flat, with no border since you want the money bundles to look as if they're sitting comfortably on the form. You'll also need to set the DragIcon property for each bundle. Remember, DragIcon determines how the mouse pointer will look during a drag operation. In this case, you'll use the icon located at c:\vb40\icons\misc\misc08.ico, so as each bundle is dragged, the mouse pointer will change to a Magnet.

Finally, you'll want to set the Tag property of each bundle to a descriptive name—Clothes, Ent, Food, Rent, Utils—which will be sent to a procedure called ShowCheck as each bundle is dropped. The ShowCheck procedure will then place a check mark (make it visible) next to the appropriate expense item.

> **Tip**   At design time, there are many ways to make your job easier. When several controls of the same type require the same property settings, for example, why not select them all? Use the Arrow pointer to surround them, or hold the Shift key and multi-click. Then set the necessary properties for all of them at once. It's also possible to use the Clipboard to cut and copy objects. When you do this, though, Visual Basic will ask if you're trying to create a control array. If you respond No, each copied control will have an incrementing number attached to its name. If you respond yes, you better skip ahead and read Chapter 34 of this book, where you'll learn how to handle control arrays.

Now it's time for the Program Overview, then you'll add some code.

Program Overview

The purpose of this program is to have a little fun working with images and Drag/Drop methods and events. As you can determine from Figure 11.2, the program's form will consist of several images, two option buttons, and various other graphical elements including some lines and an oval, drawn using Visual Basic's Line and Shape controls.

At run time, the program will allow the user to "spend" a bundle of money by dragging it to the burning bin and dropping it in, there to be consumed by a burst of flames. Each bundle is associated with a particular expense, so after the drop, a check mark appears next to the appropriate item. This particular bin is an anxious one, but polite, at least, badgering the user for food whenever a bundle is drawn near, and offering thanks when the cash is at last "deposited."

Dragging will be enabled in one of two ways, corresponding to the Immediate and Manual option button settings. When the form is first displayed, neither button will be selected, and no dragging will be allowed. When the user selects Manual mode, he or she will be able to drag a bundle in the normal way by pointing to it, clicking and holding, then dragging and releasing. In Immediate mode, the Drag event will begin automatically, as soon as the mouse pointer is brought over a bundle, with no clicking or holding required. In this mode, a single mouse-click terminates the drag, effectively "dropping" the source object.

In the next section, you'll add the code required to complete the program.

Adding Code

You'll need a couple of string variables to store the EmptyTrash and BurningTrash file names. Add this line to your form's General Declarations section:

```
Dim sEmptyTrash As String, sBurningTrash As String
```

Then you'll assign values to these variables in the form's Load event procedure:

```
Private Sub Form_Load()
sEmptyTrash = "C:\VB40\ICONS\COMPUTER\TRASH02A.ICO"
sBurningTrash = "C:\VB40\ICONS\COMPUTER\TRASH02B.ICO"
End Sub
```

As each bundle of money is burned, you'll want to place (that is, make visible) a check mark next to the appropriate expense label. A simple way to accomplish this is to write a sub procedure to do so, based upon the Tag property of the dropped object. Add the following to your form's code module:

```
Sub ShowCheck(sTag As String)              'Notice the tag coming in...

Select Case sTag                           'Read the tag....
    Case "Clothes"
        imgCheckClothes.Visible = True     '...and set the appropriate checkmark
    Case "Ent"
        imgCheckEnt.Visible = True
    Case "Food"
        imgCheckFood.Visible = True
    Case "Rent"
        imgCheckRent.Visible = True
 Case "Utils"
        imgCheckUtils.Visible = True
End Select
End Sub
```

When Immediate mode is in effect, you'll handle the drag operation from code, using the Drag method seen in the following code listing. This means that you'll not want the user to be able to initiate a drag on his or her own, so the DragMode property for each of the bundles must be set to Manual(0) Here's what optImmediate's Click procedure should look like:

```
Private Sub optImmediate_Click()           'Disable automatic drag for each picture
picClothes.DragMode = 0
picEnt.DragMode = 0
picFood.DragMode = 0
```

```
picRent.DragMode = 0
picUtils.DragMode = 0
End Sub
```

In this program, you'll get a cursory look at MouseMove events (you'll work with them extensively in Chapters 19–23). These events are triggered whenever the mouse is moved around the form or over a control. You'll add a little code to each money bundle's MouseMove procedure which, if optImmediate is True at run time, will immediately instigate a drag operation, no clicking required. The pointer will change to a Magnet, and the bundle will be dragged around the screen, until the user "drops" it with a single click.

Open a code window for picClothes, then locate MouseMove in the Proc drop-down list. Add these three lines between the Private Sub and End Sub statements, then copy them to the other four PictureBox controls. Remember to put them in the MouseMove event and to change the picXXXXX references accordingly.

```
If optImmediate Then
    picClothes.Drag 1                       'Begin the drag operation
End If
```

When the Manual Mode button is clicked, you *do* want the user to be able to select, click, and drag on his or her own. You'll make this possible by setting each picture's DragMode to 1, Automatic. Here's the listing:

```
Private Sub optManual_Click()               'Set automatic drag for each picture
picClothes.DragMode = 1
picEnt.DragMode = 1
picFood.DragMode = 1
picRent.DragMode = 1
picUtils.DragMode = 1
End Sub
```

The next step is to write the code that will move the bundle as the mouse pointer (the Magnet) is moved. You'll accomplish this by adding a line to the form's DragOver event.

DragOver events are triggered as the mouse is moved over a form or other object, *but only during a drag operation.* This is what distinguishes DragOver events from normal MouseMove events. The DragOver event procedure provides you with four very useful variables. Here's a description of each:

Variable	*Description*
Source	Refers to the object being dragged
X	The mouse pointer's X-Axis coordinate (horizontal position)
Y	The Y-Axis coordinate (vertical position)
State	0 as dragged object first enters host object borders
	1 as dragged object leaves object borders
	2 while dragged object is moved within the borders of host object

Now here's the line to add to the form's DragOver event:

```
Private Sub
Form_DragOver(Source As Control, X As Single, Y As Single, State As Integer)

Source.Move X - Source.Width / 2, Y - Source.Height / 2

End Sub
```

All you're doing here is invoking the dragged object's Move method to change its position. The Move method requires two arguments corresponding to the X and Y coordinates of the new location. In this case, you're making a purely cosmetic adjustment to the coordinates provided by the DragOver event. You want the Magnet (mouse pointer) to be centered over the dragged object, so you divide the source's width and height by two, and subtract from the X and Y coordinates, respectively.

Now you'll add some code to the imgTrash's DragOver event procedure. Remember that the "Feed Me!" balloon is supposed to become visible when a bundle is dragged within the trash bin's borders. Here are the lines to be added to imgTrash_DragOver():

```
If State = 0 Or State = 2 Then    'If you're over it...
    linFeed.Visible = True        'Show the balloon.
    shpFeed.Visible = True
    lblFeed.Visible = True
Else
    linFeed.Visible = False       'Otherwise..hide it.
    shpFeed.Visible = False
    lblFeed.Visible = False
End If
```

The final coding step is to determine what will happen when a bundle is dropped on the trash bin. You do this by adding code to imgTrash's DragDrop event. Here's what that procedure should look like, with a short discussion to follow:

```
Private Sub
imgTrash_DragDrop(Source As Control, X As Single, Y As Single)
Source.Visible = False                        'Dragged object disappears.
lblFeed.Caption = "Thanks!"                    'Change label to "Thanks!"
imgTrash.Picture = LoadPicture(sBurningTrash) 'Load burning trash picture...
Refresh                                        'To see burning trash...
lWait = Timer: While Timer < lWait + 1: Wend  'Wait for one second...
imgTrash.Picture = LoadPicture(sEmptyTrash)   'Load empty trash...
lblFeed.Caption = "Feed Me!"                   'Put label back to "Feed Me!"
linFeed.Visible = False
shpFeed.Visible = False                        'Make balloon invisible...
lblFeed.Visible = False
ShowCheck Source.Tag                           'Call check mark procedure...
End Sub
```

With documentation on almost every line, what's going on here is probably pretty clear. However, you should notice a couple of new concepts at play. Once the burning bin is displayed, you want to see it immediately, so you need to *Refresh* the form (that is, have Windows redraw it); otherwise, the form won't be redrawn until the procedure ends. If you don't force the redraw by calling the form's Refresh method, you'll never see the burning trash bin, because it becomes invisible again before the end of the procedure.

Also notice the While...Wend loop used to pause for one second while the bin is burning.

The pause is made up of three statements separated by colons, which allows them to reside on the same line. The first statement sets a variable, lWait, equal to Timer, a special Visual Basic function that returns the number of seconds elapsed since midnight. Then you loop while Timer catches up to lWait + 1, that is, for one second. This is probably not the best way to cause a delay in your program (your CPU is sort of spinning its wheels), but it will do until you learn about the Timer control in Chapter 21.

The last new idea being employed here is a simple one. You're temporarily changing your cartoon balloon's caption by setting lblFeed's Caption property to "Thanks!". Remember, although users can't change a label's caption at run time, the programmer can.

It's now time to play with, and maybe debug, your new program. You're not under oath here, so feel free to experiment and embellish. Have some fun!

Essential Summary

What   In this chapter, you learned how to display graphics by using the PictureBox and Image controls. You saw how Drag/Drop methods and events are used to provide your users with the ability to relocate items on the screen. In the process, you were introduced to many new properties, as well as the Visual Basic's Shape and Line controls.

Why   The simplest way to include graphics in your program, whether they're created at run time or loaded from disk, is to use both Image and PictureBox controls. By using Drag/Drop methods and events, you can allow your users to perform various operations in a visual way by "physically" lifting one thing onto another. You might, for example, allow them to delete a file by dropping a file icon onto a bitmap of a trash can.

How   You added to the EVB_BOOK project a new form consisting of several PictureBox and Image controls. By setting significant object properties and adding code to the MouseMove, DragOver, and DragDrop events, you created a simple game program in which the user could drag "bundles of money," representing various expenses, to a "talking" trash can for "burning."

Drive, Directory, and File List Controls

In this chapter, you'll revisit list boxes, focusing on three specialized list controls: DriveListBox, DirListBox, and FileListBox. You'll create an Image Viewer application with which you may browse your system for graphics files and view them individually, or in a timed slide-show presentation.

What Are Drive, Directory, and File List Controls?

What A *DriveListBox control* enables a user to select a valid disk drive at run time. It displays an ordered list of the user's disk drives and automatically reacts to mouse clicks to permit the user to move among them. Use this control to display a list of all the valid drives in your user's system. As you'll see, a Drive list box can be synchronized with the Directory and File list boxes to provide access to files anywhere on the user's system.

The most important property of a Drive list box is the Drive property. Assuming you have a Drive list box named Drive1 (the default), you may use it to determine the current drive at run time, as in the following:

```
CurrentDrive$ = Drive1.Drive
```

Or you may make a Directory list box display the directories of the currently selected drive by adding the following to the Drive list box's Change event:

```
Dir1.Path = Drive1.Drive
```

What
A *DirListBox control* displays an ordered, hierarchical list of the user's disk directories and subdirectories, and automatically reacts to mouse clicks to allow the user to navigate among them. You may use a Directory list box's Path property to determine the current path while a program is running, or to synchronize it with an associated File list box by adding this line to its Change event:

```
File1.Path = Dir1.Path
```

What
A *FileListBox control* locates and lists files in the directory specified by its Path property at run time. You may use this control to display a list of all files in the current directory; or you may set the Pattern property to show only certain types of files. The currently selected file is reported by the FileName property, which is available only at run time. By concatenating a synchronized Directory list box's Path property and a File list box's FileName property, you arrive at a fully qualified file identifier, which may be stored to a string variable in this way :

```
sFilename = Dir1.Path & "\" & File1.FileName
```

As with all List controls, you may set the List, ListCount, and ListIndex properties to enable a user to access items in any Drive list box, Dir list box, or File list box. Unlike the DriveList and DirList controls, however, the FileList control has a MultiSelect property which may be set to allow multiple file selection.

Why Use These List Controls?

Why
It is usually best to allow the user to manage files rather than to hard-code file access into your program. For this reason, the most common use of the DriveList, DirList, and FileList controls is to create custom File Access dialog boxes. With such dialog boxes, your user may save, open, display, and otherwise manipulate any files throughout his or her system.

How to Use Drive, Directory, and File List Boxes

How
You'll put your understanding of these new concepts to use by creating an Image Viewer program that will allow you to browse any drive on your system. The program will be designed to

help you locate and display any bitmaps, icons, or metafiles at your disposal. First, as usual, add a new form to the EVB_BOOK project. Name it frmViewer, save it, and make it the project startup form. Here is what the form should look like in design mode (see Figure 12.1):

Figure 12.1.
Design mode: the Image Viewer program.

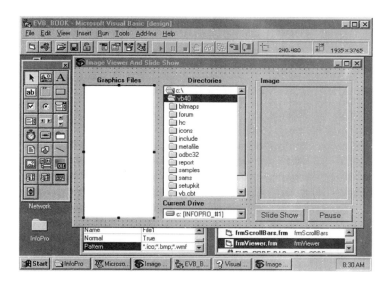

Table 12.1 shows the design time property settings of the significant controls:

Table 12.1. Design-time settings—Image Viewer program.

Visual Basic Object	Property	Design-Time Setting
Form	Name	frmViewer
	Caption	Image Viewer And Slide Show
Command Button	Name	cmdSlide
	Caption	Slide Show
	Font	Size 10
	TabStop	False
Command Button	Name	cmdPause
	Caption	Pause
	Font	Size 10
	Enabled	False
	TabStop	False
Drive List Box	Name	Drive1
Dir List Box	Name	Dir1

continues

Table 12.1. continued

Visual Basic Object	Property	Design-Time Setting
File List Box	Name	File1
	MultiSelect	2 - Extended
	Pattern	*.bmp;*.ico;*.wmf
Frame	Name	fraImage
	Caption	Image
Picture Box	Name	picImage

The only settings that might require a little comment and clarification are the File list box's MultiSelect and Pattern properties. You'll want the user to be able to select several files from any directory in order to enable the program's Slide Show feature, which is created later in this chapter. The Pattern property specifies the file types to be displayed in the list. In this case, you're only interested in graphics files with one of three, semicolon delimited, file specifications: *.bmp, *.ico, and *.wmf.

Notice also that the Pause button, cmdPause, is not enabled. This ensures that when the program is first started, the button will appear dimmed or grayed out, a visual cue to the user that it's not available. You'll enable this button when necessary, that is, when the Slide Show is running.

Program Overview

With this program, the user is able to easily navigate through the drives and directories available on his or her system, using nothing but mouse clicks. Once a graphics file of interest is located, it may be displayed by double-clicking it. The user may also select several files at once, using any of the standard multi-select techniques, then click the Slide Show button to have them displayed automatically, one-by-one, in a slide-show presentation fashion. This feature is particularly entertaining when the series of pictures, flipped through in order, create a simple animation sequence. (Once you're running, try the phases of the moon icons, located in c:\vb40\icons\elements, for example.)

Although an experienced Visual Basic programmer could create this program in a few minutes (literally), it packs an awful lot of functional bang for the buck. In fact, as a fully realized executable, it would be a welcome and useful addition to anyone's toolbox of Windows applets.

In the next section, you'll add the code needed to get this program up and running.

Adding Code

The first step is to synchronize the three list boxes. When a new drive is selected from the Drive list, you'll want the Directory list box to display the directories on that drive. Here's what the Drive list box's Change event should look like:

```
Private Sub Drive1_Change()
Dir1.Path = Drive1.Drive                          'Synchronize 'em...
End Sub
```

To get the File list box in synch with the current directory, you'll want Dir1's Change event procedure to look like this:

```
Private Sub Dir1_Change()
File1.Path = Dir1.Path                            'Synchronize 'em...
End Sub
```

Now, to display the picture associated with the selected filename, you'll add some code to File1's DblClick event. In it, you'll create a string variable containing the file's full path identifier, then pass that string to LoadPicture(), assigning the return value to picImage's Picture property. Here's the code:

```
Private Sub File1_DblClick()
Dim sFileName As String
sFileName = Dir1.Path & "\" & File1.FileName      'The full name...
picImage.Picture = LoadPicture(sFileName)         '..now load it....
End Sub
```

The next step is to create the slide-show presentation routine. Obviously, this code will be attached to the Slide Show button's Click event. Here's the annotated listing, with a brief discussion to follow:

```
Private Sub cmdSlide_Click()
Dim iImages, iImageCount As Integer               'For the display loop...
Dim sImageName As String                          'and the file name...

cmdPause.Enabled = True                           'Enable Pause button
cmdSlide.Enabled = False                          'Disable Show button

iImages = File1.ListCount - 1                      'Max side of the loop..
For iImageCount = 0 To iImages                     'The loop...
    If File1.Selected(iImageCount) Then            'If file is selected...
        sImageName = Dir1.Path & "\" & File1.List(iImageCount)
                                                   'Build the file string...
        picImage.Picture = LoadPicture(sImageName) 'Show it...
        lWait = Timer: While Timer < lWait + 1: Wend 'Wait 1 second...
        DoEvents                                    'Check for  pause..
End If
Next                                               'Do the next one.
picImage = LoadPicture()                           'Loop's done so...
                                                   'Blank the picture..
File1.Refresh                                      'And Clear selections
cmdPause.Enabled = False                           'Disable Pause...
cmdSlide.Enabled = True                            'Enable Slide Show...
End Sub
```

Some things here may be unfamiliar to you. Notice first the use of the Refresh method, three lines before the End Sub statement. In this case, you're refreshing the list control, not the form as in the last chapter. This has the effect of clearing all the selections, which provides a nice visual cue that the slide show is over. Notice also that the line previous to this calls the LoadPicture() function with no argument, blanking out the PictureBox control.

There are two other things you should notice. First, you want to be sure that when the show is running, the Slide Show button is disabled, and the Pause button becomes available. This is done by setting the command buttons' Enabled properties near the beginning of the procedure. At the end of the procedure, when the show is over, these settings are reversed.

Second, the call to Visual Basic's DoEvents procedure is very important. DoEvents turns control over to Windows so that the operating system can process other events, such as mouse clicks and key presses. Since you'll want to freeze the slide show by clicking the Pause button, Windows must process that click as it comes in. Otherwise, any code attached to the Pause button's Click event will execute *after the slide show is over*, which won't do at all.

Caution   Make sure the procedure that has given up control with DoEvents is not executed again before the first DoEvents call returns, as this could cause unpredictable results. This is another reason why it's important to disable the Slide Show button while the show is running.

The last coding step is to get the Pause button working. Here's what cmdPause's Click event should look like:

```
Sub cmdPause_Click()
Static bPause As Boolean                      'For tracking pause or continue...

If bPause = False Then
    cmdPause.Caption = "Continue"             'Set Continue caption
    bPause = True                             'Set bPause to True
    Else
    cmdPause.Caption = "Pause"                'Set Pause caption
    bPause = False                            'bPause now False...
End If

While bPause                                  'Wait, if pausing...
DoEvents                                      'Must read mouse clicks...
Wend

End Sub
```

Here you're making your command button serve double duty, as both a Pause and Continue button. First, you set up a static Boolean variable whose value will alternate between True and False with each click of cmdPause, whose Caption property is changed accordingly. Then, if you're pausing (if bPause is True), you go into a While...Wend loop and wait for another click to cmdPause, which changes bPause to False, and you drop out of the loop.

Now it's time to run your new program. While testing, notice that metafiles (WMFs) fill the entire picture box border, while bitmaps and icons are displayed at their normal sizes. See Figure 12.2 for a sample session.

Figure 12.2.
*The Image Viewer
program in action.*

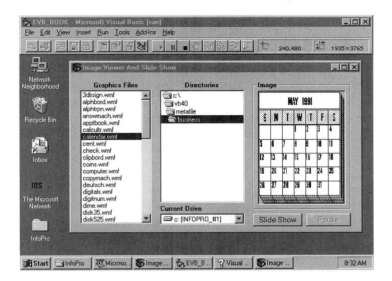

Essential Summary

In this chapter, you focused on three specialized list controls: DriveListBox, DirListBox, and FileListBox. You saw that a Drive list box can be synchronized with the Directory and File list boxes to provide access to files anywhere on the user's system.

What

The most common use of the DriveList, DirList, and FileList controls is to create custom File Access dialog boxes. With such dialog boxes, your user may save, open, display attributes, and otherwise manipulate any files throughout his or her system, avoiding the pitfalls of hard-coding file access routines into your program.

Why

By developing a simple but useful Image Viewer program, you were able to explore and utilize the most important aspects of the DriveList, DirList, and FileList controls. You also brought your skills for list box manipulation to bear, creating a Slide-Show Presentation feature by looping through a list and displaying the selected files at one-second intervals. In the process, you learned about Visual Basic's DoEvents procedure and saw what happens when you manipulate a command button's Enable property.

How

PART III

The Image Viewer Application—from Project to Executable

Managing a Project

In this short chapter, you'll learn how to manage and navigate the elements of your project by using Visual Basic's Project window and Object Browser. In addition, you'll see how to print forms, code, and other project information to assist in development, or to serve as program documentation.

What Are the Project Window and Object Browser?

What You're already somewhat familiar with the Project window. You've watched it grow with the forms and code modules of the EVB_BOOK project. If you've been working along with the book up until now, your Visual Basic IDE—with the Project window on top and a new form in the background—might look something like Figure 13.1.

Figure 13.1.
The EVB_BOOK
Project window.

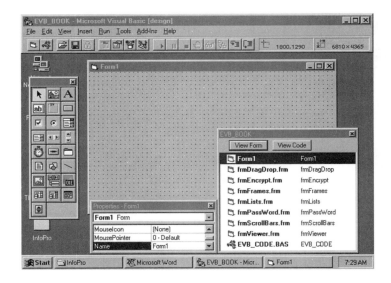

The *Project window* is a window that displays a list of your project's forms, classes, and standard modules, as well as its resource file, if you have one, and any references. Unlike previous versions of Visual Basic, in which the Project window included your program's custom controls, in Visual Basic 4.0, files with .OCX and .VBX filename extensions will not appear here.

> **Note** A *resource file* is a file in a Visual Basic project with an .RES filename extension that can contain bitmaps, text strings, or other data. Only one resource file can be associated with a project. By putting resource data in a separate file, you can enhance performance and change resource information without having to re-edit your code. Creating a resource file involves following resource source code specifications found in the Windows SDK and an additional resource compiler, such as the one shipped with Visual C++.

The information displayed in the Project window reflects most of what is contained in the Project file, a file with a .VBP extension that keeps track of the files, objects, project options, environment options, EXE options, and references associated with a project. As you might suspect, every project has its own Project File that is read from, and written to, every time you load or save your project.

You'll notice that the Project window lists both the disk filename on the left (including the proper extension) and the current value of the object's Name property on the right. You may add or remove project files (forms, code modules, classes, and resources) by selecting **A**dd File or **R**emove File from Visual Basic's **F**ile menu. You'll get a chance to experiment with this later in the chapter.

> **Tip** If you would like to automatically include certain forms, modules, or other files in every new project, you may load, edit, and save the project files named AUTO16LD.VBP or AUTO32LD.VBP for 16-bit and 32-bit development, respectively.

The Object Browser displays the classes, properties, and methods available from the modules and procedures in your project, as well as from external object libraries. Therefore, you can use the Object Browser to find and use objects you create, as well as objects from other applications.

What

In addition, you can use the Browser to select Constants in the Classes/Modules box to view the intrinsic constants for the Visual Basic object libraries. For example, if you select VB in the Libraries/Projects box and then select Constants in the Classes/Modules box, you can select one of the constants listed in the Methods/Properties box and then paste it into your code.

To open the Object Browser, choose **O**bject Browser from the **V**iew menu, press F2, or use the toolbar shortcut. Here's a summary listing of the features available in the Object Browser dialog box:

- Libraries/Projects

  Displays the libraries available to your project. You can select from available object libraries, including your own Visual Basic projects, to view the classes, modules, procedures, methods, and properties you can use in code.

- Classes/Modules

  If you select your own Visual Basic project in the Libraries/Projects box, this box displays modules from your project, including any classes you defined in the current project.

- Methods/Properties

  This box displays procedures, properties, and methods you've defined, if you've selected your own project in the Libraries/Projects box.

- The "?" Button

  Displays on-line Help for the item selected in the Classes/Modules or Methods/Properties box, along with a description and/or a procedure template.

- Show Button

  If enabled, indicates that the selected procedure contains editable code. Press the Show button to open the associated Code window.

- Paste Button

  Pastes a template of Visual Basic code for a method or property into a procedure. In the Code window, place the insertion point where you want the fragment to appear. Then select the method or property in the Object Browser and click the Paste button.

■ Options Button
Displays the Member Options dialog box, which you can use to add helpful comments about modules, procedures, classes, properties, and methods that you define in your project.

To close the Object Browser, double-click the Control-menu box.

What

Choosing **File Print** from Visual Basic's menu displays a dialog box that allows you to print forms and code to the printer specified in the Microsoft Windows Control Panel. This menu option is available only at design time, and may be accessed with the keyboard shortcut Ctrl+P.

Here's a look at some of the File Print options that may require a little explanation:

Range	Determines the range you print.
Selection	Prints the currently selected code.
Current Module	Prints the forms and/or code for the currently selected module.
Project	Prints the forms and/or code for the entire project.
Print What	Determines what you print. You can select as many options as you like, depending on what you selected as the Range.
Form Image	Prints the form images (pictures).
Forms As Text	Prints the text representation of forms. Use this feature to print all form and control properties and their values.
Code	Prints the code for the selected range.

How to Use the Project Window and Object Browser

How

For practice, you'll remove a form and standard module from your EVB_BOOK project, then add them back in again. Make sure your EVB_BOOK project is open, then in the Project window, click once on frmFrames to select it (if you double-click, the form will open, which is nice to know, but not what you want here). At this point, you may view the form or its code module by clicking the View Form or View Code buttons, accordingly. Instead, you'll remove the form from your project by following these steps:

1. Open Visual Basic's **File** menu.
2. Select **R**emove File (the form disappears from the Project window).
3. Click once on your project's code module, EVB_CODE.
4. Select Remove File from Visual Basic's File menu.

If the file you're removing has any unsaved changes, you'll be asked if you want to save them. Otherwise, the file will disappear from the Project window without asking for confirmation. But this is okay; remember that you're only removing these files from the current project, not from disk. In fact, you may add either one or both of them right back into EVB_BOOK or into any other project you wish. Follow these steps to add them back:

- Select A**d**d File from the **F**ile Menu.
- In the Add File dialog box, choose the type of file you'd like to add from the Files Of Type drop-down list.
- Locate frmFrames.frm and double-click it (or click the Open button).

You should repeat the same steps in adding the code module, EVB_CODE.BAS, back into your EVB_BOOK project.

The Object Browser

To stay within the scope of this book, you'll use the Object Browser to browse your current project. First, you'll add a description to your project. This will show up in the Object Browser, along with the project name, to help with identification. Follow these steps:

1. Open Visual Basic's Tools menu.
2. Select Options and then click the Project Tab.
3. In the box titled Application Description, type **Essential Visual Basic 4.0 Book Project.**
4. Click the OK button to save it.

Now open the **O**bject Browser by choosing it from the **V**iew menu, by pressing F2, or by using the toolbar shortcut (use your ToolTips to locate it). Make sure EVBBOOK is selected in the Libraries/Projects drop-down list (notice your project description). Complete the following steps to add a description to your Encrypt() function, which is contained in the EVB_CODE module:

1. In the Classes/Modules list box, click on EVB_CODE.
2. In the Methods/Properties list box, click on Encrypt.
3. Click the Options button.
4. In the Description text box, type **Employs simple ASCII bump encryption algorithm.**
5. Click OK to save the description and return to the Object Browser.

Your screen should now look something like Figure 13.2.

Notice your new function description adjacent to the "?" button near the bottom of the dialog box, along with the function's template. At this point, you can jump immediately to the Encrypt() function's definition by pressing the Show button, which is enabled to signify the presence of editable code. Press the Show button now. The Object Browser dialog box will close, and you'll be transported to the Encrypt() function's Code window, where you may begin editing if you like.

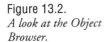

Figure 13.2.
A look at the Object Browser.

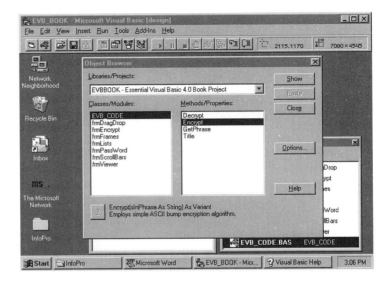

Even though the Browser is now closed, it remembers your last position. You may re-open the Object Browser to verify this. From the Object Browser dialog box, you may similarly investigate, describe, and/or quickly move to any object, property, method, or procedure in your application.

Now you'll see how to browse the Visual Basic Objects and Procedures Library for predefined constants to paste into your code. Make sure the EVB_BOOK project is still visible in the Libraries/Projects drop-down list, then follow these steps:

1. Click on frmDragDrop in the Classes/Modules list.
2. Scroll to find picUtils_MouseMove in the Methods/Properties list.
3. Click the Show button to open the Code window.

Assuming you've been following the book up to this point, you'll notice that you used the number 1 in invoking a drag operation with picUtil's Drag method. Follow these steps to look up and paste in the appropriate Visual Basic constant instead:

1. Select (highlight) the number 1.
2. Open the Object Browser.
3. Select VB in the Libraries/Projects drop-down list.
4. Select Constants in the Classes/Modules list.
5. In the Methods/Properties list, scroll down to vbBeginDrag and read the associated description near the "?" button.
6. Click the Paste button. The Browser closes, and the constant is pasted.

Essential Summary

In this chapter, you learned how to manage the elements of your project by using Visual Basic's Project window and Object Browser. You saw how to add and remove files from your project and how to print forms, code, and other project images and information to serve as program documentation or development stage reference material.

What

Windows applications of any significance may consist of many forms and code modules, and possibly several class modules, references, and one resource file. Knowledge of the Object Browser, and other project management techniques, will become invaluable as you increase the size and scope of your Visual Basic applications.

Why

You carried out a couple of simple exercises to add and remove files from (and to) the EVB_BOOK project. You used the Object Browser to add a description to one of your functions. Finally, you used the Browser to locate one of your DragDrop procedures and a Visual Basic constant, which you then pasted into your current Code window.

How

The Startup Form or Procedure

In this chapter, you'll briefly revisit the procedure for establishing your project's startup form. You'll gain a more complete understanding of insertable objects and custom controls, and you'll see how they may be added to your project. Finally, you'll see how to create a Main Sub procedure which may be used in place of a startup form and, in the process, you'll be introduced to the Printer object and several of its properties and methods.

What Is a Startup Form?

What The *startup form* is the first form displayed in your application, which is usually the first form you create in the development environment. As you've discovered, an application doesn't have to start up with the first form in the project; you can start your application with any form or a Main Sub procedure in a standard module. You can change the startup form by using the Startup Form option on the Project Options dialog box.

Here are the steps to specify a startup form:

1. From the **T**ools menu, choose **O**ptions. (Visual Basic displays the Options dialog box.)
2. Click the Project tab and select a form from the **S**tartup Form drop-down list box.
3. Choose OK.

The Startup Procedure

What

Instead of loading a form, Visual Basic can invoke a procedure to start an application. You may write a procedure called Main and use it to start up your application.

Here are the steps to specify a startup procedure:

1. Write a general Sub procedure called Main and save it in a standard module.
2. From the **T**ools menu, choose **O**ptions. (Visual Basic displays the Options dialog box.)
3. Click the Project tab and select Sub Main from the **S**tartup Form drop-down list box.
4. Choose OK.

Now, when the project starts execution, the Main Sub procedure is called immediately.

Custom Controls and Insertable Objects

What

A *Custom control* is a file with a .VBX or .OCX filename extension that, when added to a project using the Custom Controls dialog box, extends Visual Basic's Toolbox. The CommonDialog, DBCombo, and Spinner controls (you added the Spinner in Chapter 10) are examples of custom controls.

What

An *Insertable Object* is a type of Custom control which is an object from an OLE server application, such as an Excel Worksheet or Word document. You can add such objects to the Toolbox using the Custom Controls dialog box. You open this dialog box by selecting **C**ustom Controls from the Tools menu, or by using the shortcut Ctrl+T.

Here's what it looks like (see Figure 14.1).

The Available Controls list box displays the available custom controls and insertable objects. To add a control or insertable object to your Toolbox, place a check in the box next to its name. Of course, you need to clear the check box to remove the control or insertable object from your project. When you're done making selections, choose OK to update your Toolbox.

Figure 14.1.
The Custom Controls
dialog box.

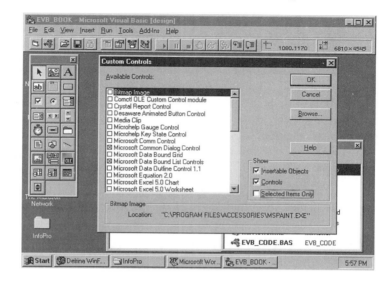

Here's a summary of the other items in the Custom Controls dialog box:

Location	Displays the full path to the currently selected control or object.
Show	Determines which items are listed in the Available Controls box. You can select either or all of the following options.
Insertable Objects	Displays insertable objects, such as a Microsoft Excel Chart.
Controls	Displays controls with .OCX and .VBX filename extensions.
Selected Items Only	Displays only those items in the Available Controls list which you have selected to include in the project.
Browse Button	Displays the Browse dialog box. To add a VBX or OLE custom control to the Available Controls box, choose the Browse button and search other directories for files with .VBX and .OCX filename extensions.

To close the Custom Controls dialog box, double-click the Control-menu box or press the Esc key. To accept the settings in the Custom Controls dialog box, choose OK.

Note You can't remove a control or insertable object that is placed on a form or otherwise referred to anywhere in your project. If you try to, you'll get a Visual Basic message stating that the control or reference is in use and cannot be removed.

Why Use Startup Procedures and Custom Controls?

The advantage of using custom controls, whether offered by a third party or developed by Microsoft, is obvious and encapsulated in the old saying, "Why re-invent the wheel?" If someone else has done it, and they're willing to give you (usually sell you) the fruits of their labor, then take advantage of it. Adding custom controls to your Visual Basic pallet is a great way to bring to your applications the power of lower-level languages, such as C.

One place where Sub Main startup procedures are useful is when your program must query the user's system, prior to displaying the first form. In the next section, for example, you'll use a startup procedure to gather information about the default printer's current settings.

How to Write and Implement a Startup Procedure

In this section, you'll add several new controls to your Toolbox, including many you'll use later in this book. You'll also create a Main Sub procedure which will query the system's default printer and output a report.

Adding Controls

Here's a list and brief description of the controls you'll add:

Control	Description
Sheridan 3D Controls	CommandButton, CheckBox, OptionButton, Frame, Panel, and Button Group Ribbon controls.
Microsoft Grid	For displaying information in a spreadsheet or tabular format.
Sheridan Tabbed Dialog	Simulates tabbed index card or file folder system.

Follow the steps outlined earlier in this chapter to add these controls to your Toolbox. Here's what your development environment might look like afterward. Compare your Toolbox to that seen in Figure 14.1.

Figure 14.2.
*Design mode: the List
Box program.*

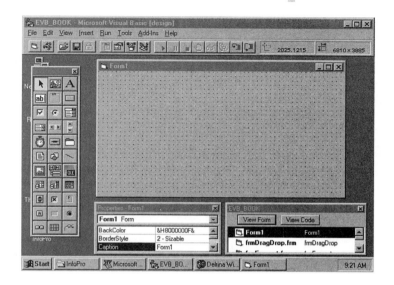

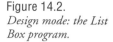

Note In Visual Basic 4.0, Microsoft has provided its own 3D command buttons, check boxes, option buttons, and frames. To be precise, an Appearance property, which may be toggled between Flat and 3D, has been added to each of these controls (32-bit only). Sheridan's SSPanel and SSRibbon controls provide some extra functionality, above and beyond mere appearance, as you'll discover in Chapter 19 of this book.

Creating a Startup Procedure

In this section, you'll add a Sub procedure called `Main` to your EVB_CODE module. Since you won't have a form to print to, `Main` will print a report to the Printer object, after determining your default printer's current settings.

The first step is to open the EVB_CODE module and enter the following on a blank line:

```
Sub Main()
```

Visual Basic will open a Code window and create a `Sub...End Sub` template. Here's what the `Main` procedure should look like:

```
Sub Main()
Dim iCounter As Integer                         'Declare variable for font
loop counter
Dim CRLF As String, sDriver As String           'Print strings...
Dim sPort As String, sOrient As String, sQual As String

CRLF = Chr$(13) & Chr$(10)

                                                'Read printer props...
sDriver = "Printer Driver: " & Printer.DriverName   'Get driver...
```

```
sPort = "Port: " & Printer.Port                         'Port...
sOrient = IIf(Printer.Orientation = 1, "Portrait", "Landscape")
'Orientation..
sOrient = "Orientation: " & sOrient
sQual = "Quality: " & Printer.PrintQuality & " DPI" & CRLF & CRLF 'Print DPI...

                                        ' Then use Print method to print 'em out...
Printer.Print sDriver
Printer.Print sPort
Printer.Print sOrient
Printer.Print sQual

Printer.Print "Available Fonts: " & CRLF            'Print heading...
    For iCounter = 0 To Printer.FontCount - 1        'Determine number of fonts.
        Printer.Print Printer.Fonts(iCounter)        'Print each font...
    Next

Printer.EndDoc                                       'Send to printer...
MsgBox "Printer Report Complete!", vbInformation, "Printer Information!"
End Sub
```

The Printer object has many more properties and methods than the few you're exploring here. Basically, all you're doing is reading some properties and printing them to the Printer object, using the Print method. In the loop, you're determining the number of fonts available to the default printer, then setting up a counter to print each of them out. Once output to the Printer object is complete, it's flushed to the printer with the EndDoc method. Finally, you're putting up a message.

Once this code is entered, you'll need to follow the steps outlined earlier in this chapter to change the project's startup form to Sub Main.

Go ahead and test your new startup procedure. Among other things, you'll notice that the procedure executes just fine, with no form in sight.

Essential Summary

What
In this chapter, you reinforced your understanding of custom controls and saw how to add them to your current project. You learned that a startup form is not necessary for your applications, and that a Sub Main procedure may be used instead.

Why
Custom controls add extra power, grace, and functionality to your program by extending Visual Basic's Toolbox. One advantage of using a startup procedure rather than a form is that it's sometimes necessary to discover information about a user's system *before* the first form is displayed.

How
You added several new controls to Visual Basic's Toolbox, some of which you will put to good use later in this book. You created a Sub Main procedure, which queried the default printer for its current settings, then printed a report.

Creating and Enhancing Menus

In this chapter, you'll make a nice cosmetic adjustment to your system by assigning icons to all of your significant forms. You'll also use Visual Basic's Menu Editor to create a typical Windows-style menu for your EVB_BOOK application. The menu will reside on a new form, frmEVBMain, and will be used to open most of the forms you've created so far. You'll learn how to enable and disable particular menu items at design time; you'll see how to establish shortcut keys for your menu items; and you'll see how to set other menu properties such as displaying and removing a menu check mark.

What Is the Menu Editor?

What The *Menu Editor* is a menu design applet included with Visual Basic. You use it to create custom menus for your application and to define their properties. To open the Menu Editor, you must have a form selected on the Visual Basic "desktop" (sometimes referred to as the *IDE*, or *Integrated Development Environment*). You may then choose **M**enu Editor from the **T**ools menu, or click the toolbar shortcut (use the ToolTips to locate it).

Here's what the Editor will look like once you've completed your menu design (see Figure 15.1).

Figure 15.1.
Visual Basic's Menu Editor.

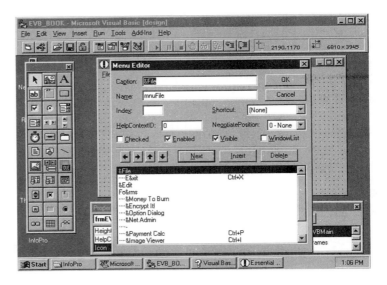

The Menu Editor consists of a *Caption* text box in which you enter the menu or command name that appears on your menu bar or in an associated drop-down menu. To allow keyboard access to the menu item, insert an ampersand (&) before a letter, as you've seen with other Caption properties. You may also use the Caption text box to create a *separator bar* (a horizontal bar serving to group related menu items) in your menu by entering a single hyphen (-).

The *Name* text box is where you enter a control name for the menu item. A *control name* (or *menu item name*) is an identifier used only to access the menu item in code; it doesn't appear in a menu. However, *every* menu item must have a name, even separator bars; and it's probably a good idea to name your menu items with an "mnu" prefix, to make them easily identifiable.

The *Index* text box is used to assign a numeric value that determines the menu item's position within a control array (control arrays will be discussed in Chapter 34).

The *Shortcut* drop-down presents a list from which you may select a shortcut key for your menu item. The Shortcut key combination will be displayed on the menu, immediately to the right of the menu caption.

The *HelpContextID* text box is where you assign the unique numeric value for the context ID. This value is used to find the appropriate Help topic in the Help file identified by the HelpFile property. (Creating help files is an advanced programming topic covered in Appendix B.)

The *NegotiatePosition* drop-down displays a list from which you can select the menu's NegotiatePosition property. This is an OLE related property and will not be covered in this book.

The four check boxes provide the following functionality.

Checked. A check box you select if you want a check mark to appear at the left of a menu item. This is generally used to indicate whether a toggle option is turned on or off.

Enabled. A check box you select if you want the menu item to respond to events. If you want the item to be unavailable and appear dimmed or grayed, clear this box.

Visible. A check box you select if you want the menu item to appear on the menu. (There are many uses for invisible menu items, as you'll see in the next chapter.)

WindowList. A check box you select if you want the menu control to contain a list of open MDI child forms in an MDI (Multiple Document Interface) application. MDI is discussed in Chapter 35.

The Menu Editor also contains a set of *outlining buttons* that enable you to move menu items to a higher or lower level, or to position them within the same level. Use the right and left arrows to adjust the sublevels of a menu. Use the up and down arrows to change the position of a menu item within the same level, that is, up or down in the menu list.

The largest element of the Menu Editor is a list box that displays a hierarchical list of menu items, a kind of visual menu template (refer to Figure 15.1). Submenu items are indented to indicate their hierarchical position or level.

Finally, the Menu Editor has the following push buttons:

Button	Description
Next	Moves selection to the next line in the template
Insert	Inserts a line above the currently selected line
Delete	Deletes the currently selected line
OK	Closes the Menu Editor and applies all changes to the last form you selected
Cancel	Closes the Menu Editor and cancels all changes

To close the Menu Editor, double-click the Control-menu box. To accept changes in the Menu Editor, choose OK. Selecting a menu item at design time opens the Code window for that item's Click event, which is how and where you'll add code to your menu objects.

Why Use Menus?

Menus are a common and powerful way to allow your users to navigate your applications; they provide an attractive and hierarchic application interface. As most Windows applications have quite sophisticated menuing systems, understanding how to create compact and efficient menus for your programs is an important part of professional applications development.

Assigning Icons to Forms

You can assign an icon to a form by setting its Icon property at design time. You use this property to specify a descriptive icon which will appear in the form's upper-left corner when it's open, as well as when the form is minimized at run time. The idea is to assign a unique icon to indicate the form's function.

The file you load into the Icon property must have the .ICO filename extension and format. If you don't specify an icon, the Visual Basic default icon for forms is used.

Here's a table suggesting the icons to be assigned to your EVB_BOOK project's forms. (You may, of course, use whatever icons you like). Remember that your Visual Basic program may be installed in a different directory.

Table 15.1. Suggested forms and icons.

Form	Complete Path to Icon	Icon Description
frmDragDrop	c:\vb40\icons\elements\fire.ico	Burning match
frmEncrypt	c:\vb40\icons\misc\secur08.ico	Shadowed key
frmFrames	c:\vb40\icons\misc\bullseye.ico	Bull's eye target
frmLists	c:\vb40\icons\comm\net01.ico	Networked computers
frmScrollBars	c:\vb40\icons\misc\house.ico	House and car
frmViewer	c:\vb40\icons\misc\eye.ico	Wakeful eye

How to Create a Menu

The first thing to do in creating your program's menuing system is to add a new form to your project. Do this now, naming it frmEVBMain, and save it as part of the EVB_BOOK project. Be sure to adjust your project's startup form option accordingly.

Start up Visual Basic's Menu Editor and refer to the following table in designing your new menu. (Refer also to Figure 15.1 to see where you're heading.)

Table 15.2. Design-time menu settings.

Menu Object	Property	Design-Time Setting
File Menu	Caption	&File
	Name	mnuFile
Exit	Caption	E&xit
	Name	mnuExit

Menu Object	Property	Design-Time Setting
	Shortcut	Ctrl+X
Edit Menu	Caption	&Edit
	Name	mnuEdit
Forms Menu	Caption	&Forms
	Name	mnuForms
First	Caption	&Money To Burn
	Name	mnuDragDrop
Second	Caption	&Encrypt It!
	Name	mnuEncrypt
Third	Caption	&Option Dialog
	Name	mnuFrames
Fourth	Caption	&Net Admin
	Name	mnuLists
Fifth	Caption	- (Menu Separator)
	Name	mnuSep1
Sixth	Caption	&Payment Calc
	Name	mnuScrollBars
	Shortcut	Ctrl+P
Seventh	Caption	&Image Viewer
	Name	mnuViewer
	Shortcut	Ctrl+I

Notice that you've named your menu items with an "mnu" prefix followed by the name of the form you intend to open, (without the "frm" prefix). This is not necessary, of course, but is simply a handy mnemonic device, as you'll see when it's time to add code.

Adding Code to Your Menu

In Design mode, you may open a Code window for a particular menu item just by clicking it. Click on File Exit, for example, and a Code window for that menu item's Click event opens. Since this is the item you'll select to exit (or end) your program, it will contain a single line between the Private Sub and End Sub statements.

```
Private Sub mnuExit_Click()
End
End Sub
```

The only other functionality you'll add to your menu system in this chapter is to open the appropriate form when one of the Forms menu items is selected. Click each of the Forms menu items and add the appropriate code.

```
Private Sub mnuDragDrop_Click()
frmDragDrop.Show
End Sub

Private Sub mnuEncrypt_Click()
frmEncrypt.Show
End Sub

Private Sub mnuFrames_Click()
frmFrames.Show
End Sub

Private Sub mnuLists_Click()
frmLists.Show
End Sub

Private Sub mnuScrollBars_Click()
frmScrollBars.Show
End Sub

Private Sub mnuViewer_Click()
frmViewer.Show
End Sub
```

The Show Method and Modal/Modeless Windows

In the previous code listing, you're using the form object's Show method to open various forms from your new menu. The Show method loads a form and displays it, or just displays it if it's already loaded but hidden (more on hiding and showing forms in Chapter 17). When a form is displayed, it may be either *modal* or *modeless*. A modal form is a window or dialog box that requires the user to take some action before the focus can switch to another form or dialog box. Visual Basic's MsgBox() and InputBox() functions display modal forms: you must click a button or otherwise close the form before processing will continue.

Modeless forms (windows or dialog boxes) do not require user action before the focus can be switched to another form or dialog box. In Visual Basic, the Toolbox, Properties window, and Project window are all examples of modeless forms. You may switch the focus to any one of them without closing the others.

When you display a form with the Show method, you may include a *style* argument in the call, using the predefined constants MODAL or MODELESS. For example:

```
frmYourForm.Show MODAL
```

or

```
frmMyForm.Show MODELESS.
```

If you omit the style argument, the form is modeless by default. Therefore, in reviewing the code you entered above, you'll see that all of the forms in your application will be modeless. (You'll work with both types of forms in Chapter 17.)

Your new menu interface is ready for testing. Be sure to verify that all your forms are modeless. You should be able to open them all at once and move freely between them. You'll be able to close any form by double-clicking its icon in the upper-left corner. Figure 15.2 shows your menu system in action.

Figure 15.2.
*Your menu system in
action.*

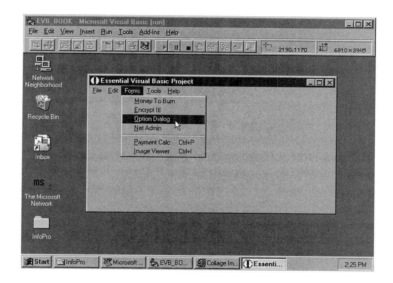

Essential Summary

In this chapter, you were introduced to Visual Basic's Menu Editor, which is used to create custom Windows-style menus for your applications. You learned that it's possible to set and remove check marks, enable and disable menu items, and even make menu items invisible, by setting their properties at design time.

What

Any commercially-viable Windows application will have a concise and efficient menu interface. Therefore, a proficiency in the use of Visual Basic's Menu Editor, along with the associated menu manipulation methods and properties (covered in Chapter 16), is a necessary condition for qualification as a serious Windows programmer.

Why

You put your hard-earned menu skills to work by creating a menu system for your EVB_BOOK project. You added a new form and used Visual Basic's Menu Editor to attach a menu to it. You wrote code for each of the Form menu's items which, when executed, displayed the associated form in a modeless style.

How

Menu Modification at Run Time

In this chapter, you'll enhance the menu system you created in Chapter 15. You'll add some new menu items, most of which will be disabled (grayed out) when they first appear. You'll add check marks to the Forms menu items, as each form is displayed, and remove them when the form is unloaded. You'll see how to create a pop-up menu that will appear with a right mouse click. Finally, you'll see how to add and remove menu items at run time.

Menu Enhancement Concepts

What In Windows programming, a check mark is often placed to the left of a menu item to indicate that it's currently in effect. All that's required to place such a check mark at run time is to set the menu item's Checked property to True; and predictably, you'd set the item's Checked property to False to remove the check. For example, assuming you have a menu item named mnuView, the following snippet would display a check mark next to it:

```
mnuView.Checked = True
```

To be precise, this snippet would work as long as it's executing from the form containing the target menu item. If you're trying to set a check mark on a menu on another form, you need to include the name of the form in the call, like the following:

```
frmThatForm.mnuView.Checked = True
```

As you might imagine, you can enable or disable a menu item in a very similar fashion. The difference is that you set the item's Enabled property to True or False, accordingly:

```
frmThatForm.mnuView.Enabled = False
```

What

Pop-up menus may literally "pop up" anywhere you want them. They need not be "dropped down" from any horizontal menu bar, and may be displayed anywhere on any form, usually with a single or double mouse click. Most serious Windows applications, and Windows itself for that matter, make good use of pop-up menus. You can point to almost any object in Windows 95, for example, and pop up a menu for it by clicking the right mouse button.

Adding pop-up menus to your program is a two-step process. First, you need to create the menu using the Editor menu. Generally, a pop-up menu will be set to invisible at design time. Once the menu is created and named, it may be displayed using the PopupMenu method, as described next.

The PopupMenu method displays a pop-up menu on any Form object at the current mouse location, unless other coordinates are specified. Here's the general syntax:

```
object.PopupMenu menuname, flags, x, y, boldcommand
```

All of the arguments, except for menuname, are optional. The object identifier is needed only when you want to pop up a menu on a form other than the one currently in focus. Here's a summary of the method's arguments.

Argument	Description
menuname	*Required.* The full name of the pop-up menu to be displayed. The specified menu must have at least one submenu.
flags	*Optional.* A value or constant used to specify the location and behavior of a pop-up menu, as described in the following section on flag settings.
x	*Optional.* Specifies the x (horizontal) coordinate where the pop-up menu is displayed. If omitted, the current mouse coordinate is used.
y	*Optional.* Specifies the y (vertical) coordinate where the pop-up menu is displayed. If omitted, the current mouse coordinate is used.
boldcommand	*Optional.* Instructs a menu control in the pop-up menu to display its caption in bold text. If omitted, no controls in the pop-up

menu appear in bold. This argument works only for applications running under Windows 95. The application will ignore this argument when running under 16-bit versions of Windows or Windows NT 3.51 and earlier.

Flag Settings

The PopupMenu method recognizes the flag settings specified in Table 16.1. There are two groups of constants: one for specifying the menu's location and one to define special menu behavior. If you'd like to send one flag constant from each group, you may OR them together.

Table 16.1. PopupMenu flag constants.

Location Constants	Value	Description
vbPopupMenuLeftAlign	0	The left side of the pop-up menu is located at the x coordinate. (Default)
vbPopupMenuCenterAlign	4	The pop-up menu is centered at x.
vbPopupMenuRightAlign	8	The right side of the pop-up menu is located at x.
Behavior Constants	Value	Description
vbPopupMenuLeftButton	0	An item on the pop-up menu reacts to a mouse click only when you use the left mouse button. (Default)
vbPopupMenuRightButton	2	An item on the pop-up menu reacts to a mouse click when you use either the right or the left mouse button. This flag can only be used in the MouseDown event.

You'll put some of these constants to use later in this chapter.

> **Note** When you display a pop-up menu, the code following the call to the PopupMenu method is suspended until the user either selects a command from the menu (in which case the code for that command's Click event is executed) or cancels the menu.

What
Adding and removing menu items at run time is another very powerful menu enhancement feature. Creating menu lists that grow or shrink as required involves working with an invisible menu separator and a menu array, as you'll see later in this chapter.

Why Use These Enhancements?

Why
The menu enhancements covered in this chapter contribute to a robust and attractive menu interface. Menu check marks and enabled or disabled appearances provide the user with important visual cues about the current state of your system.

A thoughtful use of pop-up menus—menus available, literally, at the click of a button—adds a level of functionality to your program that sophisticated users are coming to expect from all of their Windows applications. For example, a right-click on an icon representing a particular text file might pop up a menu displaying choices such as Read, Print, or Delete.

The capability to add and remove menu items at run time may pay off in many respects. In a simple contact database system, for example, you might find it convenient to keep a list of client names accessed during the current session. This list could be maintained, and manipulated, as another drop-down menu on your main menu bar.

How to Enhance Your Menu System

How
You'll begin enhancement of your menu system by adding several new menu items. Make sure your EVB_BOOK project is open, with frmEVBMain displayed and selected. Open the Menu editor and add the following items to the top of the File and Edit menus (you'll need to use the Insert button):

Table 16.2. Additions to your menu system.

Menu Object	Property	Design-Time Setting
File Menu (Done Earlier)	Caption	&File
	Name	mnuFile
Open	Caption	&Open
	Name	mnuOpen
	Shortcut	Ctrl+O
Close	Caption	&Close
	Name	mnuClose
	Enabled	No (Clear Checkbox)
Print	Caption	&Print...
	Name	mnuPrint
	Enabled	No

Menu Object	Property	Design-Time Setting
Exit (Done earlier)	Caption	E&xit
	Name	mnuExit
Separator	Caption	- (menu separator)
	Name	mnuFileList
	Index	0
	Visible	No (Clear Checkbox)
Edit Menu (Done earlier)	Caption	&Edit
	Name	mnuEdit
Undo	Caption	&Undo
	Name	mnuUndo
	Enabled	No
Cut	Caption	Cu&t
	Name	mnuCut
	Enabled	No
Copy	Caption	&Copy
	Name	mnuCopy
	Enabled	No
Paste	Caption	&Paste
	Name	mnuPaste
	Enabled	No

A few comments are in order here. Notice that most of these items will be disabled (dimmed or grayed out) at startup. That's as it should be. The Edit menu items, for example, will be usable only when something is selected for cutting or copying, or if something is in the Clipboard to be pasted. The new File menu item, mnuClose, will become enabled only after File Open has been used; that is, only when there's a file to be closed. You'll activate these features at run time as required.

Something else that's new here is the invisible separator added to the bottom of the File menu. Notice that in addition to being invisible at startup, its Index property is set to zero. This separator, mnuFileList, will be the first element in an array of menu items which will grow (and shrink) at run time. This will become a dynamic file list, tracking the open files, similar to an MRU (Most Recently Used) list seen at the bottom of many Windows File menus.

Designing a Pop-Up Menu

In this section, you'll design a pop-up menu for your program. This menu will contain two items, Zoom In and Zoom Out, and will be defined along with all the others in your system.

However, it will be invisible at startup and activated only by a right-mouse click to one of the money bundles on your Money To Burn form, frmDragDrop. You'll use it to make your money grow (or shrink).

The first step is to fire up the Menu Editor, if it's not already going, and create your new pop-up menu at the very bottom of the existing template. Here are the pop-up menu item specifications and Figure 16.1 for reference.

Table 16.3. Pop-up menu specifications.

Menu Object	Property	Design-Time Setting
Popup	Caption	Popup
	Name	mnuPopup
	Visible	No (Clear Checkbox)
Zoom In	Caption	Zoom In
	Name	mnuZoomIn
Zoom Out	Caption	Zoom Out
	Name	mnuZoomOut

Note A menu whose Visible property is set to False in the Menu Editor (so that it isn't visible on the horizontal menu bar) can still be displayed because the Visible property of the specified menu is ignored when you call the PopupMenu method.

Figure 16.1.
The Menu Editor: pop-up menu specifications.

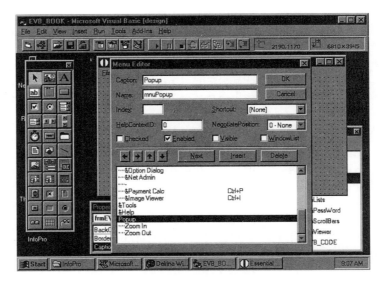

This completes the design time phase of your menu enhancements. In the next section, you'll add the code needed to make your enhancements fly.

Run Time Enabling and Checking

As you display each of your program's forms, you'll place a check next to the associated item on the form's drop-down menu. To do this, you'll need to add a single line of code to each menu item's Click event procedure. Here's what those procedures should now look like (remember, the call to the Show method was added in the last chapter):

```
Private Sub mnuDragDrop_Click()
mnuDragDrop.Checked = True          ' Check the menu...
frmDragDrop.Show                    ' Show the form...
End Sub

Private Sub mnuEncrypt_Click()
mnuEncrypt.Checked = True
frmEncrypt.Show
End Sub

Private Sub mnuFrames_Click()
mnuFrames.Checked = True
frmFrames.Show
End Sub

Private Sub mnuLists_Click()
mnuLists.Checked = True
frmLists.Show
End Sub

Private Sub mnuScrollBars_Click()
mnuScrollBars.Checked = True
frmScrollBars.Show
End Sub

Private Sub mnuViewer_Click()
mnuViewer.Checked = True
frmViewer.Show
End Sub
```

As each form is closed, in this case unloaded from memory, you'll want to remove the associated check mark from the Forms menu. You do this by adding a line to each form's Unload event. Since this involves opening several different forms and locating the Unload procedure, you might find it more convenient to use the Object Browser rather than manipulating forms in the Project window.

Here's the listing for frmDragDrop's Unload event:

```
Private Sub Form_Unload(Cancel As Integer)
frmEVBMain.mnuDragDrop.Checked = False      ' Uncheck the proper item
End Sub
```

Because the menu item you're interested in is on a different form (in this case, on your program's startup form), you need to specify the form on which the menu resides, as well as the menu item to be unchecked. Remember, you'll need to add a similar line, to the same event, in all six of your significant forms. Don't forget to change the menu item reference.

Adding and Removing Menu Items

The first thing you'll need is a form-level variable for keeping track of how many files you've opened. It must be visible to both mnuOpen and mnuClose, so declare it in frmEVBMain's general declarations section, as follows:

```
Dim iNumber As Integer
```

Now, whenever you click the File menu's Open item, you'll want to bump iNumber and use it to load the new menu item, as well as create the filename that will become the item's Caption. Here's how mnuOpen's Click event should read:

```
Private Sub mnuOpen_Click()
If iNumber = 0 Then                                 ' Get ready for first file...
    mnuFileList(0).Visible = True                   ' Show the separator
    mnuClose.Enabled = True                         ' And enable the close item...
End If

iNumber = iNumber + 1                               'Bump iNumber...
Load mnuFileList(iNumber)                           'Load new item into memory..
mnuFileList(iNumber).Caption = "File " & iNumber    'Set its caption...
mnuFileList(iNumber).Visible = True                 'And make it visible
End Sub
```

Next, you'll want each click of mnuClose to remove the latest item from your list of open files. That bit of magic is worked as follows:

```
Private Sub mnuClose_Click()
If iNumber > 0 Then                                 ' Make sure there's one left...
    Unload mnuFileList(iNumber)                     ' Unload it...
    iNumber = iNumber - 1                           ' Decrease iNumber
    If iNumber = 0 Then                             ' If no more to remove...
        mnuFileList(0).Visible = False              ' Make separator vanish...
        mnuClose.Enabled = False                    ' Disable the Close item.
    End If
End If
End Sub
```

The thing to remember here is that the horizontal separator, mnuFileList, is really the first element in a menu item array. You can load new items below it just by using iNumber as the index and calling the Load method. You remove items in a similar manner, except that you're decrementing iNumber and calling the UnLoad method.

Activating the Pop-Up Menu

The pop-up menu you'll activate is called mnuPopup, the visual design of which you completed earlier in this chapter. As you'll recall, this menu contains two items: mnuZoomIn and mnuZoomOut. You'll attach code to these items which will enlarge, or shrink, whatever object the menu is associated with. In this case, your pop-up menu will appear when the user clicks the right mouse button on any of the money bundles in frmDragDrop. Once the menu is visible, the user may select an option from it by left or right-clicking the mouse. In this way, you can make your money grow, or shrink to nearly nothing.

The first step is to locate the Click events for mnuZoomIn and mnuZoomOut. Don't be troubled by the fact that these items are not visible at design time. To get to their Click events, make sure frmEVBMain is open in design mode, then double-click anywhere on the form to open a Code window. You'll find mnuZoomIn and mnuZoomOut at the bottom of the Object drop-down list. Here's how their Click events will look, once you've added the necessary code:

```
Private Sub mnuZoomIn_Click()
Screen.ActiveForm.ActiveControl.Width = Screen.ActiveForm.ActiveControl.Width * 2
Screen.ActiveForm.ActiveControl.Height = Screen.ActiveForm.ActiveControl.Height * 2
End Sub

Private Sub mnuZoomOut_Click()
Screen.ActiveForm.ActiveControl.Width = Screen.ActiveForm.ActiveControl.Width  / 2
Screen.ActiveForm.ActiveControl.Height = Screen.ActiveForm.ActiveControl.Height / 2
End Sub
```

When you're zooming in, you're doubling the height and width of the current object, while zooming out reduces them by 50 percent. Because these procedures won't always act on the same object, you need a way to indicate that that they should be applied to the object currently in focus; that is, in this case, the money bundle that pops up the menu. You're doing that here by employing Visual Basic's Screen, ActiveForm, and ActiveControl objects. Using these objects, properly dot notated as above, you can read or set properties on the currently active object from anywhere in your system.

The last step is to add the code that will actually pop up your menu when you right-click a bundle of money. Close your menu form and open frmDragDrop. Since you want the menu to pop open only when a bundle is right-clicked, you should add the following lines to each picture's MouseDown event procedure:

```
If Button = 2 Then          ' Only on right button
PopupMenu frmEVBMain.mnuPopup, vbPopupMenuRightButton Or _
vbPopupMenuCenterAlign
End If
```

You should notice a couple of things here. Because mnuPopup is on another form, you need to specify that form in the dot path. You're also adjusting the appearance and behavior of your menu by including a couple of flag constants ORed together. The flags in this case, once the menu is popped open, will allow a menu item to be selected by clicking or releasing the right mouse button. The second flag constant makes the menu appear centered, below the mouse pointer, rather than to the left or right.

It's now time to test your new menu features. Be sure to examine all the different enhancements. You should be able to open any of your forms and see a corresponding check mark on the form's menu; the check should disappear when the form is closed. Each time you activate the File Open item, a new file should be added to the list at the bottom of the File menu; clicking File Close will remove the file list items, one at a time. Finally, be sure to enjoy your ability to make your money grow by right-clicking a money bundle and selecting Zoom In from the pop-up menu.

Figure 16.2 shows your menu enhancements in action.

Figure 16.2.
*The pop-up menu
in action.*

Essential Summary

What
You've learned that a check mark is often placed to the left of a menu item to indicate that it's currently in effect. You now know that pop-up menus may be created to appear anywhere, on any form in your application, and may be activated, and selected from, with a simple mouse click. You've also seen that it's possible to create menus whose list of items may be extended, or retracted, as required at run time.

Why
Menu check marks and menu items with enabled or disabled appearances offer the user important visual clues about their available options and the current state of your system. Pop-up menus contribute to the overall functionality of your program and add the touch of sophistication that most Windows users have come to expect.

How
In this chapter, you've added considerable functionality to your program's menu system. You added some new menu items and caused each Form menu item to be checked, or unchecked, at the proper time. You saw how to create a pop-up menu using the Menu Editor, and how to make it appear with a right mouse click. Finally, you learned one way to add and remove menu items at run time.

Custom Dialog Boxes: Modal and Modeless

In this chapter, you'll add some final touches to your EVB_BOOK project. You'll create a new form—a custom About dialog box—a common feature in Windows applications that is used to display author and copyright information. You'll get a chance to experiment further with the Show method, to see the pros and cons of hiding windows versus unloading them. You'll gain a better understanding of the differences between *modal* and *modeless* windows. Finally, you'll modify your Password form to serve as a security "front-end" to your program.

What Are Custom Dialog Boxes?

What As you've seen, Visual Basic supplies you with two somewhat limited dialog box functions, InputBox() and MsgBox(), for gathering input and displaying information, respectively. However, you have no control over the size of these boxes, extremely limited control over how they look and, in the case of `MsgBox()`, can't even determine where the box will be displayed. The good news is that you may design your own custom dialog boxes, which may look and act precisely as you want them to.

Modal versus Modeless Windows

A little clarification of terms may be in order here. In Visual Basic, the terms *form* and *window* are used interchangeably, and a *dialog box* is just a special kind of form. A *modal form (window)* is one that must be acknowledged by the user—usually by clicking some sort of termination button such as Close, OK, or Cancel—before processing can continue. A modal form prevents the user from accessing other windows in your program until it is responded to and either hidden (with the Hide method) or removed from memory (with the `Unload` command). Custom dialog boxes, designed to match the visual look and feel of your program, are usually displayed as modal forms.

In contrast to modal windows, *modeless windows* may receive or lose the user's focus at any time. Many Windows programs, including Visual Basic itself, use modeless windows as Toolboxes or Color Palettes, for example. Showing a modeless window does not prevent Visual Basic from carrying out any subsequent commands, unlike modal windows where your program freezes until the form is dispensed with.

The Show Method

What

The Show method makes an invisible form, or window, visible. If the form hasn't already been loaded (from disk into memory), it will be loaded and displayed. A window displayed with the Show method is, by default, a *modeless* window. You may display a *modal* window by passing the constant vbModal, which is predefined in Visual Basic and equal to 1. Assuming you have a form called frmGame, the following line would display it modally:

```
frmGame.Show vbModal
```

The Hide and Unload Commands

What

The Hide command (or method) makes a form vanish from view but does not unload it from the computer's memory. Any changes to the form, or its controls, that were made by the user or the program are retained for future use.

If your program has several windows, you can switch among them as necessary by Hiding and Showing them. Forms that are used frequently should be left hidden, but not unloaded, when they aren't currently needed. You can display a form much more quickly if it need not be loaded from disk. In addition, a hidden form retains the values of any static variables associated with it, as well as any property changes made during the last showing. Here's how you would hide a form called frmDone:

```
frmDone.Hide                              ' From another form or module...
```

Or just

```
Hide                              ' The form hides itself...
```

Under certain circumstances—such as when system memory is unusually low or when you're absolutely certain a form will no longer be needed—you might want to Unload forms, rather than Hide them. Unloading a form has the same effect as when a user double-clicks the form's icon in the upper-left corner, or single-clicks the X icon in the upper-right corner: the form collapses, disappears from the screen, and is removed from memory. Assuming you have a form named frmGoodBye, you may Unload it in the following manner:

```
Unload frmGoodBye                 ' From some other form or module..
```

Or, simply

```
Unload Me                         ' Called from the form itself...
```

> **Tip**   The Visual Basic reserved word Me refers to the form that is currently executing your program. This is useful in situations where you want to pass the identity of the calling form to some procedure that does things for forms in general. You might, for example, have a routine named Expand that enlarges a form by 50 percent. You could call it from within any form with the single line: Expand Me.

Why Use Custom Dialog Boxes?

The main reason for designing and using your own custom dialog boxes has already been presented; that is, by so doing you're able to overcome the limitations of Visual Basic's MsgBox() and InputBox() functions. Another reason to use your own dialog boxes is to better match the way your program looks and feels since you may set and alter any of the form's properties, including size, shape, color, icons, and position.

Modal forms are useful as dialog boxes with which the user is forced to interact. Password windows and About boxes are good examples of modal forms. Modeless forms, those displayed with a normal Show method, are used when it is desirable to leave one or many forms open without bringing your program to a halt. Modeless windows are very common in today's multitasking programs, for example, where you might monitor a communications session in one window, while typing a memo in another.

How to Create a Custom About Box

One of the standard features of just about any Windows program is the About dialog box, which is usually accessed from the system's Help menu. The About box is used to display author and copyright information, as well as program licensing and distribution restrictions.

In this section, you'll add a new form to your project, calling it frmAbout. This time you won't need to change your project's startup form since the About box will be displayed when the user selects About from frmEVBMain's Help menu. You may, of course, use your own imagination in designing your About box, but feel free to refer to Figure 17.1 for ideas.

Figure 17.1.
One possible custom About box.

The significant objects and properties of this form are summarized here, in Table 17.1.

Table 17.1. Design-time settings—a possible About box.

Visual Basic Object	Property	Design-Time Setting
Form	Name	frmAbout
	Caption	About This EVB Book System
	BorderStyle	3 - Fixed Dialog
	ControlBox	False
	MaxButton	False
	MinButton	False
Image Control	Name	imgSmile
	Picture	C:\VB40\ICONS\MISC\FACE03.ICO
Command Button	Name	cmdOK
	Caption	&OK
	Cancel	True
	Default	True

Notice that the form will display no ControlBox (or icon), nor will it have a Minimize or Maximize button; you're therefore guaranteed that the user will have only one way to close the form: the OK button. With the BorderStyle set to Fixed Dialog, the user will be able to move the form around the screen, but not resize it in any way.

An About dialog box is a perfect example of a form that should be opened modally and should be hidden, rather than unloaded, when the user is done reading it. You'll add this functionality in the following section.

The About box will be displayed when **A**bout is selected from your main form's **H**elp menu. You'll need to add that menu item now. Display frmEVBMain in Design mode, then start the Menu Editor. Refer to Figure 17.2 to see how the menu template should look.

Figure 17.2.
Adding the About menu item.

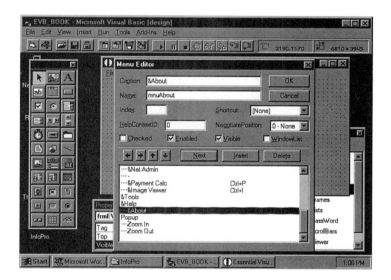

Adding Code to Activate the About Box

Once you've saved your changes and closed the Menu Editor, click on the Form menu and then the new About item to display a `Click` event Code window. All that's required to display the About form as a modal window is a single line. Here's how the event procedure should look:

```
Private Sub mnuAbout_Click()
frmAbout.Show vbModal                           ' Make it modal...
End Sub
```

Now close frmEVBMain and open frmAbout. Because the user will be able to change the location of the About form (even though he or she can't resize it), you may want to ensure that the form is centered each time it's made visible. Locate the form's `Activate` event and make it look like this:

```
Private Sub Form_Activate()                          'Center The Form When Shown

    Left = (Screen.Width - Width) / 2
    Top = (Screen.Height - Height) / 2
End Sub
```

The Activate event procedure is new to you. Because you want to center the About form every time it's displayed (not just when it's first loaded), you must attach the centering code to the Activate event, which fires off whenever the form is made visible. All you're doing here is setting the form's Left and Top properties, its X and Y screen coordinates so that the form is centered in relation to the screen's height and width (that is, you're subtracting the form's height and width from the screen's), then dividing by two.

The final step is to hide the form when the user clicks OK by adding a single line to cmdOK's Click event:

```
Private Sub cmdOK_Click()
    Hide            'Hide Me....
End Sub
```

That's it for the About form. Next you'll modify the password form you created in Chapter 7 and use it as a security "front-end" to your nearly completed project.

The New Custom Password Dialog Box

In this section, you'll make some changes to your program's password form. You're still in Design mode, so close frmAbout and open frmPassWord. Here's what it will look like (see Figure 17.3) once you've made the suggested changes:

Figure 17.3.
Design mode: the new
Password dialog box.

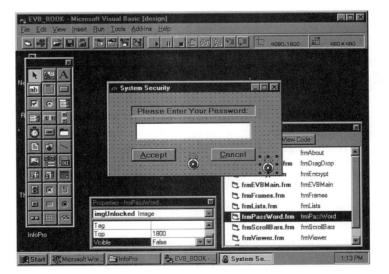

As you can see, you're going to add a couple of images, a closed and open combination lock. Only the closed lock will be visible at startup. Once the correct password is entered, the closed lock will pop open, and you'll be granted access to your system.

See Table 17.2 for significant object settings.

Table 17.2. Significant settings—the improved Password form.

Visual Basic Object	Property	Design-Time Setting
Form	Name	frmPassWord
	Caption	System Security
	BorderStyle	3 - Fixed Dialog
	ControlBox	True
Image Control	Name	imgLocked
	Picture	C:\VB40\ICONS\MISC\SUCUR01B.ICO
Image Control	Name	imgUnlocked
	Picture	C:\VB40\ICONS\MISC\SUCUR01A.ICO
	Visible	False
Command Button	Name	cmdAccept
	Caption	&Accept
	Default	True
Command Button	Name	cmdCancel
	Caption	&Cancel
	Cancel	True

The form will have neither a minimize nor maximize button, but you'll want a ControlBox to provide an alternate way to cancel and end the program. (Actually, with Windows 95, a ControlBox provides two ways of exiting; an X in the upper-right and an icon in the upper-left of the form.) Notice also that imgUnlocked's Visible property is set to False. You want to see only the closed lock when the form is first opened.

Adding and Modifying Code

It's been a while since you wrote the code that breathes life into your password form. It might be wise to review it here. Remember that you stored the correct password in the password text box's Tag property. This allowed you to compare what the user entered with txtPassword.Tag and to see whether or not access should be granted.

In the original password program, all you did was display a congratulatory message box when the correct word was submitted. In the new version, you'll pop open the combination lock, pause for a second to admire your work, then display your application's main form. Finally, since the password form will not be used again, you'll unload it from memory.

Caution There's one other thing you'll need to watch out for in the old version of your password routine. The very last line, txtPassword.SetFocus, which is meant to bring the focus back to the password text box, will cause an error in the new version when the correct password is entered. This is because *you unload the password form* when access is granted, so when that line executes, there's no txtPassword to get the focus. To get around the problem, you'll move that line up a little so that it's part of the Else clause that allows a second and third entry attempt.

Now here's a listing of the code in cmdAccept's Click event. Please note the suggested changes and additions:

```
Private Sub cmdAccept_Click()
Static iTries
If UCase(txtPassword) = txtPassword.Tag Then
    imgLocked.Picture = imgUnlocked.Picture            ' Display open lock...
    Refresh
    lWait = Timer: While lWait + 1 > Timer: Wend       ' Wait a second...
    frmEVBMain.Show                                    ' Show main form..
    Unload Me                                          ' Unload this one...
    Else
    iTries = iTries + 1
    If iTries = 3 Then
        MsgBox "Sorry...Too Many Attempts", vbCritical, "Access Denied!"
        End
        Else
        MsgBox "Press OK And Try Again", vbInformation, "Incorrect Password!"
        txtPassword.SelStart = 0
        txtPassword.SelLength = Len(txtPassword)
        txtPassword.SetFocus                           ' Moved here, from below
    End If
End If
End Sub
```

What you're doing here is employing a simple animation technique that allows one picture to be changed to another very quickly (you'll get to do more of this in Chapter 21). Rather than loading the opened lock from disk at run time, using LoadPicture(), you'll simply set imgLocked's Picture property equal to imgUnlocked's Picture property. Since imgUnlocked is already loaded (it's just invisible), the closed lock will appear to pop open, no disk access required.

One final note before testing. One of your forms, frmFrames, contains a Cancel button. You may remember that you added the End statement to that button's Click event. What this means is that if you close that form by clicking the Cancel button, the form won't just close; your program will end! This may not be what you want. It's probably a good idea to change that

End statement to Hide. You should also add a line, prior to Hide, that removes the check mark from the form's associated menu item:

```
frmEVBMain.mnuFrames.Checked = False
```

To complete the transition, you'll want the check mark to appear when the form is made visible again. Add this line to the form's Activate event:

```
frmEVBMain.mnuFrames.Checked = True
```

You're now ready to test, and possibly debug, your program. Don't forget to change your project's startup form to frmPassWord. The password used in Chapter 7 was "ROBOCOP." Of course, you may have changed it to something else, in which case you'd better check txtPassword's Tag property before you begin testing. Be sure to notice your animated lock and compare the behavior of your modal and modeless forms.

In the next chapter, you'll convert your program to a legitimate Windows executable and prepare it for distribution, using Visual Basic's Setup Wizard.

Essential Summary

In this chapter, you learned the value of custom dialog boxes. You got a chance to see the ways in which the Show and Hide methods, as well as the Unload method, may efficiently and fruitfully interact. You also acquired a solid understanding of the hows and whys of *modal* and *modeless* windows. **What**

By designing your own dialog boxes, you're able to overcome the limitations of Visual Basic's built-in dialog box functions, and to have more control over the way your program looks and feels. Modal forms are useful as Password windows, or About boxes, or anywhere the user's attention is needed. Modeless windows are commonly used as Toolboxes or Color Palettes, or in any situation where several windows must be able to acquire the user's focus at his or her discretion. **Why**

You created a modal form, a custom About box, which can be displayed from your application's Help menu. This box is shown or hidden as required, but remains in memory for the life of the program. You modified your password input form to serve as a security Cerberus, if you will, guarding your application's front gate. The form's modifications also included the addition of a simple animation technique that caused an image of a closed combination lock to pop open when the proper password was submitted. **How**

Building and Delivering the Application

Up to this point, you've run your EVB_BOOK program only within Visual Basic's *IDE (Integrated Development Environment)*. In this chapter, you'll prepare your program for delivery. First you'll create a Windows executable and see how to include with it useful documentary information. Then you'll use the Visual Basic Application Setup Wizard to create a SETUP.EXE and distribution media that will install your application on the user's system.

What Is an Executable?

What An *executable file* is a Windows-based application with an .EXE filename extension that can run outside the Visual Basic development environment. This file and other auxiliary files required by your program are delivered to the application's prospective users to be installed and executed under Windows.

Why Create an Executable?

Why

The ultimate goal of any programming project is to produce a usable, and useful, executable application. Clearly, you'll want your users to be able to launch your program directly from Windows, without Visual Basic chugging away in the background. In fact, the chances are your users won't even own a copy of Visual Basic, and wouldn't want to.

How to Create an Executable

How

Once your EVB_BOOK project is open in the development environment, the first step in creating an executable program file is to select Make EXE File from Visual Basic's **F**ile menu. This will display the Make EXE File dialog box. To open the EXE Options dialog box, click the Options button. The EXE Options dialog box, with some project information already added, is depicted in Figure 18.1.

Figure 18.1.
The EXE Options
dialog box.

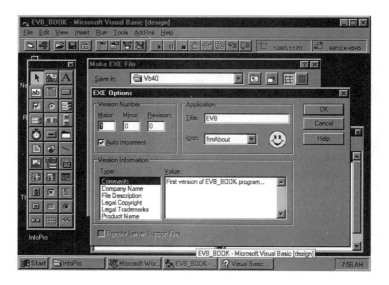

This dialog box to is used to set attributes and documentary information for the executable file you're about to make. At this point, you should go ahead and enter information pertaining to your current project. The following contains a summary description of the features available in the EXE Options dialog box.

The Version Number feature's options:

Major	The application's major release number.
Minor	The application's minor release number.
Revision	The revision version number of the application.

Auto Increment   If checked, the application's revision number will automatically be increased by one each time you run the Make EXE File command for this project.

The Application feature's options:

Title   The name of the application (may be different than the project name).

Icon   The icon for the application (select an icon assigned to one of the project's forms).

The Version Information feature's options:

Type   The type of information for which you can enter a description. You can enter information for your company name, file description, legal copyright, legal trademarks, and product name.

Value   This is where you may enter a lengthy description for the currently selected type.

Note The Remote Server Support Files check box activates an advanced feature supporting communication with an OLE server on a remote computer. When checked, Visual Basic creates an additional file, with an .REG extension and the same name as the .EXE file. This REG file contains OLE information required by the Windows registry.

To close the EXE Options dialog box and save any information you've entered, double-click the Control-menu box. Choosing Cancel closes without saving.

Once you're back to the Make EXE File dialog box, select a directory for your .EXE file (the default is the current project directory, which is usually best), then press OK to create the executable. During this phase, Visual Basic may discover problems with your code. If so, a Code window will open to show you the offending line. You may fix the problem, then restart the EXE creation process.

Caution It's possible to create and distribute more than one version of an application. Multiple versions can cause problems such as object incompatibilities between versions and the overwriting of more recent versions with older ones during setup. You might want to refer to the Visual Basic Online Help article entitled *Managing Versions of Your Application* for more information. (Search Help for "managing versions.")

You're now ready to create your application's Setup and distribution disk(s).

What Is the Application Setup Wizard?

What

The Application Setup Wizard is a tool used to create a setup program and distribution diskette(s) for your Visual Basic application. If you performed a normal installation of Visual Basic 4.0, you'll find an icon for the Wizard in your Visual Basic Group (or Folder) in the Windows Program Manager.

The first time you run the Setup Wizard, you are prompted for the location of several important files that are required for your application to run correctly. The Setup Wizard supports multiple disks and can split large files to fit on your choice of distribution media. The Setup Wizard can even copy your setup files to a hard disk directory for distribution over a network or on CD-ROM.

> **Caution** The Setup Wizard is designed to handle the common setup scenarios encountered by a Visual Basic developer and, in fact, will work fine with your EVB_BOOK project; however, some more complicated scenarios may require you to create your own custom Setup program. Refer to the Visual Basic Online Help article *Writing Your Setup Program*. (Search Help for "setup program.")

Why Use the Application Setup Wizard?

Why

The Application Setup Wizard provides an easy way to prepare your programming projects for distribution. It assists you in determining precisely which auxiliary files are required by your application, creates a Setup program that will work like any other Windows application's SETUP.EXE, compresses all required files, and writes the compressed files to the distribution media of your choice.

How to Use the Application Setup Wizard

How

Although your EVB_BOOK distribution files should fit nicely onto a single high-density disk, you might want to have a few extra blank, formatted disks on hand. Start up the Setup Wizard and work along with the book to complete the following steps:

■ Step 1. The Setup Wizard Gathers Initial Information.

Enter the path and filename for the .VBP file of the application that you want to distribute. (Your application's project file is EVB_BOOK.VBP). You may also browse the files on your disk by choosing the Select VBP File button.

If an executable file (.EXE) doesn't exist for the specified application, the Setup Wizard automatically builds it. To force a rebuild, select the Rebuild the Projects EXE file check box.

Press the Next Button to continue.

The Setup Wizard determines all the files you'll need to distribute.

■ Step 2. The Setup Wizard Gathers Data Access Information.

If your application uses the Data control or any of the data access objects (this one does not), you must select the database drivers to be included in the distribution files. For example, if your application uses Paradox 4.0 data files, select that option from the list. You can make multiple selections from this list.

Press the Next Button to continue.

Tip At any time during the rest of the setup process, you may save your work to a template file by choosing the Save Template button. A template makes it easier to interact with the Wizard in the future. You can return to the template later by choosing the Open Template button when you next start the Setup Wizard.

■ Step 3. The Setup Wizard Gathers Media Information.

If you want to distribute the application on floppy disks, select the Disk Drive option button, and then pick the drive on which you want to create your master floppy disks. Also indicate the disk capacity.

If you want to distribute over a network or on CD-ROM, you may select a destination drive and directory by clicking the Network Directory button. To distribute on CD-ROM, you can copy the distribution files from the network directory to the CD-ROM generation system.

Press the Next Button to continue.

■ Step 4. The Setup Wizard Permits You to Remove Dependency Files.

The Setup Wizard searches your project file (.VBP) to determine which files contain objects or references used in your application, and then displays them. You can add or remove files in this list by selecting or clearing the check box next to each filename (see Figure 18.2).

You'll notice that several of the files listed here are VBXs or OCXs in your project's Toolbox, even though only one of them, the spin button, is actually used by your program. You may clear the check boxes of the unused controls if you wish.

Press the Next button to continue.

Figure 18.2.
*The Setup
Wizard - Step 4.*

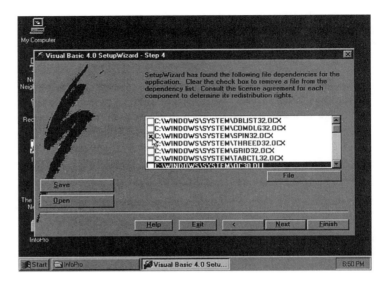

■ Step 5. You May Add or Remove Additional Files.

The Setup Wizard determines that certain files, which are displayed in this list, are required for your application to function properly. The Dependency Of field shows you which file(s) depend on the presence of any file you select in the list box. Take a look at Figure 18.3.

Figure 18.3.
*The Setup
Wizard - Step 5.*

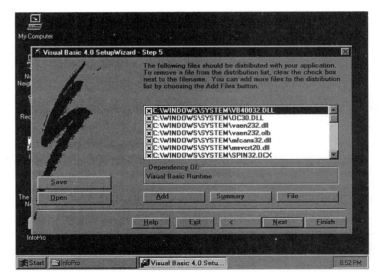

You should remove any files that you know will already be on the user's machine, or those for which you have not secured proper distribution rights. You should make a list of any files removed and distribute it with your setup disks. Again, you'll see several OCXs which are in the project's Toolbox, but are not used. However, there are many files which MUST be included if your application is to work correctly. If you're unsure, it's best not to remove any of the files displayed in this step.

Press the Next button to continue.

■ Step 6. The Setup Wizard Compresses Files.

The Setup Wizard now begins compressing your distribution files, listing them as it goes.

If you chose to distribute your application over a network or on CD-ROM, the Setup Wizard asks whether you want to delete any existing files in the destination directory before it creates the compressed files.

■ Step 7. The Setup Wizard Builds the Distribution Media.

If you selected a disk drive as the target of the setup files, the Setup Wizard notifies you of the number of blank formatted disks needed. The Setup Wizard prompts you to insert each disk, as required.

If you selected a network directory as the target of the setup files, the Setup Wizard copies the distribution files to the distribution directory.

■ Step 8. The Distribution Disks Are Complete.

The Setup Wizard notifies you when it has finished creating the distribution media and suggests that you scan the media for viruses prior to distribution.

Tip If you are distributing on floppy disks and want to create additional sets of floppy disks, choose the Back button to return to the Step 5 dialog box, and then choose Next again. The Setup Wizard creates a new set of floppy disks from the compressed distribution files.

Choose Exit to close the Setup Wizard.

If you were following along with the book, entering the appropriate information for the EVB_BOOK project, you should now have a Setup diskette for your application. It may be used like any other Windows application setup program. Give it a try.

Essential Summary

What
In this chapter, you learned that an executable is an application file that can run outside the Visual Basic development environment. You were introduced to the Application Setup Wizard, which is a tool used to create a setup program and distribution diskette(s) for your Visual Basic application.

Why
Because you'll want your users to be able to launch your program directly from Windows, an executable version of your application is a necessity. Because preparing your programming projects for distribution and installation can be a tedious and time-consuming process, the Application Setup Wizard will be a welcome addition to your Visual Basic programming environment.

How
In this chapter, you prepared your program for delivery. You created an executable version of your program, and saw how to include with it useful documentary information. Then you used the Application Setup Wizard to create a Setup and Distribution diskette for your complete application.

PART IV

Drawing, Animation, and Games

Drawing with Mouse Events and Graphics Methods

You're going to work hard in this chapter, but it will be worth it. You'll create a program that will allow you to draw with the mouse. In the process, you'll come to be quite familiar with the MouseDown, MouseMove, and MouseUp events, as well as with Visual Basic's graphics methods Line and Circle. You'll see how a PictureBox control can be used as a kind of "canvas" or easel, and how to add ToolTips to your program. Finally, you'll get a chance to use two new 3D controls: SSRibbon, which is used to create Toolbars using bitmap images; and SSPanel, a clever beveled control which can be flooded with color by percentages.

MouseDown, *MouseMove*, and *MouseUp*

What

The MouseDown and MouseUp events fire off when the user presses or releases a mouse button. Use a MouseDown or MouseUp event procedure to specify actions that will occur when a given mouse button is pressed or released. Unlike the Click event, MouseDown and MouseUp events allow you to distinguish between the left, right, and middle mouse buttons using two special incoming variables.

In all, four variables are passed to you during MouseUp and MouseDown events. Their values and uses are summarized in the following list:

- button   An integer that identifies the button (Left, Right, Middle) that was pressed (MouseDown) or released (MouseUp) to cause the event. Left =1, Right = 2, Middle = 4.

- shift   An integer that corresponds to the state of the Shift, Ctrl, and Alt keys when the button specified in the button argument is pressed or released. The shift argument equals 1 when the Shift key is down, 2 when Ctrl is down, and 4 when Alt is down. Some, all, or none of the keys may be down. If both Shift and Alt were pressed, the value of shift would be 5.

- x, y   The x-axis, y-axis coordinates specifying the location of the mouse pointer. The x and y values are always expressed in terms of the current coordinate system, the default being twips.

Testing the button or shift arguments may be made easier by using the appropriate constants listed in the Visual Basic (VB) object library in the Object Browser. These constants are summarized in Table 19.1.

Table 19.1. Shift and button constants.

Constant	Value	Description
vbLeftButton	1	Left button is pressed.
vbRightButton	2	Right button is pressed.
vbMiddleButton	4	Middle button is pressed.
vbShiftMask	1	Shift key is pressed.
vbCtrlMask	2	Ctrl key is pressed.
vbAltMask	4	Alt key is pressed.

These constants may be used in a similar manner with the MouseMove event, which is covered next.

Not surprisingly, the MouseMove event is triggered when the user moves the mouse. The MouseMove event is generated continually as the mouse pointer moves across objects. Unless another object has captured the mouse, an object recognizes a MouseMove event whenever the mouse position is within its borders.

What

The MouseMove event provides the same four variables as MouseDown and MouseUp. However, the button argument for MouseMove differs from the button argument for MouseDown and MouseUp. For MouseMove, the button argument indicates the current state of *all the buttons*; that is, a single MouseMove event can indicate that some, all, or no buttons are pressed. For MouseDown and MouseUp, the button argument indicates exactly one button per event.

The Line and Circle Methods

Visual Basic's Line method draws lines and rectangles on a Form, PictureBox or Printer object. Here's a simplified version of the syntax:

What

```
object.Line (StartX, StartY) - (EndX, EndY), color, BF
```

Here, `object` is an optional expression that evaluates to a Form, PictureBox, or Printer object. If `object` is omitted, the Form with the focus is assumed. The argument `(StartX, StartY)` is optional, consisting of single-precision values indicating the coordinates of the starting point for the line or rectangle. If omitted, the line begins at the position indicated by CurrentX and CurrentY. The Line method's only required argument, `(EndX, EndY)`, consists of single-precision values indicating the horizontal and vertical coordinates of the line's end point.

> **Note** The CurrentX and CurrentY properties return or set the horizontal (CurrentX) or vertical (CurrentY) coordinates for the next printing or drawing method. They are not available at design time. Coordinates are measured from the upper-left corner of an object, so CurrentX is 0 at an object's left edge, and the CurrentY is 0 at its top. Again, coordinates are expressed in twips by default.

The remaining three arguments are optional. The color argument is a Long integer value indicating the color used to draw the line. You may use the RGB() function or QBColor() function to specify the color. If color is omitted, the object's ForeColor property determines the color of the line.

The Line method actually serves double-duty: it may be used to draw either lines or rectangles. The B argument, if included, causes a box to be drawn using the Start and End coordinates to specify its opposite corners. The last argument, F, is used to fill the box with the same color used to draw it. You cannot use F without B. If B is used without F, the box is filled with the object's current FillColor and FillStyle.

Here's an example of how the Line method might be used to draw a line on a PictureBox control between two points with coordinates of FromX, FromY and ToX, ToY:

```
picThis.Line (FromX, FromY) - (ToX, ToY)
```

You could use the same coordinates to draw a filled green box instead. In this case, the `From` coordinates represent the box's upper-left corner, and the `To` coordinates represent the lower-right corner:

```
picThis.Line (FromX, FromY) - (ToX, ToY), QBColor(GREEN), BF
```

What

You use the Circle method to draw a circle, ellipse, or arc on a Form, Picture Box, or Printer. In this program, you're only interested in drawing circles, so here's a simplified syntax for the Circle method:

```
object.Circle (CenterX, CenterY), radius, color
```

Again object is an optional object expression representing a Form, Picture Box, or Printer. If object is omitted, the Form with the focus is assumed. The first required argument (`CenterX`, `CenterY`) indicates the coordinates for the center point of the circle. The next argument, `radius`, is also required. It represents the radius of the circle to be drawn.

The `color` argument is optional. It is a Long integer value indicating the color of the circle's outline. Again, you can use the `RGB()` function or `QBColor()` function to specify the color. If omitted, the value of `object`'s ForeColor property is used.

Tip To fill a circle, set the FillColor and FillStyle properties of the object on which the circle is drawn. The width of the line used to draw a circle or line depends on the setting of the object's DrawWidth property.

How to Draw with Visual Basic

How

In this section, you'll create your drawing program. As you've done many times before, add a new form to your EVB_BOOK project. This time name it frmDraw and make it the project's startup form. Here's what it looks like in Design mode.

Refer to Table 19.2 for a list of the design time settings for each object and complete the visual implementation of the Drawing program's main form. Since you'll be working with a couple of new controls here, remember to use Visual Basic's ToolTips to help identify them, if necessary.

Figure 19.1.
*Design mode: the
Drawing program.*

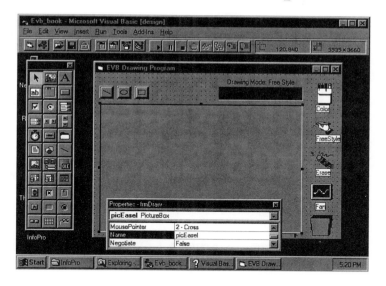

Table 19.1. Design-time settings—the Drawing program.

VB Object	Property	Design-Time Setting
Form	Name	frmDraw
	Caption	EVB Drawing Program
PictureBox	Name	picEasel
	AutoDraw	True
	MouseIcon	c:\vb40\icons\writing\erase01.ico
	MousePointer	2 - Cross
SSPanel	Name	pnlStatus
	FloodShowPct	False
	FloodType	1 - Left To Right
SSRibbon Button	Names	bmpLine,bmpCircle,bmpRectangle
	AutoSize	1 - Picture To Button
	GroupAllAllUp	True
	GroupNumber	1
	Value	False (Not Pushed)
	PictureUp	c:\vb40\bitmaps\toolbar3\ln-up.bmp
	PictureUp	c:\vb\40\bitmaps\toolbar3\ovl-up.bmp
	PictureUp	c:\vb\40\bitmaps\toolbar3\rct-up.bmp

continues

Table 19.1. continued

VB Object	Property	Design-Time Setting
Image Control	Name	imgColor
	Picture	c:\vb40\icons\writing\pens04.ico
	Stretch	True (So you can size it...)
Image Control	Name	imgDraw
	Picture	c:\vb40\icons\writing\pencil05.ico
	Stretch	True
Image Control	Name	imgErase
	Picture	c:\vb40\icons\writing\erase02.ico
	Stretch	True
Image Control	Name	imgFan
	Picture	c:\vb40\icons\industry\sinewave.ico
	Stretch	True
Image Controls	Name	imgFull
	Picture	c:\vb40\icons\computer\trash04a.ico
	Stretch	True
	Visible	False
Image Controls	Name	imgEmpty
	Picture	c:\vb40\icons\computer\trash04b.ico
	Stretch	True
Labels	Names	lblColor,lblFreeStyle,lblErase,lblFan
	Appearance	0 - Flat
	AutoSize	True
	BackColor	Light Yellow
	BackStyle	Opaque
	BorderStyle	1 - Fixed Single
	Visible	False
Label	Name	lblStatus
	Alignment	Center

> **Note** If you don't see SSPanel and SSRibbon in your Visual Basic Toolbox, you'll
> need to add them. Select Tools Custom Controls from Visual Basic's menu. In the
> Available Controls list box, locate Sheridan 3D Controls and check it, then click OK.

Adding Code

There's a lot going on in this program, so you'll need several form-level variables and constants
to help keep things straight. Open the general declarations section of your form and add the
following:

```
Dim iColor As Integer, iBackColor As Integer   ' Drawing color and background...
Dim iMode As Integer                           ' Drawing mode...drawing, erasing, etc.
Dim bDown As Boolean, bFull As Boolean         ' Mouse down?  Trash full?
Dim LastX, LastY As Long                        ' Must keep track of last mouse
                                                ' location, in order to draw...

                                                ' Constants for tracking the Drawing
                                                ' Mode...
Const DRAW_FREE = 0                             ' FreeStyle drawing...
Const DRAW_ERASE = 1                            ' Erasing...
Const DRAW_FAN = 2                              ' Fanning...
Const DRAW_LINE = 3                             ' Drawing a line....
Const DRAW_CIRCLE = 4                           ' Or a circle...
Const DRAW_BOX = 5                              ' Or a rectangle...
```

Then, in the form's Load event, you'll initialize your color variables and establish the foreground
and background colors for picEasel (the PictureBox you'll draw on):

```
Private Sub Form_Load()
iColor = 0                                      'QBColor Black
iBackColor = 15                                 'QBColor White
picEasel.ForeColor = QBColor(iColor)            ' Set easel colors...
picEasel.BackColor = QBColor(iBackColor)
iMode = DRAW_FREE                               ' Default mode...
lblStatus.Caption = "Drawing Mode: Free Style"  ' And status caption...
End Sub
```

Enabling the Drawing Modes

When imgColor is clicked, three things will happen. First, the current drawing color (iColor)
will be bumped up by one, unless it's already at the top of QBColor()'s range, which is 15. In
that case, the color is set back to 0, black. This allows the user to cycle through the palette of
available colors. The second thing that happens is that pnlStatus is flooded with the current

color, a nice visual effect that allows the user to see the color he or she will be using. The last thing to happen when imgColor is clicked is that picEasel's ForeColor property is set to iColor, so that the next stroke will be in the selected color. Here's the listing:

```
Private Sub imgColor_Click()
iColor = IIf(iColor < 15, iColor + 1, 0)     ' Bump iColor...
pnlStatus.FloodColor = QBColor(iColor)       ' Set panel's FloodColor...
For X = 0 To 100 Step 10                      ' and Flood it slowly,
pnlStatus.FloodPercent = X                    ' 10% with each iteration..
Next                                          ' for flood effect.
picEasel.ForeColor = QBColor(iColor)         ' Set the drawing color...
End Sub
```

As you may have noticed in the Form_Load event, the default drawing mode will be FreeStyle, which will allow the user to draw freely by holding the mouse down and moving it. Any time a different drawing mode is selected (by clicking one of the bitmap buttons or Image controls), the current mode will be displayed in lblStatus. All drawing modes, except for Erase, will display a Cross MousePointer when the mouse is over the PictureBox easel, picEasel. Here's the code to be placed in imgDraw's Click event:

```
Private Sub imgDraw_Click()
picEasel.MousePointer = 2                      ' Set mousepointer to Cross...
ClearButtons                                   ' Pop up all shape bitmap buttons
iMode = DRAW_FREE                              ' Set the mode..
lblStatus.Caption = "Drawing Mode: Free Style" ' And status caption....
End Sub
```

When imgErase is clicked, Erase mode will come into effect. In this case, the mouse pointer will become an eraser-tipped pencil. This is achieved by setting picEasel's MousePointer property to 99, a special setting that instructs Visual Basic to use an object's MouseIcon property as the current pointer. (You set this property for picEasel at design time.) Here's how imgErase's Click event should look:

```
Private Sub imgErase_Click()
picEasel.MousePointer = 99                      ' Use special MouseIcon...
ClearButtons                                    ' Pop the shape buttons...
iMode = DRAW_ERASE                              ' Set the mode....
lblStatus.Caption = "Drawing Mode: Erasing"    ' and status caption...
End Sub
```

A click to imgFan switches to Fan mode:

```
Private Sub imgFan_Click()
picEasel.MousePointer = 2                      ' Set back to cross...
ClearButtons
iMode = DRAW_FAN
lblStatus.Caption = "Drawing Mode: Fanning"
End Sub
```

The SSRibbon buttons are used for drawing shapes—lines, circles, rectangles. Only one button at a time may be "up" in a given group (these three were grouped together at design time). One of the great things about this Control is that all you need to do is assign a bitmap to the PictureUp property. The Control itself will modify the bitmap to make the button appear "down" or "up" when clicked. If a button is down, its Value property is True; otherwise, it's False.

Now, each of the buttons comprising the Shape Toolbar must be given some code. Here's the listing for bmpCircle's Click event:

```
Private Sub bmpCircle_Click(Value As Integer)
picEasel.MousePointer = 2                        ' Cross pointer...
If Value Then                                    ' Button down, then
   iMode = DRAW_CIRCLE                            ' Circle mode...
   lblStatus.Caption = "Drawing Mode: Circle"    ' and status caption..
      Else
   iMode = DRAW_FREE                             ' Else button up...
   lblStatus.Caption = "Drawing Mode: Free Style" ' Default to FreeStyle...
End If
End Sub
```

You should add similar code to the other two shape buttons, bmpLine and bmpRectangle, making the proper mode and caption adjustments, of course.

Creating Your Own ToolTips

Your drawing program will have *ToolTips* indicating the purpose of the significant Image controls. These tips, the labels you created and made invisible at design time, will become visible when you move the mouse pointer over one of the Drawing mode tools; as the pointer is moved away from the tool, the tip will vanish, just as they do in more sophisticated programs such as Word, Excel, and Visual Basic itself.

All that's necessary to make the tip appear is a couple of lines in the proper Image control's MouseMove event procedure. For example, here's what imgColor's MouseMove procedure should contain:

```
Private Sub imgColor_MouseMove(... ...)
ClearToolTips                        ' Clear all four tips....
lblColor.Visible = True              ' Make proper tip visible...
End Sub
```

You'll need to add similar lines to the MouseMove procedure of each of the other three related Image controls: imgDraw, imgErase, and imgFan. Of course, you'll want to make visible the appropriate tip, lblDraw, lblErase, and lblFan, respectively.

Making the tips disappear when the pointer is moved off the Image control is a little trickier. Keep in mind that moving off one control means moving onto another, or moving onto the form itself. Since you're already calling ClearToolTips (a procedure you'll define in the next section) when you move onto another drawing mode icon, you'll be fine—as long as the user slips from one drawing mode control to another. But what if they move onto the easel or form? The answer is to put ClearToolTips into the MouseMove procedure for those objects, as well.

```
Private Sub Form_MouseMove(.... ...)
ClearToolTips
End Sub
```

Later, you'll include the call in picEasel's MouseMove event, as well. Now it's time to see what the ClearToolTips procedure looks like. Place the definition in your form's general declaration section:

```
Sub ClearToolTips()                          ' Make all tips invisible...
lblColor.Visible = False
lblDraw.Visible = False
lblErase.Visible = False
lblFan.Visible = False
End Sub
```

Adding the Drawing Code

All drawing occurs in either the MouseMove or MouseUp procedures. The MouseDown procedure is used to set the values of certain very important variables. Every time the mouse is down on picEasel, you want to set bDown to True and store the current X, Y coordinates to LastX and LastY. The reason for this will become apparent later, when you add code to the MouseMove procedure. Here's the listing for picEasel's MouseDown event:

```
Private Sub picEasel_MouseDown(Button As Integer ...Y As Single)
bDown = True                            ' Mouse is down...
LastX = X: LastY = Y                     ' Store current location...

If iMode = DRAW_ERASE Then               ' If you're in erase mode...
    picEasel.DrawWidth = 10              ' make the draw width fatter...
    picEasel.ForeColor = picEasel.BackColor  ' and set the draw color to the
                                         ' the background color..

Else                                     ' Else not erasing...
    picEasel.DrawWidth = 1               ' Normal width...
    picEasel.ForeColor = QBColor(iColor) ' Normal color...
End If

End Sub
```

Code for *MouseUp*

In this program, several things may happen when a mouse button is released, depending on which drawing mode you're in. When you're in the corresponding mode, you'll draw a line, circle, or rectangle when the mouse button is released. The circle or rectangle will be filled if you're drawing with the right mouse button; otherwise they'll be empty. Here's an annotated listing of picEasel's MouseUp event procedure:

```
Private Sub picEasel_MouseUp(Button As Integer ...Y As Single)

Select Case iMode                        ' Check the current mode...
  Case DRAW_LINE                         ' If it's Line Mode....draw a line
                                         ' from the mouse down point
```

```
            picEasel.Line (LastX, LastY)-(X, Y), QBColor(iColor)   ' to the current point.

   Case DRAW_CIRCLE                                 ' In Circle Mode...
       If Button = 2 Then                           ' and right button is released
       picEasel.FillStyle = 0 'Opaque               ' Set the easel's fill style
       picEasel.FillColor = QBColor(iColor)         ' and color, to fill the circle

       Else                                         ' No right button...
       picEasel.FillStyle = 1 'Transparent          ' Don't fill circle...
       End If
                                                    ' Here's the circle...
       picEasel.Circle (LastX, LastY), Sqr((LastX - X) ^ 2 + (LastY - Y) ^ 2)
                                                    ' Center point is where the
                                                    ' mouse button went DOWN.
                                                    ' The radius is...well, see the
                                                    ' note box, below.

   Case DRAW_BOX                                    ' If Box Mode....
       If Button = 2 Then                           ' and RIGHT mouse...
                                                    ' draw and fill box...
          picEasel.Line (LastX, LastY)-(X, Y), QBColor(iColor), BF

       Else                                         ' No right button...
       picEasel.FillStyle = 1 'Transparent          ' Draw empty box....
       picEasel.Line (LastX, LastY)-(X, Y), QBColor(iColor), B
       End If

End Select

bDown = False                                       ' This happens in any case...
End Sub
```

In the preceding code, you're using a little high school geometry to supply the radius of your circle. What you're doing is taking the distance between the LastX and X coordinates, and squaring it; then you're adding it to the square of the distance between LastY and Y. Then you take the square root of that sum as the circle's radius. That is, the radius is equal to the diagonal distance you moved the mouse (with the button down), the hypotenuse of a right triangle, in fact. You're using the famous (or infamous, depending on your feelings for math) Pythagorean Theorem. The hypotenuse of a right triangle is equal to the square root of the sum of the squares of the two sides:

$$hyp = \sqrt{SideA^2 + SideB^2}$$

Code for *MouseMove*

The other drawing modes, FreeStyle, Erasing, and Fanning, are handled in picEasel's MouseMove procedure. Here's the annotated listing:

```
Private Sub picEasel_MouseMove(Button As Integer ... Y As Single)
ClearToolTips                          ' Clear tips, since you're on the easel...

If bDown Then                          ' You only draw if the mouse is DOWN...
```

```
Select Case iMode                          ' Find out which mode you're in...

    Case DRAW_FREE                   ' If FreeStyle, draw tiny line from last point
            picEasel.Line (LastX, LastY)-(X, Y)  ' to current point...and...
            LastX = X: LastY = Y            ' don't forget to update last point...

    Case DRAW_ERASE                     ' If Erasing, also draw a line.  Since the
            picEasel.Line (LastX, LastY)-(X, Y)' drawing color was set equal to the
            LastX = X: LastY = Y             ' background color, you're erasing!

    Case DRAW_FAN                          ' You fan by drawing a line and not
            picEasel.Line (LastX, LastY)-(X, Y)' resetting the LastX, LastY values.

End Select
End If
End Sub
```

The Waste Basket

Clicking the waste basket, imgEmpty, will dispose of the current drawing. If the basket is empty, it will become full (by switching pictures), just for fun. Whether the basket is empty or not, the drawing easel (picEasel) will be cleared, by invoking the Cls method. Here you go:

```
Private Sub imgEmpty_Click()
If bFull Then
    picEasel.Cls                               ' Clear the PictureBox easel...
Else
    picEasel.Cls
    imgEmpty.Picture = imgFull.Picture         ' Switch to full...
    bFull = True
End If
End Sub
```

Finally, don't forget to write the ClearButtons procedure, which simply pops up all the bitmap buttons on your shape Toolbar:

```
Sub ClearButtons()
bmpLine = False
bmpCircle = False
bmpRectangle = False
End Sub
```

Time to Draw

That's it. You'll need to play with this program a bit to get the feel of it. Just remember that you can be in only one drawing mode at a time—lines, circles, boxes, fans, free style, or erasing—as selected by clicking the appropriate Toolbar button or Image control. The current mode is always indicated by the Status Label; and a sample of the current color is always displayed in the 3D Status panel.

When drawing shapes, remember that the shape won't appear until you release the mouse button. Draw with the right button down to fill the shapes with the current color; use the left button to leave them empty of color. You'll draw freestyle lines and fans by moving the mouse with the left button down. When erasing, the mouse pointer will change to an eraser-tipped pencil, and the draw width will become very wide. Click the waste basket to completely clear the current drawing.

Here's a sample session with your drawing program, shown in Figure 19.2.

Figure 19.2.
The Drawing program in action.

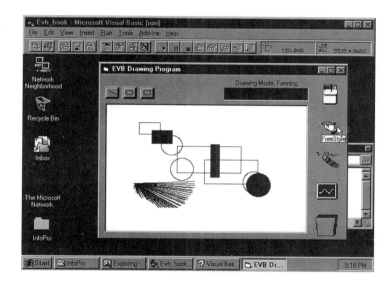

In the next chapter, you'll see how to save your drawings to disk, as well as how to retrieve and print them.

Essential Summary

In this chapter, you learned all about Visual Basic's MouseDown, MouseMove, and MouseUp events. You achieved a good understanding of the graphics methods Line and Circle. And you got a chance to use two new 3D controls, SSRibbon and SSPanel.

What

There are a multitude of uses for the very powerful graphics methods covered in this chapter. You can use the Line and Circle methods to create various background wallpaper patterns, for example. You may use them to draw specialized pie charts and bar graphs without the overhead of a custom graph control. You can create abstract art by randomizing X, Y positions and color.

Why

How

You put your understanding of these new concepts to the test by creating your own drawing program. This program allows you to draw lines, circles, rectangles, fans, and freestyle, using various mouse button and move combinations. Your program uses a PictureBox control for an "easel" and includes a bitmap Toolbar for selecting shapes. The program exhibits other visual cues as well, such as ToolTips, a 3D color panel, and a Status Label for displaying the current drawing mode.

CHAPTER 20

Saving, Retrieving, and Printing Drawings

In this short chapter (you worked hard in the last chapter, you deserve a break), you'll enhance the drawing program you created in Chapter 19 by giving users the ability to save, retrieve, and print the pictures they've created. In the process, you'll use Visual Basic's SavePicture and PrintForm statements and come to understand the full scope and purposes of the Picture and AutoRedraw properties. You'll also get a quick look at error handling, which will be covered much more extensively in Chapters 30 and 31.

What SavePicture Does

What The SavePicture statement saves a graphic from a Form object, PictureBox control, or Image control to a file. Here's the syntax:

```
SavePicture picture, filename
```

Here, `picture` is the Picture or Image property from which the graphics file is to be created, and `filename` is the name of the graphics file to be saved. If a graphic was loaded from `file` to the Picture property, either at design time or at run time, it's saved using the same format as the original file. Files created from the Image property are always bitmap (BMP) files.

Here's how you'd save a picture from a PictureBox control to a disk file called MyPic.Bmp:

```
SavePicture picEasel.Picture, "MyPic.Bmp"
```

> **Caution** When saving a new or modified picture from a Form or PictureBox, you must be sure that the Form or PictureBox's AutoRedraw property is set to True. Otherwise, you'll end up with an empty file or a blank picture.

What The AutoRedraw property applies only to Form or PictureBox objects. It returns or sets a Boolean value indicating how the output from a graphics method to a persistent graphic (see Note) is handled, and how and when object repainting occurs. Here are the two possibilities:

True   Enables automatic repainting of a Form object or PictureBox control. Graphics and text are written to the screen *and to an image stored in memory*. The object is repainted when necessary, using the image stored in memory.

False   (Default.) Disables automatic repainting of an object and writes graphics or text only to the screen. In this case, Visual Basic invokes the object's Paint event when it becomes necessary to repaint the object.

> **Note** A *persistent graphic* is the output from a graphics method—Line, Circle, and Pset—that is stored in memory. Persistent graphics are automatically retained when certain kinds of screen events occur; for example, when a form is redisplayed after being hidden behind another window. Graphics are persistent if they are drawn when the AutoRedraw property is set to True.

An understanding of the AutoRedraw property is crucial to working with the graphics methods covered in the last chapter, as well as the Point, Print, and Pset methods. Setting AutoRedraw to True automatically redraws the output from these methods in a Form object or PictureBox control when, for example, the object is resized or redisplayed after being hidden by another object.

> **Caution** If you set the BackColor property of a drawn upon object, all graphics and text, including the persistent graphic, are erased. In general, all graphics should be displayed using the Paint event unless AutoRedraw is set to True.

You've already used the Picture property many times. The Picture property returns or sets a graphic to be displayed in a control. When setting the Picture property at design time, the graphic is saved and loaded with the form. If you create an executable file, the file contains the image. When you load a graphic at run time, the graphic isn't saved with the application. At run time, the Picture property can be set to any other object's DragIcon, Icon, Image, or Picture property, or you can assign it the graphic returned by the LoadPicture() function. You'll put the LoadPicture() function and the Picture property to good use in this chapter.

What

The PrintForm method provides a relatively simple way to get a printed copy of a form. If the form contains nothing but a picture, *voila*, you've got a simple way to print your drawings, icons, bitmaps, and metafiles. What PrintForm does is send a bit-by-bit image of a Form object to the printer. It couldn't be easier to use. To print the form which currently has the focus, use the following:

What

```
PrintForm
```

To print some other form in your system, even one that's currently invisible, use the following:

```
frmOther.PrintForm
```

PrintForm prints all visible objects and bitmaps of the Form object. PrintForm also prints graphics added to a Form object or PictureBox control at run time if the AutoRedraw property is True when the graphics are drawn. The printer used by PrintForm is determined by the Windows Control Panel settings.

> **Caution** Unless you set the form's AutoRedraw property on, any drawn graphics (those created with the Line and Circle methods, for example) will not be printed with PrintForm. Bitmaps, icons, and metafiles will print even if AutoRedraw is left off, its default.

Why Save and Print Images As Forms?

There are many reasons why you'd want to save and/or print images which are created, modified, or simply used by your programs. You may use SavePicture in your own painting applications, or in other programs involving graphics, to create reusable disk files. In this way, you can later view or modify them. You can use Printform to print copies of the visual and design aspects of your project, or to print any pictures you've created for fun or artistic expression.

Why

How to Save, Load, and Print Images

In this section, you'll enhance the drawing program created in Chapter 19, adding the functionality necessary to save, retrieve, and print your drawings. To begin, you'll add a new form, frmPrintImage, to your EVB_BOOK project. But this time you *will not* make it the startup form. You'll use this form to print your picture, as you'll see. You'll need to modify the layout frmDraw, which will remain the startup form. Figure 20.1 is what the enhanced form will look like.

Figure 20.1.
*Design mode: enhanced
Drawing program.*

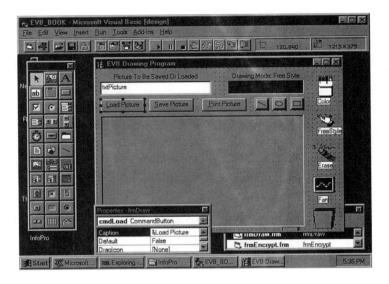

> **Caution** Make sure frmPrintImage is large enough to contain any picture you might draw in picEasel, and that its AutoRedraw property is set to True. No other properties are important, since frmPrintImage will never be visible, as you'll see.

Table 20.1 can be used in implementing the visual modifications to your drawing program.

Table 20.1. Design-time settings—the improved Drawing program.

Visual Basic Object	Property	Design-Time Setting
Form	Name	frmDraw (Still)
	Caption	EVB Drawing Program (Still)
Text Box	Name	txtPicture
Label	Name	lblPicture
	Alignment	Center
	Caption	Picture To Be Saved Or Loaded

Visual Basic Object	Property	Design-Time Setting
Command Button	Name	cmdLoad
	Caption	&Load Picture
Command Button	Name	cmdSave
	Caption	&Save Picture
Command Button	Name	cmdPrint
	Caption	&Print Picture

Enhancement Overview

Now you'll be able to save your beautiful drawings and retrieve them at any time for admiration or modification. To save, type a valid filename in the txtPicture text box, including a path and extension. If you omit the path, the file will be saved in the Visual Basic home directory. Once you've entered a name, click the Save Picture button.

Caution If another file with the same name exists in the same directory, it will be overwritten. So beware. You might say you need some enhancements to your enhancements, but that comes later. In the meantime, be careful when saving.

As long as you know the name of the file you want to load (retrieve), that process will be just as simple. Type the name of the desired file into the Picture text box, then click Load Picture. To print the currently displayed drawing, just click the Print Picture button.

Adding Code

Here's what frmDraw's modified `Form_Load` procedure should look like:

```
Private Sub Form_Load()
iColor = 0      'Black
iBackColor = 15 'White
picEasel.ForeColor = QBColor(iColor)
picEasel.BackColor = QBColor(iBackColor)

lblPicture.Caption = "Picture To Be Saved Or Loaded" ' Set Caption...
txtPicture = ""                                      ' Blank the text box...
Load frmPrintImage                                   ' Load but don't show the form
                                                     ' to be used for printing...
End Sub
```

Here's what happens when cmdLoad is clicked:

```
Private Sub cmdLoad_Click()
Dim sPicture As String                          ' Variable to hold filename...

On Error Resume Next                            ' Set up error trapping...
                                                ' not a bad idea
                                                ' whenever you access a disk..

If txtPicture = "" Then                         ' Complain if no filename...
   MsgBox "You haven't specified a load file name!", vbCritical, "Draw Program
Error!"
   Exit Sub                                     ' Exit this sub...
End If

lblPicture.Caption = "Picture To Be Loaded"     ' Set text box caption...
sPicture = txtPicture                           ' Get name of file to load...

If MsgBox("Ready To Load Picture?", vbQuestion + vbYesNo,
➥"Will Load Picture " & sPicture) = vbYes Then    ' Ask if it's Ok to continue...
picEasel.Picture = LoadPicture(sPicture)          ' If so, load the picture....
End If

                                                ' If there's an error, display it..
If Err Then MsgBox (Error$(Err)), vbCritical, "Save Error Message"

End Sub
```

The Save Picture routine is similar, but uses the SavePicture statement rather than LoadPicture().

```
Private Sub cmdSave_Click()
Dim sPicture As String

On Error Resume Next

If txtPicture = "" Then
   MsgBox "You haven't specified a save name!", vbCritical, "Draw Program Error!"
   Exit Sub
End If

sPicture = txtPicture
lblPicture.Caption = "Picture To Be Saved"

If MsgBox("Ready To Save Picture?", vbQuestion + vbYesNo,
➥"Will SavePicture "& sPicture) = vbYes Then

SavePicture picEasel.Image, txtPicture           ' Here's the save....
End If

If Err Then MsgBox (Error$(Err)), vbCritical, "Save Error Message"
End Sub
```

Finally, here's the code that handles the printing:

```
Private Sub cmdPrint_Click()
On Error Resume Next

SavePicture picEasel.Image, "Image.Prn"          ' First save it to a temp file...

frmPrintImage.Picture = LoadPicture("Image.Prn")  ' Load it into frmPrintImage...

frmPrintImage.PrintForm                           ' And print the form...

If Err Then MsgBox (Error$(Err)), vbCritical, "Save Error Message"
End Sub
```

Tip Your programs need to be *error aware*, especially when you're doing things like accessing a disk file, where all sorts of things can go wrong. The file you're looking for may not exist, or a drive door may be open or contain a disk with the wrong capacity. The hard drive itself may be full or otherwise inaccessible. Any of these unexpected conditions may bring your program to a screeching halt. The simple error trapping you've installed in the preceding code will display a relevant message, then gracefully exit the sub procedure.

Figure 20.2 shows a session with your new and improved Drawing program.

Figure 20.2.
Your new Drawing program in action.

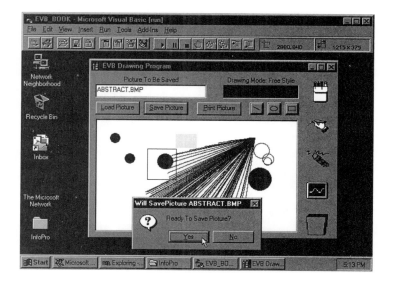

Essential Summary

What
In this chapter, you gained an understanding of Visual Basic's SavePicture statement, as well as a new familiarity with the Picture and AutoRedraw properties. You saw how to make a kind of photocopy of your forms by calling upon the PrintForm method. You also took a peek at error handling, as a sort of teaser of what's to come in Chapters 30 and 31.

Why
You may use SavePicture in your own painting applications, or in other programs involving graphics, to create reusable disk images, which may viewed or modified at a later date. The Printform method is a simple way to print copies of the visual and design aspects of your project for reference or user documentation.

How
You made use of the power behind the SavePicture and PrintForm statements, as well as the familiar LoadPicture() function, in adding to your drawing program the capability to save, retrieve, and print your drawings.

Animation Techniques: Timer and Move Methods

In this chapter, you'll learn how to add simple animation to your programs by using Timer controls and the Timer event. You'll also receive a formal introduction to the Move method, as well as a peek at Visual Basic's random number generator (which will be covered thoroughly in the next chapter). You'll put these ideas to use by creating a new game-like form which has the Earth being pelted by randomly generated, rampaging meteors.

What Is the Timer Control?

What The Timer control, invisible to the user, is a powerful and sophisticated clock which is useful for background processing. Once started, a Timer works independently and constantly, no matter what else might be happening in your Visual Basic program, or in Windows itself. This is the meaning of *multitasking*, more than one thing happening at the same time.

A Timer allows you to execute code at regular intervals by firing off a Timer event. A Timer event occurs when a Timer's preset interval has elapsed. The interval's frequency is stored in the control's Interval property, which specifies the length of time between events in milliseconds (thousandths of a second).

Tip Timers are far superior to loops for measuring duration. If you build a pause into your program using `For I = 1 To 30000 : Next I`, the amount of time the loop takes to finish will depend on the speed of the user's computer. A Timer is better because it will delay the same amount of time on any machine. It uses the computer's vibrating crystal clock, so the time it measures is nearly absolute (well, as absolute as time can get in our post-Relativity, post-Quantum Mechanics, post-Chaos Theory universe).

Even when you're using a loop and the system's clock to create your delay (as you've done earlier in this book), a Timer is better because it runs in the background. Although the delay loops you created earlier were for a precise amount of time, your system stopped responding to everything else for the duration.

You may use the Timer's event procedure to tell Visual Basic what to do after each Timer control interval has elapsed. You may stop, or suspend, Timer events in one of two ways: by setting the Timer's Enabled property to False, or setting its Interval property to 0. To resume execution of Timer events, set Enabled to True. It's also possible, and often convenient, to increase or decrease a Timer's Interval at run time. You might, for example, have an animated stop light in your program, where, presumably, you'd want the Yellow light to be displayed for a shorter time than Red and Green. In fact, you can make a Timer do pretty much anything you want that involves duration, delay, and repetition, by manipulating the Interval and Enabled properties in various ways.

Note Timers may seem a little confusing at first. They are called controls but they are unlike any others found in Visual Basic. Most controls have more than a dozen properties; Timers have only eight. Most controls have at least 10 events, where Timers have only one. Other controls are accessed, and their events triggered, by the user or the program; Timers work in the background, ticking away, completely independent of the user.

What Is the Move Method?

The Move method moves and optionally sizes a Form or control. Here's the general syntax:

```
object.Move left, top, width, height
```

The object is an optional object expression that evaluates to a valid control or form name. If object is omitted, the current form (the form with the focus) is assumed to be object. The first argument, left, is the only required argument. It is a single-precision value indicating the horizontal (x-axis) coordinate for the left edge of whatever is being moved. top is an optional value indicating the vertical (y-axis) position for the top edge of the object being moved. You may also set the object's height and width by passing along the third and fourth arguments.

Although only the left argument is required, to specify any other arguments, you must include all arguments that appear in the syntax prior to the argument you want to specify. You can't specify width, for example, without specifying left and top.

> **Note** As mentioned earlier, the default screen coordinates are measured in device independent twips (twentieth of a printer's point). So, roughly, there are 1440 twips per inch. Moving a form on the screen or moving a control in a frame is always relative to the origin (0,0), which is the upper-left corner. When moving a control on a Form object or in a PictureBox or other container, the coordinate system of the container object is used.

An alternative way to move an object is to manipulate its Top and Left properties. At design time, these properties are set automatically as you arrange your controls on the form. They correspond to the y-axis and x-axis screen coordinates, as described earlier, and may be set accordingly at run time.

> **Tip** Although you can relocate objects by merely changing their Left and Top properties, the Move method is better for diagonal movements. Producing a diagonal movement by changing the Left and Top properties results in an abrupt, uneven transition. You could likewise shrink or stretch an object by changing its Width and Height properties, but if you want to resize the object in both directions at once, then Move produces a smoother effect.

Why Use Timer and Move Methods?

There's no way to provide a Visual Basic program with convincing animation effects without using Timers and the Move method, but both are useful in other ways, as well. The Move method can be used to enlarge or shrink a control in response to current program conditions. For example, you could use Move to shrink an icon when it cannot be selected as a viable option, providing the user with a visual cue to that effect.

The things you can do with Timers are limited only by your imagination. You may use a Timer to cause a delay so that a message appears on-screen for a few seconds, then disappears. You can use Timers to cause events to repeat at prescribed intervals, such as saving a user's work on a regular basis. You can use a `Timer` event to look at the computer's built-in battery-powered clock, to see if it's time for the user to do something, such as go to a meeting or make a phone call. A Timer can be used like a stopwatch to measure the passage of time and report the time that some procedure takes to complete. You can even use a timer to pelt the earth with meteors, as you'll see next.

How to Add Animation Using Timers

How

In this section, you'll put your new understanding of Timers and the Move method to use. You'll create a game program in which randomly generated "meteors" bombard the earth. You'll need to add a new form to the EVB_BOOK project. Name it frmAnimation and make it the project's startup form. Here's a look at the form in Design mode (see Figure 21.1).

Figure 21.1.
Design mode: the
Meteor Collision
program.

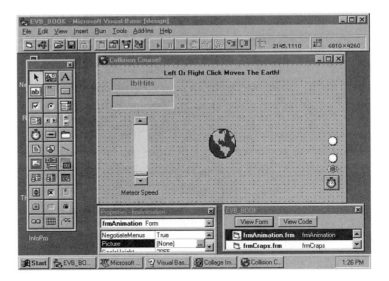

Table 21.1 summarizes the design time specifications of your new program's significant objects. Use it to finish your new form's design.

Table 21.1. Design-time settings—Collision Course!

Visual Basic Object	Property	Design-Time Setting
Form	Name	frmAnimation
	Caption	Collision Course!
Image Control	Name	imgEarth
	Stretch	True
	Picture	c:\vb40\icons\elements\earth.ico
Image Controls	Name	imgMeteor, imgMeteor2
	Stretch	True
	Picture	c:\vb40\icons\elements\moon05.ico
	Visible	False
Image Control	Name	imgBurst
	Stretch	True
	Picture	c:\vb40\icons\misc\misc15.ico
	Visible	False
Labels	Name	lblHits, lblMisses
	Alignment	Center
	Appearance	3D
	BorderStyle	Fixed Single
	Font	10 Bold
	ForeColor	Red, Green
Label	Name	lblCollision
	Caption	Left Or Right Click Moves The Earth
	Font	Bold
Vertical ScrollBar	Name	vsbSpeed
	Max	30 (Less than Min for upward increase)
	Min	360
	LargeChange	18
	SmallChange	5
	Value	36
Timer	Name	Timer1
	Interval	1000 (One second)

Program Overview

As this game begins, the Earth is being pummeled by meteors. The program keeps track of hits and misses. The player may simply sit back and enjoy the onslaught, or click the left and right mouse buttons to move the earth accordingly, in order to minimize the hits. As the Earth is moved, however, the meteor shower seems to follow it, so it's not safe to remain too long in any one place. The player may also use the vertical scroll bar, vsbSpeed, to increase or decrease the speed at which the meteors travel. The game is ended, mercifully, when the player closes the form.

Adding Code

You'll need a few form-level variables to keep track of things and events. Open a Code window for the form's general declarations section and add the following lines:

```
Dim iHits As Integer, iMisses As Integer    ' Record hits and misses
Dim OriginX As Long, OriginY As Long        ' The center of the earth
Dim MeteorX, MeteorY As Long                ' The meteor's current position...
Dim lHitWidth, lHitHeight As Long           ' Rectangular hit zone around the
                                            ' center of the earth.
Dim lShift As Long                   ' Random shift of meteor path...
Dim iSpeed As Integer                ' For monitoring meteor speed...

Const INCH = 1440                    ' A useful constant when dealing
                                     ' with Twips...1440 per screen inch.
```

As usual, the Form_Load Event is a good place to initialize variables. Here's what it should look like:

```
Private Sub Form_Load()
lHitWidth = (imgEarth.Width / 2) - 72    ' Establish the hit zone, which is
lHitHeight = (imgEarth.Height / 2) - 72  ' not quite the full width and height
                                         ' of the earth. (You need to allow for
                                         ' misses in the third dimension.)

lblHits.Caption = "Hits: "               ' Blank the hits and misses labels
lblMisses.Caption = "Misses: "

iSpeed = 36                              ' Set meteor speed...and...
vsbSpeed = 36                            ' synch it with the scroll bar.
End Sub
```

Now, all of the action is Timer generated. You start with a Timer Interval of 1000 (one second), but you must alter it, randomly, as the program runs. (Otherwise, the meteors will come at predictable intervals and be easy to avoid.) Double-click on the Timer and enter the following:

```
Private Sub Timer1_Timer()
Randomize                                ' Seed the random number generator...
Timer1.Interval = (Rnd * 1000)           ' Set the interval to some fraction of a
                                         ' second.

Randomize                                ' Plant another seed...
```

```
lShift = (Rnd * INCH)       ' Get a random x-axis shift, some fraction of an INCH

If Rnd < 0.5 Then           ' Shift meteor start point right or left
lShift = -lShift            ' (plus or minus), randomly..
End If

SetMeteor                   ' Set meteor's starting position...
SendMeteor                  ' Then send it...

lblHits = "Hits: " & CStr(iHits)          ' Record hit, if there is one...
lblMisses = "Misses: " & CStr(iMisses)    ' Otherwise, record miss...
End Sub
```

As you probably guessed, the SetMeteor and SendMeteor sub procedures are defined by you. Add them to the general declarations section of your form. Here they are:

```
Sub SetMeteor()
OriginX = imgEarth.Left + lHitWidth      ' Set center of earth, its Left and Top
OriginY = imgEarth.Top + lHitHeight      ' position, minus the hit zone...

MeteorX = OriginX + (2 * INCH) - lShift  ' Set next meteor's starting point, two
MeteorY = OriginY - (2 * INCH)           ' inches to the left (randomly shifted)
                                         ' and two inches above the earth.

imgMeteor.Picture = imgMeteor2.Picture   ' Set fresh meteor picture, in case
                                         ' the last one hit and burst...

imgMeteor.Move MeteorX, MeteorY          ' Move meteor to starting gate..
imgMeteor.Visible = True                 ' Make it visible....
End Sub
```

Once the next meteor is in position, it's time to send it. (Remember, this is happening at continuous, though random, intervals.) Create a new procedure, SendMeteor, in your form's general declarations section. Here's the code that moves the meteor:

```
Sub SendMeteor()
For iTmes = 1 To 200                 ' Should be enough to get it across.

DoEvents                             ' If the player clicks to move the
                                     ' earth, you want to catch it....

MeteorX = MeteorX - iSpeed           ' Set new X and Y location, allowing
MeteorY = MeteorY + iSpeed           ' for speed adjustment. Remember, the
                                     ' meteor is moving from upper right
                                     ' to lower left.  That is, X decreases
                                     ' while Y increases.

imgMeteor.Move MeteorX, MeteorY      ' Move and refresh the meteor..
imgMeteor.Refresh

If IsHit(CLng(MeteorX), CLng(MeteorY)) Then  ' Was there a Hit?  If so,
    imgMeteor.Picture = imgBurst.Picture     '  burst the meteor...
    imgMeteor.Refresh                        ' Refresh so you can see it, briefly.
    imgMeteor.Visible = False                ' Meteor is gone...
    iHits = iHits + 1                        ' iHits is bumped.
    Exit Sub                                 ' Exit
End If
```

```
Next                                        ' If no hit, keep moving ....
iMisses = iMisses + 1                       ' Then record a miss...
End Sub
```

So what about this new IsHit() function? You'll write it to return a Boolean True if the meteor moves into the predefined hit range; otherwise, it will return False. The only way this function will know if the meteor is in the hit zone is if you pass to it the meteor's current location. The function therefore expects two arguments, corresponding to the meteor's X and Y position. Here's the listing:

```
Function IsHit(lX As Long, lY As Long) As Boolean
IsHit = False               ' Starts out no hit...

If (lX >= OriginX - lHitWidth And lX <= OriginX + lHitWidth) And  _  ' If in the
➥zone...
➥ (lY >= OriginY - lHitHeight And lY <= OriginY + lHitHeight) Then

    IsHit = True                    ' IsHit() returns True.
End If
End Function
```

To allow the user to move the earth, you'll need to add some code to the form's Click event. When the player clicks the right mouse button, the earth will jump an inch to the right, that is, its Left property will increase by 1440 twips. A left mouse click, on the other hand, will shift the earth to the left by the same distance, in this case, decreasing the Left property. Add the following lines to the form's MouseDown event, between the Private Sub and End Sub statements:

```
If Button = 2 Then                          ' On right click...
    imgEarth.Left = imgEarth.Left + INCH    ' Move to the right...
Else
    imgEarth.Left = imgEarth.Left - INCH    ' Otherwise...left..
End If
OriginX = imgEarth.Left + lHitWidth         ' Reset the earth's origin, so the
OriginY = imgEarth.Top + lHitHeight         ' meteors can zero in on it...
```

The last thing is to get the speed scroll bar working, which is simple. When you change the scroll bar, the iSpeed variable is changed accordingly. Here are the program's final listings:

```
Private Sub vsbSpeed_Change()
iSpeed = vsbSpeed
End Sub

Private Sub vsbSpeed_Scroll()
vsbSpeed_Change
End Sub
```

It's time to test, or play, depending on your frame of mind. Keep your feet on the ground, but cast your eyes skyward. Figure 21.2 shows a sample session.

Figure 21.2.
*Collision Course
program in action.*

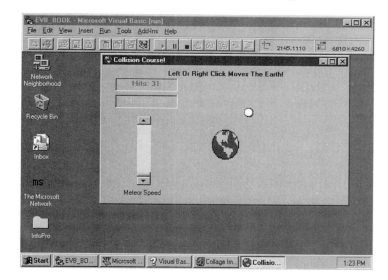

Essential Summary

In this chapter, you learned some simple animation techniques using the Timer control and Timer event, as well as Visual Basic's Move method. You also got a quick look at how to generate random numbers, a subject covered in greater detail in the next chapter.

What

The Move method, and Timer controls in particular, have a multitude of uses. You may use Timers to cause delays or repeat procedures at prescribed intervals, or to act like a stopwatch or appointment calendar. Both Timers and the Move Method are invaluable in the creation of animation effects.

Why

You put your grasp of these new ideas to the test by creating a game which has the Earth being pelted by a randomly generated meteor shower. Not entirely merciless, you wrote your program to allow the user to "move the Earth" with a simple mouse click.

How

Random Numbers, Animation, and Games

In this chapter, you'll learn more about how random numbers may be generated by using Visual Basic. You'll gain a thorough understanding of the Randomize statement and the Rnd() function, and see how they interact. Finally, you'll create a computerized gambling game (a game of Craps) to see one way that random numbers may be used in computer programming.

What Are Random Numbers?

What From a statistical or scientific standpoint, a *random number* is a number whose probability of occurrence is completely undetermined and equal to that of any other number in its group or predefined range. Given this definition, a sequence of computer-generated numbers *can never be truly random!* The reason for this is that a computer program, no matter how sophisticated or complex, still *determines* the behavior of the computer.

If a computer is spitting out a particular number, it's because it's being told to—somehow, somewhere, subtly within the inner recesses of its code—even if the number appears to be random to mere mortals.

> **Note** Number theorists say that there may be no such thing as a truly random series, even in nature. Mathematicians cannot even agree on a definition of *randomness*. So far, the value of pi has been calculated out a few million decimal places without any discernible pattern of repetition. So pi might be a true example of randomness, but no one can prove it. At five million decimal places, pi could start producing a letter-for-letter copy of the I Ching, complete with mathematical descriptions of all its hexagrams. There's just no way to know.

Now for the good news. You won't let this stop you. To make random (or pseudorandom) numbers useful in computing, all that's required is that they be sufficiently unpredictable for the program's purposes. Visual Basic provides two commands, Randomize and Rnd, which work together to generate number sequences with an extremely high level of unpredictability. As long as what you're simulating is the toss of dice or the luck of the draw—instead of something tougher, like sub-atomic particle placement or global weather patterns—Randomize and Rnd will do quite nicely.

What The Randomize statement initializes, or seeds, Visual Basic's random-number generator, Rnd. The computer can provide a series of random numbers when you use the Rnd() function alone. However, each time you run your program, the series will repeat itself. To avoid this, you use the Randomize statement to provide a random seed for the Rnd function. Here's the syntax:

```
Randomize number
```

Here, *number* is optional and may be any valid numeric expression. If you omit *number*, the value returned by the system timer is used as the new seed value. If Randomize is not used, the Rnd() function (with no arguments) uses the same number as a seed the first time it is called, and thereafter uses the last generated number as a seed value. This is why that without Randomize, Rnd() produces the same sequence of numbers.

What The Rnd function returns a random number whose value is less than 1 but greater than or equal to 0. Here's its syntax:

```
Rnd(number)
```

number is an optional argument (in fact, with this function, even the parentheses are optional), which can be any valid numeric expression. The value of number determines how Rnd generates a random number. If number is less than zero, then Rnd returns the same number every time, using number as the seed. If number is equal to zero, Rnd returns the most recently generated number. If number is greater than zero (or omitted), then the next random number in the sequence is returned.

> **Tip** To produce random integers in a given range, use this formula: `Int( (upper - lower + 1) * Rnd + lower )`, where *upper* is the highest number in the range, and *lower* is the lowest number in the range. So, to toss a die, you'd use the following: `Int( 6 * (Rnd + 1))`.

Why Use Random Numbers?

You need random numbers whenever you want things to happen by chance, in games, simulations, scientific or statistical analysis, even in art and design. You must use random numbers any time you want to introduce a little chaos into the relentlessly orderly world of the computer.

For example, you might want to create a screen saver program that splashes spots on the screen in chance locations. Or you might design a stock market simulation system that provides for a "crash" every once in an unpredictable while. In games, you might want to shuffle a deck of cards or have alien spaceships appear at random times in random places. Or, as you do in the next section, you might want to simulate the toss of dice.

How to Use Random Numbers

In this section, you'll experiment with random numbers by creating a computer program that simulates a game of Craps. Add a new form to your EVB_BOOK project. Name it frmCraps and make it the startup form. Here, in Figure 22.1, is how the Crap Game program looks at design time.

Figure 22.1.
Design mode: a game of Craps.

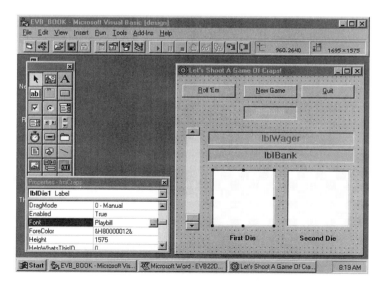

Table 22.1. Design-time settings—a game of Craps.

Visual Basic Object	Property	Design-Time Setting
Form	Name	frmCraps
	Caption	Let's Shoot A Game Of Craps!
	Icon	c:\vb40\icons\misc\bullseye.ico
Command Button	Name	cmdRoll
	Caption	&Roll 'Em
Command Button	Name	cmdNew
	Caption	&New Game
Command Button	Name	cmdQuit
	Caption	&Quit
Vertical Scroll Bar	Name	vsbWager
	Min	100 (Clicking upward will increase)
	Max	1
	LargeChange	10
	SmallChange	1
Label	Name	lblPoint
	Font	Size 10, Bold
	ForeColor	Green
	Visible	False
Label	Name	lblWager
	Font	Size 12, Bold
	ForeColor	Red
Label	Name	lblBank
	Font	Size 12, Bold
	ForeColor	Blue
Labels	Names	lblDie1, lblDie2
	Alignment	Centered
	Captions	First Die, Second Die
	Font	Playbill, Size 72, Bold
	BackColor	Light Yellow

Program Overview

This program simulates a game of Craps, using the same rules you would encounter in any casino. Craps is a gambling game in which the player places a wager, then rolls (throws) two dice. A first throw of 7 or 11 wins, while a first throw of 2, 3, or 12 loses. A first throw of any other number (called *point*) must be thrown again to win before a 7 is thrown, in which case the player loses both the bet and the dice.

In this computerized version of the game, the player starts out with a bankroll of $500. He or she may place a bet of any amount from $1 to $100 (using the wager scroll bar), as long as there's enough money in the bank to cover it. The dice are "thrown" by clicking the Roll 'Em button. A win or loss on the first roll is reported immediately, and the bankroll is adjusted accordingly. If the player is required to make point, a message is displayed, indicating the point to be made. If point is made, the bank increases by the wager amount; if point is lost (7 is rolled first), the bank is decreased. The game is over when the bank is $0 or less, or when the player decides to start a new game or quit.

Adding Code

You'll need a few form-level variables to keep track of important values. Open a Code window for your form's general declarations section and enter the following lines:

```
Dim iDie1, iDie2 As Integer                       ' For the values of the dice...
Dim iBank As Integer                              ' Amount in the bank...
Dim iWager As Integer                             ' The bet amount..
Dim iPoint As Integer                             ' To track the current point...
Dim bWon As Boolean, bLost As Boolean, bFirst As Boolean   ' Some useful
➥Booleans...
```

Now you'll initialize some of the variables in the form's Load event:

```
Private Sub Form_Load()
bFirst = True
iBank = 500                                   ' Put $500 in the bank...
lblBank = "Bank = " + Format(iBank, "Currency")' and display it...
End Sub
```

You'll get the program's wager scroll bar working by adding the following code to vsbWager's Change event:

```
Private Sub vsbWager_Change()
If bFirst Then                          ' Allow the wager if ready for first roll...
    iWager = vsbWager                   ' Set and display the wager...
    lblWager.Caption = "Wager = " & Format(iWager, "Currency")

Else                                    ' Can't change wager...Show message...
   MsgBox "You Can't Change Your Wager!", vbInformation, "Sorry...You're Mid-
➥Point!"
End If
End Sub
```

As usual, you'll want the player to be able to increase and decrease the wager by dragging the scroll bar's thumb. Make sure that vsbWager's Scroll event calls its Change event:

```
Private Sub vsbWager_Scroll()
vsbWager_Change
End Sub
```

Most of your program's functionality is accomplished when the dice are rolled. Here's an annotated listing of the code contained in cmdRoll's Click event:

```
Private Sub cmdRoll_Click()
Dim iRoll As Integer          ' To hold the value of the current roll...

If iWager > iBank Then        ' Player can't bet more than what's in the bank....
    MsgBox "Reduce Your Bet!", vbCritical, "Not Enough In The Bank!"
    Exit Sub
    ElseIf iWager = 0 Then        ' But player must bet something...
    MsgBox "Make Your Bet!", vbInformation, "You Forgot To Make A Wager!"
    Exit Sub
End If


RollEm                        ' Sets random values for each die...

iRoll = iDie1 + iDie2         ' Current roll ...

lblDie1 = iDie1               ' Show the die values...
lblDie2 = iDie2

If bFirst Then                ' If it's the first roll...

Select Case iRoll
    Case 7, 11                ' And it's 7 or 11....Winner!
    MsgBox CStr(iRoll) & "'s A Winner!", vbExclamation, "Congratulations!"
    BumpBank                  ' Increase the bank...

    Case 2, 3, 12                                      ' Its a loser...
    MsgBox "Sorry, Craps Loses!", vbCritical, "Better Luck Next Time!"
    DingBank                  ' Decrease the bank...

    Case Else                 ' Otherwise, set the point
    iPoint = iRoll            ' and display the point...
    lblPoint.Caption = "Point Is " & CStr(iPoint)
    lblPoint.Visible = True
    bFirst = False            ' No longer the first roll...
End Select

Else                          ' Wasn't the first roll...so the player
                              ' must be trying for point.

Select Case iRoll             ' Now evaluate the roll...
    Case iPoint               ' If it equals the point...Winner!
    MsgBox "Winner On Point!", vbExclamation, "Congratulations!"
    BumpBank                  ' Increase the bank...

    Case 7                    ' 7 before point loses....
```

```
      MsgBox "Sorry, 7 Loses!", vbCritical, "Failed To Make Your Point!"
      DingBank                    ' Decrease the bank...
   End Select
   End If
End Sub
```

Of course, you must write the auxiliary procedures RollEm, BumpBank, and DingBank. Create them in the form's general declarations section. Here are their listings:

```
Sub RollEm()              ' Simulates a roll of the dice
Dim iTimes As Integer     ' Want the dice to "tumble" several times
Randomize                 ' Seed the generator...

For iTimes = 1 To Int(10 * (Rnd + 1))  ' Tumble each die from 1 to 10 times...
   iDie1 = Int(6 * (Rnd + 1))             ' New random number each tumble...
   lblDie1.Caption = iDie1                ' Show the tumbling...
   lblDie1.Refresh
   iDie2 = Int(6 * (Rnd + 1))
   lblDie2.Caption = iDie2
   lblDie2.Refresh
Next
End Sub


Sub BumpBank()                   ' Increases the bank by wager amount...
iBank = iBank + iWager           ' and display new balance...
lblBank = "Bank = " & Format(iBank, "Currency")
lblDie1.Caption = ""             ' Blank out the dice....
lblDie2.Caption = ""
lblPoint.Visible = False         ' Make point box invisible...
bFirst = True                    ' Ready for next "First" roll...
End Sub

Sub DingBank()                   ' Decreases the bank...
iBank = iBank - iWager           ' and displays new balance...
lblBank = "Bank = " & Format(iBank, "Currency")
lblDie1.Caption = ""
lblDie2.Caption = ""
lblPoint.Visible = False
bFirst = True

If iBank <= 0 Then               ' If out of money, the game is over!
   Beep                          ' Pathetic "Beep"
   MsgBox "You're Out Of Money!", vbCritical, "The Game Is Over!"
End If
End Sub
```

The last coding step is to get the New Game and Quit buttons working. Add the following lines to their Click events:

```
Private Sub cmdNew_Click()       ' Starts a new game....
bFirst = True
iBank = 500
iWager = 0
lblBank.Caption = "Bank = " & Format(iBank, "Currency")
lblWager.Caption = ""
lblPoint.Visible = False
End Sub
```

```
Private Sub cmdQuit_Click()          ' Quits the game, with player's permission..
If MsgBox("Are You Sure?", vbQuestion + vbYesNo,
➥"Ready To Quit This Session?") = vbYes Then
End
End If
End Sub
```

That's it. It's time to test and have some fun, but don't lose your shirt. Here's a sample session in Figure 22.2.

Figure 22.2.
Crap game program in action.

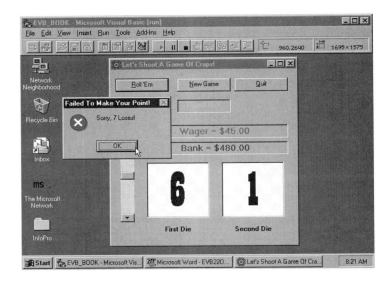

Essential Summary

What

In this chapter, you learned more about random numbers than you probably wanted to know. Although it may be that a sequence of truly random numbers is not possible, you saw how to use Visual Basic's Randomize statement and Rnd() function to produce a more than reasonable facsimile.

Why

Random numbers are necessary whenever you want things to happen by chance in your computer programs. They are commonly used in games, for example, where a card must be selected at random or an entire deck must be shuffled. As computers are relentlessly logical and orderly machines, you must use random numbers any time you want to introduce a little unpredictability into your computer programs.

How

Finally, you put your new understanding of random numbers to use by creating a computerized version of the game of Craps. Your program used random numbers, as well as some simple animation techniques, to simulate the tumbling roll of the dice.

A Game of Concentration

It's time to relax again. In this chapter, you'll create a game program that employs many of the random number, animation, and timer techniques you've learned in the previous few chapters. It won't all be fun and games, however (sorry about that), because you'll also become familiar with a new concept, the Control variable. You'll see how to declare and assign references to Control variables by using the Control data type and Visual Basic's Set statement.

The Set Statement and Control Variables

What One type of variable you've not yet encountered in this book is the Control type. You may dimension a variable of type Control by following the standard variable naming conventions, in the following manner:

```
Dim ctlMyCheckBox As Control          ' Local variable....
```

The Dim, Private, Public, ReDim, and Static statements declare only a variable that refers to an object, in this case a Control. No actual control is referred to until you use the Set statement to assign a specific object. The Set statement assigns a control (or other object) reference to a variable. Here's a simplified version of the syntax:

```
Set  controlvar  =  controlexpression
```

Here, `controlvar` is the name of the variable. To the right of the equal sign is `controlexpression`, an expression consisting of the name of a control, another declared variable of the same type, or a function or method that returns a control of the same object type. (You'll see more sides to the Set statement later, in Part V, "A Simple Database Program.")

Why Use Control Variables?

There are many uses for Control variables. Whenever you create a function or procedure that sets some property or invokes some method for controls in general (rather than a particular control specified by name), you'll need to declare, set, and manipulate Control variables.

For example, you might want to create a procedure that receives a variable containing a reference to a Grid control, in order to facilitate a uniform design for all the grids in your system. The procedure might define the grid's headings, as well as the number of rows and columns, row heights and column widths, and other properties. The game you'll be creating in this chapter would be much more difficult to write, if not impossible, if you were unable to deal with controls as variables, as you'll see.

Creating the Game of Concentration

In this section, you'll put your newly acquired game design skills, as well as your understanding of Control variables, to fruitful use. You'll need to add another form to your EVB_BOOK project. Name it frmConcentrate and set it as the project's startup form.

Program Overview

This program is a roadside rendition of the classic Concentration game. The player is presented with a board displaying 16 identical pictures. The player clicks on the pictures in sets of two to reveal the randomly assigned road signs beneath (in this program, the random signs are attached to the Picture Box's Tag property). If the two signs match, they remain displayed; if not, they're flipped back over. The goal of the game is to reveal all eight matches in as short a time as possible. Clicking the Shuffle button "shuffles the deck" and starts the clock running on a new game. The program maintains and displays the highest score (the fewest number of seconds required for revealing all the signs) for each session.

Figure 23.1 shows what the game looks like in Design mode.

Figure 23.1.
*Design mode: A game of
Concentration.*

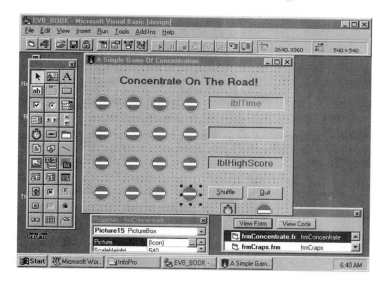

Notice how the Timer and one Picture Box, picBack, have slipped below the lower sill of the window. This is okay because these controls will not be visible at run time. Refer to Table 23.1 for a list of the program's significant objects.

Table 23.1. Design-time settings—Concentration game.

VB Object	Property	Design-Time Setting
Form	Name	frmConcentrate
	Caption	A Simple Game Of Concentration
	Icon	c:\vb40\icons\traffic\trffc09.ico
Labels	Names	lblTime,lblMatches,lblHighScore
	Alignment	Centered
	Appearance	3D
	BorderStyle	Fixed Single
	Font	Size 12, Bold
	ForeColor	Red, Green, Blue
PictureBoxes(16)	Names	Picture0-Picture15
	Appearance	Flat
	BorderStyle	None
	BackColor	Gray (same as form)
	Picture	c:\vb40\icons\traffic\trffc13.ico

continues

Table 23.1. continued

VB Object	Property	Design-Time Setting
Picture Box	Name	picBack
	Visible	False (other properties same as above)
Command Button	Name	cmdShuffle
	Caption	&Shuffle
Command Button	Name	cmdQuit
	Caption	&Quit
Timer	Name	Timer1
	Enabled	False
	Interval	1000 (One second)

Although you might be tempted to use Image controls rather than Picture Boxes, there's an important reason why you should not. Although an Image control can receive a click, it cannot receive the *focus*; that is, you'll never be able to refer to it as Screen.ActiveControl, which means the code you'll enter later won't work. So put aside that temptation and use Picture Boxes. Create the first one, name it Picture0, and set its properties according to Table 23.1. Then copy it 15 times. Or better, copy it three times, make a row of four, then copy the row four times. Or...well, fulfill your own fantasies of geometric progression here.

> **Tip** You probably noticed that you're not using the *pic* prefix for these Picture Boxes. You're breaking with convention here for a good reason. As you copy the pictures, and decline making a control array, the copies will be named Picture1, Picture2, and so on. That is, you won't have to mess with changing each copy's name, which in this case will save quite a bit of time.

> **Caution** Beware the eccentricities of the `PictureBox` control! Because a Picture Box may be a container for other controls, the process of copying them can be a bit tricky. If you draw a Picture Box, select it, then Copy and Paste, the copy will be created *inside* the original. You won't be able to get it out, which might prove mildly annoying. To prevent this, select the original and Copy it but don't Paste. Click anywhere on the open form, then perform the Paste operation. The control will appear in the upper-left corner of the form, from where you may drag it to the desired location.

Once you've completed the visual implementation of your new form, it's time to add the code that will get your game going.

Adding Code

First, you'll need some form level variables to manage different aspects of your program. Add the following declarations to the form's general declarations section:

```
Dim saSigns(8) As String              ' To hold matching road signs...
Dim sCheck As String                  ' For tracking signs during shuffle

Dim ctlFirstSign As Control           ' Special Control Variables for
Dim ctlSecondSign As Control          ' for first, second signs flipped.

Dim bOneShowing As Boolean, bShowingBoth As Boolean ' Track how many showing...

Dim iMatches As Integer               ' Track matches, time, score...
Dim iSeconds As Integer
Dim iHighScore As Integer
```

You'll initialize most of these variables, and begin the game, in the Form_Load event:

```
Private Sub Form_Load()
lblTime.Caption = ""                  ' Blank out label captions...
lblMatches.Caption = ""
lblHighScore.Caption = ""
bOneShowing = False                   ' None showing, at first...
iHighScore = 30000                    ' Set unlikely high score so first
                                      ' score will beat it, and be displayed

saSigns(0) = "C:\vb40\icons\traffic\trffc01.ico" ' Fill the signs array....
saSigns(1) = "C:\vb40\icons\traffic\trffc02.ico"
saSigns(2) = "C:\vb40\icons\traffic\trffc03.ico"
saSigns(3) = "C:\vb40\icons\traffic\trffc04.ico"
saSigns(4) = "C:\vb40\icons\traffic\trffc05.ico"
saSigns(5) = "C:\vb40\icons\traffic\trffc06.ico"
saSigns(6) = "C:\vb40\icons\traffic\trffc07.ico"
saSigns(7) = "C:\vb40\icons\traffic\trffc08.ico"

cmdShuffle = True                     ' Push the shuffle button to begin.
End Sub
```

And here's what happens when the Shuffle button is clicked:

```
Private Sub cmdShuffle_Click()
MousePointer = 11                     ' Change pointer to HourGlass...
sCheck = ""                           ' Empty the check string...
FlipSigns                             ' Flip and enable the signs...
EnableAll
Picture0.Tag = saSigns(MixSigns())    ' Call MixSigns for random number,
Picture1.Tag = saSigns(MixSigns())    '   using it as an index to randomly
Picture2.Tag = saSigns(MixSigns())    '   assign pictures from
Picture3.Tag = saSigns(MixSigns())    ' saSigns array.
Picture4.Tag = saSigns(MixSigns())
Picture5.Tag = saSigns(MixSigns())
Picture6.Tag = saSigns(MixSigns())
Picture7.Tag = saSigns(MixSigns())

sCheck = ""                           ' Empty check string...
Picture8.Tag = saSigns(MixSigns())    ' and do it again for next eight
Picture9.Tag = saSigns(MixSigns())    ' pictures...
Picture10.Tag = saSigns(MixSigns())
Picture11.Tag = saSigns(MixSigns())
```

```
Picture12.Tag = saSigns(MixSigns())
Picture13.Tag = saSigns(MixSigns())
Picture14.Tag = saSigns(MixSigns())
Picture15.Tag = saSigns(MixSigns())
MousePointer = 0                       ' Mousepointer back to normal...
iSeconds = 0                           ' Reset seconds...
Timer1.Enabled = True                  ' Start the clock...
End Sub
```

MixSigns() is a function that returns a random integer between 0 and 7, to be used as an index to one of the saSigns array's elements. For each set of 8 calls to MixSigns(), you'll want to be sure that you get a random mix of all the integers between 0 and 7, with no duplicates. Here's the listing of the MixSigns() function, which you'll add to the form's general declarations section.

```
Function MixSigns() As Integer
Dim iCurNum                            ' Need a variable for random num...

Do While True                          ' Keep generating...
    Randomize Timer                    ' Seed based on number of seconds
                                       ' since midnight.

    iCurNum = Int(8 * Rnd)             ' Get number between 0 and 7...

    If InStr(sCheck, CStr(iCurNum)) = 0 Then   ' If it's not already assigned...
        sCheck = sCheck & CStr(iCurNum)        ' add it to the check string...
        Exit Do                                ' and return it...
    End If
Loop                                   ' Otherwise loop to generate another
MixSigns = iCurNum
End Function
```

Once the shuffle is complete, the clock is started and the game begins. The next step is to add a couple of lines to each (all 16) of the game board's Picture Boxes. Whenever a picture is clicked, you'll load into it the road sign image, which has been randomly assigned to its Tag property; that is, you'll flip the sign over to reveal its "back side" for matching. Then you'll call the CheckSign sub procedure to determine if this is the first or second sign to be flipped in the matching process. Here's a listing of the first, and last, picture's Click event. Don't forget to copy to and adjust the other 14.

```
Private Sub Picture0_Click()
Picture0.Picture = LoadPicture(Picture0.Tag) ' Flip it...
CheckSign                                     ' Check it...
End Sub

Private Sub Picture15_Click()
Picture15.Picture = LoadPicture(Picture15.Tag)
CheckSign
End Sub
```

The CheckSign procedure checks to see if only one sign or both are showing during the matching process. If one sign is showing, you want to Set a control variable equal to the sign (Picture Box) that's just been clicked (the screen's active control). If two signs are showing, then you

Set the second control variable and call `CheckForMatch` to see if they're matching. Here's the listing:

```
Sub CheckSign()
If bOneShowing Then                                  ' If one sign already visible
    Set ctlSecondSign = Screen.ActiveControl  ' Set second control variable...
    CheckForMatch                                    ' And check for match.
    bOneShowing = False                              ' Now both are showing..
    Else
    Set ctlFirstSign = Screen.ActiveControl   ' If this is the first sign...
    ctlFirstSign.Enabled = False              ' Disable it, so it can't be clicked
    bOneShowing = True                        'again... bOneShowing now true.
End If
End Sub
```

If you've got a match, you want to bump iMatches and display the current number of matches in lblMatches. You also want to disable both of the matching signs, so they can't be clicked again. If iMatches equals 8, then the game is over. At this time, you shut off the timer, then check and display the score. Here's the listing for `CheckForMatch`:

```
Sub CheckForMatch()
If ctlFirstSign.Tag = ctlSecondSign.Tag Then                  ' If Tags are the same...
    iMatches = iMatches + 1                                   ' You've got a match...
    lblMatches.Caption = "Matches: " & CStr(iMatches)
    ctlFirstSign.Enabled = False                             ' Disable controls...
    ctlSecondSign.Enabled = False
    If iMatches = 8 Then                                      ' Is game over?
        Timer1.Enabled = False                               ' If so, stop the clock..
        If iSeconds < iHighScore Then                        ' Check for high score...
            MsgBox "New High Score!", cbExclamation, "Congratulations!"
            iHighScore = iSeconds                            ' Set new high, if so...
            lblHighScore = "High Score: " & CStr(iSeconds) & " Seconds"
        End If

    End If
    Else                                                     ' No match...
    bShowingBoth = True                                      ' Set variable to True...
End If
End Sub
```

Now, when two signs are revealed but don't match (bShowingBoth is True), you'll want to display them for a while so the player can get a look at them. Rather than using another timer, you'll keep the revealed pictures visible until the player moves his or her mouse. Attach the following code to the form's `MouseMove` event:

```
If bShowingBoth Then
    ctlFirstSign.Enabled = True              ' Enable the controls...
    ctlFirstSign.Picture = picBack.Picture   ' And flip 'em over...
    ctlSecondSign.Picture = picBack.Picture
    bShowingBoth = False                     ' Don't forget this...
End If
```

Finally, you need to add a couple of auxiliary procedures which are called by the Shuffle routine. The first one, `EnableAll`, sets the matches to 0, blanks out the Matches Caption, and enables all pictures for the next round. Here's the code to be added to your form's general declarations section (don't forget to copy and paste whenever convenient):

```
Sub EnableAll()
iMatches = 0
lblMatches.Caption = ""
Picture0.Enabled = True
Picture1.Enabled = True
Picture2.Enabled = True
Picture3.Enabled = True
Picture4.Enabled = True
Picture5.Enabled = True
Picture6.Enabled = True
Picture7.Enabled = True
Picture8.Enabled = True
Picture9.Enabled = True
Picture10.Enabled = True
Picture11.Enabled = True
Picture12.Enabled = True
Picture13.Enabled = True
Picture14.Enabled = True
Picture15.Enabled = True
End Sub
```

The last procedure to be added, FlipSigns, does just that: it flips all the revealed road signs over so you're seeing the same-sign "back" of each "card," and the board is again ready for play. Here's the listing:

```
Sub FlipSigns()
Picture0.Picture = picBack.Picture   'Flip to picBack picture...
Picture1.Picture = picBack.Picture
Picture2.Picture = picBack.Picture
Picture3.Picture = picBack.Picture
Picture4.Picture = picBack.Picture
Picture5.Picture = picBack.Picture
Picture6.Picture = picBack.Picture
Picture7.Picture = picBack.Picture

Picture8.Picture = picBack.Picture
Picture9.Picture = picBack.Picture
Picture10.Picture = picBack.Picture
Picture11.Picture = picBack.Picture
Picture12.Picture = picBack.Picture
Picture13.Picture = picBack.Picture
Picture14.Picture = picBack.Picture
Picture15.Picture = picBack.Picture
End Sub
```

That's it for the game of Concentration. It's time to play!

Figure 23.2.
*The Concentration game
in action.*

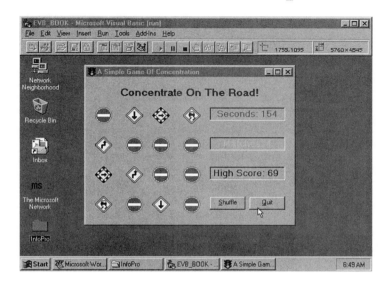

Essential Summary

In this chapter, you created a game program, reinforcing the random number, animation, and timer techniques you learned earlier. You were introduced to a powerful new programming concept, the Control variable. You learned how to declare such variables and how to assign values to them using the Set statement.

What

Because there are many uses for Control variables, not just in games but any programs, it's important to understand what they are and how to use them. Whenever you write a function or procedure that sets some property for controls in general, you'll need to create and manipulate Control variables.

Why

Finally, you put your conceptual grasp of Control variables, as well as your recently acquired game design skills to, hopefully, a pleasant use. You created your own roadside rendition of the popular game Concentration.

How

PART V

A Simple Database Program

The Data Manager and Data Control

In this chapter, you'll change gears a little and take the first steps toward an understanding of data management with Visual Basic. First, you'll be introduced to the Data Manager, a Visual Basic add-in for creating and managing databases. You'll use it to build a simple address book for keeping track of business and personal contacts. Then you'll be introduced to the Data Control, which will be your gateway to accessing your new address book through a Visual Basic form.

What Is the Data Manager?

What The *Data Manager*, available on Visual Basic's Add-In menu, allows you to create new Microsoft Jet (Access) databases. Data Manager also permits you to examine the *structure* (sometimes called *mapping*) of existing external databases in a variety of formats. You can use Data Manager to create or map databases in the formats shown in the following list:

Database Type	Access Allowed
Access	Create and Map
Btrieve	Map only
dBASE III and IV	Map only
FoxPro 2.0 and 2.5	Map only
Paradox 3.X and 4.X	Map only

Since Visual Basic shares its database engine with Microsoft Access, databases created with Visual Basic or Data Manager can be manipulated with Access, and databases created with Access can be managed through Visual Basic and the Data Manager. Throughout this chapter, and the rest of the book, the term *database* will refer to *Visual Basic* or *Jet database*, meaning one that was created with Visual Basic, Microsoft Access, or the Data Manager application.

What

A *database* is made up of at least one table and usually several tables. Each table is defined as a set of one or more *fields*, with each field describing the kind of data to be stored by specifying the data type, size, and other attributes.

Tables allow you to group related data together. For example, in the phone book you'll create in this chapter, information about each contact is stored in the Contacts table. The Contacts table will consist of several fields (or columns) such as Company, Address, Contact, and Phone. Each new contact added to your database will take up an entire row (or record) in the Contacts table.

Creating a New Database

Following are the general steps to be followed in creating a new database. (Just read them for now. You'll create a real database and table in the next section.) Once the Data Manager is started, follow these steps:

1. Select the **N**ew Database option from the Data Manager's **F**ile menu. Select a directory and enter a name for your new database file. This file can reside on a local drive or on a network drive if your system supports it. Click the Save button.

2. The Database window will open, displaying six command buttons, only two of which will be enabled. Here's a summary description of those buttons:

Button	Description
Open	Opens an existing table and view its data.
New	Creates a new table in the current database.
Delete	Removes an existing table from the current database.

Button	Description
Design	Views and/or modifies an existing table's structure.
Attach	Attaches remote tables (advanced).
Relations	Defines how data is related between tables (advanced).

3. Click the New button to define your database's first table. In the Name box, enter the name of your new table. Then define the table's fields, one at a time, by entering a field name, selecting a data type, and specifying the size of the field, if required. Once a field is defined, click the right arrow button (>) to add it to the field list box.

As the field list is built, you may use the Up and Down buttons, to the right of the list box, to change a field's position within the table. You may use the Left Arrow button (<) to remove a field from the list. The Double Left Arrow (<<) will remove all fields from the list box. Once all fields are designed, click the OK button to save your table definition. You'll then be returned to the Database Tables window, which will now contain your new table name. A new window, SQL Statement, will also be visible.

You may repeat Step 3 for every table to be included in your database.

Caution You can add additional fields to a database table, as well as change the names of existing fields. You cannot, however, modify field sizes or other attributes without losing the data contained therein. For this reason, it's wise to design your tables carefully.

The *Data control* is a built-in control used to connect a Visual Basic application with a selected data source. Data controls provide an easy, visual way to navigate through the fields, records, and tables of one or more databases. They are also used to "bind" other controls—text boxes, labels, picture boxes, and so on—to fields from selected tables in your database. Once a control, such as a text box, is bound to a particular field, any changes to the contents of the text box are automatically recorded in the associated field. In short, bound data controls enable you to create data access applications that require little or no coding, as you'll see in the following chapters.

What

Bound Data Controls

There are ten bound controls in addition to the Data control provided with Visual Basic. These controls are listed and described here:

Data*	Used to provide access to data in databases through bound controls on your form. Creates and manages Database and Recordset objects (discussed in Chapter 26) for use by bound controls. Required for use with all other bound controls.

DBCombo*	Used to create a bound combination list box and text box, or simple drop-down list. The list can be filled automatically from a Data control.
DBList*	Used to display a Data control-generated list of items from which the user can choose one. The list can be filled automatically from a Data control.
DBGrid*	Used to draw a bound grid composed of multiple records. The grid can be filled automatically from a Data control. The user can either choose an item from the grid or enter a value in the new record.
Label	Can be used to provide display-only access to a specified text data field.
TextBox	Can be used to provide read/write-access to a specified text data field.
CheckBox	Can be used to provide read/write-access to a specified Boolean or bit data field.
ComboBox	Must still be filled with the AddItem method. As a bound control, can be used to provide read/write-access to a specified text data field selected from the list. (The DBCombo control is the better choice for bound data management.)
ListBox	The list is filled with the AddItem method. When bound, may be used to provide read/write access to a specified text data field selected from the list, but the DBList control is a better choice.
PictureBox	Used to display a graphical image from a bitmap, icon or metafile on your form. As a bound control, it can be used to provide read/write access to a specified image/binary data field from one of your tables
Image	Images displayed in an Image control are only decorative and use fewer resources than a picture box. As a bound control, it can be used to provide read/write access to a specified image/binary data field.

Again, to use any of these "data-aware" controls, you need to place one or more Data controls on your form. The Data control establishes a link between the database and any bound controls used to manipulate the data.

The Toolbox displays all of these standard Visual Basic controls, including the Data control. If the bound control you need is not displayed in the Toolbox, use the Tools Custom Controls dialog box to add them to your project.

> **Note** To write code that references the data access objects (DAO) that a Data control creates, you may need to use the Tools References dialog box to activate the Microsoft DAO 2.5 Object Library. The controls listed with an asterisk (*) in the preceding list have libraries that require activation using this dialog box.

How to Create a Database Table

In this section, you'll create the Contacts Database, which will be comprised of a single table, also called Contacts. First, select Data Manager from Visual Basic's **Add-In** menu. (At this point, you may see a dialog box asking if you want to add SYSTEM.MDA to Data Manager's .INI file. Security is not an issue with this simple database, so just say No.) From Data Manager's **F**ile menu, select the **N**ew Database option. Select a directory and enter the name of your new database file: **Contacts**. Click the Save button.

You'll now see the empty Database Tables window. Click the New button to begin definition of the Contacts table. In the Name box, enter **Contacts**. Then define the table's fields, one at a time, by entering a Field Name, selecting a Data Type, and specifying the Size of the field, if required. Once a field is defined, click the Right Arrow button (>) to add it to the field list box. You'll keep things simple here, using only the Text Data Type. Table 24.1 shows the structure of the Contacts table.

Table 24.1. The Contacts table structure.

Field Name	Data Type	Size
Code	Text	5
Company	Text	30
Address	Text	30
City	Text	20
State	Text	2
Zip	Text	5
Contact	Text	30
Phone	Text	15

When all the fields have been defined, your screen should look something like Figure 24.1.

Once you're satisfied with the field definitions, click the OK button to save your new table structure. You'll then be returned to the Database Tables window, which will now contain your new table name.

Figure 24.1.
The Data Manager: defining the Contacts table.

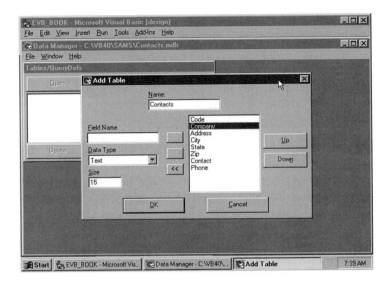

Adding Records to an Existing Table

You may use Visual Basic's Data Manager to add or edit records in your database tables. From the Database Tables window, choose the name of an existing table, in this case, Contacts. Now click the Open button. At this point, you may perform any of the following operations:

- Add a new record to the end of your table by clicking Add and filling in the fields. Click Update to complete the Add.

- Select an individual field and change its contents. Click the Update button to save your changes.

- Delete the current record by clicking Delete. The record is immediately deleted and cannot be recovered.

- Locate a particular record by clicking the Find button and entering a search expression.

- Retrieve the records again using Refresh. (This is used in a multiuser environment where others may be editing the table at the same time.)

- Press the Close button when finished.

Now, following the steps outlined here, please add some sample records to your Contacts table. You may add as many records as you like, but for testing purposes in later chapters, please include the ten records specified in Table 24.2.

Caution Unless you have allowed for Zero-Length strings in your field definitions (the default setting for this attribute is No), you must enter data into each field before the Data Manager will allow you to Update a record.

Table 24.2. Test data for the Contacts database.

Code	Company	Address (City, ST, Zip)
ABI	Albatross Industries	1111 First Avenue South
		Seattle, WA 98111
	Contact: Mariner, Andrew	Phone:(206) 555-1111
BBB	Best Books Bindery	2222 Second Avenue, #222
		Seattle, WA 98222
	Contact: Bates, Byron	Phone:(206) 555-2222
CCC	Crazy Castle Corp.	3333 Third Avenue
		Tacoma, WA 98333
	Contact: Carson, Cathy	Phone:(206) 555-3333
DDD	Drew Davis Designs	4444 Fourth Street, #4
		Olympia, WA 98444
	Contact: Davis, Drew	Phone: (360) 555-4444
EEE	ExcellEd Entertainers	5555 Fifth Avenue
		New York, NY 10555
	Contact: Edwards, Earl	Phone:(201) 555-5555
FFF	Farrah's Fast Food	6666 Sixth Street, #666
		Los Angeles, CA 90666
	Contact: Finley, Farrah	Phone: (203) 555-6666
GGG	Giant Gifts Galore	7777 Seventh Street West
		Seattle, WA 98777
	Contact: Grant, Gary	Phone: (206) 555-7777
HHH	Half Hilton Hotel	8888 Eighth Avenue
		New York, NY 10888
	Contact: Harris, Steven	Phone: (201) 555-8888
III	Illinois Industries, Inc.	9999 Ninth Street
		Olympia, WA 98999
	Contact: Ivans, Ivana	Phone (360) 555-9999
JJJ	Jerry's Juke Joint	1010 Tenth Street SW
		Tacoma, WA 98101
	Contact: James, Jerome	Phone: (206) 555-1010

Figure 24.2 shows what your screen will look like after you've entered the first record.

Figure 24.2.
The Data Manager:
Sample data in the
Contacts table.

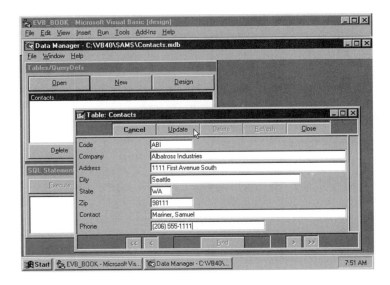

That's it for this chapter. In Chapter 25, you'll see how to use a Data control and other bound controls to access your Contacts data from Visual Basic.

Essential Summary

What

In this chapter, you gained an understanding of some basic database concepts. You learned that a *database* is a collection of one or more *tables* which, in turn, are made up of rows (or *records*) divided into fundamental units of information called *fields*. You learned how to use Visual Basic's Data Manger to create a database and its tables, and how to add and edit data therein. Then you read about the Data control, which, along with special "bound" controls, will be your gateway to accessing databases from within Visual Basic applications.

Why

There's an entire branch of computer systems development devoted to the creation and management of databases. Whether you're tracking recipes in your own kitchen or managing mission-critical information systems for interplanetary space flight, you'll find the exact same database concepts at work.

How

You used the Data Manger to create a database file called Contacts.MDB (the .MDB extension was added by Data Manager because this is an Access database), to which you added a single table definition, also called Contacts. You added some sample data to the Contacts table, which will be used in subsequent chapters as you learn how to connect to and manipulate your new database from within a Visual Basic form.

Forms and Bound Controls

In this chapter, you'll see how to access your new database using nothing but a form, a Data control, and eight text boxes, each bound to a field in your Contacts table. You'll be able to view and edit data, browse backward and forward through the records, or jump to the first or last record with a single mouse click. All of this will be possible just by setting various control properties at design time. No code required!

Data and Other Bound Control Properties

What The Data control has many Properties, nine of which are listed and summarized here.

Align	Returns or sets an integer value (0–4) that determines whether the Data control is displayed in any size anywhere on a form (0) or whether it's displayed at the top, bottom,

left, or right of the form (1–4) and is automatically sized to fit the form's width.

Caption	A descriptive phrase displayed on the Data control itself.
Database	Returns a reference to the Data control's underlying Database object.
DatabaseName	Returns or sets the name and location of the source of data for a Data control. This is often a string expression indicating the fully qualified path to the database.
Exclusive	Returns or sets a Boolean value that indicates whether the underlying database for a Data control is opened for single-user or multi-user access. Default is False, allowing multi-user access.
ReadOnly	Returns or sets a Boolean value indicating whether the data can be edited. Default is False, to allow editing.
Recordset	Returns or sets a Recordset object defined by a Data control's properties. (More on Database and Recordset objects in Chapter 26.)
RecordsetType	Returns or sets an integer value (0–2) indicating the type of Recordset object you want the Data control to create: Table, DynaSet, or SnapShot. The default is 1, DynaSet.
RecordSource	Returns or sets the underlying table or SQL statement for a Data control. This property determines which records will be displayed by the Data control.

> **Tip** In placing a Data control on your form, it's a good idea to set the DatabaseName property immediately. If you have a valid connection to your database, you'll be able to access a list of tables from the Data control's RecordSource property, saving you the trouble of having to remember table names.

Data Control Methods

There are three particularly useful methods associated with a Data control: Refresh, UpdateControls, and UpdateRecord. Each is discussed in turn.

The *Refresh method* is used to rebuild and redisplay the set of records associated with the Data control. Assuming you have a Data control called dtaMyData, you would invoke its Refresh method in the following way:

```
dtaMyData.Refresh
```

The Refresh method is often used in multi-user environments, in which other users may change the database, to ensure that the current user is viewing the most recent data. Even in an exclusive use environment, a Data control's RecordSource property may be changed at run time (you might want to display only your Contacts from the state of Washington, for example). In this case, the Data control would need to be refreshed in order for the change to take effect.

The *UpdateControls method* gets the current record from a Data control's Recordset object and displays the appropriate data in controls bound to the same Data control. Here's how you use this method to update controls bound to dtaMyData:

```
dtaMyData.UpdateControls
```

Use this method to restore the contents of bound controls to their original values, such as when a user makes changes to data and then decides to cancel the changes. This method produces the same effect as making the current record current again.

The *UpdateRecord method* saves the current values of all bound controls to their respective data fields. Here you're updating the current record associated with dtaMyData:

```
dtaMyData.UpdateRecord
```

Use this method to save the current contents of bound controls to the database during the Validate event without triggering the Validate event again. The UpdateRecord method has the same effect as executing a Recordset's Edit method, changing a field, and then executing the Update method, except that no events occur.

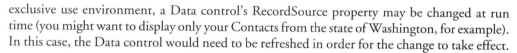

In designing your new form, you'll use several text boxes as bound controls. Associating a control such as a text box with a Data control on the same form will allow you to bind the control to a specific field from your Contacts table. Once the properly configured Data control is in place, two properties must be set in each text box to complete the binding.

The DataSource property sets a value that identifies the Data control through which the current control is bound to a database. This property must be set at design time, as it is not available at run time. Clicking the DataSource property in the Properties window will display a list of available Data controls (valid controls on the current form) from which you may choose one.

To complete the connection with a field in the Recordset managed by the Data control, you must also provide the name of a Field object in the DataField property, which is discussed next.

The DataField property returns or sets a value that binds a control to a field in the current record. The setting is a string expression that evaluates to the name of one of the fields in the Recordset specified by a Data control's RecordSource and DatabaseName properties. If the DataSource is properly set, clicking the DataField property at design time will display a list of fields from which you may select one.

In summary, bound controls provide easy access to specific data in your database. Bound controls typically display the value of one field in the current record. The DataSource property of a bound control specifies a valid Data control name, and the DataField property specifies a field name in the set of records created by the Data control. Together, these properties determine what data appears in the bound control.

> **Caution** Make sure the DataField property setting is valid for each bound control. Since it's possible to change the setting of a Data Control's RecordSource property and then use Refresh, the new Recordset may not contain the field expected by your bound control. This will invalidate the DataField setting of your bound controls and produce a trappable error.

Accessing Data from Visual Basic

How

In this section, you'll create a new form containing a Data control and other bound controls. You'll use it to access information from your Contacts database. The first step is to add a new form to your EVB_BOOK project. Name it frmContacts and make it the project's startup form. Refer to Figure 25.1 and Table 25.1 to complete the visual implementation of your form.

Figure 25.1.
Design mode: the Contact Manager form.

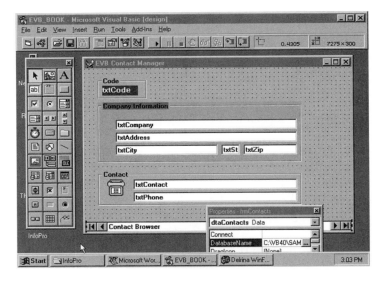

Table 25.1. Design-time settings—Contact Manager program.

Visual Basic Object	Property	Design-Time Setting
Form	Name	frmContacts
	Caption	EVB Contact Manager
	Icon	c:\vb40\icons\comm\handshak.ico
Data Control	Name	dtaContacts
	Align	2 - Align Bottom

Visual Basic Object	Property	Design-Time Setting
	Caption	Contact Browser
	DatabaseName	c:\vb40\sams\contacts.mdb
	RecordSource	Contacts
Text Box	Name	txtCode
	DataField	Code
	DataSource	dtaContacts
Text Box	Name	txtCompany
	DataField	Company
	DataSource	dtaContacts
Text Box	Name	txtAddress
	DataField	Address
	DataSource	dtaContacts
Text Box	Name	txtCity
	DataField	City
	DataSource	dtaContacts
Text Box	Name	txtState
	DataField	State
	DataSource	dtaContacts
Text Box	Name	txtZip
	DataField	Zip
	DataSource	dtaContacts
Text Box	Name	txtContact
	DataField	Contact
	DataSource	dtaContacts
Text Box	Name	txtPhone
	DataField	Phone
	DataSource	dtaContacts
Picture Box	Name	picPhone
	Appearance	Flat
	BackColor	Gray
	BorderStyle	None
	Picture	c:\vb40\icons\comm\phone01.ico

Caution   Remember that the exact location of your database and icons may be different from those given in the preceding table. Be sure to use the fully qualified paths relevant to your system.

Once the proper control properties have been set, your Contact Manager will be ready to test. Start the program and notice how simple it is to browse forward and backward through your contacts table, just by clicking the appropriate arrows on the Data control. You may also edit the contents of any field, then move to another record to write the changes into your database. All of this functionality, as promised, and you haven't written a single line of code!

Figure 25.2 shows how your Contact Manager looks in action.

Figure 25.2.
Bound Data controls in action.

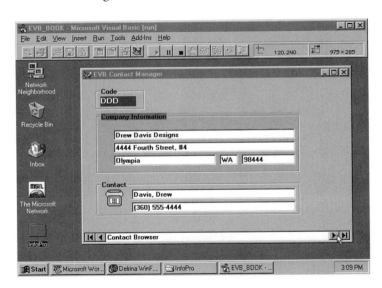

In the next chapter, you'll add still more functionality, including the capability to add and delete records, and to locate particular contacts by selecting their names from a drop-down list.

This *will* require a little code, but not much, really.

Essential Summary

In this chapter, you learned about many of the Data control's properties and methods. You saw how to connect a Data control to a database by specifying its DatabaseName and RecordSource properties. You learned how to "bind" other controls, such as text boxes, to specific fields in a database by setting their DataSource and DataField properties.

What

Using the Data control and other bound controls is a simple yet powerful way to access and manipulate existing databases. The Data control is like a periscope at sea—there's a large and powerful machine beneath it. It's not only a gateway to your databases, it provides access to a whole specialized data management language built into Visual Basic.

Why

You created a new program to access your Contacts database using nothing but a form, a Data control, and text boxes. You bound the text boxes to fields associated with the Data control's current Recordset. Once your program was running, you were able to view and edit data from your Contacts table, browsing backward and forward through the records with a single mouse click.

How

Database and Recordset Objects

In this chapter, you'll learn all you need to know, for now, about Database and Recordset objects. You'll employ what you learn in adding new functionality to your Contact manager system. You'll be able to add and delete records, and locate specific contacts using the "data-aware" DBCombo control. You'll also see how, why, and when to add indexes to your database.

What Are Database and Recordset Objects?

What A Database object is a logical representation of a physical database which may be assigned to, and manipulated by, a variable of the Database type. A *database*, as you've already seen, is a set of data related to a specific topic or purpose. Although a simple database, such as your Contacts.MDB, contains only a single table, databases often contain not only tables but report formats, queries, indexes, table relationships, and field validation criteria.

Once you've added a valid Data control to your applications, you're already working with a Database object. You may remember from the previous chapter that a Data control has a Database property (not the same as the DatabaseName property), which contains a reference to the Database object associated with the current control.

In your programs, you may declare variables of the Database type and set them equal to the Database property of a particular Data control; or you may assign values to them by using the OpenDatabase() function, which is discussed next.

The OpenDatabase() function opens a specified database and returns a reference to the Database object that represents it. Here's the simplified syntax:

```
Set dbVariable = OpenDatabase(dbName)
```

Here, dbVariable is a variable of the Database object data type that represents the Database you're opening. The argument dbName is a string expression that is the name of an existing database file. If the database filename has an extension, you must include it. If your network supports it, you can also specify a fully-qualified network path, such as \\MYSERVER\MYDIR\MYDB.MDB. If dbName doesn't refer to an existing database, or if it refers to a database that is already open for exclusive access by another user, an error occurs. If you wanted to open your Contacts database from code, rather than with a Data control, here's a snippet of code that would do the trick:

```
Dim dbContacts As Database                               ' Declare variable
Set dbContacts = OpenDatabase("c:\vb40\sams\contacts.mdb")   ' And Set it...
```

Note Although the OpenDatabase() function is fine for simple database systems, such as the one you're developing here, it is included in Visual Basic 4.0 for backward compatibility with earlier versions. In more complex systems, where you have multiple users and sessions, it's recommended that you use the OpenDatabase method with the Workspace object instead.

Once you've got a valid Database variable, you can use it to execute Database methods such as Execute, which executes an SQL statement against the specified Database, or OpenRecordset, which creates a new Recordset object. For example you could gain access to your Contacts table by adding the following lines to the previous code:

```
Dim rsContacts As Recordset                          ' Variable of type Recordset
Set rsContacts = dbContacts.OpenRecordset("Contacts")   ' Set it...
```

Which brings you to the next topic of discussion, Recordset objects.

A Recordset object is a logical set of records associated with a physical Database. It represents the records in a base table or the records that result from running a query. Recordset objects are the primary means by which you interact with the data contained in your databases.

What

All Recordset objects are constructed using records (rows) and fields (columns) from existing database tables. There are three types of Recordset objects:

Table-Type — A representation of a base table that you can use to add, change, or delete records from a single database table.

Dynaset-Type — The result of a query that can have updatable records. A dynaset-type Recordset is a dynamic set of records that you can use to add, change, or delete records from an underlying database table or tables.

SnapShot-Type — A static copy of a set of records that you can use to find data or generate reports. A snapshot-type Recordset can contain fields from one or more tables in a database but can't be updated.

You can choose the type of Recordset object you want to create using the type argument of the OpenRecordset method, which is discussed next.

Note If your project doesn't reference the Data Access (DA) object library in the Object Browser, none of the data access objects mentioned earlier are available. To make these objects available, choose **R**eferences from the **T**ools menu and select the appropriate DAO Component Object Library in the References dialog box.

The OpenRecordset method is used to create a new Recordset object associated with the current database. Here's the simplified syntax:

What

```
Set rsVariable = dbVariable.OpenRecordset(Source, Type)
```

Here rsVariable is a declared variable of type Recordset; dbVariable is a variable of type Database that has been set to a currently valid database object. The required argument Source is a string expression specifying the source of the records for the new Recordset. Source can be a table name, a query name, or an SQL statement that returns records. For table-type Recordset objects, Source can only be a table name.

The Type argument is optional and is used to indicate one of the three Recordset types. If Type is omitted, Visual Basic (through the Microsoft Jet database engine) attempts to create a table-type Recordset. If this isn't possible, a dynaset-type or snapshot-type Recordset is created. The Type argument may be one of the following integer constants:

dbOpenTable — Opens a table-type Recordset.

dbOpenDynaset — Opens dynaset-type Recordset.

dbOpenSnapshot — Opens a snapshot-type Recordset.

Once you've established a Recordset variable, (or "latched" on to the Recordset associated with a particular Data control), you can use the MoveNext, MovePrevious, MoveFirst, and MoveLast methods to navigate the records. For dynaset-type and snapshot-type Recordsets, you can also use the Find methods, such as FindFirst, to locate a specific record based on a criterion. You'll put these ideas to use later in this chapter.

Why Use Database and Recordset Objects?

Why Even though your Contact Manager program will not require an elaborate use of the Database and Recordset objects (you will use them, indirectly, through manipulation of the Data control), a thorough understanding of them is absolutely essential if you intend to develop industrial-strength database systems. There will be times when you'll want to simultaneously manage multiple databases including many tables, strictly from code; that is, with no Data or other bound controls anywhere in the picture. In those situations, WorkSpace, Database, and Recordset objects are, literally, the only way to go.

Managing a Data Control's Recordset

How In this section, you'll add some command buttons and a DBComboBox control to your Contact Manager form. You'll use the command buttons to Add and Delete records, and later to run SQL queries and print a report. The bound ComboBox will be used as a drop-down list to quickly locate a specific contact. You'll add code to the buttons and ComboBox which will manipulate the Data control's Recordset object.

Here, in Figure 26.1, is what the enhanced Contact Manager form looks like in Design mode.

Now, referring to Figure 26.1 and Table 26.1, complete the visual modification of the Contact Manager's form.

Table 26.1. Design-time settings—the new Contact Manager.

Visual Basic Object	Property	Design-Time Setting
DBCombo	Name	dbcContacts
	BoundColumn	Contact
	DataSource	dtaContacts
	ListField	Contact
	RowSource	dtaContacts
	Style	2 - DropDown List
Command Button	Name	cmdAdd
	Caption	&Add

Visual Basic Object	Property	Design-Time Setting
Command Button	Name	cmSave
	Caption	&Save
	Enabled	False
Command Button	Name	cmdCancel
	Caption	&Cancel
	Enabled	False
Command Button	Name	cmdDelete
	Caption	&Delete
Command Button	Name	cmdQuery
	Caption	&Query
Command Button	Name	cmdReport
	Caption	&Report

Figure 26.1.
*Design mode: The
Contact Manager form.*

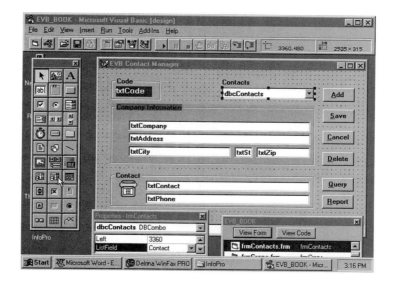

The DBCombo control is new to you and warrants a little discussion. It looks and works very much like a normal unbound ComboBox, but it has a lot more database-related functionality. You may use it to display a list of the contacts in your database just by setting the DataSource and RowSource properties to dtaContacts, the Data control. You then set the BoundColumn and ListField properties to the field whose contents you want displayed in the list, in this case, Contact. That's it. No need to mess with the AddItem method or stepping through all the records in your table. When you run the form and drop down the list, you'll see the names of your Contacts.

Part V

> **Tip** The DBCombo, and other so-called "data-aware" controls such as DBList and DBGrid, are easy to locate in Visual Basic's Toolbox. They look just like their non-data-aware counterparts, except that they have two overlapping golden circles in the lower-left corner. Use your ToolTips to absolutely identify them. If they're not there, you can add them from the Custom Controls dialog box.

Adding Code to Your Program

You'll need a string variable for marking your place in a Recordset, using the Recordset's Bookmark property, as you'll see. Declare it in the general declarations section of your form, as in the following:

```
Dim sLastRecord As String
```

The form's Activate event will contain a line that serves a purely cosmetic function. It makes the drop-down list box display the first Contact name in the database. Without this line, the edit area of the list would, at first, be empty. Here's the listing:

```
Private Sub Form_Activate()
dbcContacts.Text = dtaContacts.Recordset("Contact")
End Sub
```

You're simply setting the list's Text property equal to whatever name is contained in the first record's Contact field. In this case, the Recordset is the one created by your Data control.

Now, when the Add button is clicked, you want to prepare the Data Control's Recordset to receive a new record. This is done by calling the Recordset's AddNew method, which in effect creates a memory buffer for the new record, and blanks out the bound text boxes. At this point, the user may fill in the new information, then click the Save button to complete the add. If the user decides not to add the record after all, he or she may click the Cancel button instead. (Notice that neither the Save nor Cancel button is available until the Add button is clicked.) Here's cmdAdd's Click event procedure:

```
Private Sub cmdAdd_Click()
    sLastRecord = dtaContacts.Recordset.Bookmark    ' Mark your place in the
Recordset
    cmdAdd.Enabled = False                          ' Disable the Add button...
    cmdSave.Enabled = True                          ' Enable the Save and
    cmdCancel.Enabled = True                        ' and cancel buttons...
    dtaContacts.Recordset.AddNew                    ' Add new record ...
    txtCode.SetFocus                                ' Move to the first field...
End Sub
```

A Recordset's Update method posts a newly added record. Here's what happens when the user clicks the Save button:

```
Private Sub cmdSave_Click()
    dtaContacts.Recordset.Update                         ' Post the record...
    cmdSave.Enabled = False                              ' Disable Save and Cancel...
```

```
        cmdCancel.Enabled = False
        cmdAdd.Enabled = True                          ' Enable the Add button.
    End Sub
```

Should the user decide to cancel the Add operation, he or she will press the Cancel button instead of Save. Because the AddNew method appends a record to the bottom of the table, you'll want to use your Bookmark to return to your previous place in the Recordset. Here's the code for cmdCancel's `Click` event:

```
Private Sub cmdCancel_Click()
    cmdCancel.Enabled = False                    ' Disable Cancel and Save...
    cmdSave.Enabled = False
    cmdAdd.Enabled = True                        ' Enable Add.
    dtaContacts.Recordset.Bookmark = sLastRecord  ' Set the Recordset's Bookmark
End Sub                                         ' Property equal to your bookmark
                                                ' variable. This will return the user
                                                ' to the record he or she was on
                                                ' when the Add button was pressed.
```

Deleting a record from a Recordset is a two-step process. First, you call the Recordset's Delete method, and then you move off of the deleted record. Here's the code for the Delete button's `Click` event:

```
Private Sub cmdDelete_Click()
 If MsgBox("OK To Delete?", vbQuestion + vbYesNo, "Deleting " _
    ➥& txtContact) =  vbYes Then               ' First, ask if it's OK to delete...

    dtaContacts.Recordset.Delete                ' If so, delete it...
    dtaContacts.Recordset.MovePrevious          ' and move up a record.
 End If
End Sub
```

In both Adding and Deleting a record, you'll notice that the list of names displayed in the Contacts drop-down list is automatically updated to reflect the latest changes. This is another advantage of using a data-aware control rather than a regular list box.

The last coding step is to get the drop-down list working as a quick Contact locator. This is done by adding a few lines to the control's `Click` event. You'll want the user to be able to pick a name from the list and have the corresponding record immediately displayed, no browsing required. There are a number of ways in which this can be accomplished. You'll explore the two most expedient ways next.

The first way is to use the Recordset's FindFirst method to locate the proper Contact record. The FindFirst method requires a single argument, a string expression which evaluates to an SQL WHERE clause (more on SQL in Chapter 28). In this case, you'll be looking for the record whose Contact field is equal to the name selected from the drop-down list. If you're looking for "Harris, Steven" for example, the search criteria would be:

```
Contact = 'Harris, Steven'
```

Here's the listing for dbcContact's `Click` event:

```
Private Sub dbcContacts_Click(Area As Integer)
Dim sCriteria As String                         ' Variable for search string
```

```
sCriteria = "Contact = '" & dbcContacts & "'"        ' Build search string...
dtaContacts.Recordset.FindFirst sCriteria            ' Find it in the Data Control's
End Sub                                              ' Recordset.
```

Please pay particular attention to the way the search criteria string is concatenated. You must include the *single* quotes around the name displayed in dbcContacts, the Contacts list. Notice also that the literal components of the string are enclosed with *double* quotes, as usual. This may seem a little tricky at first, but you'll get use to it. You'll do a lot of SQL string manipulation in Chapter 28.

Now, the second way to perform this little magic is easier but can only be done when you're using a data-aware bound list control, as you are here. Here's the listing:

```
Private Sub dbcContacts_Click(Area As Integer)
dtaContacts.Recordset.Bookmark = dbcContacts.SelectedItem
End Sub
```

This single line packs a lot of wallop. The DBCombo and DBList controls have a special property, SelectedItem, which returns a Bookmark to the record corresponding to the item currently displayed in the list. So all you have to do when a Contact is picked from the list, is set the Data control's Recordset Bookmark equal to the list's SelectedItem property.

It's time to run your program, and thoroughly explore all the new features you've added. Here, in Figure 26.2, is a sample session.

In testing, you may have noticed that your drop-down list of Contacts is not displayed in alphabetical order and that when records are added, the new Contact name is simply appended to the bottom of the list. This is because your Contacts table is not indexed. In the next section, you'll revisit the Data Manager to add an index to your database.

Figure 26.2.
The new Contact Manager in action.

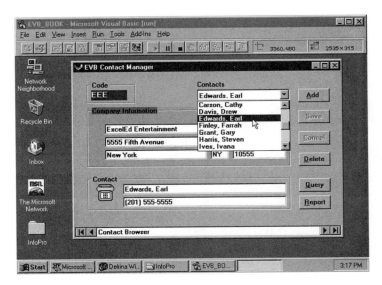

Indexing Your Data

The simplest way to have your contact list displayed alphabetically is to add an index to your database. Indexes are also used to improve performance and to eliminate duplicate records in your table, so it's a good idea to know how to create them. Start the Data Manager and open the Contacts database, then follow these steps to create an index based on the Contacts field:

1. Select the Contacts table, then click the Design button to open the Table Editor window.

2. Click the Indexes button to open the Indexes window. At this point, no indexes are listed. Click Add to create a new one.

3. Type **Contact**, the new index's name, in the Add Index window.

4. Choose the field Contact in the Fields In Table list.

5. Choose either Add (Asc) or Add (Dec) to designate whether the table is to be sorted in ascending or descending order. Here, in Figure 26.3, is what your screen should look like.

6. Click OK to create the index and return to the previous screen. From there you may "Close" your way back to the Data Manager's Main window and exit.

   Now run your program and verify that your drop-down list of contacts is sorted in ascending alphabetical order.

Figure 26.3.
Data Manager:
Indexing your data.

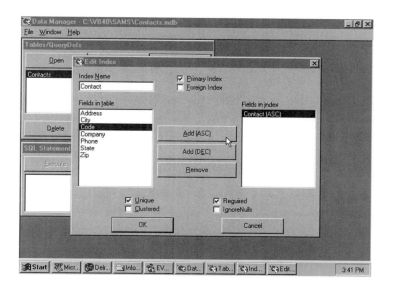

Essential Summary

What In this chapter, you learned probably more than you wanted to know about Database and Recordset objects. You were introduced to a new control, DBCombo, which allowed you to easily display a drop-down list of Contacts in your database. You revisited the Data Manager in order to add a useful index to your database.

Why A thorough understanding of Database and Recordset objects is a must if you intend to develop commercially viable database systems. Managing multiple sessions, databases, tables, and possibly hundreds of users is just not feasible using Data controls alone. In those situations, WorkSpace, Database, and Recordset objects are, literally, the only way to go.

How You put your new knowledge to use by adding new functionality to your Contact Manager system. You're now able to add and delete records, and to locate specific contacts using the data-aware DBCombo control. Finally, you added a new index to your contacts databases, making it possible to efficiently sort and search the Contact field.

The Grid Controls: Viewing Tabular Data

The plain ol' vanilla Grid control, not data-aware, not able to be bound to a data table, is useful nevertheless. You'll get a chance to use it in this chapter, and in the process, see how to access your data without a Data control, using only the Database and Recordset objects. You'll also see how the powerful DBGrid control works to easily load and display your data in an attractive and editable tabular format.

What Are Grid and DBGrid?

What A Grid control displays a series of rows and columns. The intersection of a row and column is a called a *cell*. You can read and set the contents of each cell in a grid by evaluating (or setting) its Text property. In this way, you may put either text or a picture in any cell of a grid.

Part V

The size of the grid, the number of rows and columns, is established by setting its Rows and Cols properties. This particular grid control can't have more than 2000 rows or 400 columns. Do not confuse the Rows and Cols properties with the singular Row and Col, which are used to specify and move to a particular cell. You can specify the current cell in code, or a user can change it at run time using the mouse or the arrow keys. For example, if you wanted to place the word "Wages" in the cell located at Row 3, Column 5, you would do so like this:

```
grdMyGrid.Row = 2                      ' Rows and columns are numbered from zero...
grdMyGrid.Col = 4
grdMyGrid.Text = "Wages"
```

If the text in a cell is too long to be fully displayed, it wraps to the next line within the same cell. To display the wrapped text, you must increase the cell's column width and/or row height by adjusting the grid's ColWidth or RowHeight properties. You may set a column's width at run time by using the TextWidth() function, as you'll see.

A grid may have zero, one, or many *fixed* columns or rows. A fixed column or row is shaded and located at the left or top of the grid, and will not scroll off the screen as the user clicks the grid's horizontal or vertical scroll bars. A standard grid has one fixed column and one fixed row by default, but the number may be adjusted at design time or run time by setting the grid's FixedCols and FixedRows properties.

What

The DBGrid control displays and enables data manipulation of a series of rows and columns representing records and fields from a Data control's Recordset object. It requires more overhead than the standard grid control, but the added functionality and attractive appearance is well worth it in most cases.

Although the data-aware DBGrid control appears similar to the standard Grid control, you can set the DBGrid control's DataSource property to a Data control so that the grid is automatically filled, and its column headers set, from the Data control's Recordset. The DBGrid control is really just a collection of columns and rows, the dimensions of which are determined by the number of fields and records in the associated Recordset.

> **Note** Before you can use the Apex Data Bound Grid control, you need to add the control to the project using the Add Custom Controls dialog box and register the DAO library using the Add References dialog box. To have these controls loaded automatically into every new project, load and edit the AUTOLOAD.VBP file accordingly.

As with the standard grid, the Row and Col properties specify the current cell in a DBGrid control. The contents of the current cell may be set or displayed by manipulating its Text or Value property. Each cell of a DBGrid can hold either text or picture values, but not linked or embedded objects.

As with the standard grid, you can specify the current cell in code, or the user can change it at run time using the mouse or the arrow keys. Cells in a DBGrid can be edited interactively by typing into the cell, unlike the standard grid, where producing a similar effect would require much coding. Since the grid represents a dynaset bound to a table from your database, any changes the user makes are recorded in the underlying table.

You may read the DBGrid control's Columns Count property and the Recordset object's RecordCount property to determine the number of columns and rows in the control. A DBGrid control can have as many rows as the system resources can support and about 1,700 columns, a huge increase in capacity over the standard Grid control. Each column of the DBGrid control has its own font, border, word-wrap, color, and other attributes that can be set without regard to other columns.

When initially created at design time, the DBGrid control displays two columns and two rows. Using the Properties window, you can change any of the grid's visible attributes. When you set the DataSource property, the DBGrid control accesses the Recordset created by the Data control and displays the columns, including headings, and rows from the current Recordset. Columns are numbered according to the position of the fields in the underlying Recordset (minus 1, as usual). Rows are numbered starting from zero, but, unlike the standard Grid, the header is not included. That is, Row 0 corresponds to the first record in the underlying dynaset.

DBGrid's Run-Time Appearance

Using an attractive 3-D chiseled effect, the DBGrid control displays records from a Data control's Recordset at run time. As long as there are records in the Recordset, there is always a single current record in the DBGrid control, even if multiple rows in the control are selected. Although more than one column may be selected, there is only one current column.

Within a single row, individual cells can be selected, and the selection can be extended to include any number of contiguous cells in the same row or in adjoining rows. If the user clicks on a column header, the HeadClick event is generated (where you can add code to handle it), but the column selection isn't affected.

If a column's AllowSizing property and the DBGrid's RecordSelectors property are both True, the user can drag the border between rows to resize the row height. If DBGrid's HeadLines property is greater than or equal to 1 (default) and the current column's AllowSizing property is True (default), the user can drag the column border to resize the column width.

Note Among Visual Basic's controls, both the standard Grid and DBGrid controls are in a class by themselves. They include many specialized properties and are thus virtually separate, functional programs. Of their scores of properties, most are unique to grid controls and are highly specific, such as AllowAddNew, TopRow, ColWidth, and RowDividerStyle. Covering each of these Grid-specific properties individually would require a small book in itself. However, the properties are not difficult to work with, and you should refer to the Visual Basic manuals and online Help for detailed information and examples.

Why Use Grid Controls?

You may use Grid controls to make traditional spreadsheet applications. However, the advent of OLE technology, whereby a spreadsheet program such as Excel may operate as an OLE server, allowing you to almost literally drop a spreadsheet onto your form, makes this use nearly obsolete. It may be that your users will not want their programs to involve Excel or some other OLE compliant spreadsheet application. In such cases, a Grid control can be used to provide simple spreadsheet functionality.

The graphic's capabilities of Grids may be used to display thumbnail sketches of bitmap or icon graphics. The user could then click on a particular picture to assign it to a toolbar, for example, or to use it as an icon representing personal files. Perhaps the most common use of Grid controls is to create and manipulate tables of information that may be input programmatically, or drawn from a database, as you will see in the next section.

How to Use Grid Controls

In this section, you'll use Visual Basic's standard Grid control to display a table view of your Contacts information. Rather than using a Data control, however, you'll declare Database and Recordset variables and use them to access your database. To begin, create a new form named frmGrid, which will contain only a standard Grid control called grdContacts (this form will be opened from frmContacts, so don't make it the startup form). Table 27.1 contains the design time specifications.

Table 27.1. Design-time settings—Contacts Grid form.

Visual Basic Object	Property	Design-Time Setting
Form	Name	frmGrid
	Caption	Contacts Table View
	Icon	c:\vb40\icons\computer\msgbox04.ico
	Height	3555 (suggested size)
	Width	9330
	Left	120 (suggested position)
	Top	2940
Grid	Name	grdContacts
	Height	3015
	Width	8895

You don't need to set any other properties at design time. Specifying the column headers and widths, and filling the grid, will be handled in code.

Adding Code to Populate the Grid

You'll put all the code required to fill your grid, and set its column widths and headers, into frmGrid's Load event procedure. There are quite a few lines, introducing a couple of new ideas, which will be discussed in the annotation. Here's the listing of the code:

```
Private Sub Form_Load()

Dim dbContacts As Database                              ' Need a Database variable...
Dim rsContacts As Recordset                             ' and a recordset variable.

Dim iRowCount As Integer, iColCount As Integer  ' For determining the size of the
➥grid.
Dim iColIndex As Integer, iRowIndex As Integer  ' For looping...

Set dbContacts = OpenDatabase("C:\vb40\sams\contacts.mdb")      ' Open the database
Set rsContacts = dbContacts.OpenRecordset("Contacts", dbOpenDynaset) ' And dynaset

iColCount = rsContacts.Fields.Count                     ' Get number of columns...
rsContacts.MoveLast                                     '  Move to last record in the set..
iRowCount = rsContacts.RecordCount                      '  to get the number of records.
rsContacts.MoveFirst                                    ' Don't forget to go back to top...

grdContacts.FixedCols = 0                               ' Grid will have no fixed columns..
grdContacts.Cols = iColCount                            ' Set the number of columns...
grdContacts.Rows = iRowCount + 1                        ' Set the number of rows, plus
                                                        ' one for the fixed header.

'Estimate/Set The Column Widths...                      ' Here you're using the
grdContacts.ColWidth(0) = TextWidth("Code")            ' the TextWidth function,
grdContacts.ColWidth(1) = TextWidth("Company") * 4     ' which returns the number of
grdContacts.ColWidth(2) = TextWidth("Address") * 4     ' twips needed to display the
grdContacts.ColWidth(3) = TextWidth("City") * 4        ' sample of text passed to it.
grdContacts.ColWidth(4) = TextWidth("State")           ' You're setting the width of
grdContacts.ColWidth(5) = TextWidth("Zip Code")        ' each column based on
grdContacts.ColWidth(6) = TextWidth("Contact") * 4     ' estimate of what it may
grdContacts.ColWidth(7) = TextWidth("Phone") * 3       ' contain.

' Now set the headers by looping through the RecordSet's columns, and reading their
For iColIndex = 0 To iColCount - 1                      ' Name Properties.
    grdContacts.Row = 0                                 ' First row only...
    grdContacts.Col = iColIndex                         ' Set the column number..
    grdContacts.Text = rsContacts(iColIndex).Name       ' and read it's Name.
Next                                                    ' Do the next column...


' Now fill the grid with the contents of the recordset.
iRowIndex = 0                                           ' Set row index to 0...

Do Until rsContacts.EOF                                 ' Loop until end of set

    For iColIndex = 0 To iColCount - 1                 ' For each column....
        grdContacts.Row = iRowIndex + 1                ' starting in row 1...
        grdContacts.Col = iColIndex                    ' starting with first column...
        grdContacts.Text = rsContacts(iColIndex)       ' Set the text property
                                                        ' of the current cell equal to
                                                        ' the contents of the
                                                        ' recordset's current field.
```

```
        Next iColIndex                          ' Then do the next field.

        rsContacts.MoveNext                     ' Move to next record...
        iRowIndex = iRowIndex + 1               ' Bump the row index....
Loop                                            ' and loop...
End Sub
```

As you've probably surmised by perusing the preceding annotation, you may access the contents of a Recordset by reading (or setting) field values in the following way:

```
varFieldValue = rsMyRecordSet(iFieldNumber)
```

where *iFieldNumber* is a numeric expression representing a field's ordinal position in the set (starting with 0). You may also reference a particular field by name, like so:

```
varFieldValue = rsMyRecordSet(sFieldName)
```

where *sFieldName* is a valid string expression. Here's an example:

```
sContactName = rsContacts("Contact")
```

You should save your work and close frmGrid, then open frmContacts. You don't have a Table button (although you could add one if you like) on your startup form, frmContacts, so you'll display your Table view by double-clicking anywhere on the form. Here's what frmContacts' DblClick event will look like:

```
Private Sub Form_DblClick()
frmGrid.Show
End Sub
```

Feel free to test. Double-clicking the Contact Manager form should produce something similar to the screen displayed in Figure 27.1.

Figure 27.1.
The Contacts Manager Table view.

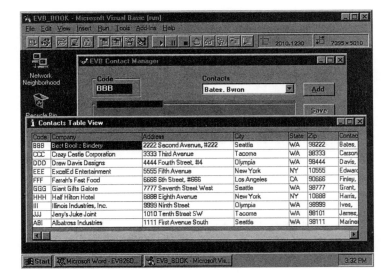

The data-aware DBGrid control is much easier to use, at least as far as getting it to display data from one of your tables. Add a second new form to your project and name it frmQuery. This form will be used here and in the following chapter where you'll learn to query your database using SQL. Table 27.2 contains the design-time settings.

Table 27.2. Design-time settings—the Contacts Query form.

Visual Basic Object	Property	Design-Time Setting
Form	Name	frmQuery
	Caption	Contacts Query Form
	Height	3120 (suggested size)
	Width	9210
	Left	390 (suggested position)
	Top	3390
	Icon	c:\vb40\icons\computer\msgbox02.ico
DBGrid	Name	DBQueryGrid
	Caption	Query Results
	DataSource	dtaQuery
	Height	2055 (suggested size)
	Width	8535
Data Control	Name	dtaQuery
	DatabaseName	c:\vb40\sams\contacts.mdb
	RecordSource	Contacts
	Visible	False
Command Button	Name	cmdQuery
	Caption	"Process Query"
	Default	True
Text Boxes	Names	txtCity, txtState

Refer to the preceding table and to Figure 27.2 to complete the visual design of your new form.

Now you'll add a little code (very little code) to get your query form working.

Figure 27.2.
Design mode: the
Contacts Query form.

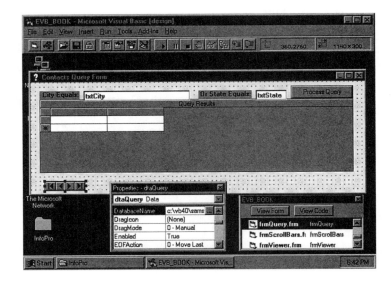

Adding Code

One of the great strengths of DBGrid is that it may be indirectly bound to a particular table in your database, allowing for a tabular display of data without writing any code at all. Because you've set DBQueryGrid's DataSource property to dtaQuery, the Data control bound to your Contacts table, the grid will automatically be filled when the form is opened. The code you'll enter now will be for purely cosmetic purposes—specifically, to blank the City and State text boxes since you won't use them until the next chapter, when you'll experiment with SQL. Here's the Form_Load event procedure:

```
Private Sub Form_Load()
txtCity = ""
txtState = ""
End Sub
```

You'll display frmQuery when the Query button is clicked. Here's all you need:

```
Private Sub cmdQuery_Click()
    frmQuery.Show
End Sub
```

It's time to test. You should be able to open both of your new forms from within the Contact Manager program. Since the forms are modeless, there's no reason why you can't have them both open at once. Be sure to verify that you can actually change data in your Contacts Table, using DBQueryGrid, by typing directly into a cell. Figure 27.3 shows your new Contact Manager program in action.

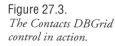

Figure 27.3.
The Contacts DBGrid
control in action.

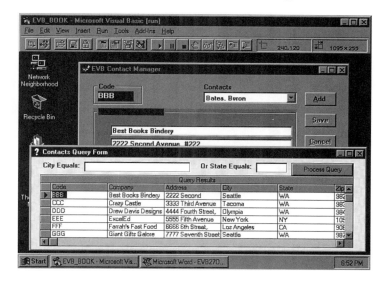

Essential Summary

In this chapter, you were introduced to two new Visual Basic controls, Grid and DBGrid, the standard and data-aware grids. You saw that both may be used to display information in a tabular format, but that DBGrid is designed specifically to display data contained in the Recordset of a bound Data control. You also got a chance to see how Database and Recordset objects may be used to access a database directly from code, with no Data control in sight.

What

You may use Grid controls to perform spreadsheet functions, although this is no longer the most common use, as OLE technology has advanced to the point whereby you may simply "drop" a real spreadsheet object onto your form. The graphic's capabilities of grids may be used to display bitmaps or icons, so a user could pick one for a variety of purposes. The most common use of Grid controls is to create and manipulate tables of information, which is what you've done in this chapter.

Why

By adding two new forms to your EVB_BOOK project and opening them from your Contact Manager program, you were able to display data from your Contacts database in a concise tabular format. To achieve this by using the standard Grid control, it was necessary to write some code; the data-aware DBGrid control, on the other hand, was made functional simply by setting a few of its properties.

How

Querying the Database with SQL

In this short chapter, you'll receive a crash course in *SQL (Structured Query Language)* in order to get your Contact Management program's query form up and running. You'll see how to build and execute SQL statements in code, on the fly, and in relation to the current state of other program elements, such as controls and variables.

What Is SQL?

What *Structured Query Language (SQL)* is a language used in querying, updating, and otherwise managing relational databases. It can be used to retrieve, filter, and sort database information. You can use SQL SELECT statements anywhere a table name, query name, or field name is accepted. For example, you can use an SQL statement in place of a table name in the OpenRecordset method:

```
Dim dbCDLibrary As Database
Dim rsBlues As Recordset
Dim sSQL As String

sSQL = " SELECT * FROM BLUES"                    ' Select all fields from Blues table
Set dbCDLibrary = OpenDataBase("CDisks.MDB")
Set rsBlues = dbCDLibrary.OpenRecordset(sSQL,dbOpenDynaSet) ' Pass the statement.
```

An *SQL statement* is a string expression that begins with a Structured Query Language command, such as SELECT, UPDATE, or DELETE, and may include filtering and sorting clauses such as WHERE and ORDER BY. SQL statements, sometimes referred to as *queries*, are divided into two categories: *select queries* and *action queries*.

A select query asks the database for a set of records matching specified criteria, and receives a Recordset in return; an action query performs a specified operation on a set of records that match specified criteria. In either case, you may use an SQL statement to define which records you want to retrieve or act upon, and how you want them ordered and grouped. Here's an example of a select query that might be used with your Contacts database:

```
SELECT Code, Contact, Phone FROM Contacts WHERE State = 'NY' ORDER BY Code
```

If you wanted to remove all California contacts from your Contacts table, you would use the following action query:

```
DELETE FROM Contacts WHERE State = 'CA'
```

If you use an SQL query to retrieve data, Visual Basic's database engine (the Microsoft Jet engine) creates a dynaset-type or snapshot-type Recordset, never a table-type. Once the Recordset is built, you may further refine it by using one of the Find methods, or set up a loop to step through the records one at a time. There are a number of ways to execute SQL queries, which are summarized here:

- Use an SQL statement as an argument to the OpenRecordset method.
- Set the RecordSource property of a Data control and use the Refresh method.
- Use an existing QueryDef (discussed later in this chapter) in the Data control's RecordSource property.
- Use an SQL action query as an argument to the Execute method.
- Create and execute a custom QueryDef object.
- Execute an existing QueryDef with the OpenRecordset method.

You've already seen an example of the first way, passing the query as an argument to the OpenRecordset method, in the sample code earlier. You'll use the second way later in this chapter. The others require an understanding of the QueryDef object and the Database object's Execute method, which will receive a cursory examination later but will not be employed in this book.

Setting a Data Control's RecordSource Property

You may create a Recordset by setting a Data Control's RecordSource property to an SQL query string. Here are the general steps to follow when using an SQL query with a Data control:

1. Design your SQL query so it returns only the records you want.

2. Enter the query's SQL statement in the Data control's RecordSource property. You can do this at design time or run time. For example, at run time, you can use this code:

```
dtaQuery.RecordSource = "SELECT * FROM Contacts  WHERE State = 'NY'"
```

3. At run time, use the Refresh method to recreate the Recordset:

```
dtaQuery.Refresh
```

Using an Existing QueryDef in the RecordSource Property

A *QueryDef* is a database object created by you that contains an SQL statement for fetching data from one or more tables using a specific filter and sort order. Generally, you can use a QueryDef anywhere you can refer to a table. To retrieve data specified by the QueryDef using the Data control, follow these steps:

1. At design time or run time, enter the name of the QueryDef in the RecordSource property. At run time, your code might look like this:

```
dtaQuery.RecordSource = "NYContacts"          ' You defined NYContacts
earlier.
```

2. At run time, you'll need to rebuild the associated Recordset by calling the Refresh method:

```
dtaQuery.Refresh
```

Using an Action Query and the Execute Method

If you need to execute an action query to perform an operation that doesn't return records—as when you insert, delete, or update records—you can use an SQL statement as an argument to the Execute method. The Execute method can be used with a Data control or an open

Database object as long as the query doesn't return records. For example, to delete all of the records from a table matching specific criteria, you can use the following code:

```
dbContacts.Execute "DELETE FROM Contacts WHERE City = 'Tacoma'"
```

Constructing the SQL Query Statement

When your program is ready to build an SQL statement, use the concatenation operator (&) to join portions of the statement with the contents of controls or variables in your application. In this case, avoid using the plus operator (+), which implies addition of the arguments. If your substituted arguments must be bounded by quotes in the SQL query, your logic and concatenation must provide quotes on both ends of the string. This is why you see the use of single quotes within double quotes in the previous examples.

Caution Beware of arguments passed from the user that contain single or double quotes because these may break the quote pairing in your SQL statement. You can use either single (') or double (") quotes to frame quoted strings, as long as they are used in matched and properly balanced pairs.

For example, the following procedure accepts a Database variable, the name of a column to search, and a comparison operator—such as "=" or "<>"—and inserts them into an SQL query. The code then completes the SQL query based on the arguments, and the contents of a text box named txtSearch then creates a Recordset and places the name of the first selected Contact into a text box named txtFound:

```
Sub FindContact (dbIn as Database, sColumn as String, sOperator as String)
Dim sSQL as String
Dim  rsContacts as Recordset

sSQL = "SELECT * FROM Contacts"                  ' Build the query string...
sSQL = sSQL    & " WHERE " & sColumn & sOperator ' Don't miss space before WHERE
sSQL = sSQL & "'" & txtSearch.Text & "'"         ' Don't forget bounding quotes.

Set rsContacts = dbIn.OpenRecordset(SQL,dbOpenSnapshot)  ' Open the recordset...

If rsContacts.RecordCount <> 0 Then                 ' If you got one...
     txtFound.Text = rsContacts(Contact)           ' show it...
Else
     txtFound.Text = "(Contact Not Found)"          ' else not found
End If

End Sub
```

If you call this procedure with "City" as the column argument, "=" as the operator argument, and txtSearch.Text contained "Kansas City", the SQL statement generated is:

```
SELECT * FROM Contacts WHERE City = 'Kansas City'
```

> **Caution** Watch out for spaces before and after the arguments provided, especially when you break your string into more than one line. Without the space before the WHERE clause, the SQL statement would read SELECT * FROM ContactsWHERE..., which would throw an error.

Why Use SQL?

In many environments, SQL, in one flavor or another, is the only way to retrieve, sort, or in other ways manage a relational database. If your intention is to use Visual Basic to develop anything but the most trivial database applications, you *will* encounter situations where a thorough grasp of SQL is absolutely essential.

How to Query Your Database

In this section, you'll make some modifications to the query form you created in the last chapter. As it stands now, the query form displays all fields and all records contained in the Contacts table. You'll add some code to build various SQL statements in response to the contents of the text boxes txtCity and txtState. To be precise, your user will be able to ask for contacts in particular states or cities.

Adding Code

You haven't opened your code module EVB_CODE for a while. Do so now and add a couple of useful MousePointer constants to its general declarations. You'll need these in the following procedure, as well as in others in the remainder of this book. Here's the modified listing:

```
'Global Variables...
Global sPhrase As String

'Global constants...
Global Const CHECKED = 1            'For check boxes
Global Const RED = 4
Global Const GREEN = 2              'QBColor Constants
Global Const BLUE = 1

Global Const HOURGLASS = 11         ' MousePointer constants..
Global Const NORMAL = 0
```

Now here's what happens when your query form's Process Query button is clicked:

```
Private Sub cmdQuery_Click()
MousePointer = HOURGLASS                 ' Some queries may take a while,
                                         ' so it's a good idea to put up the
                                         ' the hourglass.
Dim SQLString As String, SQLWhat As String, SQLWhere As String   ' To build the
➡final query string
```

Part V

```
Dim bCity As Boolean, bState As Boolean      ' Anything in txtState, txtCity?
Dim iRecords As Integer                      ' Number of records returned.

SQLWhat = "Select * From Contacts "          ' Select WHAT clause

bCity = IIf(txtCity <> "", True, False)      ' True, if not empty...
bState = IIf(txtState <> "", True, False)

                                             ' Now build the WHERE clause
If bCity And bState Then                      ' Something in both...

   SQLWhere = "Where City = '" & txtCity & "' Or State = '" & txtState & "'"

     ElseIf bCity And Not bState Then         ' City but no State
        SQLWhere = "Where City = '" & txtCity & "'"

     ElseIf bState And Not bCity Then         ' State, but no City...
        SQLWhere = "Where State = '" & txtState & "'"
End If                                        ' If neither, WHERE clause
                                             ' will be empty.

SQLString = SQLWhat & SQLWhere               ' Add WHAT to WHERE

dtaQuery.RecordSource = SQLString            ' Set the RecordSource
dtaQuery.Refresh                             ' and build the new Recordset.

iRecords = dtaQuery.Recordset.RecordCount    ' See how many records...
                                             ' and Set the Grid's caption.
DBQueryGrid.Caption = CStr(iRecords) & " Record(s) Match Your Conditions"

MousePointer = NORMAL                        ' Pointer back to normal.
End Sub
```

Time to test. Be sure to try several City/State combinations. In Figure 28.1, you see the Recordset generated for contacts in Los Angeles or anywhere in New York state:

Figure 28.1.
*The Contact Manager
Query form.*

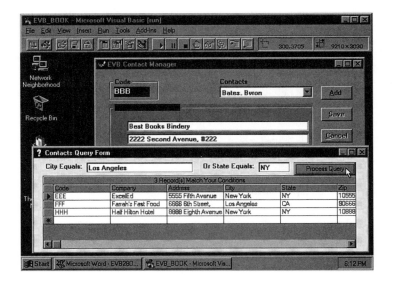

Essential Summary

In this chapter, you were dunked, ever so briefly, into the pool of SQL programming. You learned that Structured Query Language (SQL) is used in querying, ordering, and otherwise caressing the information stored in relational databases.

What

A solid grounding in the art and intricacies of SQL programming is a requirement if you intend to use Visual Basic to develop commercially-viable database applications—whether for the desktop, LAN, WAN, or Client/Server environments.

Why

You added code to your Contact Manager's Query form that allows the user to retrieve records that meet very specific City/State conditions. In the process, you learned how to build and execute SQL statements in code that took into consideration the current state of your program's controls and variables.

How

Designing and Printing Reports

In this chapter, you'll work with the Crystal Reports add-in program. You'll get a look at how database reports are created, and see that using the Crystal Reports Report Designer is very similar to many other Windows-based report formatting systems. Finally, you'll see how to print your reports from within Visual Basic by dropping the Crystal Reports control onto your form and manipulating its properties at run time.

The Crystal Reports Add-In

What You can think of the Crystal Reports add-in as containing two separate elements: The Crystal Reports program and the CrystalReport custom control. Used together, these two elements give you the ability to generate custom reports, transparently, via your Visual Basic application.

The Crystal Reports program is a powerful Windows report writer that you can use to design a nearly endless variety of custom reports. As you'll see, the program comes with a complete set of intuitive design tools that allow for dragging and dropping of report elements such as fields and other variables, grouping and subtotaling, and simple font formatting of literal as well as variable text. Using Crystal Reports, you can easily design the report or reports you want your users to be able to run from your application.

The CrystalReport custom control allows you to access the report-writing capabilities of the Crystal Reports add-in quickly and easily by simply including the control in your Visual Basic project. The CrystalReport custom control is a set of tools that makes it easy for you to build the connection between your application and the print engine. Using these tools, you can have your application generating reports in a very short time. The CrystalReport custom control is visible at design time but invisible at run time. When you place the control on your form and set the properties, you add advanced reporting functionality to your application without writing a lot of additional code.

You add the CrystalReport custom control to your project in the same way you've added other controls, through the Custom Controls dialog box. Here are the steps:

1. Open the Custom Controls dialog box by selecting **C**ustom Controls from the Tools menu, or use the shortcut key combination, Ctrl+T.
2. In the scrollable list box, locate Crystal Report Control and check it.
3. Close the dialog box, and the control will be added to your Toolbox.
4. When you want to add Crystal Reports capabilities to your program, double-click the control, or click it and place the control in the usual manner. The control will be added to the current form but will be invisible at run time.

Using the CrystalReport Custom Control

Once you have the CrystalReport custom control object on your form, you build the connection between your application and the reports you've designed by setting the object's properties in the usual way; that is, via the control's Properties list. The Properties you may specify include:

ReportFileName	A string expression indicating the name of the report you want to print in response to an application event.
Destination	The report's destination: window =0, file = 1, or printer = 2.
CopiesToPrinter	If your report is going to the printer, the number of copies you want to print.
PrintFileName	The filename, if you're printing to disk.

You may also set many properties relating to the appearance, size, and position of the report window, should you decide to print to the screen. Here are the related properties:

WindowBorderStyle	An integer expression between 0 and 3, corresponding to None, Fixed Single, Sizable, and Fixed Double.
WindowControlBox	True or False, if you want one or not.
WindowMaxButton	True or False.
WindowMinButton	True or False.
WindowTitle	A string expression to be displayed in the report window's title bar.
WindowTop	Set the Y position of window in pixels.
WindowLeft	Set the X position of window in pixels.
WindowHeight	Set the height of the report window in pixels.
WindowWidth	Set the width of the report window in pixels.

Why Print Reports?

Attractive and readable printed output is an indispensable part of any database program. The Crystal Reports Report Designer and Control are therefore powerful additions to the Visual Basic IDE (Integrated Development Environment). Learning to use them efficiently will save you uncountable hours of development time.

Why

How to Use Crystal Reports

You start the Crystal Reports Report Designer by selecting **R**eport Designer from Visual Basic's **A**dd-Ins menu. Do so now. At this point, you may want to register the program or bypass an advertisement for the latest version of Crystal Reports. Click the Proceed button to continue.

How

The Crystal Reports design area includes a Toolbar and text formatting Ribbon similar to those seen in many word processing and spreadsheet programs. (In Crystal Reports, ToolTips are displayed at the bottom of the main window.) The right side of the Toolbar shows ten buttons that pertain to the report design process. These ten tools are described here:

Insert a Database Field	Displays a dialog box containing fields from the attached database table; you may select a field and place it into your report template.
Insert a Text Field	Opens a dialog box into which you may type text for placement in your report.
Insert a Formula Field	Opens a dialog box into which you enter the name of

your formula field. Clicking OK opens another window into which you type your formula directly or build it by selecting Field, Function, and Operator elements. Upon checking and clicking the Accept button, you may place the formula field anywhere on your report.

Insert a Summary Field	Once you've placed a database field in the details section of your report template, you may select it and press this button to create a related summary field that might report the count, minimum, or maximum. If the database field you've selected is numeric, it may also be totaled or averaged.
Insert A Graphic Item	Opens a dialog box from which you may select a graphic item to be included in your report.
Insert An OLE Object	Opens the Insert Object dialog box from which you may select an OLE object to be included in your report.
Draw A Line	The mouse pointer becomes a "pencil" with which you may draw a line anywhere on your report. Once you've drawn the line, you may right-click it to adjust its format, including color, width, and style.
Draw A Box	The mouse pointer becomes a "pencil" with which you may draw a rectangle anywhere on your report. Once you've drawn the box, you may right-click it to adjust its format, including fill color, border color, width, and style.
Sort The Report	Opens the Record Sort Order dialog box from which you may select the field or fields to sort by in ascending or descending order.
Set Record Selection Criteria	Opens the Record Selection Formula edit box, which may be used to build a selection formula such as Contacts.City = "Seattle".

Creating a New Report

It's time to design a simple report that will list the Contacts in your database. To begin a new report, select **New** from the **File** Menu, then select **Report** (or simply click the New Report button on the Toolbar). This will display the New Report dialog box. Make sure you're creating a new Report from a Data file, then click OK. In the Choose Database File window, locate Contacts.MDB, then click Open.

A new report design template consisting of three bands will now be visible, along with the Insert Database Field dialog box. The three bands are *Page header, Details*, and *Page footer*. The template's bands represent three areas of your report: the page header, record detail, and page footer. Anything entered into the page header or page footer bands will be repeated at the top or bottom of every page in the report. Headers are typically used to display report descriptions, column labels, and print dates. Footers may be used to display page numbers, for example, or specially formatted group and/or report summary fields.

The Details band contains the field information you want printed for every record in the attached database table. It is here that you will place the Code, Company, Contact, and Phone fields from the Contacts table. To do so, select the fields in the Insert Database Field dialog box and click Insert (or just double-click the field names). This will allow you to drag the field to the desired location. Take a look at Figure 29.1 to get an idea of where you're heading.

Figure 29.1.
Crystal Reports designer:
Design mode.

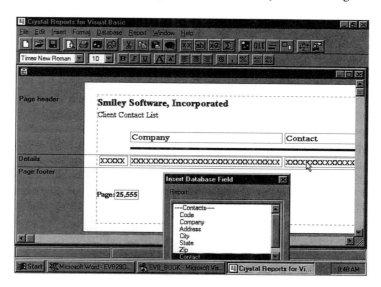

As you place the fields, side by side, in the Details section, Crystal Reports places the corresponding field name above each field in the Page header area. Once all four fields are in place, you'll add a report title, make some cosmetic adjustments to the field names, and insert some special fields for printing page numbers and the current date.

Feel free to add a title to the upper-left corner of the page, like the one displayed in Figure 29.1. You place literal text on your report just by placing the I-Beam where you want it and typing; or you may use the Insert Text Field button as described earlier. Text may be selected and formatted using the format Ribbon. Notice that each time you press Enter within the header band, a new line is added. This is a simple way to increase the number of lines available in the header. You may remove unwanted lines by selecting them and pressing Delete.

> **Tip** The advantage of inserting literal text as a field is that it may be easily selected for formatting, or relocated by dragging and dropping. The disadvantage is that all text within the field must be formatted the same; that is, you can't mix font styles and sizes.

Notice that Crystal Reports displays the column headers in a kind of pathetic underlined format. You may select all of the headers at once (hold Shift and click them), then click the Underline button on the formatting ribbon to remove the underlining. Now drag the column headers up a line, leaving a space below them. While the headers are still selected, click the Bold button and bump the Font Size up to 12, to give them a little substance. The last adjustment to the column labels will be to draw a thick underline across the page beneath them. Click the Draw Line button and draw the line, then right-click it to adjust its width. Again, refer to Figure 29.1.

The last step in your report design will be to add two special fields. From the Insert menu, select Special Field and then Print Date Field, and place the field in the upper-right corner of the page header. Add the caption "Run Date:" to the left of the date field. Now, in a similar manner, add a page number to the page footer band.

You may see what your report looks like at any time during the design phase by printing it to screen or paper. Click the Print Preview button on the Toolbar and examine your new report. Refer to Figure 29.2 for a comparison.

Figure 29.2.
Crystal Reports Design mode: Report Preview.

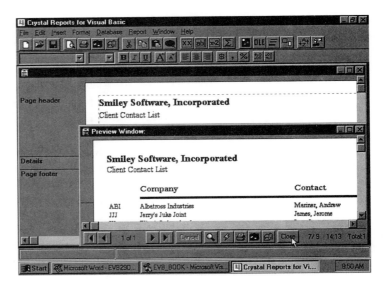

That's it for the design phase. Save your report as Contacts, using the suggested file extension .RPT, then exit the Report Designer. In the next section, you'll create code to print your new report to a custom report window, from where the user may send it to the printer, if he or she chooses.

Adding Code

Before adding code to access your new report, you'll need to add the Crystal Reports Custom Control to your Contact Manager form. Open that form, frmContacts, in Design mode, then double-click the Crystal Reports Control in the Visual Basic Toolbox. This will install the control on the form. (Remember, it will be invisible at run time, so it doesn't matter where it's placed on the form.) In this case, you'll accept the default name of the control, CrystalReport1. All other properties will be set at run time, in the Report button's Click procedure, which is listed and annotated here:

```
Private Sub cmdReport_Click()

Dim V_INCH, H_INCH As Long              ' Because the CR control expects pixels,
                                        ' not twips, we'll need to do a little
                                        ' conversion...

H_INCH = 1440 / Screen.TwipsPerPixelX   ' Divide 1440 twips by screen twips per
V_INCH = 1440 / Screen.TwipsPerPixelY   ' pixel to get an inch worth of pixels...

CrystalReport1.Destination = 0          ' Send to report window....

CrystalReport1.ReportFileName = "C:\VB40\SAMS\CONTACTS.RPT"   ' Report file...

CrystalReport1.WindowTitle = "Contact Manager: List Of Current Contacts" ' Win
Title

CrystalReport1.WindowTop = 2.25 * V_INCH   ' Position window 2.25 inches from top
CrystalReport1.WindowLeft = 0.1 * H_INCH   ' of screen, a tenth of an inch to the
                                           ' left.

CrystalReport1.WindowHeight = 2.4 * V_INCH    ' Size it 2.4 inches high...
CrystalReport1.WindowWidth = 6.5 * H_INCH     ' and 6.5 inches wide...

CrystalReport1.Action = 1                     ' Set Action To 1 To Print

End Sub
```

You complicated things here a little by deciding to modify the default window's size and position. But it wasn't that complicated, really, and you got a chance to see how and why the Screen object's TwipsPerPixel properties are used.

That's all there is to it. Run your program and click the Reports button. Your screen should look something like Figure 29.3.

Figure 29.3.
The Contact Manager
Report Window.

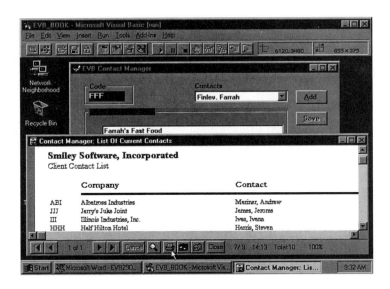

Essential Summary

What
In this chapter, you were introduced to the Crystal Reports Report Designer and Custom Control. You saw that producing database reports is a two-step process, first defining the report format then printing the report itself in response to a programming event.

Why
Until a totally paperless and inkless environment is achieved, printed output will be required of your database systems and other programs. The Crystal Reports Control and Report Designer make the process of designing and producing such output relatively easy and efficient.

How
You used the Crystal Reports program to design a simple list of the Contacts contained in your database. You added the Crystal Reports Control to your Contact Manager form, which, through run time manipulation of its properties, allowed you to generate and send the report to a customized window, from where it might be examined and printed.

PART VI

Error Handling and Debugging

Simple Error-Handling Techniques

In this chapter, you'll acquire an understanding of the types of errors you're likely to encounter in your Visual Basic programming efforts, as well as the types of errors your users may encounter. You'll learn the difference between *design-time errors*, *run-time errors*, and *logic errors* or *bugs*. You'll see how Visual Basic's On Error GoTo and Resume statements, along with the Err() and Error$() functions, may be used to create simple error-handling routines.

What Are Errors?

What Even the best programmers make errors. In fact, the longer and more complex a program is, the more likely it is to produce errors. Errors come in several different types: *design-time errors*, which occur when you mistype a command or leave out an expected phrase or argument; *run-time errors*, which are caused by circumstances beyond the program's control, such as a drive door left open, or a file not found; and *logic errors* or *bugs*, which cause your program to produce incorrect or unexpected results.

Visual Basic itself handles the first type, design-time errors, by detecting syntax problems as you enter them, refusing to run until they are fixed. When design-time errors are encountered, Visual Basic even offers its assistance in the form of explanations and Help messages. The other two types, run-time errors and bugs, must be fixed by you, the programmer. Handling run-time errors is the subject of this chapter and Chapter 31. Logic errors are dealt with in Chapters 32 and 33, where you'll see how to use the Visual Basic Debugger.

In Visual Basic, run-time errors are referred to as *trappable errors;* that is, Visual Basic recognizes that an error has occurred and enables you to trap it and take some corrective action. If you don't deal with trappable errors in your code, any run-time error that occurs will be fatal; that is, Visual Basic will simply display a curt and probably meaningless error message to your user, then crash your program. Not very nice.

> **Note** If you're running your program from the Visual Basic development environment and a run-time error occurs, a dialog box displays the error and gives you a chance to end the program and go right to the Debugger.

What The way to deal with trappable errors is to use Visual Basic's On Error GoTo statement. Here's the general syntax:

```
On Error GoTo label
```

Here, *label* is another location in the current procedure. A *label* is a way of identifying the beginning of a block of code; it is simply a word on a line by itself, followed by a colon (:). Assuming you have a form containing a button called cmdTest, here's how error trapping would be initiated for that button's Click event:

```
Private Sub cmdTest_Click()

On Error GoTo HandleIt                      ' If there's an error, jump to HandleIt..

MsgBox "I'm Clicked..."

Exit Sub

HandleIt:                                   ' Here's the error handler..
        MsgBox "Whoops! There's an error!"
        Resume
End Sub
```

Now, if Visual Basic throws a trappable error during this procedure, control will branch to the specified label—in this case, HandleIt. So the general idea is to execute the On Error GoTo statement first, to set up your error-handling routine. In the preceding lines, please notice that you exit from the Sub procedure before reaching the HandleIt label, so that you do not inadvertently execute the error-handling code.

Because the code in an error-handling routine is in the same procedure where the error occurs, the error code shares all the variables visible to the rest of the procedure. This means that your error routine will have access to variables that may be of value in fixing the error.

The Resume statement lets you retry the operation that caused the error. This may or may not be what you want, depending on the nature of the error. In fact, if the error was due to something the user can do nothing about, the previous Resume statement could result in an infinite loop.

What

The Resume statement may also be used to return control to the statement immediately following the one that caused the error (Resume Next), or to branch to another line or label elsewhere in the procedure (Resume label). If you use a Resume statement anywhere except in an error-handling routine, an error occurs.

> **Caution** When an error-handling routine is active and the end of a procedure is encountered before a Resume statement is encountered, an error occurs because a logic error is assumed to have been made inadvertently. However, if an Exit Sub or Exit Function statement is encountered while an error handler is active, no error occurs because it is considered a deliberate redirection of flow.

A user-friendly error handler will display the error number and description, and offer some choices on how to proceed after the error is encountered. The Err() and Error$() functions are used to report the error number and the message associated with it. Err() returns the Visual Basic error number associated with the current error condition. The Error$() function takes an error number as its argument and returns a string description of the error. Both are used in the error handler you'll see later.

What

The following listing shows an enhanced error-handling routine that puts up a message box containing information about the error, as well as the Abort, Retry, and Ignore Buttons. If, for example, the error is due to a drive door being open, the user may simply close the door and click the Retry button to try the operation again. If the problem is not so easily resolved, the user may elect to Abort or Ignore.

```
Private Sub cmdTest_Click()

On Error GoTo  HandleIt            ' If there's an error, jump to HandleIt..

MsgBox "I'm Clicked..."

Exit Sub

HandleIt:                          ' Here's the error handler..

Dim iResponse As Integer           ' Variable to get user's response

Dim sMsg As String, sTitle As String  ' To build error message box...
Dim iType As Integer
```

```
sMsg = Error$(Err)                          ' Show the error message...
iType = vbCritical + vbAbortRetryIgnore     ' Use Abort, Retry, Ignore Buttons...
sTitle = "Error Number " & CStr(Err) & "!" ' Display error number in title bar...

iResponse = MsgBox (sMsg,iType, sTitle)     ' Display and get response...

Select Case iResponse

    Case vbAbort                            ' Abort means exit sub...
    Exit Sub

    Case vbRetry                            ' Retry means Resume...
    Resume                                  ' with the line that caused the error

    Case vbIgnore                           ' Ignore means skip the line
    Resume Next                             ' that caused the error and try
                                            ' the next one.

End Select

End Sub
```

You'll put this error-handling routine to real use later in this chapter. In the meantime, Table 30.1 displays the commonly encountered Visual Basic error numbers and their meanings. This table will be useful in this chapter and in Chapter 31 where you'll write a more powerful, custom error-handling routine.

Table 30.1. Common Visual Basic run-time errors.

Error Number	Description
3	Return without GoSub
5	Invalid procedure call
6	Overflow
7	Out of memory
9	Subscript out of range
10	This array is fixed or temporarily locked
11	Division by zero
13	Type mismatch
14	Out of string space
16	Expression Too Complex
17	Can't perform requested operation
18	User interrupt occurred
19	No Resume
20	Resume without error
28	Out of stack space
35	Sub, Function, or Property not defined

Error Number	Description
47	Too many DLL application clients
48	Error in loading DLL
49	Bad DLL calling convention
51	Internal error
52	Bad file name or number
53	File not found
54	Bad file mode
55	File already open
57	Device I/O error
58	File already exists
59	Bad record length
61	Disk full
62	Input past end of file
63	Bad record number
64	Bad file name
65	File previously loaded
66	Duplicate procedure definition
67	Too many files
68	Device unavailable
70	Permission denied
71	Disk not ready
72	Disk-media error
74	Can't rename with different drive
75	Path/File access error
76	Path not found
91	Object variable or With block variable not set
92	For loop not initialized
93	Invalid pattern string
94	Invalid use of Null
427	Object is not the Printer object
428	Object is not a control
429	Object is not a form

continues

Table 30.1. continued

Error Number	Description
430	There is no currently active control
431	There is no currently active form
452	Invalid ordinal
453	Specified DLL function not found
456	Get and Put cannot be used with arrays in Variants
457	This key is already associated with an element of this collection
460	Invalid Clipboard format
461	Specified format doesn't match format of data
480	Can't create AutoRedraw image
481	Invalid picture
482	Printer error
483	Printer driver does not support specified property
484	Problem getting printer information
485	Invalid picture type
520	Can't empty Clipboard
521	Can't open Clipboard

Why Error Handling Is Important

You must be prepared to handle run-time errors whenever your program will come into contact with something outside itself—the printer, a disk drive, another program via a DDE or OLE link, the Windows Clipboard—whenever there is some chance that the outside entity will be contacted incorrectly, respond too slowly, or be called upon after it has been killed, deleted, or otherwise removed from existence. What you want to avoid is generating an error that crashes your program, or worse, causes the computer to hang or lock up and become unresponsive, requiring the system to be powered down. To a programmer, this is a catastrophic and embarrassing collapse of craft.

Error handling provides a way for your program to deal with failed attempts. Without an error handler specifying what you want done in the event of a bad disk, insufficient memory, or an overflow or internal error, Visual Basic will completely shut down your program. That's an over-reactive, some might even say rude, way to tell your user that they've mistyped a filename.

How to Include Simple Error Handling

You already have a form in your EVB_BOOK project that contains an error just waiting to happen. Open the project and change the startup form to frmViewer. Open frmViewer and, temporarily, comment out the following line in its Unload event:

```
Private Sub Form_Unload(Cancel As Integer)
' frmEVBMain.mnuViewer.Checked = False      ' Comment out this line....
End Sub
```

This is necessary if you're going to use the form as a stand-alone startup form since frmMain won't be available to have its menu items checked or unchecked. The real potential for error in the Viewer program is when the user tries to access a floppy drive that is not closed or contains an unformatted or otherwise unreadable disk. To verify that this is a problem, open a floppy drive and then run the program and try to access it. You'll get an abrupt error message, and the program will end.

Adding Error-Handling Code

Here's what Drive1's Change event should look like once the preceding error-handling routine has been adjusted to work with it:

```
Private Sub Drive1_Change()
On Error GoTo DriveChangeError             ' If there's an error, jump to handler....

Dir1.Path = Drive1.Drive                   ' Here's the proc code...
Exit Sub                                   ' Don't forget this...

DriveChangeError:                          ' Here's the error handler..

Dim iResponse As Integer                   ' Variable to get user's response

Dim sMsg As String, sTitle As String       ' To build error message box...
Dim iType As Integer

sMsg = Error$(Err)                         ' Show the error message...
iType = vbCritical + vbAbortRetryIgnore    ' Use Abort, Retry, Ignore Buttons...
sTitle = "Error Number " & CStr(Err) & "!" ' Display error number in title bar...

iResponse = MsgBox(sMsg, iType, sTitle)    ' Display and get response...

Select Case iResponse                      ' Make decision...based on response

    Case vbAbort                           ' Abort means exit sub...
    Exit Sub

    Case vbRetry                           ' Retry means Resume...
    Resume                                 ' with the line that caused the error

    Case vbIgnore                          ' Ignore means skip the line
    Resume Next                            ' that caused the error and try
                                           ' the next one.
End Select
End Sub
```

It's time to test your new error handler. Run the program and force an error by deliberately accessing an empty drive. Here, in Figure 30.1, is a sample session.

Figure 30.1.
The error handler in action.

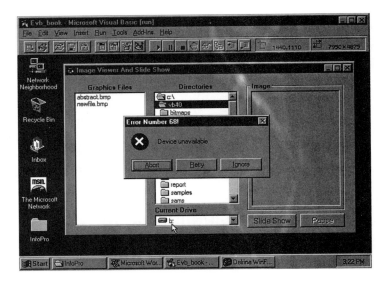

This routine will efficiently trap any run-time errors that might occur during the Drive1_Change event, allowing the program to recover and continue normally. If an error occurs in another procedure, however, this error handler would, obviously, have no effect. In the next chapter, you'll see how to create a generic, custom error handler that may be called from any procedure.

Essential Summary

What

In this chapter, you gained an understanding of the types of errors you must deal with in programming with Visual Basic. You learned the difference between design-time errors, run-time errors, and logic errors or *bugs*. You saw how to use On Error GoTo, Resume, Err(), and Error$() in handling run-time errors.

Why

Things go wrong. Screws fall out all the time. The world is an imperfect place. Any time your program comes into contact with the world outside itself, it must be able to handle run-time errors in a graceful and efficient, if not friendly, manner. Without good error handling, Visual Basic will simply shut down your program whenever something unexpected occurs.

How

You created a simple error-handling routine that displays an error message and number, and presents to the user a choice of actions he or she may make in response to the current error condition. You adapted this routine to work with the Image View program you created in Chapter 12, where it now traps any errors generated during an attempt to access your system drives.

A Custom Error-Handling Procedure

In this chapter, you'll learn what a custom error handler is and why it can be an invaluable addition to your Toolbox of reusable Visual Basic code. You'll then create your own custom error-handling procedure which may be added to any project and called from any procedure in any form or code module. You'll also add a new form to your EVB_BOOK project which will be used to thoroughly test your new ErrorHandler() function.

What Is a Custom Error Handler?

What A *custom error handler* is an error handler designed to handle a wide variety of errors but still provide the user with as much error-specific information as possible. A good custom error handler will allow the user a viable choice of alternative actions, as determined by the nature of the current error. More important, it should be flexible enough to behave serviceably, no matter what part of a program calls it into action.

Why Create a Custom Error Handler?

Why Since efficient error handling is a requirement of any commercially viable computer program, having a custom error-handler routine on hand—one that can be plugged into a project and used with only minor adjustments, if any—can be a real time and aggravation saver.

How to Create a Custom Error Handler

How In this section, you'll create a custom error handler you can call from any procedure or function. The handler itself will be a function that returns one of three values equal to the built-in Visual Basic constants vbAbort, vbRetry, or vbIgnore, depending on what the user wants to do in response to a particular error condition.

You'll want your custom error handler to be available throughout your application. This means that it must be stored in a standard code module, such as EVB_CODE. Open EVB_CODE and create a new function called `ErrorHandler()`. Here's the listing and annotation:

```
Function ErrorHandler(ErrorIn As Integer) As Integer   ' Returns response as integer

Dim sMsg As String                           ' Variables for creating error
Dim iType As Integer                         ' message dialog box.
Dim sTitle As String

Dim NL As String                             ' New line characters
NL = Chr$(13) & Chr$(10)

iType = vbCritical + vbAbortRetryIgnore      ' Use Critical icon, and Abort,
                                             ' Retry, Ignore buttons.

Select Case ErrorIn                          ' Evaluate the error...

Case 1 To 6, 9 To 11, 13 To 49, 59, 90, 94   ' It's a program error...

    sTitle = "Programming Error!"            ' Message box title...

    sMsg = "An unexpected error condition has occurred." & NL & NL   ' Build the
➥message
    sMsg = sMsg & "Error Number: " & CStr(ErrorIn)
    sMsg = sMsg & ", " & Error$(ErrorIn) & NL & NL
    sMsg = sMsg & "Please write down the number and message " & NL
    sMsg = sMsg & "then call Smiley Software at 1-800-555-1212 " & NL
    sMsg = sMsg & "to report the error to our support personnel."

    MsgBox sMsg, vbInformation, sTitle        ' Display the message, no choice
                                              ' of buttons in this case...

    ErrorHandler = vbAbort                    ' Return vbAbort.
```

```
    Case 7                                      ' Out of Memory...

        sTitle = "Out Of Memory Error!"         ' Set the title...and build message..
        sMsg = "Not enough memory to complete the operation!" & NL
        sMsg = sMsg & "Save your work! Then close any open "
        sMsg = sMsg & "programs and try again."

        MsgBox sMsg, vbInformation, sTitle       ' Display message, no choices.
        ErrorHandler = vbAbort                         ' Return vbAbort

    Case 51                                      ' Internal error...
        sTitle = "Internal System Error!"
        sMsg = "Report error to System Administrator..."
        MsgBox sMsg, vbInformation, sTitle
        ErrorHandler = vbAbort

    Case 52 To 56, 58, 60, 62 To 66, 69 To 70, 73 To 76        ' File Errors...

        sMsg = Error$(ErrorIn)                    ' Message is error message...

        sTitle = "System File Error Number " & CStr(Err) & "!"   ' Title displays error
    ➡number...

        ErrorHandler = MsgBox(sMsg, iType, sTitle)        ' Return user's choice of
                                                          ' Abort, Retry, Ignore

    Case 61                                      ' Disk Full..

        sMsg = "Disk Is Full!" & NL & NL         ' Build message...
        sMsg = sMsg & "Change disks or delete " & NL
        sMsg = sMsg & "unwanted files!"

        sTitle = "System Disk Error!"            ' Set dialog box title...

        ErrorHandler = MsgBox(sMsg, iType, sTitle)        ' Return user's choice...


    Case 57, 68, 71 To 72                        ' Disk Not Ready Errors...

        sMsg = "Disk Not Ready Or Unavailable!" & NL & NL  ' Build message...
        sMsg = sMsg & "Check the disk before continuing."

        sTitle = "System Disk Error!"            ' Set title....
        ErrorHandler = MsgBox(sMsg, iType, sTitle)        ' Return choice...

    Case 67                                      ' Too many files open...

        sMsg = "Not enough file handles to complete the operation! " & NL ' Build Msg...
        sMsg = sMsg & "Increase the FILES = number in your config.sys file."

        sTitle = "File Handles Error!"           ' Set title...

        MsgBox sMsg, vbInformation, sTitle       ' Display message, with no
        ErrorHandler = vbAbort                   '  choice this time.

    Case 281 To 297                              ' DDE Errors
```

```
        sMsg = Error$(ErrorIn)                    ' Message, no choices...
        sTitle = "System DDE Error!"

        MsgBox sMsg, vbInformation, sTitle
        ErrorHandler = vbAbort

    Case 340 To 344                               ' Control Array Errors

        sMsg = Error$(ErrorIn)                    ' Message, no choices..
        sTitle = "Control Array Error!"

        MsgBox sMsg, vbInformation, sTitle
        ErrorHandler = vbAbort

    Case Else                                     ' Catch the rest...
                                                  ' and report to programmers...

        sTitle = "General Error Condition!"       ' Message box title...

        sMsg = "An unexpected error condition has occurred." & NL & NL   ' Message...
        sMsg = sMsg & "Error Number: " & CStr(ErrorIn)
        sMsg = sMsg & ", " & Error$(ErrorIn) & NL & NL
        sMsg = sMsg & "Please write down the number and message " & NL
        sMsg = sMsg & "then call Smiley Software at 1-800-555-1212 " & NL
        sMsg = sMsg & "to report the error to our support personnel."

        MsgBox sMsg, vbInformation, sTitle        ' Info only, no choices...
        ErrorHandler = vbAbort                    ' Return abort...
End Select
End Function
```

The general idea here is to evaluate whatever error is coming into the function, then decide whether or not the user will be able to do anything about it. If it's a disk access or filename error, for example, the user should have a chance to correct the problem and retry the operation, if he or she chooses. On the other hand, if a program error is involved, the operation cannot be completed, so a Telephone Support Line message is displayed, and the procedure that caused the error is gracefully exited. Obviously, this function could be expanded to include many more specific errors and error-specific messages. There are currently hundreds of predefined error numbers in Visual Basic, with room to grow; in fact, the first 1,000 numbers are reserved for future use by Visual Basic.

Now you'll add a new form to your project, frmErrorTest, which will be used to thoroughly test your custom error handler. For the purposes of testing, you'll want to set frmErrorTest as the startup form. The design-time specifications appear in Table 31.1.

Table 31.1. Design-time settings—the Error Testing form.

Visual Basic Object	Property	Design-Time Setting
Form	Name	frmErrorTest
	Caption	EVB Error-Handler Test
Form		

Visual Basic Object	Property	Design-Time Setting
Frame	Name	fraErrors
	Caption	Errors To Test For
Option Buttons	Name, Caption	optProgram, Programming
	Name, Caption	optMemory, Memory
	Name, Caption	optInternal, Internal
	Name, Caption	optFile, File
	Name, Caption	optDisk, Disk Full
	Name, Caption	optNotReady, Disk Not
Ready		
	Name, Caption	optHandles, File Handles
	Name, Caption	optRandom, Random
Command Button	Name	cmdTest
	Caption	&Test
	Default	True
Command Button	Name	cmdCancel
	Caption	&Cancel
	Cancel	True

Complete the visual design of this form, using Figure 31.1 as a guide. Don't forget to draw the frame first, then draw each option button separately, to ensure the proper containership. Figure 31.1 shows what the form looks like in Design mode.

Figure 31.1.
Design mode: the Error Testing form.

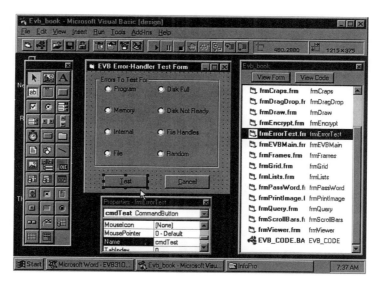

Adding Code

The purpose of the error testing program is to generate random error numbers within the ranges specified for the selected error group. That random number is used, along with Visual Basic's Error statement, to deliberately cause an error, which will be passed along to your ErrorHandler() function. In this way, you may thoroughly evaluate the effectiveness of your custom error handler.

Although the ErrorHandler() function is defined in the standard code module EVB_CODE, the following code will be local to the error testing form. Make sure frmErrorTest is open in Design mode.

Here's frmErrorTest's Load event:

```
Private Sub Form_Load()
Randomize                                ' Seed VB's random number generator
optProgram = True                        ' Set the first option button ON
End Sub
```

You'll need a random error generator which will return an error number within the range specified by the currently selected option button. Which button is selected will be determined outside the RandomError() function, as you'll see, and will be passed in as an integer value between 1 and 8. The RandomError() function contains quite a few lines, but should require little explanation. Enter the following code in the form's general declarations section (don't forget to copy and paste wherever possible):

```
Function RandomError(iSeed As Integer) As Integer    ' Receives Integer...and...
                                                     ' returns an error number integer
Dim iError, iGroup As Integer

Select Case iSeed                        ' iSeed is 1-8, depending on which
    Case 1                               ' group of errors is selected...

        iGroup = Int(Rnd * 6) + 1        ' There are six ranges of program
                                         ' errors, so you'll randomly select
                                         ' one of six

        Select Case iGroup               ' Then pick a number from the
            Case 1                       ' the randomly selected range...
                iError = Int(Rnd * 6) + 1    ' to set iError's value..
            Case 2
                iError = Int(Rnd * 2) + 9
            Case 3
                iError = Int(Rnd * 36) + 13
            Case 4
                iError = 59
            Case 5
                iError = 90
            Case 6
                iError = 94
        End Select

    Case 2                               ' Memory error is 7
        iError = 7
```

```
    Case 3                                  ' Internal error is 51
        iError = 51

    Case 4
        iGroup = Int(Rnd * 4) + 1           ' For ranges of File errors...so pick
                                            ' one randomly.

        Select Case iGroup                  ' Then pick an error from the
            Case 1                          ' random group...
                iError = Int(Rnd * 4) + 52
            Case 2
                iError = Int(Rnd * 8) + 58
            Case 3
                iError = Int(Rnd * 1) + 69
            Case 4
                iError = Int(Rnd * 3) + 73
        End Select

    Case 5                                  ' Disk full...
        iError = 61

    Case 6
        iGroup = Int(Rnd * 4) + 1           ' Four different
                                            ' Disk Not Ready errors.
        Select Case iGroup
            Case 1
                iError = 57
            Case 2
                iError = 68
            Case 3
                iError = 71
            Case 4
                iError = 72
        End Select

    Case 7                                  ' Too many files...
        iError = 67

    Case 8                                  ' Random error 1 - 500
        iError = (Rnd * 499) + 1
End Select

RandomError = iError                        ' Don't forget to return the
                                            ' error value!
End Function
```

Now to put your `ErrorHandler()` and `RandomError()` functions to the test, literally, you'll add the following code to cmdTest's `Click` event:

```
Private Sub cmdTest_Click()
Dim iWhich As Integer                       ' Which option button is selected
On Error GoTo LocalHandler                  ' Enable error trapping...

iWhich = IIf(optProgram, 1, iWhich)         ' iWhich will be 1 - 8...
iWhich = IIf(optMemory, 2, iWhich)
iWhich = IIf(optInternal, 3, iWhich)
iWhich = IIf(optFile, 4, iWhich)
```

```
iWhich = IIf(optDisk, 5, iWhich)
iWhich = IIf(optNotReady, 6, iWhich)
iWhich = IIf(optHandles, 7, iWhich)
iWhich = IIf(optRandom, 8, iWhich)


iWhich = RandomError(iWhich)                 ' Now iWhich becomes random
                                             ' error number...

Error iWhich                                 ' Force the error...
                                             ' (You'll return here on Retry)

MsgBox "Error Ignored", vbInformation, "Error Testing Message"     ' Here, on
Ignore

Exit Sub                                     ' Don't forget this...

LocalHandler:                                ' Here's local handler...
Dim iResponse As Integer

iResponse = ErrorHandler(Err)                ' Which calls custom handler
                                             ' and stores user response...

Select Case iResponse                        ' Process the response....

    Case vbAbort                             ' Exit if abort...
        Exit Sub

    Case vbRetry                             ' If Retry, try error line again...
        Resume

    Case vbIgnore                            ' If Ignore, skip error line,
Resume Next                                  ' resume at next line...

End Select
End Sub
```

That's about it. Run your error-testing program and put it through its paces. Here, in Figure 31.2, is a sample session.

Once you're satisfied with your ErrorHandler, you may add it to any project and call it from any procedure in any form, as long as it's stored in one of your project's standard code modules. Your ErrorHandler may be set up and called in exactly the same way in every procedure. First, you have the On Error GoTo LocalHandler statement, followed by normal procedure statements, followed by an Exit Sub or Exit Function, and then the LocalHandler label and code, exactly as it appears in cmdTest's Click event procedure.

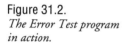

Figure 31.2.
*The Error Test program
in action.*

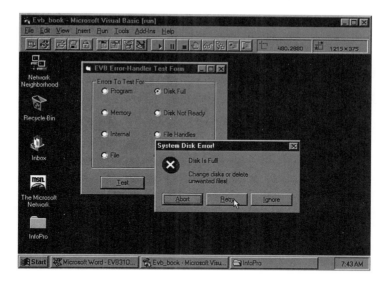

Essential Summary

In this chapter, you received a good look at what a custom error handler is, and can be. You learned that a custom error handler is one that can cope with a wide range of errors, yet provide as much error-specific information as possible. It should be flexible enough to behave helpfully and predictably, no matter what part of a program calls it into action.

What

Because graceful and efficient error handling is a requirement of any serious computer program, a "plug-and-play" custom error handler can save you hours of development time. A custom handler may be used repeatedly as is, or modified to fit the expected error-handling requirements of the current project.

Why

By creating your own custom error-handler function, `ErrorHandler()`, you got a chance to explore more error-handling concepts. You also added to your programmer's Toolbox a reusable error-handling routine that may be added to any project and called from any procedure in any form or code module.

How

The Visual Basic Debug Environment

In the last two chapters, you've seen how to trap and handle run-time errors. In this chapter, you'll learn how to use Visual Basic's debugging tools to locate the third and most insidious type of programming error, the *logic error* or *bug*. A logic error may be buried deep within a long interwoven web of statements, each of which may interact with one another and the program environment in subtle but complex ways. Providing an environment for unraveling the code, for getting to the bug and swatting it, is what Visual Basic's Debugger is all about.

What Is the Debugger?

What The Visual Basic *Debugger* is really a collection of tools you can access from the Tools and Run menus, or by using the appropriate keyboard or Toolbar shortcuts. The debugging tools you'll read about and explore in this chapter are Add Watch, Breakpoint, Single-Stepping, the Immediate or Debug Window, and Calls.

What The Add Watch option on the Tools menu is a highly valuable debugging tool, probably used more than any other. When you add a "Watch

Point" or just "Watch" to your program, you're telling Visual Basic to look for some specific condition while your program is running. For example, you might want to know when the value of a particular variable changes or reaches a certain point; when this happens, Visual Basic will interrupt or "break" into your program, allowing you to observe your watch values and use other debugging tools, such as single-stepping and the Debug Window, to poke around in the current environment.

What   Rather than wait for a particular condition, you may set a *breakpoint* on almost any line in your program. While looking at your code in the Code Window, Press F9, or click the "Stopping Hand" on the Toolbar. The line containing the cursor will be highlighted in red, indicating that it has become an active breakpoint. Then, when you run your program, Visual Basic will stop when it gets to that line, and you'll be able to use the Debug Window to check the values of variables and other expressions.

You may hard-wire a break into your program by using the Stop statement, which causes Visual Basic to behave exactly as if it had hit a breakpoint in your code. The disadvantage here is that you must look for and remove Stop statements when they're no longer needed. Breakpoints, on the other hand, may be easily toggled on or off (using F9), or you may press Ctrl+Shift+F9 to clear all breakpoints at once.

What   While at a breakpoint, you may execute your program one line at a time by pressing F8 or by clicking the Step Into button on the Toolbar. Not surprisingly, this process is called *single-stepping*; it allows you to observe changes in your program as they occur, either by watching your forms or by using the Debug Window and Watch Pane as described later. If you come to a Sub procedure or function that you know is working, press Shift+F8, and you'll jump over it. This is called *procedure-stepping*.

While single-stepping your program, you may step through several lines at a time by using the Step To Cursor feature (Ctrl+F8) found on the Run menu. With this, you may simply click on a line anywhere below your current point of execution and press Ctrl+F8. The program will run through every line up to the cursor location, then stop.

In a large application, it's sometimes difficult to remember the order of execution of various program routines. Single-stepping and procedure-stepping are therefore useful in observing the overall *flow* of your program—the pathways it takes as it runs from one Sub procedure, function, or event to another.

What   As you've observed by now, the Debug Window opens automatically whenever you launch your program from the Visual Basic IDE. If you close it, or if it's hidden by another window, you may get to it by selecting **D**ebug Window from the **V**iew menu, or by pressing Ctrl+G. When you've established watch points, you'll see them displayed in a separate pane at the top of the Debug Window. The Debug Window itself is used to check the values of variables and other program expressions. To do this, you simply type **? VarName** or **? Expression**, and their values will be printed on the next line.

The Debug Window may also be used to receive printed output from your programs. This feature is probably used less often than other debugging tools because it's most useful within a loop; that is, where you might want to see a list of variables changing over time. A useful alternative is to continuously update a special form devoted to showing the value of variables while the program runs. Or just use a Watch, and observe the changes in the Watch pane of the Debug Window.

What

The Tools menu's Calls option (Ctrl+L) reports which procedures—Subs, Functions, Events—in your program are still *active*, that have not reached their respective End Sub and End Function commands, and are still in effect when the break occurs. Calls helps you to untangle the labyrinthine situation in which you have nested procedure calls; that is, where you've put them one inside another like Russian dolls. If you've written your program in such a fashion that one procedure calls upon the services of another, which calls a function, which calls another function, which calls a procedure.... Well, you get the idea. If you're big on nesting procs and love recursion, you'll find the Calls option a lifeline, a veritable Ariadne's Thread, when your program vibrates out of control.

How to Use the Debugger

In this section, you'll add another small form to your EVB_BOOK project. Name it frmDebugger and make it the project's startup form. You'll use it here, and in Chapter 33, to explore the debugging process. Table 32.1 shows the new form's size and position specifications. They're not carved in stone, but you'll want the form to be small enough to view it and the Debug and Code Windows simultaneously.

Table 32.1. Design-time settings—the Debug Practice form.

Visual Basic Object	Property	Design-Time Setting
Form	Name	frmDebugger
	Caption	EVB Debugger Practice
	Height	2100
	Width	4200
	Left	1800
	Top	1300

To see how to work with the Watch Window, add the following code to frmDebugger's Click event:

How

```
Private Sub Form_Click()
Dim Temp1, Temp2 As Integer

Temp2 = 5000
For Temp1 = 1 To 5000
    Temp2 = Temp2 - 1
    Cls
```

```
        Print "Temps: " & Temp1 & " " & Temp2
        DoEvents
    Next
    End Sub
```

Nothing too mysterious here. All you're doing is monitoring two variables—one increasing and one decreasing as you loop—and printing their values to the form. Now, focusing on the Code Window, select (highlight) the variable Temp1 (it doesn't matter which occurrence). From the **T**ools menu, select **A**dd Watch. The Add Watch dialog box will appear, with *Temp1* in the Expression box. In the Context frame, you'll see that the current procedure and module are indicated. The Watch Type frame contains three option buttons. Make sure Watch Expression is selected, then press OK.

At this point, notice that the Debug Window contains two panes. The upper pane, the Watch Window, has three columns: Expression, Value, and Context. The upper pane is where your Watch variables will be displayed.

Now add a second Watch, this time for Temp2. Go back to your Code Window and click anywhere to remove the highlighting of Temp1. As you'll see, it's not necessary to select a variable, or expression, before making it a Watch. Just select **A**dd Watch from the **T**ools menu and type the variable name into the Expression box, then click OK. Do this now, setting a Watch for variable Temp2. Similarly arranged, your screen should look something like Figure 32.1.

Figure 32.1.
Establishing Watch points.

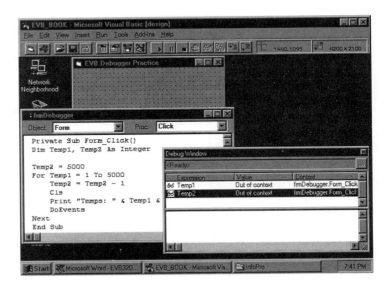

Now run your program and click the form. The numbers will flip by pretty quickly, but you should be able to see Temp1 and Temp2 approach and pass one another, like two speedboats in the night. You can pause (or break) the program at any time by clicking the Break button on the Toolbar (it's the one with two vertical lines, between Run and End). When you do, the

Debug Window will spring to the front, and the Watch Pane will display the current values of Temp1 and Temp2.

Now, end the program by clicking the End button or by selecting **End** from the **Run** menu. Rather than force the break yourself, you can have Visual Basic cause the break when the value of a Watch expression becomes True or changes. Go back to your Code Window and select Add Watch. The Expression this time will be Temp1 = Temp2. Then, in the Watch Type frame, select Break When Value Is True. Press OK, and the new Watch expression will be added to the Debug Window's Watch Pane.

Run your program and click the form. You might be surprised to discover that the break occurs immediately. This is because when Temp1 and Temp2 are first declared, they *are* equal; that is, until they're assigned values, they're equal to 0. Click the Continue button, and the program will begin to flash its numbers and stop when Temp1 and Temp2 hit 2500. You may verify this by checking their current values, displayed in the Watch Pane. Your screen may look something like Figure 32.2.

Figure 32.2.
The Watch Pane revisited.

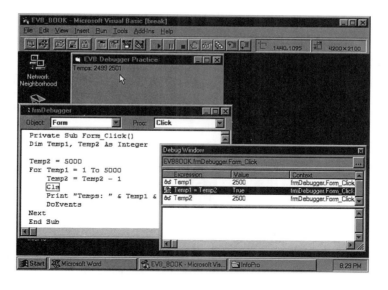

There are several interesting things to notice here. You'll see in the Code Window that the line Cls has a border around it. This indicates that it's the next line to be executed. Look in the Watch Pane, and you'll see that Temp1 and Temp2 are indeed equal. They became equal an instant before the form was to be cleared and the new values printed. This is why, although Temp1 and Temp2 are equal, the form does not yet reflect that fact. Your program broke precisely when Temp1 became equal to Temp2.

Now, end your program. You may select any one of the Watch Expressions in the Watch Pane, then edit or remove it by opening the Edit Watch Window (Ctrl+W). Select Temp1 = Temp2 and press Ctrl+W. In the Watch Window, press the Delete button, and the expression will be removed from the Watch Pane.

> **Tip** In addition to the ways described here, you may Add, Edit, or Delete Watch points by right-clicking in the Watch Pane, or on a particular expression in the pane. This will pop up a menu. You may also Continue or End from this menu, as well as Hide the Debug Window or keep it always on top.

How To set a breakpoint yourself, go to your Code Window and place the cursor on the line that reads Temp2 = Temp2 - 1. Press F9 (or click the Hand on the Toolbar), and the line will be highlighted in red, indicating the point is set. Now run the program (don't forget you need to click the form to get things rolling). The program will stop at the breakpoint, and you'll see in the Watch Pane that the values of Temp1 and Temp2 are 1 and 5000, respectively. This is the first time through the loop. Click the Continue button or press F5, and the program will continue to the next breakpoint—in this case, the same line—the next time through the loop. Now Temp1 and Temp2 are 2 and 4999, respectively.

You may set as many breakpoints as you like. In the Code Window, place the cursor on the line that prints the values to the form and press F9. Press F5 to continue on to the new breakpoint. Press F5 again. The values will be printed, and you'll stop at the first breakpoint in the loop.

You may remove breakpoints individually by selecting them and pressing F9, or you may remove all breakpoints at once by pressing Ctrl+Shift+F9. Alternatively, you may toggle a breakpoint by right-clicking it and selecting Toggle Breakpoint from the popup menu. For now, remove the second breakpoint only, then press F5 to loop around to the first break you created.

How At this point, you may begin single-stepping through your program. To execute one line at a time, press F8 or click the Step Into button on the Toolbar. Press F8 a few times to cycle through the loop. As you go, notice that the line that is about to be executed has a border around it. Notice also that you may keep an eye on the Watch Pane to monitor the values of Temp1 and Temp2.

While single-stepping, you may continue running the program at any time by pressing F5. Or if your focus is on the Debug Window, you may right-click and select Continue as described earlier. In this way, you can use single-stepping, along with breakpoints, to zero in on an area that's behaving erratically and therefore requires closer scrutiny.

How As you've seen, the Debug Window contains the Watch Pane. The area below the Watch Pane may be used during a breakpoint to evaluate variables or expressions that may not be associated with a Watch. You might, for example, want to know the value of the expression Temp1 + Temp2 / Temp1. In the Debug Window, below the Watch Pane, type a **?** (or the word **Print**), followed by the expression. The result will be displayed on the next line. Compare your screen with Figure 32.3.

Figure 32.3.
Evaluating an expression in the Debug Window.

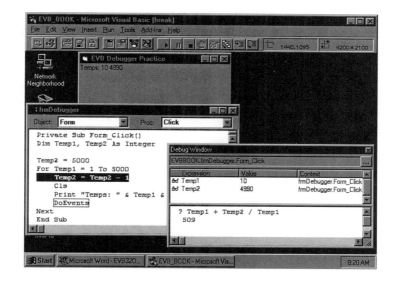

To see how the Calls tool works, you'll need to complicate your program a little. What you'll do is write a Sub procedure, which calls a function you've written. You'll then call the Sub procedure from your test program and watch what happens as you step through it. In the general declarations section of your form, create the new procedure and function listed here:

How

```
Sub CallProc()
Static iTimes As Integer                ' To keep track of times called..
iTimes = iTimes + 1                     ' Bump it each time..
X = CallFunction()                      ' Call the function...
End Sub

Function CallFunction()
Static iTimes As Integer                ' Track times called...
iTimes = iTimes + 1
End Function
```

Now you'll need to add a line to your form's Click event procedure. Here's the complete listing, with the new line boldfaced:

```
Private Sub Form_Click()
Dim Temp1 As Integer, Temp2 As Integer

Temp2 = 5000
For Temp1 = 1 To 5000
    Temp2 = Temp2 - 1                   ' Set break point here...
    Cls
    Print "Temps: " & Temp1 & " " & Temp2
    DoEvents
    CallProc                           ' Call your procedure...
eNext
End Sub
```

If you've been working along with the book, your breakpoint should still be set.

If not, set it where indicated earlier, then run your program (don't forget to click the form). When the breakpoint is encountered, single-step to the CallProc line. At this point, you may press Shift+F8 to step over it, if you like. Instead, go ahead and step into it by pressing F8. The Code Window will change, showing you the CallProc procedure. Continue stepping, then step into your function, CallFunction, and see its code listed in the Code Window. Continue stepping and watching the Code Window, until you're back to your breakpoint.

Now, begin stepping again, but this time when you get to the end of your function, after iTimes has been incremented, click the Calls button or press Ctrl+L to open the Calls Window. Your screen should look something like Figure 32.4.

Figure 32.4.
Debugging with the Call Window.

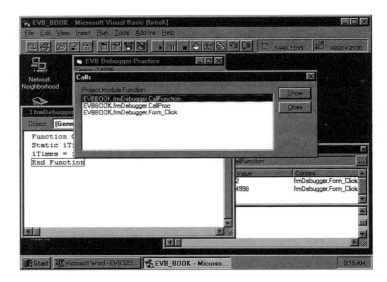

The Calls Window displays a list of all active Sub procedures, functions, and events. You may, at this point, jump to any listed procedure by double-clicking it, or by clicking the Show button. For now, just close the Calls Window.

At this point in your program, the function's Static variable iTimes is within scope, so you could use the Debug Window to see its current value. Notice that there's no problem in having an iTimes variable in both the procedure and the function. Even though they're *Static* (they maintain their values through multiple calls), they are private to their host procedures.

In the next chapter, you'll write a real program, a simple sorting routine, that will contain several bugs. You'll use your newly acquired debugging skills to get it working properly. For now, feel free to experiment further with the debugging environment. When you're finished, be sure to remove all breakpoints and Watches, then end your program and save your work before continuing on to the summary.

Essential Summary

In this chapter, you learned that logic errors, or bugs, may be buried deep within a chain of statements, each of which may interact with one another in a complex and web-like way. You saw that the Visual Basic Debugger is a collection of useful tools that may be used to assist you in finding and fixing such errors.

What

Because all programmers make errors, some of which may be subtle and extremely difficult to eradicate, an understanding of the Debug environment and a proficiency with its tools will be powerful additions to your repertoire of Visual Basic skills.

Why

To experiment with the Debug environment and tools, you added a new form to your EVB_BOOK project. You wrote a simple looping program, as well as a test function and procedure, which you used to explore the Watch, Debug, and Calls Windows; you also saw how to set breakpoints and single-step, as well as procedure-step, through your program.

How

Debugging an Application

In this short chapter, you'll write a program, a simple sorting routine, which will contain a few very common bugs. You'll then use some of your newly acquired debugging skills to get it working properly.

Creating the Program

You'll want to enlarge your Debugger form a little. Open frmDebugger in Design mode and add two command buttons to it. Here's a table showing the new form specifications:

Table 33.1. Design-time settings—the modified Debugger form.

Visual Basic Object	Property	Design-Time Setting
Form	Name	frmDebugger
	Caption	EVB Debugger Practice
	Height	3400
	Width	4200
	Top	1350
	Left	1800
Command Button	Name	cmdSort
	Caption	&Sort 'Em
	Default	True
Command Button	Name	cmdQuit
	Cancel	True
	Caption	&Quit

The Quit button will...well, quit the program. Put the End statement in its Click event. In the Click event of the Sort 'Em button, type the code listed here. (This code has three very common bugs in it, so be sure to type it exactly as it appears.)

```
Private Sub cmdSort_Click()
Static saClowns(10) As String            ' Declare clown array...
Cls                                      ' Clear the form...

saClowns(1) = "Yackles"                  ' Put some clowns in the array
saClowns(2) = "Jangles"
saClowns(3) = "Chuckles"
saClowns(4) = "Ferris"
saClowns(5) = "Bozo"
saClowns(6) = "BigShoes"
saClowns(7) = "LittleShoes"
saClowns(8) = "Amos"
saClowns(9) = "Waffler"
saClowns(10) = "Zeppo"


For iOuter = iOuter To 10                          ' Here you're using a
                                                   ' common sorting technique
                                                   ' consisting of an inner
                                                   ' and outer loop..

    For iInner = iOuter To 10

        If saClowns(iOuter) > saClowns(iInner) Then    ' If the second is
                                                       ' "lighter"
            Temp$ = saClowns(iOuter)                   ' swap them...
            saClowns(iInner) = saClowns(iInner)
            saClowns(iInner) = Tmp$
```

```
        End If

    Next iInner

Next iOuter

For iCounter = 1 To 10                          ' Here you print the list
    Print saClowns(iCounter)
Next

End Sub
```

This procedure creates a string array and fills it full of clowns. You then use a common sorting technique called a *bubble sort,* whereby each element in a list is compared to all the others, and the "lighter" elements, the ones higher in the sort order, are allowed to "bubble" to the top of the list. Note that you are using the > logical operator to compare strings, which is perfectly legal in Visual Basic; this allows you to determine the alphabetical order of the strings. Finally, you print the (hopefully) sorted list to the form.

Now run the program and click the Sort button. Unfortunately, the resulting list will look a little incomplete, with Yackles at the top, Zeppo at the bottom, and nothing in between! It's time to debug.

How to Debug It

You can start debugging without even stopping the program. To do this, select the Code item from Visual Basic's View menu, then drop down the Object list to locate cmdSort. You may now browse the code for errors while the program is running. Often you can spot obvious errors immediately. In this case, you'll notice that when you switch elements around in the array, you swap them into a variable named Temp$; when you swap them back into the list, you use a mistyped variable Tmp$. Examine Figure 33.1.

You may actually fix this problem without stopping the program. Just click the Break button (or select Break from the Run menu) to pause the program temporarily. Now you'll be able to edit the code (in a limited way). In this case, change Tmp$ to Temp$.

> **Tip** Misspelling a variable's name is probably the most common type of bug. Visual Basic does not complain about such errors at compile-time because it assumes that you're implicitly declaring a new variable, and sets it to an empty string or 0 if it's a number. If you'd like to be notified of such errors at compile-time, use the Option Explicit statement in the general declarations section of your module. Visual Basic will then balk at any undeclared variables, which is one way to detect misspellings before they become bugs.

Figure 33.1.
*Debugging the Clown
Sort program.*

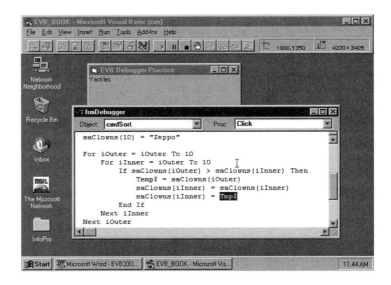

You can allow the program to continue now by pressing F5 or by clicking the Continue button. Then click the Sort button to view the list. You'll notice that things have changed...but they're still not right! End the program and open a Code Window for cmdSort's Click event.

The problem seems to be that the elements of the saClowns() array are not being filled correctly. To see what is happening, you need to observe the array elements as they are being switched around. You need to set a breakpoint on the first line of the inner loop, as displayed in Figure 33.2.

Figure 33.2.
*Setting a breakpoint
within the Sort loop.*

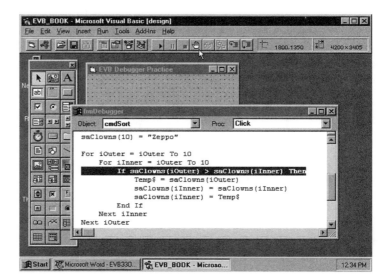

Now run the program. When the break occurs, you can check the values of saClowns(iOuter) and saClowns(iInner) by jumping to the Debug Window and entering a ? followed by the expression you're investigating. Here, in Figure 33.3, is what the Debug Window shows.

Figure 33.3.
Checking values in the Debug Window.

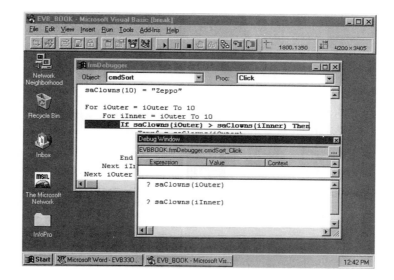

When you check the values of saClowns(iOuter) and saClowns(iInner), you see that they are empty! The line containing the If statement is comparing nothing. At this point, both iOuter and iInner should be pointing to the first element of the clown array; that is, they should both be equal to 1. When you check the value of iOuter, you'll see that it's equal to 0, not 1. The problem is that iOuter is never initialized to 1 at the beginning of the outer loop. Here's the listing, with the corrected line boldfaced.

```
Private Sub cmdSort_Click()
Static saClowns(10) As String
Cls
saClowns(1) = "Yackles"
:
:

For iOuter = 1 To 10                            ' iOuter needs a starting value

For iInner = iOuter To 10
        If saClowns(iOuter) > saClowns(iInner) Then
            Temp$ = saClowns(iOuter)
            saClowns(iInner) = saClowns(iInner)
            saClowns(iInner) = Tmp$
        End If
    Next iInner
Next iOuter
```

```
For iCounter = 1 To 10
    Print saClowns(iCounter)
Next
End Sub
```

Now toggle off the breakpoint and run the program. You get a list full of Yackles and one Zeppo! Obviously, there's still a problem, so end the program and open the Code Window. The thing to do at this point is to examine the part of the program where the array elements are swapped. Put a breakpoint at the end of the element-swapping section, on the line before the End If.

The exchange of array elements goes like this: You place the value in saClowns(iOuter) into Temp$. Then you copy what's in saClowns(iInner) to saClowns(iOuter). Finally, you move Temp$ into saClowns(iInner). When the program breaks, you've not completed the last step of the swap, so saClowns(iOuter) should be equal to saClowns(iInner).

You can set Watches for both of those variables to see if this is indeed what happens. In the Code Window, select saClowns(iOuter) and a Watch for it by selecting **A**dd Watch from the **T**ools menu. Do the same for saClowns(iInner), or use one of the other methods for adding a Watch point as discussed in the last chapter. Now run the program and jump to the Debug Window to see the following (see Figure 33.4).

Figure 33.4.
Using Watch points to debug the program.

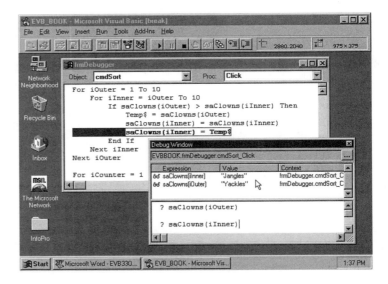

The two array elements are not the same. Something is wrong. If you look back one line in your code, above the breakpoint, you'll see the following line:

```
saClowns(iInner) = saClowns(iInner)
```

And there's the problem! It is clear that this line should be :

```
saClowns(iOuter) = saClowns(iInner)
```

Make the change, remove your breakpoint, then run the program again. Clicking the Sort button produces the properly sorted list, as in Figure 33.5.

Figure 33.5.
The debugged Clown
Sorter in action.

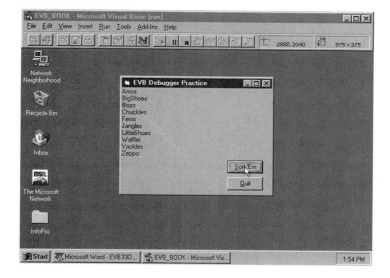

Congratulations! Your program has been debugged.

Essential Summary

In this chapter you learned how to use Visual Basic's debugging tools to track down and swat some pesky but common bugs. You saw how to make good use of breakpoints and watch points, and how to check the values of significant variables in the Debug Window.

What

Even though you used only a few of the debugging tools available in Visual Basic, it should be clear that a thorough familiarity with the Debug environment will be invaluable in ferreting out those nasty logic errors—the ones that have you pulling out your hair or considering another line of work.

Why

You created a simple sorting program that contained a few deliberate but common bugs. You then used the debugging skills you acquired here and in Chapter 32 to get it working properly. With a few modifications, the bubble sort routine you developed in this chapter may be converted to a generic sorting function, which might make a nice addition to your Toolbox of reusable code. Or you can leave it like it is and when that little car hits the center ring, and all those clowns come tumbling out, you'll be all set to restore some order.

How

Advanced Programming Topics

Creating and Using Control Arrays

In this chapter, you'll receive a thorough grounding in the creation and use of Control arrays. You'll see what Control arrays are and why they'll be an invaluable addition to your own "array" of Visual Basic skills. Finally, you'll create a new program to explore the Control array mechanism in detail, using an array of command buttons and an array of Image controls.

What Are Control Arrays?

What Just as you may have arrays of strings or numbers, Visual Basic also allows you to create arrays of controls, where each element (control) may be accessed by a unique index. *Control arrays* are a convenient way to handle groups of controls that perform a similar function. For example, imagine that you have a number of option buttons, say, OptionA, OptionB, OptionC, and OptionD. In this case, you would have to write a completely separate event procedure for each button (as you've been doing throughout this book). That is, you'll have `OptionA_Click`, `OptionB_Click`, `OptionC_Click`, and `OptionD_Click`. Jumping between these procedures is awkward and time-consuming if the buttons perform essentially the same actions, as is usually the case with groups of controls.

An easier and more sensible way to handle such a group of buttons is to give them all the same name. If you do, Visual Basic automatically assigns them different *index* numbers, which are stored in the Index property for each control. For example, if you name each button optColor, Visual Basic gives the first one an index of 0, the next an index of 1, and so on. These buttons may now be referred to as optColor(0), optColor(1), and so on, just as you would refer to the individual elements of any other array.

> **Tip** Another way to create a Control array is to set the Name property (using the same name), then adjust the Index property of the arrayed controls as you create them at design time.

The beauty here is that now, instead of four different event procedures, there will be only one procedure for each event, to which Visual Basic will kindly pass an Index value corresponding to the button that was clicked. If your form contained the four buttons described in the preceding discussion, optColor(0) through optColor(3), you could double-click on any one of them, in Design mode, and see the following event procedure template:

```
Private Sub optColor_Click(Index As Integer)
End Sub
```

The usual thing to do between the two lines seen here is to set up some sort of construct—often a `Select Case` or `If...Then` block—in which you would evaluate `Index` to determine which button was pressed, and perform the proper action accordingly. (This is all very abstract at this point; you'll get to see this in action soon.)

> **Note** A control array has at least one element and can grow to as many elements as your system resources and memory permit; the maximum size of a Control array also depends on how much memory and Windows resources each control requires. With 32-bit Windows platforms, the maximum index you can use in a control array is 32767, and approximately 16000 with 16-bit Windows platforms.

Why Use Control Arrays?

Control arrays are efficient. Grouping and naming controls in this way lets you manipulate their properties and methods *mathematically*. Because they're now labeled with numbers, not text names, you can refer to them in Loops and other structures as a single entity, easily executing the same method, or changing the same property, in each control by using a single loop.

These are not the only reasons to use Control arrays. By using Control arrays, you may create new controls while your program is running. (In fact, Control arrays are the only way to do this.) To create a new member of a Control array, you use the Load command. To remove members, you use Unload. In this way, the Control array mechanism allows you to employ the power of *inheritance* in defining event procedures for controls created at run time. That is, each newly loaded control (each new element in your array) *inherits* its event procedures, and most of its properties, from the array's original element. For example, if you want a form to contain several PictureBox controls that each display a particular picture, you can create a single picture box at design time, making it the first element of an array, then add multiple elements to the array at run time, so that all of the picture boxes share the same Picture property.

By using Control arrays, you may work with several Controls of the same type as a single entity. Since the elements of a Control array may be referred to by their numeric Indexes, you are able to manipulate their properties and methods *mathematically*, by incrementing an index in a loop, for example. Another great advantage of Control arrays is that you may write a single block of code to handle the same event for each of the array's elements; you simply use the incoming Index variable to determine which control in the array was activated.

A third and very powerful advantage of the Control array mechanism is that it allows you to add or remove controls while your program is running; in fact, using Control arrays is the *only* way you can do this in Visual Basic. If you need to add or delete menu items at run time, for example, or fill the screen with images, as you might do with a screen saver or wallpaper program, Control arrays provide the required punch and flexibility.

How to Create Control Arrays

How

If you want to create a new control at run time, that control must be a member of an existing Control array. With a Control array, each new element inherits the common event procedures of the first element, as well as most of its properties and methods. In this section, you'll add a new form to your EVB_BOOK project. Call it frmControl and make it the project's startup form.

As you'll see from the upcoming table and figure, your new form will contain two control arrays. The first, cmdChange(), is an array of four command buttons, indexed 0 through 3. The second array, imgWallPaper(), is an Image Control array that will have only one element at design time. At run time, you'll use imgWallPaper() to fill your form with pictures of hardware components or storage devices—CD-ROMs, floppy disks, mice, Macs—creating a wallpaper background with a computer motif.

Please complete the visual design of the Control Array form, referring to Table 34.1, Figure 34.1, and the following Tip for guidance.

Table 34.1. Design-time settings—the WallPaper program.

Visual Basic Object	Property	Design-Time Setting
Form	Name	frmControl
	Caption	EVB Control Array Form
	Icon	c:\vb40\icons\computer\cdrom01.ico
Command Button Array	Name	cmdChange
	Index	0
	Caption	CD Rom
	Index	1
	Caption	Disk
	Index	2
	Caption	Mouse
	Index	3
	Caption	Mac
Image Control Array	Name	imgWallPaper
	Index	0
	Picture	c:\vb40\icons\computer\cdrom01.ico
	Stretch	True
	Height	615
	Width	615
Image Control	Name	imgCDRom
	Picture	c:\vb40\icons\computer\cdrom01.ico
Image Control	Name	imgDisk
	Picture	c:\vb40\icons\computer\disk12.ico
Image Control	Name	imgMouse
	Picture	c:\vb40\icons\computer\mouse01.ico
Image Control	Name	imgMac
	Picture	c:\vb40\icons\computer\mac04.ico

Figure 34.1.
Design mode: the
WallPaper program.

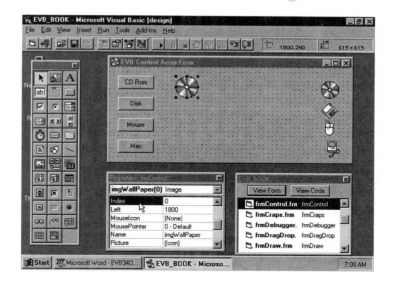

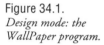

> **Tip** A great way to create Control arrays at design time is to draw the first control, give it the name you want to use for the array, and set any inheritable properties—size, fonts, colors, pictures, icons. Then Copy it and Paste as many times as you like. On the first Paste, Visual Basic will ask you if you want to create a Control array, to which you'll respond Yes. With each new Paste (the Ctrl+V keyboard shortcut is particularly handy here), a new control will be added to your array, its Index automatically set by Visual Basic. You'll find the new controls "stacked" one on top of another in the upper-left corner of the form. Just drag them to the desired locations.

Program Overview

When first executed, your new WallPaper program will flood the form with pictures of a CD-ROM. But you'll be able to change the wallpaper by clicking one of the buttons in the cmdChange() Control array. As you'll see in the following section, there's only one Click event associated with these buttons, which is exactly what you'd expect and want. You'll have one block of code for handling clicks to any of the buttons.

As an extra fun-time at run-time bonus, you'll be able to double-click on individual pictures and have them change right before your eyes. In this way, you can mix and match to design your own custom wallpaper.

Adding Code

First, declare some helpful variables and constants in your form's general declarations section:

```
Dim iRows As Integer, iCols As Integer, iTotalPics As Integer   ' For tracking rows,
➥columns, pictures

Const CDROM = 0                                    ' Constants equal to the Index
Const DISK = 1                                     ' of the corresponding command
Const MOUSE = 2                                    ' buttons in the cmdChange()
Const MAC = 3                                      ' control array.
```

In the Load event, you'll establish the number of rows and columns of pictures. You may set iRows and iCols to anything you like, even if they'll fill more, or less, than the entire form. The values here will work fine if you've used the height and width suggested for imgWallPaper().

```
Private Sub Form_Load()
iRows = 10
iCols = 15
iTotalPics = iRows * iCols
WallPaper                                          ' Run your WallPaper procedure, as
End Sub                                            ' defined below.
```

Now here's the procedure that floods the form with pictures. It uses the Load method to add new controls to the imgWallPaper() array. In addition to adding the controls, you need to figure out where to place them. To do this, you're using two variables to store the height and width of the control, plus 100 extra twips for breathing room. These variables will then be used to set the Top and Left properties of each new image control as it's loaded and made visible.

Add this code to frmControl's general declarations section:

```
Sub WallPaper()
MousePointer = HOURGLASS                           ' Might take some time...

Dim iPic As Integer                                ' Local variables for tracking
Dim iRow As Integer, iCol As Integer               ' the current picture, row,
                                                   ' and column.

Dim lMoveDown As Long, lMoveOver As Long           ' You'll be  moving down or over
                                                   ' to set the position of the
                                                   ' current control.

lMoveDown = imgWallPaper(0).Height + 100           ' How far to move down,
lMoveOver = imgWallPaper(0).Width + 100            ' or over....

imgWallPaper(0).Visible = False                    ' Should already be false,
                                                   ' but just in case...

For iRow = 0 To iRows - 1                           ' Loop through the rows,

    For iCol = 0 To iCols - 1                       ' and columns...
```

```
            iPic = iPic + 1                              ' New control index...
            Load imgWallPaper(iPic)                      ' Load it...
            imgWallPaper(iPic).Top = lMoveDown * iRow    ' Position it...
            imgWallPaper(iPic).Left = lMoveOver * iCol
            imgWallPaper(iPic).Visible = True            ' Make it visible.

        Next iCol                                        ' Next column...

    Next iRow                                            ' Next row.

    MousePointer = NORMAL
End Sub
```

To add code for your command buttons, all you have to do is double-click any one of them. Since they're all part of the same Control array, you'll be transported to the one and only code window for their mutual `Click` event. Notice that Visual Basic is passing you an integer variable containing the Index of whichever button was clicked. You'll use this to decide which picture to switch to. Here's the code for cmdChange's `Click` event:

```
Private Sub cmdChange_Click(Index As Integer)     ' Index coming in...

Select Case Index                                 ' Evaluate it...

    Case CDROM                                     ' CDROM button was clicked

    For X = 1 To iTotalPics                        ' Fill the array with
        imgWallPaper(X).picture = imgCDRom.picture ' CDROM pictures.
    Next


    Case DISK                                      ' Disk was clicked...

    For X = 1 To iTotalPics                         ' Fill with Disk pics.
        imgWallPaper(X).picture = imgDisk.picture
    Next


    Case MOUSE                                     ' User wants mice...

    For X = 1 To iTotalPics                         ' So...
        imgWallPaper(X).picture = imgMouse.picture  ' bring in the mice....
    Next


    Case MAC                                       ' Mac button clicked

    For X = 1 To iTotalPics                         ' So...
        imgWallPaper(X).picture = imgMac.picture    ' a multitude of Macs.
    Next

End Select
End Sub
```

The last code to be added allows you to double-click a wallpaper image and cycle through all four possible pictures, giving you a chance to mix and match. Even though, at design time, imgWallPaper() contains only one control, you may add code to its DblClick event which will work with any of its descendants generated at run time. The DblClick event procedure will be inherited from the original "parent." Here's the listing:

```
Private Sub imgWallPaper_DblClick(Index As Integer)

Dim iPic As Integer                        ' Will represent the current picture,
                                           ' that is the picture in the control
                                           ' that was double-clicked.

iPic = IIf(imgWallPaper(Index).picture = imgCDRom.picture, CDROM, iPic) ' Which pic
iPic = IIf(imgWallPaper(Index).picture = imgDisk.picture, DISK, iPic)   ' was
iPic = IIf(imgWallPaper(Index).picture = imgMouse.picture, MOUSE, iPic) ' clicked?
iPic = IIf(imgWallPaper(Index).picture = imgMac.picture, MAC, iPic)


Select Case iPic                                           ' Now evaluate it...

    Case CDROM                                             ' If it was CDROM...
        imgWallPaper(Index).picture = imgDisk.picture      ' switch to DISK.

    Case DISK                                              ' If it was DISK...
        imgWallPaper(Index).picture = imgMouse.picture     ' switch to MOUSE.

    Case MOUSE                                             ' If it was MOUSE...
        imgWallPaper(Index).picture = imgMac.picture       ' switch to MAC.

    Case MAC                                               ' If it was MAC,
        imgWallPaper(Index).picture = imgCDRom.picture     'switch back to CDROM.
End Select
End Sub
```

It's time to test your WallPaper program. Don't forget to double-click on some pictures to make sure you're able to cycle through them. Here, in Figure 34.2, is a sample session with the WallPaper program.

Note In testing your WallPaper program, you're probably thinking that Control arrays would have been a better way to handle the pictures involved in the Game Of Concentration you created way back in Chapter 23. You're right. In fact, Control arrays should be used whenever possible for handling groups of related images or pictures, option buttons, command buttons, check boxes, Menu Items—any collection of controls that provide similar but distinct functionality.

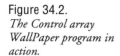

Figure 34.2.
The Control array
WallPaper program in
action.

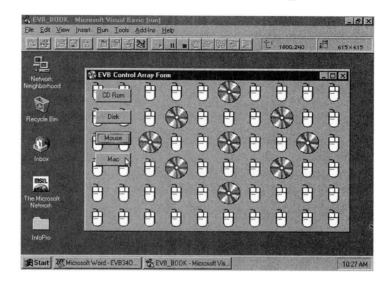

Essential Summary

In this chapter, you learned that a Control array is a group of controls that share a common name and type, as well as event procedures, properties, and methods.

What

You saw that Visual Basic allows you to create Control arrays where each element (control) may be accessed and manipulated using a unique index. You also learned that Control arrays are a convenient and powerful way to handle groups of controls that perform a similar but distinct function.

Control arrays are both efficient and powerful. Since the controls in a Control array may be referred to by their numeric indexes, you are able to manipulate their properties and methods by incrementing an index in a loop, for example. In Visual Basic, Control arrays offer the only mechanism whereby you may add or remove controls while your program is running. Another advantage of Control arrays is that you may write a single block of code to handle the same event for each of the array's elements, thereby preventing unnecessary fragmentation of your code.

Why

You explored the Control array mechanism in detail by creating a new form containing an array of command buttons and an Image control array which, at design time, contained but a single element. You then wrote a program that flooded the form with computer-related pictures, by adding a screenful of elements to the Image Control array at run time, creating a kind of cybernetic wallpaper. You also made it possible for the user to modify the wallpaper by clicking a command button to display a different base image, or by double-clicking individual images to cycle through four picture possibilities, thus allowing a mix-and-match approach to wallpaper design. All of this was accomplished with a minimum of fuss by making a thoughtful use of only two Control arrays.

How

Multiple Document Interface (MDI) Applications

In this chapter, you'll learn about *MDI (Multiple Document Interface)* applications by creating one. Your MDI application will contain an MDI parent form and two MDI children (also forms), and you'll get a chance to see just exactly how they interact. Of course, you'll need a good working definition of just what an MDI form is, and that will come first.

What Is an MDI Form?

What An *MDI parent form* is a container for other forms. Many Windows applications are MDI programs. Excel, for example, may display many different sheets and charts within its main window, all under the same umbrella, so to speak; Word may have several documents opened at once. Specifically, an MDI parent is a window that acts as the background of an application and is the container for other forms that have their MDIChild property set to True.

The MDI *parent* window (a form) encloses *child* windows (other Forms). Child windows can be open, iconized, resized, moved, and otherwise treated as if they were normal windows. However, the child windows always remain within the parent window: they cannot be dragged outside the parent. Even when you reduce the "children" to icons, they do not move to the bottom of the screen, but rather to the bottom of the parent window. When you minimize the parent, the children are folded up along with it. The children are contained within the parent as if the parent was the entire screen!

You create an MDI form (the parent) by choosing MDI Form from the Insert menu. An application can have only one parent form. An MDI form cannot be Modal and can contain only Menu objects, picture boxes, or a custom control, such as SSPanel, that has an Align property. However, you can place other controls in the picture box or panel. Picture boxes and panels may be aligned to the Top, Bottom, Left, or Right of the MDI parent. Aligned to the Top or Bottom, a picture box or panel on an MDI parent has the same width as the form, but they may have any height up to the Height of the form. Similarly, when aligned Right or Left, they'll conform to the height of the form, but allow their widths to be adjusted. Typically, picture boxes and panels are used to create Toolbars at the top or message/status areas at the bottom or sides of the form.

> **Tip** Although you cannot use the Print method to display text on an MDI parent directly, you may use it to print to a picture box contained on the parent form.

Visual Basic's Arrange command is peculiar to the MDI parent form. It allows you or the user to determine whether the child windows will be of random sizes and in random positions, or arranged so that each is visible and of the same size (*tiled*), or *cascaded* so that each overlaps another like a fanned deck of playing cards. The Arrange command may also be used to organize and iconize child windows within the parent; you'll see the Arrange command in action later, when you create your MDI application.

What   Although an application may have only one MDIForm parent, it may have many MDI child forms. MDI child forms are designed independently of the MDI form, but are always contained within the MDI form at run time. In fact, an MDI child is just another form in your project, except that its MDIChild property is set to True.

If an MDI child form has menus, the child form's menu bar automatically replaces the MDIForm object's menu bar when the MDI child form is active. That is, the menu bar designed for an MDI child form is displayed on the MDI parent form at run time when the MDI child form is active, even though it appears on the child form at design time.

When an MDI child form is the startup form, the MDI form is loaded automatically; but MDI child forms are loaded only when specified as the startup form, when explicitly referenced in code, or when specified in a Load statement.

If you want several child forms to function identically, you can use multiple instances of a single form, or an array of forms of a single type, rather than making copies of the same form at design time. You can load and create instances of MDI child forms dynamically at run time using the Dim statement to establish a new Form Object variable. After creating a new instance of a form, you can change that instance's properties without affecting other forms. You can use the Me keyword to reference the currently active instance of a form or the currently active form array element. Similarly, the ActiveForm property of the MDI form specifies the MDI child form that has the focus, or was most recently active. (Again, be patient. You'll put all of these perhaps hazy, abstract theoretical considerations to a good practical use in the following sections.)

Why Create an MDI Application?

Why

An MDI application is like a miniature version of Windows within your Windows screen. For word processing, file management, graphic file viewing, and other applications it's often desirable to contain related windows within a larger window. Any time you need to view several documents, sheets, charts, or pictures at once—or if you need to mix many different types of forms under the same "umbrella"—an MDI application provides the perfect environment for their simple arrangement and organization.

How to Create an MDI Program

How

In this section, you'll add three new forms to your EVB_BOOK project. You'll design two MDI child forms: a Memo form, and a limited Spreadsheet form which will allow you to enter and edit data in a Grid control. The third form you'll create will be your program's MDIForm object, the parent form, which will contain the application's menu. (So you'll get a chance to refresh the Menu Editor skills you developed back in Chapter 15.)

Here, in Table 35.1, are the design-time specifications for the Spreadsheet child form.

Table 35.1. Design-time settings—the Sheet MDI Child.

Visual Basic Object	Property	Design-Time Setting
Form	Name	frmSheet
	Caption	MDI Sheet
	MDIChild	True
	Icon	c:\vb40\icons\computer\monitr01.ico
Grid Control	Name	grdSheet
	FixedCols	1
	FixedRows	1

continues

Table 35.1. continued

Visual Basic Object	Property	Design-Time Setting
	Top	480
	Left	120
Label Control	Name	lblEdit
	Caption	Edit:
	Visible	False
TextBox Control	Name	txtEdit
	Visible	False

The Top and Left Properties establish the grid's position relative to the form. This will become important, as you'll want the grid's height and width to change as the form is resized. The design-time size of the grid (and of the form, for that matter) is not relevant, as long as the form is big enough to display the grid at the Top and Left coordinates specified in Table 35.1. The label and text box will be used to enter, or edit, the contents of the current cell. They should be invisible at startup. Here, in Figure 35.1 is what the form may look like at design time.

Figure 35.1.
The MDI child:
Spreadsheet form.

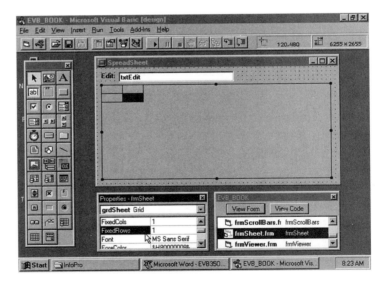

Tip When you're designing an MDI Child form, it's a good idea to set it as the startup form and keep its MDIChild property set to False. That way, you can press F5 to easily see the form in action during the design phase. Once you're satisfied with how it looks and works, you can then set its MDIChild property to True.

Adding Code to the Spreadsheet Form

You'll use the Spreadsheet child's Load event to set the grid's dimensions, fill in the alphabetic column headings, and number the rows. Make sure frmSheet is open in Design mode. Double-click anywhere on the form and add the following code:

```
Private Sub Form_Load()                         ' frmSheet's Load Event Proc
Dim iRow As Integer, iCol As Integer

grdSheet.Rows = 100                             ' Size the grid...
grdSheet.Cols = 27

For iCol = 1 To 26                              ' Loop through the columns
    grdSheet.Row = 0                            ' in Row 0, the fixed header.
    grdSheet.Col =  iCol
    grdSheet.Text = Chr$(iCol + 64)             ' Adding 64 to iCol, and
Next                                            ' converting to CHR, results
                                                ' in the proper letter of the
                                                ' alphabet.


For iRow = 1 To 99                              ' Now number the rows
    grdSheet.Row = iRow                         ' in the first, fixed, column.
    grdSheet.Col = 0
    grdSheet.Text = CStr(iRow)
Next
End Sub
```

Now, when the Spreadsheet form is resized, you want the grid to be resized accordingly. This is handled in the form's Resize event procedure. Open a code window, select Form from the Object drop-down, then locate Resize in the Proc drop-down list. Here's the listing:

```
Private Sub Form_Resize()                       ' frmSheet's Resize Event

If Me.Height > 1000 Then                         ' As long as the form is not
grdSheet.Height = Me.Height - 1000              ' too short, adjust the height
End If                                          ' of the grid in proportion.

If Me.Width > 360 Then                          ' As long as the form is not
grdSheet.Width = Me.Width - 360                 ' radically narrow, adjust the
End If                                          ' width of the grid.

End Sub
```

An error will occur if either the Height or Width of the grid go negative. You're preventing this by using the two If...Then constructs you see in the preceding code. They'll keep the grid to a realistic size so that you'll be able to resize, or even minimize, the form without any problems.

Now, you're going to allow your user to edit the contents of any cell in the grid. They'll be able to select a cell, then double-click it (or press Enter), to open an editing window (txtEdit) on top of the grid. They may enter or edit text in txtEdit, then press Enter to store the contents in the current cell. Add the following code to frmGrid's DblClick event (be sure you're adding it to the grid, not the form):

```
Private Sub grdSheet_DblClick()

txtEdit.Width = grdSheet.Width - 720    ' Adjust the width of txtEdit...
txtEdit = grdSheet.Text                 ' Display the contents of the current cell...
lblEdit.Visible = True                  ' Make the edit box and label visible...
txtEdit.Visible = True
txtEdit.SelStart = 0                     ' With any text selected...
txtEdit.SelLength = Len(txtEdit)
txtEdit.SetFocus                         ' Move the cursor there...

End Sub
```

To open the edit window when Enter is pressed anywhere on the grid, add the following code to grdSheet's KeyPress event:

```
Private Sub grdSheet_KeyPress(KeyAscii As Integer)

If KeyAscii = 13 Then                    ' If they pressed ENTER...
    grdSheet_DblClick                    ' it's as if they'd double-clicked...
End If

End Sub
```

Another little cosmetic touch is to close the edit window whenever the user clicks on another cell. In this case, the contents of the edit window will not be transferred to the current cell. Here's what the grid's Click event will look like:

```
Private Sub grdSheet_Click()

lblEdit.Visible = False                  ' The edit window and
txtEdit.Visible = False                  ' label disappear.

End Sub
```

The final bit of coding is to monitor the keystrokes coming into the edit window. When the user presses Enter, you'll want to store the current contents of txtEdit to the grid's current cell, and then close the edit window. Here's the listing for txtEdit's KeyPress event:

```
Private Sub txtEdit_KeyPress(KeyAscii As Integer)

If KeyAscii = 13 Then                    ' If ENTER is pressed...
    grdSheet.Text = txtEdit              ' Update the grid...
    txtEdit = ""                         ' Dump the text in the edit box...
    txtEdit.Visible = False              ' and make it invisible.
    lblEdit.Visible = False

End If

End Sub
```

That's it for the Spreadsheet MDI child form. Test it to make sure it looks and acts the way you want it to, then set its MDIChild Property to True. Save this form and go on to the next section.

Your application's second child form will contain an array of four TextBox Controls to be used as a kind of MemoPad. Add a new form to your project, frmMemo, and make it the startup form. The Memo form will receive and display text in four boxes labeled To, Date, From, and Subject. Here are the design-time settings:

Table 35.2. Design-time settings—the Memo MDI child.

Visual Basic Object	Property	Design-Time Setting
Form	Name	frmMemo
	Caption	MDI Memo
	MDIChild	True
	Icon	c:\vb40\icons\writing\note03.ico
TextBox Control Array	Name	txtMemo
	Index, TabIndex	0 (To TextBox)
	Index, TabIndex	1 (Date TextBox
	Index, TabIndex	2 (From TextBox)
	Index, TabIndex	3 (Subject TextBox)
	MultiLine	True
	ScrollBars	2 - Vertical
	Top	1320
	Left	1080
Labels	BackStyle	0 - Transparent
	BorderStyle	0 - None

Here, too, the position of the Subject TextBox, txtMemo(3), is important, so its Top and Left Properties have been included in the preceding table. Notice also that you're setting the TabIndex property of the text boxes, as well as the array Index. The TabIndex property determines the order in which controls on a form will receive the focus as the user presses the Tab key (or Shift+Tab to move backward). The Control with a TabIndex of 0 has the focus when the form first opens. Also note that the Subject TextBox is a multi-line box with Vertical scroll bars. Figure 35.2 shows how the Memo form might look at design time.

Figure 35.2.
The MDI child: Memo form.

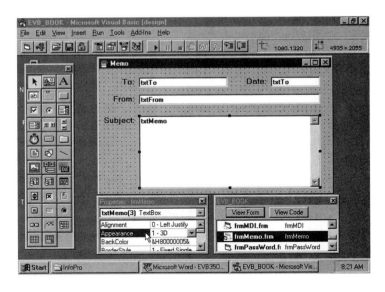

Adding Code to the Memo Form

When the Memo form is loaded, you want to be sure its text boxes are empty. Because they are part of a Control array, it's a simple matter to loop through their Indexes, setting each of their Text properties to an empty string. Here's the listing for frmMemo's Load event:

```
Private Sub Form_Load()                            ' frmMemo's Load Event
For X = 0 To 3
    txtMemo(X).Text = ""                           ' Empty each box in the array.
Next
End Sub
```

Now allow for resizing the Subject TextBox in proper relation to the form:

```
Private Sub Form_Resize()                          ' frmMemo's Resize Event

If  Me.Height > 1875 Then
txtMemo(3).Height = Me.Height - 1875               ' Adjust the Subject TextBox
End If

If Me.Width > 1440 Then
txtMemo(3).Width = Me.Width - 1440
End If

End Sub
```

That's all there is to the Memo MDI child form. Test it to make sure it looks and behaves the way you expect it to, then don't forget to set its MDIChild property to True. In the next section, you'll create your applications MDIForm Object, the Parent.

How   To create the MDI Parent form, select MDI Form from Visual Basic's Insert menu. Call this form frmMDI and make it the project's startup form. You'll notice that you cannot have more than one MDI form per project: as soon as this one is added, the MDI Form menu item is disabled. In your program, all of the code associated with the MDI parent will be executed from the menu you will create for it. Table 35.3 contains the design-time settings for the form and menu.

Table 35.3. Design-time settings—the MDI Parent form.

Visual Basic Object	Property	Design-Time Setting
Form	Name	frmMDI
	Caption	EVB MDI Application
	WindowState	2 - Maximized
Menu Item	Name	mnuFile
	Caption	&File
SubMenu	Name	mnuNew
	Caption	&New
Sub-SubMenu	Name	mnuMemo
	Caption	&Memo
Sub-SubMenu	Name	mnuSheet
	Caption	&SpreadSheet
SubMenu	Name	mnuSep
	Caption	- (Separator)
SubMenu	Name	mnuExit
	Caption	E&xit
Menu Item	Name	mnuEdit
	Caption	&Edit
SubMenu Array	Name	mnuEdItem
	Index	0
	Caption	Cu&t
	Index	1
	Caption	&Copy
	Index	2
	Caption	&Paste
Menu Item	Name	mnuWindow
	Caption	&Window
	WindowList	Checked

continues

Table 35.3. Design-time settings—the MDI Parent form.

Visual Basic Object	Property	Design-Time Setting
SubMenu Array	Name	mnuWinItem
	Index	0
	Caption	&Cascade
	Index	1
	Caption	&Horizontal Tile
	Index	2
	Caption	&Vertical Tile
	Index	3
	Caption	&Arrange Icons

Notice that the File menu contains three items, including the separator. The first item, mnuNew, contains two additional submenu choices, mnuMemo and mnuSheet. This may be the first time you've gone to a third level of menus, so keep that in mind during the design phase.

Notice also that the Edit and Window menus contain Menu Control arrays, mnuEdItem() and mnuWinItem(). Remember to create these arrays by filling in the proper index value in the Menu Editor.

> **Caution** In designing Menu Control arrays, you might be tempted to assign an Index of zero to the menu object one level above the first item in the array, thinking, for example that mnuEdit or mnuWindow should be the array's first element. Menu Control arrays may not span across menu levels, and their elements must be contiguous in the menu hierarchy. That is, you may not have two items in the array, then a separator that's not part of the array, then more array items below the separator. It *is* possible to have nonsequential index numbers in a Control array, as long as they're in ascending order—though no one so far has come up with a good reason for doing so.

The indexes assigned to the mnuWinItem() array are of particular importance. They will be used later in this chapter, along with the Arrange command, to provide for the cascading and tiling of child windows. The last thing to notice is that mnuWindow's WindowList check box is checked. This will cause a list of open child forms to be displayed at run time, a handy feature for navigating quickly between many open windows. To help you visualize what's going on here, take a look a Figure 35.3.

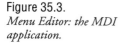

Figure 35.3.
Menu Editor: the MDI application.

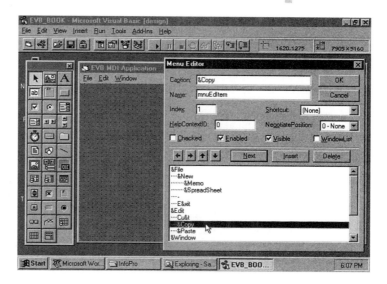

Adding Code to the MDI Parent Form

Amazingly, little code is required to get the MDI parent form working properly. As mentioned earlier, all code associated with the form is executed through menu selections.

When the user selects **N**ew from the **F**ile menu, then picks Memo from the corresponding submenu, a new instance of frmMemo will be created. Here's the listing:

```
Private Sub mnuMemo_Click()

Static iMemos As Integer            ' To keep track of how many memo
iMemos = iMemos + 1                 ' windows are open...Bump It..

Dim NewMemo As New frmMemo          ' Create a new instance of the frmMemo
                                    ' class of objects....(see discussion)

NewMemo.Caption = "Memo " & iMemos  ' Set the caption property of the new
NewMemo.Show                        ' form, and make the form visible.
End Sub
```

There's a little bit of class magic going on here. To Visual Basic, a form is just another object, a single instance of a new class which you, the programmer, have created and made available to the environment. You don't need to make several different memo forms, one for each memo window you open; you just "clone" them as you need them, using the Dim and New statements as seen in preceding code. You're creating a variable and assigning to it a reference to a new object, in this case, of the frmMemo class. You may then use the variable to manipulate the form's properties and methods.

When your user wants to create a new Spreadsheet child, you're doing the exact same thing, only you're using a different class of forms, the frmSheet class:

```
Private Sub mnuSheet_Click()

Static iSheets As Integer
iSheets = iSheets + 1
Dim NewSheet As New frmSheet
NewSheet.Caption = "Sheet " & iSheets
NewSheet.Show

End Sub
```

To get the parent form's Edit menu working, you'll need to learn a little about the Clipboard object. The Clipboard may be used to transfer text and pictures between different forms and controls, just as it's used in Windows itself. You may transfer text to the Clipboard by using its SetText method. Use the Clear method to empty the Clipboard of all contents. To retrieve text, you use the GetText() function, as you'll see in the following code. Remember that mnuEdItem() is a Menu control array, so each of its elements shares the same Click event procedure. Here it is:

```
Private Sub mnuEdItem_Click(Index As Integer)
On Error GoTo LocalHandler                        ' Minimum error handling...

Select Case Index                                 ' Which menu item was clicked?

 Case 0                                           ' If Cut...
  Clipboard.Clear                                 ' Clear the ClipBoard...
  Clipboard.SetText Screen.ActiveControl.SelText  ' and transfer to it whatever
                                                  ' text is selected, if any, in the
                                                  ' the active control.

  Screen.ActiveControl.SelText = ""               ' Replace the selected text
                                                  ' and empty string, thus
                                                  ' cutting it from the active
                                                  ' control.

 Case 1                                           ' If Copy...do the same thing
  Clipboard.Clear                                 ' but don't cut the selection
  Clipboard.SetText Screen.ActiveControl.SelText  ' from the active control...

 Case 2                                           ' If Paste...transfer whatever's
  Screen.ActiveControl.SelText = Clipboard.GetText()' in the ClipBoard to the
End Select                                        ' to the cursor location
Exit Sub                                          ' in the active control.

LocalHandler:                                     ' Local error handler
Exit Sub                                          ' just exits.

End Sub
```

You may remember from Chapters 30 and 31 on error handling that it's a good idea to think about error trapping whenever you access something outside your program. That's what you're doing when you reach out to the Clipboard object. In this case, you're setting up the barest skeleton of an error handler, one that merely keeps your program from crashing if something goes wrong. If there's an error, you simply exit the Sub procedure. (Don't forget the Exit Sub *before* the handler, either.)

The last bit of code is a clever little ditty that packs a heck of a wallop. It's a single line that will Cascade or Tile your child windows, either vertically or horizontally, depending on which menu item in the mnuWinItem() array is clicked. It will also arrange any wayward iconized children into neat little rows at the bottom of the parent window. All of this functionality in a single line! Here's how mnuWinItem's Click event should look:

```
Private Sub mnuWinItem_Click(Index As Integer)
Arrange Index
End Sub
```

This works because the Arrange command requires an integer argument from 0 to 3. Here's what Arrange does with each of those four values:

> 0 - Cascade all open child windows.
>
> 1 - Tile all open child windows horizontally.
>
> 2 - Tile all open child windows vertically.
>
> 3 - Arrange any iconized child windows along the bottom sill of the parent.

Each number happens to correspond exactly with the Index of the appropriate mnuWinItem() element! So all you have to do is pass Index to Arrange. Magic.

It's that time again. Fire up your new program and test it thoroughly. Figure 35.4 shows a sample session.

Figure 35.4.
The MDI application in action.

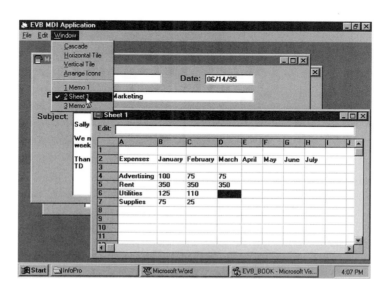

Part VII

Essential Summary

What

In this chapter, you learned that an MDI parent form is a container for other forms. Specifically, an MDI parent is a window that acts as the background of an application and is the container for other forms, created by you, that have their MDIChild property set to True.

Why

MDI applications provide an organized and easily managed multi-window environment whenever you need to view, exchange data between, or otherwise manipulate several documents, sheets, charts, or pictures, at once—or if you need to mix many different types of forms to be worked with as a group within a single application window.

How

Finally, you created a fully functional MDI application of your own. This application can display multiple instances of two "classes" of forms: a Memo and a Spreadsheet. These child forms, or windows, are able to easily exchange data through the Clipboard object. No matter how messy your "desktop" gets, with child forms randomly arranged in various sizes and positions, a simple selection from the Windows menu will whip them into shape.

Sequential and Random File I/O

This is a long and fast-moving chapter, so hold on to your hats! In the following pages, you'll learn how to create disk files containing contact and setup information from your Contact Manager Program; you'll also see how to read those files at run time, making their data available to your application. In the process, you'll encounter several new Visual Basic commands, statements, and functions, and you'll get a chance to work with a new Custom Control, CommonDialog, which allows you to make use of Windows' own predefined dialog boxes.

What Is File I/O?

What *File Input/Output (I/O)* is a general term for the mechanisms by which you may read and write disk files from within your programs. Disk files are used to store whatever kinds of data your program generates or manipulates and wants to save for later use. As you know, disk files hold all kinds of information—pictures, text, numeric data, even programs that can be run. The Visual Basic command, Open, is your gateway to the computer's disk drives and the files thereon; using this command is like pulling open a file drawer that allows you to place new folders (files) into the cabinet, as well as open existing folders for inspection or modification.

Opening Files

What

The Open command is designed to work with data, information of some kind, not executable programs. You use LoadPicture and SavePicture when working with images, as you did in Chapter 20. All that's left is information, usually in alphanumeric form, such as shopping lists, letters, poetry, or records such as those maintained by your Contact Manager program.

A file must be opened with the Open command before any I/O operation can be performed on it. The Open command is used to allocate a buffer (reserved memory) for I/O to the file, and to determine the mode of access to use with the buffer. There are three ways, or *modes*, you may use in opening a disk file: *binary*, *sequential*, and *random*. Here's the simplified syntax for the Open command:

```
Open sPathName  For Mode  As #FileNumber  Len=RecLength
```

Here sPathName is a string expression that specifies the file to be opened; it may include a directory and drive. If the file specified by sPathName doesn't exist, it is created when a file is opened for Append, Binary, Output, or Random modes. If the file already exists, and it's opened for Output, it will be overwritten, so be sure to use Append if you want to add to it.

Mode is one of five Visual Basic keywords specifying the mode in which the file will be opened. To specify sequential mode you use Append, Input, or Output, depending on whether you're adding data to an existing file, reading a file, or creating a new file and writing to it. To open a file in Binary or Random mode, you use the keywords Binary or Random, accordingly.

The FileNumber argument must be a valid file number in the range 1 to 511, inclusive. In the Binary, Input, and Random modes, you may open a file using a different file number without first closing the file. In Append and Output modes, however, you must first close a file before opening it with a different number.

The expression RecLength is a number less than or equal to 32,767 (bytes). For files opened for random access, it corresponds to the length of one record, as you'll see later in this chapter.

> **Tip** If you plan on having several files opened at once, you should set your FileNumber equal to Visual Basic's FreeFile function. The FreeFile function returns the next file number available for use by the Open statement; it's used when you have to supply a file number and you want to make sure the file number is not already in use.

Closing Files

When you're finished reading or writing a file, you may close it using the Close statement. Close concludes input/output to a file opened using the Open statement. Its syntax is very simple:

```
Close FileNumberList
```

The optional *FileNumberList* can be one or more file numbers separated by commas. If you omit *FileNumberList*, all active files opened by the Open statement are closed. When you close files that were opened for Output or Append, any buffered data for that file is written to the file before closing. When the Close statement is executed, the association of a file with its file number ends, and all buffer space associated with the closed file is released back to the memory pool.

The Three File Modes

As mentioned earlier in the "Opening Files" section, there are three ways (or modes) in which you may open a disk file: binary, sequential, and random access. Each of these modes is discussed in turn in the following sections.

Binary File Access

Of the three modes, Binary is the least automated, meaning the programmer must handle more of the detail work as to location within the file, and the number of characters (individual bytes) to be read or written. For this reason, Binary is used less frequently than the other two modes, and will not be covered in this chapter.

Sequential Access Files

A file opened for sequential access allows for simpler I/O by way of the Line Input # and Print # commands. Although you can read a single byte, Sequential mode is more commonly used to read in (or write out) entire lines at a time. Reading and writing complete lines simplifies the I/O process considerably because you can use Line Input # to read an entire line into a single string variable, or use Print # to write the contents of a variable to its own line in the file. You don't need to keep track of where you are in the file because Visual Basic knows to move to the next line with each successive call to Line Input # or Print #. This makes sequential access great for working with files made up of lines of varying lengths, such as autoexec and special config files, or Windows INI files, where each line represents a distinct program setting or feature. The Line Input # and Print # statements are discussed next.

The Line Input # statement reads a line from an open sequential file and assigns it to a string variable. Here's the syntax:

```
Line Input #FileNumber, sVarName
```

where `FileNumber` is the number of the sequential access file you wish to read, and `sVarName` is a valid string variable name. The Line Input # statement reads from a file one character at a time until it encounters a carriage return (Chr(13)) or carriage return-linefeed (Chr(13) + Chr(10)) sequence. However, the CRLF sequence is not included in the character string.

The following code shows how you might read the first 10 lines of your WIN.INI file and print them to a form:

```
iFileNumber = FreeFile                                  ' Get a free number...
Open "C:\Windows\Win.Ini" For Input As #iFileNumber     ' Open the file...

For X = 1 To 10                                         ' Read and print
    Line Input #iFileNumber, sCurrentLine$              ' the first 10 lines...
    Print sCurrentLine$
Next
Close #iFileNumber                                      ' Close when done.
```

What   The Print # statement writes data, one line at a time, to a sequential file opened for Output or Append. Here's its syntax:

```
Print #FileNumber, OutputList
```

where `FileNumber` is the number of the sequential access file you wish to write to, and `OutputList` is the string or numeric expression, or list of expressions, you wish to print. If you omit `OutputList` and include only a comma after `FileNumber`, a blank line is printed to the file.

As an example of the Print # statement, let's say you wanted to create a disk file containing the list of clowns you worked with in Chapter 33. The clown names were kept in an array called `saClowns()`, as you'll recall. Here's how you'd write the contents of that array to disk:

```
iFileNumber = FreeFile                                  ' Get a free number...
Open "C:\VB40\Clowns.Dat" For Output As #iFileNumber    ' Open the file...

For X = 1 To 10                                         ' Write each clown
    Print #iFileNumber, saClowns(X)                     ' to the file.
Next
Close #iFileNumber                                      ' Close when done.
```

Random Access Files

Files opened for random access are anything but random in structure. In fact, the name "random" is somewhat misleading because this is the most strict and inflexible of the three modes in which you can open a file. It's called "random" because data is stored as "records" of a fixed size, which may be accessed *randomly* without having to read through any preceding data.

Here's how this is accomplished. One piece of information you include in opening a file for random access is the size of each record. Once Visual Basic knows the size of a record, it's a simple bit of multiplication to determine the precise point in the file where a particular record is located. That is, if each record is 50 characters long, and you want record 12, Visual Basic will jump right to byte 600 and begin reading. For this reason, the computer need not search through such a file *sequentially*, looking for carriage returns or other codes to let it know when it has a complete chunk of data. Instead, it can *randomly* access any record in the file.

> **Tip** A good way to remember the distinction between *sequential* and *random* file access is to think of music on tape versus compact discs. When you want the sixth cut on a tape, you have to pass through the preceding five cuts to get to it, even if you're fast-forwarding. A CD, on the other hand, allows you to jump almost instantly from one tune to another. That is, tapes require sequential access but compact discs may be accessed randomly.

Once a file is opened for Random (or Binary) access, it may be written to and read from using Visual Basic's Put # and Get # statements. They are discussed next.

What

The Put # statement writes from a variable to a disk file opened for either Random or Binary access. Here's how it's used:

```
Put [#]FileNumber, RecNumber, VarName
```

Here, *FileNumber* is the valid number of the file you want to write to. The *RecNumber* argument is the record number (in Random mode) or byte number (in Binary mode) at which the writing is to begin. *VarName* is the name of the variable containing the data to be written to disk.

The Get statement reads data from a disk file opened for Random or Binary access into a variable. Here's how it works:

What

```
Get [#]FileNumber, RecNumber, VarName
```

The arguments here are exactly the same as for the Put # statement, except that *VarName* is the name of the variable to *receive* the incoming data.

In the next section, you'll put the Open, Close, Line Input #, Print #, Put #, and Get # statements to good use in adding special File I/O features to your Contact Manager program.

How to Access Sequential and Random Files

In this section, you'll use the Open, Close, Line Input #, Print #, Put #, and Get # statements to add File I/O functionality to your Contact Manager program. Specifically, you will add a file Export/Import feature which will allow you to write your contact data to disk in a random access format which may be imported into your own or other programs. You'll also allow your users to define a program configuration file which may be read at run time and used to display personalized user name and company information in the program's main title bar.

Your first step is to make some design modifications to your Contact Manager program. Open your EVB_BOOK project, then open frmContacts in Design mode. (You should make frmContacts the project startup form at this time.) Now use the Menu Editor to add the short File Menu you'll see in Figure 36.1. Here are the new menu specifications:

How

Table 36.1. Design-time settings—the Contact Manager File menu.

Visual Basic Object	Property	Design-Time Setting
Menu Item	Name	mnuFile
	Caption	&File
SubMenu	Name	mnuImport
	Caption	&Import
SubMenu	Name	mnuExport
	Caption	&Export
SubMenu	Name	mnuSep1
	Caption	- (Separator)
SubMenu	Name	mnuSetup
	Caption	&Program Setup
SubMenu	Name	mnuSep2
	Caption	- (Separator)
SubMenu	Name	mnuExit
	Caption	E&xit

Figure 36.1.
The Contact Manager File menu.

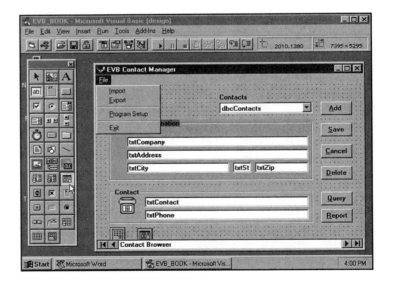

You'll notice in Figure 36.1 that a new Custom Control has been placed on the form, as well. This is the CommonDialog control, and it allows you to use Windows' own built-in dialog boxes, such as the File Open and File Save boxes you see in almost every Windows application.

You should go ahead and place this control on your form, accepting the default name of CommonDialog1. You won't need to set any properties at design time, and the control will not be visible at run time, so it really doesn't matter where you place it.

Adding Code

The first thing to do, by way of adding code, is to create a new user-defined data type which will be perfect for writing your contact records to disk, as well as for reading them during the import process. You may recall from Chapter 3, lo so many chapters ago, that you're not limited to the data types provided by Visual Basic. You may create your own specialized types which are custom-tailored for your program's purposes. The way to do so is by using the Type...End Type construct. Custom data types must be defined in a standard code module, such as EVB_CODE. Open that module now, and add the following lines to its general declarations section:

```
Type ContactRecord              ' User-defined type in EVB_CODE module

    Code As String * 5          ' The ContactRecord type will contain elements
    Company As String * 30      ' which correspond exactly with the fields found
    Address As String * 30      ' in your Contacts table.  In this case, all of the
    City As String * 20         ' elements are of the string type, and you'll notice
    State As String * 2         ' that they are sized precisely, to make the most
    Zip As String * 5           ' efficient use of memory.
    Contact As String * 30
    Phone As String * 15

    NewLine As String * 2       ' Since your records will be stored on separate
                                ' lines in the disk file,  you're including a couple
                                ' of bytes for the CRLF characters.
End Type
```

Now you'll be able to declare variables of this special type whenever you need them. They'll come in handy in both the export and import procedures, as you'll see. For now, close the EVB_CODE module and save your changes.

The rest of the new code will be added to frmContacts, the Contact Manager's main form, which you should open now. You may remember the following event procedure from the earlier version of the Contact Manager program:

```
Private Sub Form_Activate()
'dbcContacts.Text = dtaContacts.Recordset("Contact")      ' Comment out this line!
End Sub
```

This procedure was used to perform a purely cosmetic function involving what was first displayed in the Contacts drop-down list. For now, comment out the single line in this procedure, because it will give you headaches later during testing.

The real work of the new file import and export features will be accomplished in two special Sub procedures which should be added to frmContact's general declarations section. As these procedures will be accessing the disk, they will contain simple error-handling routines to provide a little information, and keep your program from crashing should something unfavorable occur.

> **Tip** During development, it's not a bad idea to disable your custom error-handlers, either by commenting out the On Error GoTo lines or changing them to On Error GoTo 0. The reason for this is that when you're running your program in the development environment, Visual Basic will provide its own error-trapping and will even allow you to jump right into the debugger and to the very line that caused the error! This is a terrific feature of which you should take full advantage. You can, and should, enable your own error-handlers when you're ready to build and deliver the completed application.

Here's the annotated listing of the file export procedure. Again, it should be added to the Contact Manager form's general declaration's section.

```
Sub ExportFile(sFileOut As String)              ' Will be passed  the name of the
                                                ' file to receive the exported data.

Dim dbContacts As Database                      ' Need database...
Dim rsContacts As Recordset                     ' and recordset variables.

Dim iFileNumber As Integer                      ' For file number...
Dim iRecordNumber As Integer                    ' For tracking number of records...

Dim NL As String                                ' Carriage return, line feed...

Dim CurrentRecord As ContactRecord              ' Declare a variable of your
                                                ' custom type, ContactRecord.

On Error GoTo LocalHandler                      ' Set up error-trapping. Might
                                                ' want to disable this for now.

NL = Chr$(13) & Chr$(10)                         ' CRLF

Set dbContacts = OpenDatabase("c:\vb40\sams\contacts.mdb")   ' Open database and...
Set rsContacts = dbContacts.OpenRecordset("Contacts", dbOpenDynaset) ' recordset...

rsContacts.MoveFirst                            ' To top of recordset...

iFileNumber = FreeFile                          ' Get a file number...
                                                ' and open it...
Open sFileOut For Random As #iFileNumber Len = Len(CurrentRecord)

Do Until rsContacts.EOF                         ' Loop until no more records...

    iRecordNumber = iRecordNumber + 1           ' Bump the record number...
                                                ' then copy the contents of each
    CurrentRecord.Code = rsContacts("Code")     ' field into the corresponding
    CurrentRecord.Company = rsContacts("Company") ' element of the custom data
    CurrentRecord.Address = rsContacts("Address") ' data variable.
    CurrentRecord.City = rsContacts("City")
    CurrentRecord.State = rsContacts("State")   ' Notice how you're able to refer
    CurrentRecord.Zip = rsContacts("Zip")        ' to the different elements of your
    CurrentRecord.Contact = rsContacts("Contact") ' custom variable by using dots.
    CurrentRecord.Phone = rsContacts("Phone")
```

```
        CurrentRecord.NewLine = NL                          ' And add CRLF...

        Put #iFileNumber, iRecordNumber, CurrentRecord  ' Write CurrentRecord to file.

        rsContacts.Delete                                   ' Delete the record, so you can
                                                            ' import it later and avoid
                                                            ' duplicate keys...

        rsContacts.MoveNext                                 ' Next record, please...
    Loop

    dtaContacts.Refresh                                     ' No records to show
    Close #iFileNumber                                      ' Close the export file...
    rsContacts.Close                                        ' Close recordset
    dbContacts.Close                                        ' and database.

    MsgBox "Table Has Been Emptied!", vbInformation, "Data Export Successful!"

    Exit Sub                                                ' Put up a nice message, and exit.

    LocalHandler:                                           ' Local handler...
      MsgBox Error$(Err), vbCritical, "File Export Error"
      Exit Sub
    End Sub
```

Normally, you'd want to export data without deleting records from the database, unless you were performing some sort of purging-to-archive operation. In this case, you'll remove the records as you export them so that you can test the import routine in the following code, without receiving key violation errors.

Now here's the corresponding import routine. It's very similar to the export routine—you're just transferring data in the opposite direction:

```
Sub ImportFile(sFileIn As String)                       ' Import file name comes in...

Dim dbContacts As Database                              ' Same as before...
Dim rsContacts As Recordset
Dim iFileNumber, iRecordNumber As Integer
Dim iFileSize, iTotalRecords As Long
Dim CurrentRecord As ContactRecord

On Error GoTo LocalHandler

Set dbContacts = OpenDatabase("c:\vb40\sams\contacts.mdb")
Set rsContacts = dbContacts.OpenRecordset("Contacts", dbOpenDynaset)

iFileNumber = FreeFile

Open sFileIn For Random As iFileNumber Len = Len(CurrentRecord)

iFileSize = LOF(iFileNumber)                            ' This is different.  You're using
                                                        ' the length-of-file function to
                                                        ' see how many bytes are in
                                                        ' the import file.

iTotalRecords = Int(iFileSize / Len(CurrentRecord))     ' Then you compute the number
                                                        ' of records in the file,
                                                        ' which is
```

```
                                                    ' just the file size divided
                                                    ' by the
                                                    ' length of a record.

iRecordNumber = 1                                   ' Then you count the records as
Do While iRecordNumber <= iTotalRecords             ' you bring them in.

    Get iFileNumber, iRecordNumber, CurrentRecord   ' Read the record with Get...

    rsContacts.AddNew                              ' Add a new record to recordset...

    rsContacts("Code") = CurrentRecord.Code         ' and read it in via the
    rsContacts("Company") = CurrentRecord.Company   ' CurrentRecord variable.
    rsContacts("Address") = CurrentRecord.Address
    rsContacts("City") = CurrentRecord.City
    rsContacts("State") = CurrentRecord.State
    rsContacts("Zip") = CurrentRecord.Zip
    rsContacts("Contact") = CurrentRecord.Contact
    rsContacts("Phone") = CurrentRecord.Phone

    rsContacts.Update                               ' Post the record to the set...

    iRecordNumber = iRecordNumber + 1               ' and bump the record number.

Loop                                                ' Do the next one, till there
                                                    ' aint no more....

rsContacts.Close                                    ' Close the set..
dbContacts                                          ' and the database reference.

dtaContacts.Refresh                                 ' Now admire the new records...
                                                    ' after reading a nice message.
MsgBox "New Records Have Been Added!", vbInformation, "Data Import Successful!"
Exit Sub

LocalHandler:
  MsgBox Error$(Err), vbCritical, "File Import Error"

Exit Sub
End Sub
```

OK, now that you have the export/import procedures in place, it's time to see how to call them. This is where the CommonDialog control comes in. When the File Export menu is clicked, you'll display a dialog box, borrowed from Windows, which may be used to enter the name of the file to be imported; or if your user doesn't remember the name, the box may be used to browse the current disk environment to locate it. As you'll see, the CommonDialog control has many properties which may be set to select a particular dialog box and control the way it looks and acts. Here's the annotated listing of mnuExport's `Click` event procedure:

```
Private Sub mnuExport_Click()
Dim sFileName As String                 ' String variable for selected filename.
On Error GoTo LocalHandler              '  To handle cancel button error, if clicked

CommonDialog1.CancelError = True        ' Cancel button will generate error...

CommonDialog1.DialogTitle = "Enter Export File Name"  ' Title of box....and, on the
                                                      ' next line, available file
                                                      ' filters...
```

```
CommonDialog1.Filter = "Export Data Files (*.DAT)¦*.DAT¦All Files (*.*)¦*.*"
CommonDialog1.FilterIndex = 1                ' Default to first filter...

CommonDialog1.DefaultExt = "DAT"             ' Default file extension...

CommonDialog1.InitDir = "C:\VB40\SAMS"       ' Initial directory, when the
                                             ' dialog box first opens...

CommonDialog1.Action = 2                     ' Open the Save As...
                                             ' dialog box...

sFileName = CommonDialog1.Filename           ' And store the entered or
                                             ' or selected name to the
                                             ' sFileName variable...


If sFileName <> "" Then                      ' If it isn't empty...
    ExportFile sFileName                     ' pass it to the export
End If                                        ' routine.
Exit Sub

LocalHandler:                                '  In this case, an error means
Exit Sub                                     ' the Cancel button was
End Sub                                      ' clicked...so exit.
```

Here's a very similar listing which displays the Windows File Open dialog box, so that the user may select a file for importing:

```
Private Sub mnuImport_Click()
Dim sFileName As String

On Error GoTo LocalHandler

CommonDialog1.CancelError = True

CommonDialog1.DialogTitle = "Select Data File For Import"    ' Different title, same
➥filters
CommonDialog1.Filter = "Import Data Files (*.DAT)¦*.DAT¦All Files (*.*)¦*.*"
CommonDialog1.FilterIndex = 1

CommonDialog1.InitDir = "C:\VB40\SAMS"
CommonDialog1.Action = 1                     ' This time, show File Open...

sFileName = CommonDialog1.filename           '  And, if it's not empty,
If sFileName <> "" Then                      ' send the filename to
    ImportFile sFileName                     ' the file import procedure.
End If
Exit Sub

LocalHandler:                                ' In case they click Cancel...
  Exit Sub
End Sub
```

By setting the CommonDialog control's CancelError property to True, you're forcing Visual Basic to throw an error if the user decides to click the dialog box's Cancel button, thus providing an easy way to tell if the import (or export) procedure should be aborted. You just trap the error, then exit the procedure.

The use of the Filter and FilterIndex properties might require a little more explication. What you're doing is defining which types of files will be displayed in the dialog box's file list. In effect, you're creating a list of filters from which the user may choose.

The Filter string is made up of one or more two-part components: the filter description and the actual filter specification. These components are separated by the pipe character (|), and you must be careful not to include any unwanted spaces. The Filter string in the preceding code indicates that the user will have two filters available: one that limits the file list to files with an extension of DAT and another that will display all files (*.*) in the current directory. The FilterIndex property, in this case, specifies that the first filter will be in effect when the box opens, although the user may select the other filter if he or she desires. A little visual reinforcement is probably in order here. Take a look at Figure 36.2 to see the File Import dialog box in action.

Figure 36.2.
The File Import dialog box in action.

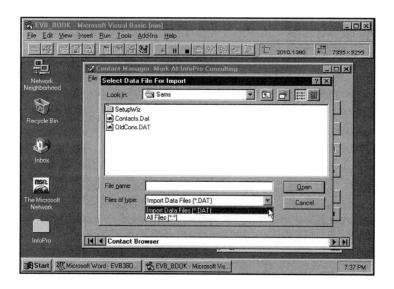

That's all there is to creating, reading, and writing random access files. At least, that's all that's necessary to import and export from your Contact Manager program. Now it's time to see how to work with sequential access files.

How

Your enhanced Contact Manager program will have a Setup routine that will allow users to create a customized configuration file to store personalized information, in this case the user's name and company. This information will be read into the program at startup and displayed in the main form's title bar. Here's the code for the Setup procedure, which should be attached to mnuSetup's Click event:

```
Private Sub mnuSetUp_Click()

Dim sUser, sCompany As String          ' For user name and company....
Dim iFileNumber As Integer             ' and for file number.
```

```
On Error GoTo LocalHandler                      ' Accessing the disk, so setup
                                                ' error handling.

                                                ' Now ask for user's name...
sUser = InputBox$("Please Enter Your Name: ", "Program Setup Information")

If sUser = "" Then Exit Sub                     ' If canceled, or no response...Exit

sCompany = InputBox("Please Enter The Name Of Your Company: ", "Program Setup
Information")                                    ' Ask for company...

If sCompany = "" Then Exit Sub                  ' Exit if no response...

iFileNumber = FreeFile                          ' Get next available file number...
                                                ' and open the file for Output.
Open "C:\vb40\sams\Contacts.Cfg" For Output As #iFileNumber

Print #iFileNumber, sUser                       ' Write user name to file..
Print #iFileNumber, sCompany                    ' Write company to file..
Close #iFileNumber                              ' Close the file...and set the set
                                                ' the form's new caption.
Me.Caption = "Contact Manager: " & sUser & " At " & sCompany

Exit Sub                                        ' Don't forget to exit, before you
                                                ' hit the error-handler.

LocalHandler:                                   ' Display error, then exit...
  MsgBox Error$(Err), vbCritical, "Error Creating Setup File"
  Exit Sub

End Sub
```

The last step is to have frmContact's Load event search the disk for the configuration file. If it finds one, the file is opened, and the personalized information is displayed in the title bar. If no configuration file is available, or if it's empty, then the title bar will display the default caption. Here's how frmContact's Load event will look:

```
Private Sub Form_Load()

Dim iFileNumber As Integer                      ' Need some variables...including
Dim sCompany As String, sUser As String, sConfigFile As String     ' one for the
➥config filename.

On Error GoTo LocalHandler                      ' Set up error trapping...

sConfigFile = Dir("C:\vb40\sams\contacts.cfg")    ' Dir() returns the name of the
                                                ' file, if it's found in the specified
                                                ' directory. Otherwise, an empty
                                                ' string.

If sConfigFile = "" Then                        ' If no config file...
    Me.Caption = "EVB Contact Manager"          ' use default caption...
Else
    sConfigFile = "C:\vb40\sams\" & sConfigFile     ' If there is one, specify its
                                                    ' complete path...

    iFileNumber = FreeFile                          ' Get a file number...
```

```
    Open sConfigFile For Input As #iFileNumber    ' Open it for Input, that is,
                                                  ' to be read.

    If LOF(iFileNumber) > 0 Then                  ' If the file's not empty...

        Line Input #iFileNumber, sUser            ' Read the first line into sUser...
        Line Input #iFileNumber, sCompany         ' Second line into sCompany...

        Close #iFileNumber                        ' Close....then set the customized
                                                  ' caption in the title bar.
        Me.Caption = "Contact Manager: " + sUser + " At " + sCompany

    Else                                          ' Config File is empty...
        Close #iFileNumber                        ' So close it...
        Me.Caption = "EVB Contact Manager"        ' and set the default caption.
    End If
  End If
Exit Sub                                          ' Don't for get this...

LocalHandler:                                     ' Display error, and exit.
  MsgBox Error$(Err), vbCritical, "Error Reading Setup File"
  Exit Sub

End Sub
```

That, at long last, is it. It's time to test all the new features of your Contact Manager program. You should be able to export your contact records to a file of your choice. Since the export procedure also removes the records from your database, you'll be able to import them immediately, without any concern for duplicate keys. If you try to import them again, you'll receive an error message indicating a key violation, which is fine. (Once your custom error-handler is activated, this message will not shut down the program.) You could use your favorite text editor to edit the exported data file directly, changing the Contact fields to avoid duplication, then import the edited file. A more practical use for the import feature would be to import a completely new list of contacts, which might be created in a text editor, or spreadsheet program, or even exported from a different database system.

You'll also be able to run the Setup routine and provide your own name and company information. Watch the title bar change as the new information is displayed. Notice also that you may quit and then restart the program, and the personalized information will still be displayed. The program automatically reads the configuration file at startup. You may delete Contacts.CFG to return the title bar to its default caption.

You've worked hard in this chapter. In the next, much shorter chapter, you'll add one more feature to your Contact Manager program. If you have a modem, you'll be able to use it to automatically dial a contact's phone number.

Essential Summary

In this chapter, you learned that the Open statement lets you create and access disk files directly. You discovered that the Open statement provides three types of file access: Sequential, Random, and Binary. Once a file was opened, you saw that it may be written to, or read, using the Line Input #, Print #, Put #, and Get # statements. Finally, you were introduced to CommonDialog, a custom control that allows you to "borrow" Windows' own predefined dialog boxes and modify them for your own purposes.

What

Sequential access files are commonly used for writing text files, such as error logs and reports, as well as special configuration files such as Windows INI files. Sequential access is best when you're dealing with files composed of lines of varying lengths, but each line represents a distinct unit of information.

Why

Random access mode is used whenever you need to read and write data to a file without closing it, and file data is stored in records of a specific length. Random file access is an excellent technique for manipulating database data since the information is already organized into fields and records.

Binary access (Binary mode) is used less frequently than the other two, but may come in handy in specialized cases where you need to read or write to any byte position in a file, such as when storing or modifying a bitmap image, and the image manipulation tools provided by Visual Basic don't quite fill the bill.

You exercised your new File I/O skills by adding new features to your Contact Manager program. You added a file Export/Import utility which allows you to write your contact data to disk in a random access format which may be imported into your own or other programs. You also wrote a Setup routine that allows your users to define a configuration file that is read at run time and is used to display personalized name and company information in the program's title bar.

How

Serial Communications

After the last chapter, you can use a breather. In this short but fun chapter, you'll see how to manipulate your system's COM ports, using the MSComm communications control. Specifically, you'll add a special phone dialing feature to your Contact Manager program; this will allow you to autodial the selected Contact by clicking the Telephone icon. This chapter assumes you have a modem installed in your system. If not, read along anyway, and you'll be ready to autocall once you have the proper hardware.

What Is the Communications Control?

What The *Communications control* provides serial communications for your application by allowing the transmission and reception of data through a serial port. Each communications control you use corresponds to one serial port, so if you need to access more than one serial port in your application, you must use more than one Communications control.

As you may know, *modems* are serial communications devices; if you have one, it's connected to a serial port on your computer (even if you have an internal modem, it's still regarded by your system as a serial port), so the Communications control is perfect for performing modem operations such as dialing the phone.

> **Note** Many entire books are dedicated to the subject of serial communications. A complete exploration of all that can be accomplished using serial communications, and the MSComm custom control, is beyond the scope of this book.

Although the Communications control has many important and powerful properties, you'll require a minimal understanding of only a few in order to accomplish your goal in this chapter. Here's a summary list, with a slightly more detailed discussion to follow.

Table 37.1. Communications control properties.

Properties	Description
CommPort	Sets and returns the communications port number.
Settings	Sets and returns the bps rate (bits per second), parity, data bits, and stop bits as a string.
PortOpen	Opens or closes a serial port for communications.
Input	Returns and removes characters from the receive buffer.
Output	Writes a string of characters to the transmit buffer.
InBufferCount	Counts characters received in the input buffer.
OutBufferCount	Counts characters waiting to be transmitted.

The CommPort property sets and returns the communications port number. You can set the CommPort property to any number between 1 and 99 at design time, and the default is 1. However, the communications control generates a Device Unavailable error 68, if the port does not exist, when you attempt to open it with the PortOpen property. You must set the CommPort property before opening the port.

The Settings property sets and returns the bps rate, parity, data bit, and stop bit parameters. This property expects a parameter string in the following format:

```
"BBBB,P,D,S"
```

Where BBBB is the bps rate, P is the parity, D is the number of data bits, and S is the number of stop bits. The default setting for this property is 9600,N,8,1. If the setting is not valid when the port is opened, MSComm generates error 380, indicating an Invalid Property Value. Refer to Table 37.2 for valid settings.

Table 37.2. Valid settings: property values.

Bps or Baud	Parity Settings	Data Bits	Stop Bits
110	E - Even	4	1 (Default)
300	M - Mark	5	1.5
600	N - None (Default)	6	2
1200	O - Odd	7	
2400	S - Space	8 (Default)	
9600 (Default)			
14400			
19200			
38400 (Reserved)			
56000 (Reserved)			
128000 (Reserved)			
256000 (Reserved)			

The PortOpen property sets and returns the state of the communications port (open or closed, True or False). This property is not available at design time. Setting the PortOpen property to True opens the port. Setting it to False closes the port and clears the receive and transmit buffers. The communications control automatically closes the serial port when your application is terminated.

The Input property returns and removes a string of characters from the receive buffer. This property is not available at design time and is read-only at run time. The InputLen property determines the number of characters that are read by the Input property. Setting InputLen to 0 (the default) causes the Input property to read the entire contents of the receive buffer.

The Output property writes a string of characters to the transmit buffer, where they are received by the associated COM port. This property is not available at design time.

The InBufferCount property returns the number of characters waiting in the receive buffer. InBufferCount refers to the number of characters that have been received by the modem and are waiting in the receive buffer for you to take them out. You can clear the receive buffer by setting the InBufferCount property to 0. This property is often used to wait for a valid response string from the modem, and is not available at design time.

The OutBufferCount property returns the number of characters waiting in the transmit buffer. You can also use it to clear the transmit buffer by setting the property to 0. This property is not available at design time.

> **Caution** Be careful not to confuse the InBufferCount and OutBufferCount properties with InBufferSize and OutBufferSize. The Size properties reflect, or set, the total size of the receive and send buffers, not just how many characters are currently contained there.

Following is an example of how these properties may be used to initialize a modem attached to your system's COM2 port. If you're driven to try this example for yourself, add a new form to your EVB_BOOK project and make it the startup form. Drop an MSComm Communications control on it, and add the code to your form's Click event. If your modem is not on COM2, make the proper adjustment. Then run the program and click the form. If your modem is working and is properly connected, you'll get a response of OK.

```
Dim sResponse As String          ' For storing the modem response...
MSComm1.CommPort = 2             ' Use COM2.
MSComm1.Settings = "9600,N,8,1"  ' 9600 baud, no parity, 8 data, and 1 stop bit.
MSComm1.InputLen = 0             ' Read entire buffer when Input is used...

MSComm1.PortOpen = True          ' Open the port.

MSComm1.Output = "AT" + Chr$(13) ' Send the attention command to the modem.

Do                               ' Wait for the modem's response...
        Dummy = DoEvents()
Loop Until MSComm1.InBufferCount >= 2 ' Until there's at least two characters back..

sResponse = MSComm1.Input        ' Read the response data in the serial port.

MsgBox sResponse,vbInformation,"Modem Response"    ' Display the response...

MSComm1.PortOpen = False                            ' Close the serial port.
```

Why Use Serial Communications?

You use serial communications whenever you need to both send and receive information via one of your system's COM ports. By using the Communications control, you may directly manipulate standard serial hardware such as modems, some printers, mice, joysticks, as well as a whole world of a specialized hardware from simple trackballs to computerized pumps and compressors, to satellite signaling devices. Your program must be capable of serial communications if you intend to engage in on-line communications sessions or otherwise take control of any serial ports and connected peripheral devices available to your system.

How to Use the Communications Control

If you haven't already done so, open your Contact Manager form in Design mode. You may need to add the MSComm Custom control to your Toolbox. If so, press Ctrl+T to open the Custom Control dialog box, and check the entry labeled "Microsoft Comm Control." Click OK, and the control will now be available. Place it anywhere on your form, and retain the default Name of MSComm1. (Be sure frmContacts is the startup form.)

Here, in Figure 37.1, is what the modified form will look like in Design mode.

Figure 37.1.
The modem-aware
Contact Manager
program.

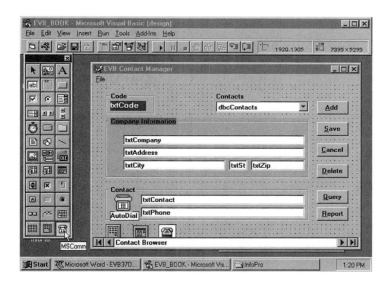

Notice the new Communications control on the form and the arrow indicating what the control looks like in the Toolbox. You might also notice the ToolTip beneath the telephone. It's just a friendly touch to let your user know what the Telephone icon is for.

Table 37.3 contains the design-time settings for the new controls in your Contact Manager program.

Table 37.3. Design-time settings—the enhanced Contact Manager.

Visual Basic Object	Property	Design-Time Setting
MSComm Control	Name	MSComm1
Label Control	Name	lblPhone
	Caption	AutoDial

continues

Table 37.3. Design-time settings—the enhanced Contact Manager.

Visual Basic Object	Property	Design-Time Setting
	Appearance	Flat
	AutoSize	True
	BorderStyle	Fixed Single
	BackColor	Light Yellow
	Visible	False

Adding Code

You'll need to add a little code to get your program's autodial feature working. First, create a new procedure called DialOut, which will be stored in the form's general declarations section. Here it is:

```
Sub DialOut(sCallNumber As String)          ' Will receive a number to dial...

On Error GoTo LocalHandler                  ' You're reaching out of your
                                            ' controlled programming
                                            ' environment, so error trapping
                                            ' is a must.

MSComm1.CommPort = 2                         ' Adjust for your modem port...

MSComm1.Settings = "9600,N,8,1"             ' and settings....

MSComm1.InputLen = 0                         ' Read all of  receive buffer, later

MSComm1.PortOpen = True                      ' Open the port....

MSComm1.Output = "AT" + Chr$(13)            ' Get the modem's attention,

Do                                           ' And wait until you receive
    Dummy = DoEvents()                      ' a response...
Loop Until MSComm1.InBufferCount >= 2

MSComm1.InBufferCount = 0                     ' Clear the InBuffer....

MSComm1.Output = "ATDT" + sCallNumber + Chr$(13)     ' Send the dial command and
                                                     ' the number, and simulate
                                                     ' pressing ENTER.

                                                     ' Display a message
MsgBox "Pick Up The Phone And Click OK", vbExclamation, "Dialing: " & sCallNumber &
➥ "..."
                                            ' User should wait till dialing
                                            ' is through, then click OK.
```

```
MSComm1.PortOpen = False                          ' Close the port.
Exit Sub

LocalHandler:                                     ' In case of problems...
  MsgBox Error$(Err), vbCritical, "Modem Communications Error!"
  Exit Sub

End Sub
```

All that's needed now is a little code to prepare the number to be sent to the DialOut procedure. This will be executed when the user clicks the Telephone, so add the following code to picPhone's Click event:

```
Private Sub picPhone_Click()

Dim sPhoneNumber As String                        ' Variable for phone number...
sPhoneNumber = dtaContacts.Recordset("PHONE")     ' Get it from the Data
                                                  ' Control's recordset.

If Mid(sPhoneNumber, 1, 1) = "(" Then             ' Add a 1, if an area code
    sPhoneNumber = "1-" + sPhoneNumber            ' is included..
End If

DialOut sPhoneNumber                              ' Send the number to DialOut...

End Sub
```

That's it for the autodial routine. If you've got a modem, give it a try. You might want to make sure your contacts have valid phone numbers. And remember that a 1 will be automatically added to the calling string if the first character is a left parenthesis (( ); otherwise, it's not. Also, all non-numeric characters will be ignored by the modem.

> **Note** It's up to you to get your ToolTip working. You'll want it to become visible when the mouse is moved over the Telephone; but it should be invisible otherwise. (Hint: you did some ToolTipping in Chapter 19.)

Here, in Figure 37.2, is your auto-dialing routine in action.

Figure 37.2.
The Contact Manager
program's Auto-Dialer.

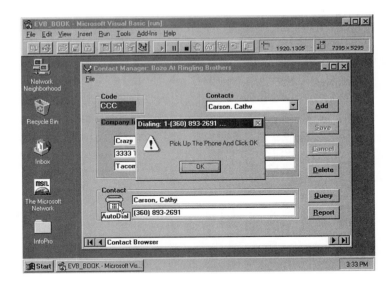

Essential Summary

What   In this chapter, you learned how to manipulate your system's modem by using the MSComm Communications control. You saw that it's possible to send and receive data via your modem, or serial ports in general. And you received a brief overview of the Communications Control properties used in getting a modem to dial a telephone number from within your Contact Manager program.

Why   Your program must be capable of serial communications if you intend to engage in on-line communications sessions or otherwise take control of any serial ports and connected peripheral devices available to your system. By using the Communications control, you may directly manipulate serial hardware such as modems, some printers, mice, trackballs, joysticks, and other digitizing equipment.

How   You put your new serial communications skills to use by adding a special phone dialing feature to your Contact Manager program; this new feature allows you to autodial the selected Contact by clicking the Telephone icon.

Object Linking and Embedding (OLE)

It's time to see how to bring the power of other applications into your own programs. In this chapter, you'll explore one of the most exciting parts of Visual Basic—the OLE Control—which, among other things, allows you to directly *link* or *embed* objects from OLE server applications into your Visual Basic programs. And of course, you'll create a new program in which you'll explore linking and embedding, as well as some of the more advanced ideas behind OLE Automation Objects.

What Is OLE?

What The acronym *OLE* stands for *Object Linking and Embedding*, which represents the technology that enables a programmer of Windows-based applications to create a program that can display data from many different applications, and enables the user to edit that data from within the application in which it was created. Rather than simply paste a range of Excel spreadsheet cells into your Visual Basic program, OLE allows you to paste in an entire sheet, with all the power of Excel itself behind it. By using OLE, you can give your users complete word processing capabilities, rather than a mere multi-line TextBox control, by linking in or embedding a Word or WordPad document.

What
The term *OLE Object* refers to a discrete unit of data supplied by an application. An application can provide (or *expose*) many types of objects. For example, a spreadsheet application can expose a worksheet, macro sheet, chart, cell, or range of cells, all as different types of objects. A word processor such as Word 6.0 might expose a document or picture object. An application that receives and displays an object's data is a *container* application. For example, a Visual Basic application that uses an OLE container control to embed or link data from another application is a container application.

What
The data associated with *linked objects* is stored by the application that supplied the object. The application only stores link references that display a snapshot of the source data. When you *link* an object, any application containing a link to that object can access the object's data and change it. For example, if you link a bitmap file to a Visual Basic application, the bitmap can be modified by any application linked to it, or by anyone who opens the file, by using the application that created it, such as Microsoft Paint, for example. The modified version will appear in all documents linked to the original bitmap file. You must use the OLE control to create a linked object in your Visual Basic application.

What
When you create an *embedded object*, all the data associated with it is contained in the object itself. For example, if a spreadsheet were an embedded object, all the data associated with the cells would be contained in the OLE control (or insertable object), including any necessary formulas. Because the name of the application that created the object is saved along with the data, if a user selects the embedded object while working with your application, the spreadsheet application can be started automatically so the user can edit those cells.

> **Tip** When an object is embedded in an application, no other application has access to the data in the embedded object. You should use embedded objects when you want only your application to maintain data that is produced and edited in another application.

There are three ways to create an OLE object in Visual Basic, the last two of which will be explored in this chapter. You can:

- Add the object to the Toolbox using the Custom Controls dialog box, and then draw the object directly on a form. This technique *embeds* the object within the form in your application.

- Embed or link the object within an OLE Custom control. This technique is required if you plan to change objects on the form at run time, create linked objects, and/or bind the OLE control to a Data control. (See following discussion.)

- Use the CreateObject() or GetObject() functions to create and manipulate an OLE Automation object in code, at run time. With this technique, an object variable is declared and Set equal to the reference returned by the CreateObject() or GetObject() functions, which are discussed later.

The *OLE control* enables you to add insertable objects to the forms in your Visual Basic applications. With the OLE control, you can create a placeholder in your form for an object such as a spreadsheet, document, or picture. At run time, you can create the object that is displayed within the OLE control, or change an object you placed there at design time. You can also use the OLE control to create a linked object in your application, or to bind the OLE control to a database field via the Data Custom control.

Each time you draw an OLE control on a form, the Insert Object dialog box is displayed. You may use this dialog box to create a linked or embedded object, as you'll see later in this chapter. If you choose Cancel, no object is created. At design time, right-click the OLE control to display a pop-up menu. The commands displayed on this pop-up menu depend on the state of the OLE Container control as summarized in Table 38.1.

Table 38.1. The OLE control's pop-up menu.

This Menu Item	Is Enabled in the Menu When
Insert Object	Always enabled....
Paste Special	The Clipboard contains a valid OLE object.
Delete Embedded Object	The OLE control contains an embedded object.
Delete Linked Object	The OLE container control contains a linked object.
Create Link	The SourceDoc property is set.
Create Embedded Object	The Class or SourceDoc property is set.

An OLE container control can contain only one object at a time, but you can create a linked or embedded object in several ways. You may use the Insert Object or Paste Special dialog boxes at either run time or design time. At design time, you may set the OLE Control's Class property in the Properties window, then click the control with the right mouse button and select the appropriate command. Or you may use the appropriate OLE control method.

> **Tip** You can find a list of OLE class names available to your application by selecting the Class property in the Properties window and clicking the ellipsis (...). The Insert Object dialog box doesn't display a precise list of class names; instead, it displays user-friendly names for each class of object, which are generally longer and more easily understood.

Just in case you think you understand all of this, here's a little twist. OLE Automation is a technology that enables applications to provide objects in a consistent way to other applications, not just for simple linking and embedding purposes, but to be created and manipulated as run-time objects of their unique class. What this means is that if an application supports OLE Automation, the objects it exposes can be accessed by Visual Basic, and your Visual Basic programs may manipulate these objects by invoking their methods and setting their properties. You could, for example, create an Excel spreadsheet object, place several ranges of labels and numbers on it, mathematically manipulate the numbers and create a chart, then print both the sheet and chart, without your user even seeing the Excel application itself!

The objects, functions, properties, and methods supported by an OLE Automation application are defined in the application's object library. This is why you must be sure to include a reference to the application's object library if you intend to take advantage of OLE Automation. This will also allow you to use Visual Basic's Object Browser to familiarize yourself with the available objects, properties, and methods.

What
The CreateObject() function creates an OLE Automation object at run time. Here's the syntax:

```
Set ObjectVariable = CreateObject(sClass)
```

Here, ObjectVariable is a valid variable of the Object Type. The sClass argument is a string expression formatted as follows: AppName.ObjectType, where AppName is the name of the application providing the object, and ObjectType is the type of object to create.

To create an OLE Automation object, assign the object returned by CreateObject() to an object variable. Here's an example:

```
Dim ExcelObject As Object
Set ExcelObject = CreateObject("Excel.Sheet")
```

When this snippet is executed, the application creating the object (Excel in this case) is started. If it is already running, a new instance of the application is started, and an object of the specified type is created. Once an object is created, you reference it in code using the object variable you defined and the dot notation techniques you've come to love. In the preceding example, you access properties and methods of the new object using the object variable, ExcelObject:

```
ExcelObject.Range("A1")  =  "Hello, world."  ' A friendly message in Cell A1
ExcelObject.PrintOut                          ' Print the sheet...
```

What
The GetObject() function retrieves an OLE Automation object from a file.

You use it like this:

```
Set ObjectVariable = GetObject(sPathName, sClass)
```

Here sPathName is the full path and name of the file containing the object to be retrieved. If sPathName is omitted, sClass, which is a string expression representing the class of the object as described earlier, is required. If sPathName is a zero-length string (""), GetObject() returns a new object instance of the specified type. If the sPathName argument is omitted entirely, GetObject() returns a currently active object of the specified type. If no object of the specified type exists, an error occurs.

You'll have a chance to use both of these functions very soon.

Why Use OLE?

To cover everything that can be accomplished using the latest OLE technology, this book would have to be dedicated to that subject alone, and be three times as big. On the simplest level, OLE is a way to pass data between programs, an attempt to reduce the need to copy and paste between applications by using the Clipboard.

According to Microsoft, the ultimate goal of OLE technology (which is still in a process of evolution) is to provide a seamless integration between applications. OLE will eventually make communication between programs instantaneous and efficient. Data will no longer be "located" within a particular application, but will be able to exist simultaneously in a Visual Basic program, a Word document, and an Excel spreadsheet. If you make changes to that data in one of those applications, the change will appear in all of them. OLE is not quite to the "seamless" and "instantaneous" stage yet, but the road to it is well-mapped and becoming less bumpy all the time.

How to Use OLE

For this section you'll need to create a Microsoft Paint bitmap object, or select an existing one, to use as a linked file for your new application. (You'll find Paint in the Windows Accessories group.) You might take a minute to do that now; it doesn't need to be anything elaborate. Save it as LOGO.BMP in whatever directory you like. While you're at it, if you have Excel available on your system, create an Excel sheet called TSTSHEET.XLS, which will be used later when you experiment with OLE Automation Objects. (Those of you who don't have Excel should still be able to read along and enjoy the ride.)

Now it's time to add another form to your EVB_BOOK project. Name it frmOLE and make it the project's startup form. This form will contain two OLE controls, a command button, and a few labels, with the significant controls listed in Table 38.2. Here, in Figure 38.1, is how the form looks in Design mode.

As you draw the OLE Controls, the Insert Object dialog box will be displayed. For now, just press Cancel and assign the Class and OLETypeAllowed properties from the Properties window. Refer to Table 38.2 for the correct settings.

Table 38.2. Design-time settings—the OLE form.

Visual Basic Object	Property	Design-Time Setting
Form	Name	frmOLE
	Caption	Object Linking And Embedding
OLE Control	Name	oleWordPad
	Class	WordPad.Document.1
	OLEType	0 - Embedded

continues

Table 38.2. continued

Visual Basic Object	Property	Design-Time Setting
OLE Control	Name	olePaint
	Class	Paint.Picture
	OLEType	1 - Linked
Command Button	Name	cmdSheet
	Caption	Sheet Object

Figure 38.1.
Design mode: the OLE Practice form.

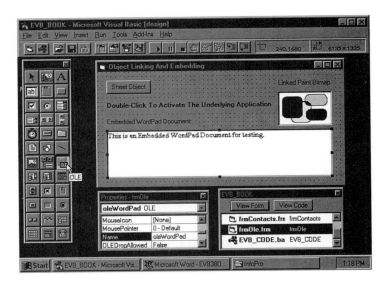

Once the OLE controls and other objects are in place, you'll complete the visual design of your form by linking and embedding as follows:

1. Select oleWordPad, then right-click the mouse.

2. From the pop-up menu, select Create Embedded Object. A small WordPad window will open. Notice that WordPad's menu is displayed at the top of your form.

3. Type something in the WordPad window; for example, **This is an Embedded WordPad Document for testing....** Then click anywhere outside the window, and the OLE control will be updated.

4. Select olePaint, then right-click to get its pop-up menu.

5. Select Insert Object to display the Insert Object dialog box. The Create From File option button should be selected. Locate your LOGO.BMP and click OK.

6. The LOGO bitmap is now displayed in the OLE control. You may right-click and select Edit, or just double-click olePaint to edit your logo at either run time or design time.

Adding Code

The final touch to your OLE experiment will be to see what OLE Automation Objects are all about. You won't be able to complete this section unless you've got Excel installed on your system. (And those of you who do have Excel, make sure the Microsoft Excel 5.0 Object Library is checked in the Tools, References dialog box.)

Now, add this code to cmdSheet's Click event:

```
Private Sub cmdSheet_Click()
Dim SheetObject As Object                    ' You'll need an object variable...

On Error GoTo LocalHandler:                  ' You'll want an error-handler...

MousePointer = HOURGLASS                     ' Might take awhile...

Set SheetObject = CreateObject("excel.sheet")   ' Create an Excel Sheet Object...

SheetObject.Range("A1").VALUE = "This sheet object created from scratch..."
SheetObject.PrintOut                         ' Place a message in cell A1,
                                             ' and print the sheet.

Set SheetObject = GetObject("c:\vb40\sams\tstsheet.xls")   ' Use the same variable
➡to open
heetObject.Range("A1").VALUE = "This was a pre-existing sheet..."
                                             ' a pre-existing sheet.

SheetObject.PrintOut                         ' and print it...

MousePointer = NORMAL                        ' Normal pointer...
Exit Sub                                     ' and goodbye...

LocalHandler:                                ' Just in case...
  MousePointer = NORMAL                      ' Normal pointer...

  MsgBox Error$(Err), vbCritical, "Possible OLE Error"     ' OLE error message...
  Exit Sub

End Sub
```

Don't forget to include the proper paths for the bitmap and sheet you created. They're probably different from those listed here.

That's it. Run your program. You'll be able to double-click, or right-click and get a menu, in order to edit your bitmap and document. Because your bitmap is a linked object, you may edit it outside your Visual Basic application, and any changes will be reflected the next time you run your program. Don't forget to turn your printer on and click the Sheet Object button. Here, in Figure 38.2, is OLE in action.

Figure 38.2.
OLE in action.

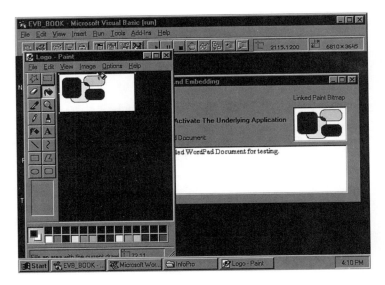

Essential Summary

What In this chapter, you received a brief glimpse of what OLE is and will become. You saw how it may be used to bring the power of other applications into your own Visual Basic programs. You saw that simple object linking and embedding may be accomplished by way of the OLE Custom control, and that more powerful OLE techniques become available through the use of OLE Automation Objects.

Why The simplest use of OLE is to provide a way for your applications to share data without messing with the Clipboard. At another level, it allows you to add the power of external programs to your own applications, even though those applications take time to load and sometimes take over the screen in clumsy and unattractive ways. But the goal of OLE technology is to provide a seamless and simple integration between applications; you will, in effect, enter an alternative computer realm of free-floating objects. You can't now, but some day you'll be able to think, not in terms of *this data* and *that application*, but simply of *my computer*.

How Putting your new OLE skills to the test, you created a program in which you accomplished object linking and embedding by using the OLE control to connect to Microsoft's Paint and WordPad programs. And finally, you got a taste of some of the more advanced ideas behind OLE Automation Objects by creating and printing your own Excel spreadsheets, with Excel working behind the scenes, nowhere in sight.

Calling External Functions: The Windows API

In this chapter, you'll take a brief excursion beyond Visual Basic itself. The reason for the detour is that there are things that Visual Basic just can't do. For example, there is no Visual Basic command to crop or smear or reverse a picture. To accomplish this sort of thing, and others, you'll need to tap into the power of Windows itself. You'll need the keys to the engine room of the submarine running beneath Visual Basic, the Windows API, and that's what this chapter is all about.

What Is the API?

What The *Windows API (Application Programming Interface)* consists of the functions, messages, data structures, data types, and statements you can use in creating applications that run under Microsoft Windows; that is, the types of applications you create with Visual Basic 4.0.

The most-often used parts of the API are code elements included for calling API functions from Windows. These include: procedure *declarations* for API functions; user-defined *types*, for data structures passed to those functions; and *constants*, for values passed to and returned from those functions. In order to access the API, you need to use the Declare statement, which is discussed next.

What

The *Declare statement* is a powerful Visual Basic tool; it's what opens the door to the Windows API. The *Declare* statement is used at module level to declare references to external procedures in a dynamic-link library (DLL), such as those used by Windows itself. The general syntax for the *Declare* statement is as follows:

```
Declare Sub SubName Lib "LibName"(ArgList)
```

Or, to access an external function:

```
Declare Function FunctionName Lib  "LibName"(ArgList) As VarType
```

Here, *SubName* and FunctionName are the procedures you want to call, and LibName is the name of the DLL that contains them. Both may receive arguments, and usually do. In the case of a function, you also need to indicate the Type of value to be returned, if there is one.

Sounds simple. Using the Declare statement can be a little tricky, however. The reason is that the list of arguments can make the statement unbelievably long. Here, for example, is the declaration for the BitBlt function, which allows you to manipulate bitmap images:

```
Declare Function BitBlt Lib "gdi32" (ByVal hDestDC As Long, ByVal X As Long, ByVal
Y As Long, ByVal nWidth As Long, ByVal nHeight As Long, ByVal hSrcDC As Long, ByVal
xSrc As Long, ByVal ySrc As Long, ByVal dwRop As Long) As Long
```

This is a single declaration! And it MUST be entered on a single line in the general declarations section of a standard code module, precisely as it appears here, without the word wrapping, of course. Fortunately, Visual Basic 4.0 provides a sweet little applet called the *API Text Viewer*, which makes this process a little less painstaking. You'll see how it's used later, when you create this chapter's program.

Why Use the API?

Why

The reason you turn to the Windows API is that there are things that Visual Basic just can't do. There is no Visual Basic command to dither, invert, crop, or smear a picture, for example. Also, your Visual Basic program will recognize mouse clicks only if they're on an open form. What if you wanted to draw a rectangle that overlapped several forms, and cut the enclosed image into the Clipboard? What if you want to make your computer's speaker wail like a siren or titter like a flock of angry birds? Visual Basic's Beep command emits a single annoying sound of one pitch and one duration, so something else is needed. What's needed is the API.

How to Use the API

In this section, you'll create a form containing two PictureBox controls, two CommandButtons, and an OptionButton array of eight elements. You'll load a bitmap image of your choice into the first PictureBox, then select an option button to determine how the image will be copied into the second PictureBox. As you'll see, you'll be able to contort the image into different shapes, as well as invert and reverse its colors.

How

To do this, you'll need to access the Windows API. Open your EVB_CODE module to the general declarations section.

The API Text Viewer is located in the Visual Basic 4.0 group. In fact, there may be two of them there, one for 16-bit development and one for 32-bit projects. Open the proper one for your environment. From the Viewer's File menu, select Load Text File and load Win32Api.Txt (or Win16Api.Txt). This will take a while, so be patient. There's a lot of stuff here.

How

Caution After the API Text file is first loaded, you may be asked if you'd like to convert the text file to a database for faster loading. In the Beta copy of Visual Basic 4.0, answering Yes to this question caused the system to hang. The problem may well be fixed in your version of VB 4.0, but...well, you're on your own here.

Once the file is loaded, select Declares from the API Type drop-down list. In the Available Items list, locate SetStretchBltMode and double-click it to add it to the Selected Items list. Do the same for StretchBlt. Your screen should look something like Figure 39.1.

Figure 39.1.
The Windows API Text Viewer.

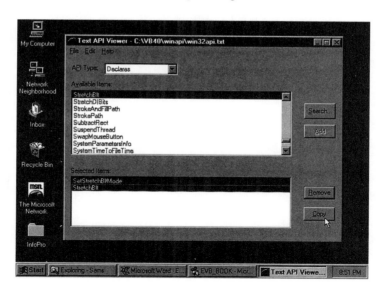

Once the functions are selected in the Selected Items list, click the Copy button to copy them to the Clipboard. Then switch to your EVB_CODE module and paste them in. That's all there is to it. This way you're assured of getting an accurate declaration, no matter how long and cumbersome the statement. Just minimize the API Text Viewer for now—you'll need it again later.

Now it's time to add another form to your EVB_BOOK project. Call it frmAPI and make it the startup form. Table 39.1 contains the design-time specifications.

Table 39.1. Design-time settings—the API Interface program.

Visual Basic Object	Property	Design-Time Setting
Form	Name	frmAPI
	Caption	EVB Windows API Exercise
PictureBox Control	Name	picSource
	Picture	C:\vb40\sams\logo.bmp
PictureBoxControl	Name	picDestination
CommandButton	Name	cmdStretch
	Caption	&Picture Play
	Default	True
CommandButton	Name	cmdQuit
	Cancel	True
Frame Control	Caption	Copy Mode
OptionButton Array	Name	optMode()
	Index	0
	Caption	Copy
	Index	1
	Caption	Paint
	Index	2
	Caption	And
	Index	3
	Caption	Invert
	Index	4
	Caption	Erase
	Index	5
	Caption	Negative
	Index	6

Visual Basic Object	Property	Design-Time Setting
	Caption	Not Erase
	Index	7
	Caption	MergePaint

Here, in Figure 39.2, is what your form may look like in Design mode. Feel free to adjust the size of the boxes and load whatever bitmap image you desire.

Figure 39.2.
Design mode: the API exercise.

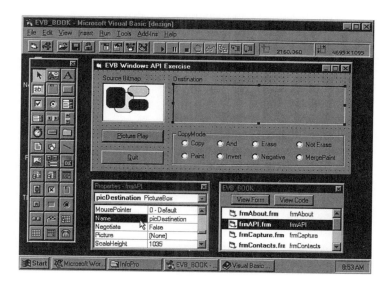

Adding Code

Now you'll put your newly declared Windows functions to use. First, you'll need a few constants to make setting the copy mode easier. (You could use the API Text Viewer here but sometimes, for short entries, it's easier just to type 'em in. It's up to you.) Add these lines to EVB_CODE's general declarations section:

```
Global Const SRCCOPY = &HCC0020           'In EVB_CODE general declarations..
Global Const SRCPAINT = &HEE0086
Global Const SRCAND = &H8800C6
Global Const SRCINVERT = &H660046
Global Const SRCERASE = &H440328
Global Const NOTSRCCOPY = &H330008
Global Const NOTSRCERASE = &H1100A6
Global Const MERGECOPY = &HC000CA
```

And here are the function declarations, which you pasted in earlier (remember that these must each appear on a single line):

```
Declare Function SetStretchBltMode Lib "gdi32" (ByVal hdc As Long, ByVal
nStretchMode As Long) As Long          ' On one long line.....
```

```
Declare Function StretchBlt Lib "gdi32" (ByVal hdc As Long, ByVal X As Long, ByVal
Y As Long, ByVal nWidth As Long, ByVal nHeight As Long, ByVal hSrcDC As Long, ByVal
xSrc As Long, ByVal ySrc As Long, ByVal nSrcWidth As Long, ByVal nSrcHeight As
Long, ByVal dwRop As Long) As Long      ' On one very long line...
```

Now close the EVB_CODE module and open frmAPI. You'll need some variables in the form's general declarations section:

```
Dim CopyMode As Long, I As Integer
Dim SourceWidth As Long, SourceHeight As Long
Dim DestinationWidth As Long, DestinationHeight As Long
```

The picture is actually copied and manipulated in cmdStretch's Click event, based on the currently selected option button:

```
Private Sub cmdStretch_Click()

Dim RetVal As Long                          ' To call functions...

MousePointer = HOURGLASS                     ' First time takes a while...

picDestination.picture = LoadPicture()       ' Clear the last picture..

For I = 0 To 7                               ' Loop through the option
    If optMode(I) = True Then                ' buttons to see which is
        CopyMode = I                         ' selected.
    End If
Next

Select Case CopyMode                         ' Then set the CopyMode

Case 0                                        ' accordingly....
    CopyMode = SRCCOPY

Case 1
    CopyMode = SRCPAINT

Case 2
    CopyMode = SRCAND

Case 3
    CopyMode = SRCINVERT

Case 4
    CopyMode = SRCERASE

Case 5
    CopyMode = NOTSRCCOPY

Case 6
    CopyMode = NOTSRCERASE

Case 7
    CopyMode = MERGEPAINT
```

```
Case Else                                            ' Case no button...
    CopyMode = SRCCOPY                               ' Normal copy and stretch...

End Select

picSource.ScaleMode = 3                              ' Set Proper scale mode
picDestination.ScaleMode = 3                         '  for pictures. API wants
                                                     ' pixels.

SourceWidth = picSource.ScaleWidth                   ' Get pixel height and width
SourceHeight = picSource.ScaleHeight                 ' of source picture.

DestinationWidth = picDestination.ScaleWidth         ' Height and width of
DestinationHeight = picDestination.ScaleHeight       ' destination picture.


RetVal = StretchBlt(picDestination.hdc, 0, 0, DestinationWidth, DestinationHeight,
picSource.hdc, 0, 0, SourceWidth, SourceHeight, CopyMode)          ' One line call....

MousePointer = NORMAL                                ' Back to normal..
End Sub
```

Try this out. Depending on the size and colors involved in your source picture, the effects of stretching and color masking can be quite startling. (See Figure 39.3.) Try it with different PictureBox sizes and pictures. You may also add and subtract values from the source's ScaleHeight and ScaleWidth properties to get some interesting cropping effects. Clearly what you have here is the beginning of a photo-retouching or other image modification program.

Figure 39.3.
The API Bitmap Stretch exercise.

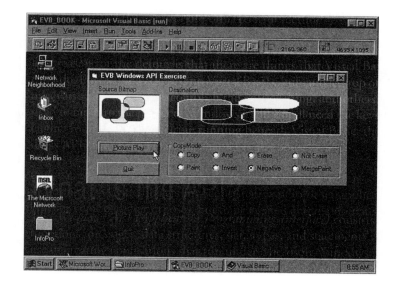

How

One last bit of API magic. You know that your Visual Basic programs recognize mouse clicks, but only if the click is to one of your open forms. What you'll do in this section is create a program that will respond to a click anywhere on the screen, inside or outside of a form. Not only that, but the response will be to capture an image of the current screen, from the upper-left corner to the mouse position, and paste it into your form!

Add one last form to your project. Call it frmCapture and make it the startup form. Be sure to set the form's ScaleMode property to 3 - Pixel. You're going to be sending lots of screen information to Windows, and the API expects pixels, not twips. Open EVB_CODE again, and define the following user type:

```
Type APIPOINT
    X As Long
    Y As Long
End Type
```

Now you're going to need several function declarations. Use the API TextViewer to paste the following Declares into your code module:

```
MoveToEx
SetROP2
CreateDC
ClientToScreen
SetCapture
ReleaseCapture
DeleteDC
BitBlt
```

And here they are:

```
Declare Function MoveToEx Lib "gdi32" (ByVal hdc As Long, ByVal X As Long, ByVal Y
As Long, lpPoint As APIPOINT) As Long

Declare Function SetROP2 Lib "gdi32" (ByVal hdc As Long, ByVal nDrawMode As Long)
As Long

Declare Function CreateDC Lib "gdi32" Alias "CreateDCA" (ByVal lpDriverName As
String, ByVal lpDeviceName As String, ByVal lpOutput As String, lpInitData As Any)
As Long

Declare Function ClientToScreen Lib "user32" (ByVal hwnd As Long, lpPoint As
APIPOINT) As Long

Declare Function SetCapture Lib "user32" (ByVal hwnd As Long) As Long

Declare Function ReleaseCapture Lib "user32" () As Long

Declare Function DeleteDC Lib "gdi32" (ByVal hdc As Long) As Long

Declare Function BitBlt Lib "gdi32" (ByVal hDestDC As Long, ByVal X As Long, ByVal
Y As Long, ByVal nWidth As Long, ByVal nHeight As Long, ByVal hSrcDC As Long, ByVal
xSrc As Long, ByVal ySrc As Long, ByVal dwRop As Long) As Long
```

Close the code module and access your new form. (Don't forget to set the form's ScaleMode to Pixel.) Now add the following to the form's General Declarations section:

```
Dim Anchor As APIPOINT               ' For anchor point, and current point...
Dim Current As APIPOINT
Dim Down As Boolean                  ' When mouse goes down...
Dim RetVal As Long                   ' For calling API functions...
```

Here's the form's Load event:

```
Private Sub Form_Load()
    RetVal = SetCapture(hwnd)        ' You're telling Windows to capture to form
    Down = False                     ' by passing the form's hWnd property.
End Sub
```

Now here's the form's MouseDown event:

```
Private Sub Form_MouseDown(Button As Integer, Shift As Integer, X As Single, Y As
Single)

If Button <> 2 Then                  ' If Right button, clear the form...Else

    Anchor.X = X                     ' Set anchor
    Anchor.Y = Y
    ClientToScreen hwnd, Anchor      ' Convert to screen coordinates...
    Down = True                      ' Mouse is down...

Else
Cls                                  ' Right button clears the form
End If
End Sub
```

Most of the magic occurs when the mouse is released. It will probably appear to you to really *be* magic, as some of these lines are likely to be mysterious, if not impenetrable. But type them in anyway; it'll be fun. Here's the MouseUp event procedure:

```
Private Sub Form_MouseUp(Button As Integer, Shift As Integer, X As Single, Y As
Single)

Dim hDCScreen As Integer

If Down Then
    ReleaseCapture
    Down = False
    Current.X = X
    Current.Y = Y

    ClientToScreen hwnd, Current

    hDCScreen = CreateDC("DISPLAY", ByVal 0&, ByVal 0&, ByVal 0&)

    RetVal = SetROP2(hDCScreen, 6)
    RetVal = MoveToEx(hDCScreen, Anchor.X, Anchor.Y, Anchor)

    MapWidth% = Abs(Anchor.X - Current.X)
    MapHeight% = Abs(Anchor.Y - Current.Y)

    RetVal = BitBlt(hdc, 0, 0, MapWidth%, MapHeight%, hDCScreen, 0, 0, &HCC0020)
    RetVal = DeleteDC(hDCScreen)
End If
End Sub
```

Well, that's really it. Fire up your program, and click anywhere on the screen. You're likely to see something like Figure 39.4.

Figure 39.4.
The Screen Capture program in action.

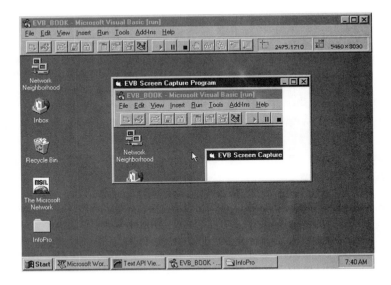

To really understand what's going on here, you'll need to become thoroughly familiar with each of these Windows API functions. That alone would take a chapter or two—or three. You're best bet, if you're really interested in the inner workings of the Windows environment, is to obtain one of many books on Windows API Programming. Such books are written for C Programmers and may be a little tough if you're not comfortable with C. But you don't need to know exactly *why* things work to *make* them work. There's nothing wrong with learning and experimenting—and having fun, using the monkey-see, monkey-do approach. In time and with practice, things tend to become clearer, and the monkey will be seeing, doing, *and* understanding.

Essential Summary

In this chapter, you wandered out of Visual Basic itself and into the powerful nether world of the Windows API. You learned what the API is and how its functions and procedures may be accessed through Visual Basic's Declare statement. You also learned how to use a handy tool, the API Text Viewer, which makes the painstaking process of declaring API functions a little easier.

You turn to the Windows API when what you want to do is just not in Visual Basic's bag of tricks. For example, there is no Visual Basic command to dither, crop, or smear a picture. To bring sounds other than Visual Basic's annoying Beep into your programs, you must directly manipulate the computer's speaker or sound card. This can be done through the API. In short, you use the Windows API to bring the power of C into your Visual Basic programs. **Why**

You created two new mini-programs, both of which borrowed their thunder from the Windows API. The first program allows you to stretch, crop, even contort a bitmap image, as well as manipulate its colors. The second program uses several API calls to allow mouse-clicks outside the form, in the Windows desktop itself, to be recognized and acted upon. With it, you're able to capture a portion of the screen and paste it into your form. **How**

Simple Help Files

Most commercially-viable Windows Applications provide their own Help Systems. Adding the custom Help Compiler to your applications might seem like a tall order, almost like writing another whole program. However, most applications use the built-in Windows Help System, and only provide a Help file (HLP) which that system can use. In this chapter, you'll see how to create such a Help file for your Contact Manager program.

What Are Help Files?

What A Windows *Help file* is a specially compiled file with the HLP extension; it may be used with the built-in Windows Help System to display Help Compiler information pertaining to your Visual Basic application. The user may select an item from the Help Contents, then view, search, and navigate the various Help screens by jumping from one topic to another. In addition to "topic-jumping," custom Help Systems often provide pop-up windows that give more detailed information about a particular keyword, without actually jumping to another Help Compiler page.

The Four Steps

The process of creating your own custom Help file can be broken down into four distinct steps. They are:

1. Create the Help Text File (or Topic File) in RTF format.
2. Create the Help Project File (HPJ).
3. Compile the Help File using the Help Compiler and Project File.
4. Attach the Help File to your Visual Basic application.

Each of these steps is discussed and demonstrated in this chapter.

What The Help Text or Topic File is created with an editor, such as Microsoft Word, that is capable of saving text in the RTF format; it contains topics that are linked together via hypertext "jump phrases" or special hypergraphics (see Chapter 42). Without linking, the topics in a Help file would be isolated islands of information; a user could not move from one topic to another. The most convenient way of linking topics is to create hypertext that enables users to jump between topics or display a pop-up window. Such topic-jumps serve a purpose similar to cross-references in a book. These jumps consist of specially coded text or graphics that cause the WinHelp application to display another topic in the main Help window.

What The Project File is a simple ASCII text file, with an extension of HPJ. The project file is used to pass information regarding the current Help project to the Help Compiler. This information includes the name and location of the RTF Topic file or files, the directory location of any required bitmaps, error log specifications and warning levels, context-sensitive Help Compiler information, and the location, size and color of the Help System window.

How to Create the Help Text: Contacts.RTF

How To create the Help Text file, you must use an editor that is capable of saving files in the Rich Text Format (RTF). Microsoft Word is such a program and will be used here. You're going to be working with underlined (Ctrl+U), double-underlined (Ctrl+Shift+D), and hidden text (Ctrl+Shift+H), so it's not a bad idea to reveal all formatting codes while you create your RTF file.

In the Topic file, jump phrases (hypertext jumps) are double-underlined; they are followed immediately by a "tag" phrase (or context string), which is formatted as hidden text. In the Help window, hypertext jumps appear underlined and on color monitors, they appear green. For example, a double-underlined phrase <u>Export A File</u> appears as <u>Export a File</u> in green text to the user.

Here, in general, are the steps required to establish a word or phrase as a jump in the topic file:

1. Place the insertion point at the place in the text where you want to enter the jump phrase.
2. Select the double-underline (or strikethrough) feature of your editor.

3. Type the jump word or words in double-underlined format.

4. Turn off double-underlining and select the editor's hidden text feature.

5. Type the context string (or jump tag) assigned to the topic that is the target of the jump.

Caution When coding jumps, be careful not to include spaces between the double-underlined text and the hidden text. Also be careful not to format paragraph marks accidentally as hidden text. If you do, a compiler error or warning will occur.

Now it's time to start Word and create your new Help System's topic file. Here's the Contact Manager Help Contents screen, the first page of Contacts.RTF (see Figure 40.1).

Figure 40.1.
The Help Text file:
Contents screen.

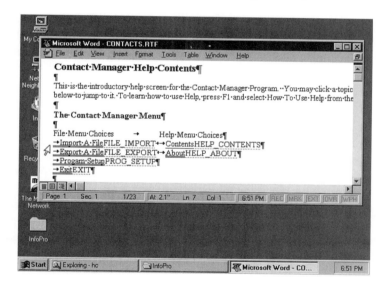

The first thing to notice here is the use of double-underlining. As already mentioned, words or phrases that are double-underlined here will appear as green, single-underlined jump phrases (or hypertext) in your Help System. When the user clicks on them, control will jump to the page represented by the "jump tag," which is the hidden label immediately following the double-underlined jump phrase. (All codes are revealed here, so hidden text shows up with a light, dotted underline, as you can see in Figure 40.1.) This is important: the jump tag must follow the jump phrase immediately, no spaces, and it must be hidden. In the example seen in Figure 40.1, Import A File is the jump phrase, FILE_IMPORT is the hidden tag; Export A File is the phrase, FILE_EXPORT is the tag, and so on.

Once your Help Contents screen is completed, start a new page (in Word press Ctrl+Enter). The text for each jump page must be written on a separate word processing page. You connect the jump page text to the jump phrase by using the jump tag with a custom footnote symbol. In fact, there are three custom footnote symbols you may use, each invoking a different Help System feature. These features are summarized in Table 40.1 and are discussed in detail immediately after.

Table 40.1. Help Text file: custom footnote symbols.

Symbol	Description
#	Connects a jump page to its jump phrase by referencing the jump tag.
$	References the jump page title, which will then appear in the Help System's Search list box.
K	References a keyword with which the user may search for a topic.

The (#) footnote symbol is used to connect a Help Compiler topic page with its related jump tag. In this way, jump tags identify each topic in the Help System. Each tag must be unique—you can assign it to only one topic in the Topic File. Assigning a jump tag gives a topic an identifier that you can use to create jumps to that topic or to display it in a pop-up window. Although the Help Compiler can successfully compile topics that don't have a jump tag, the user of the Help System can't display them unless they contain keywords (see the next section). Although a jump tag has a practical limitation of 255 characters, you should keep the tags short so they are easier to enter into your Topic Files.

The ($) footnote symbol is used to identify a Help Topic Title. In your custom Help System, the title of a topic usually appears at the beginning of the topic, and in the Bookmark menu and Search list box if the topic contains keywords. To place the title at the beginning of the topic, type it as the first paragraph. You must define code for the title in a footnote for the title to appear correctly in the Bookmark menu and the Search dialog box. Although the Help Compiler doesn't require that a topic have a title footnote, only those topics in the main Help window or a secondary window that do have a title footnote appear correctly in the Bookmark menu.

The (K) footnote symbol specifies topic keywords, which may be used to search for related topics. The WinHelp application lists matching topics by their titles (as defined in the title footnote) in the Search dialog box. The keyword search facility serves the same purpose as the index in a book. Because a keyword search is often the fastest way for users to access Help topics, you'll probably want to assign keywords to most topics in your Help system. You may specify more than one keyword per topic by separating them with semicolons in the topic footnote. Here's how a keyword footnote for a topic entitled Opening Text Files might appear:

```
K open;opening;text file;ASCII;existing;text only;documents
```

Tip You should specify a keyword footnote only if the topic has a title footnote because the title of the topic appears in the Search dialog box when the user searches for the keyword. Topics that do not have titles but that are accessible through keywords are listed as >>Untitled Topic<< in the list at the bottom of the Search dialog box.

Now take a look at Figure 40.2, which shows the primary jump pages and associated footnote symbolism you should add to Contacts.RTF.

Figure 40.2.
The Help Text file: jump screens.

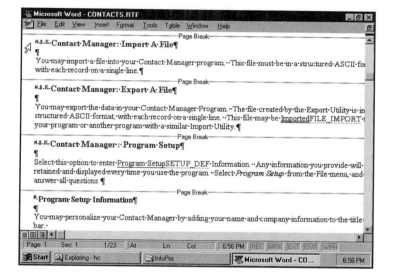

As you can see, the custom footnote symbol(s) must be the first item(s) on the jump page, followed by the Help Topic Title, and any other Help Compiler text. To place a footnote using Word, you select Footnote from the Insert menu, which brings up the Footnote and Endnote dialog box. You want to use a Custom symbol here, so click the Custom Mark option button and enter one of the three symbols described in Table 40.2 (the # is required to connect a tag to a jump phrase and should be entered first). When OK is clicked, the screen will split into two windows, with the jump page above and footnotes below. You may then enter the appropriate jump tag, if you're inserting the # footnote, or any other text reference, such as a title or search keyword. Look at Figure 40.3 for comparison.

Here, the arrow is pointing to the first of three footnotes associated with the Program Setup Help screen. Notice the actual footnote symbols, side by side, in the Program Setup text page in the upper window. This is a valid jump page; its title will appear in the Help Search list box, and Setup will serve as a search keyword.

Figure 40.3.
The Help Text file:
inserting custom
footnotes.

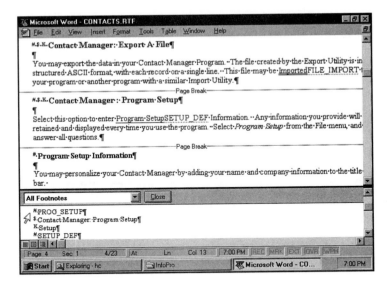

There's something else to notice in Figure 40.3. In the Contact Manager: Program Setup page, the phrase `Program Setup` is single-underlined, and there's a hidden tag `SETUP_DEF` associated with it. When a phrase is single-underlined in your RTF file, the phrase will appear in green, with a light dotted underline, in your running Help System. Rather than jumping to another page, a click to this phrase will pop up a small window displaying a definition or additional information. The phrase's hidden tag must still be referenced in a footnote on a separate page containing the pop-up window's text. (You can see this clearly in Figure 40.3.)

> **Note** Pop-up windows need not be limited to definitions, although it's important to keep the text brief since the main purpose of a pop-up window is to display definitions or notes that don't distract the user from the main topic.

Okay, that's it for the first version of your Help Text file (you'll add much more to this file over the next three chapters). If you're working along with this chapter, you should save the file as Contacts.RTF (again, it must be saved in the RTF format). The next step is to create the Help Project file.

Creating the Help Project File: Contacts.HPJ

The Help Project file is a simple text file that contains information to be passed to the Help Compiler. You may use your favorite text editor to create it. Here, in Figure 40.4, is what it looks like for the first version of your new Help System.

Figure 40.4.
The Help Project file:
Contacts.HPJ.

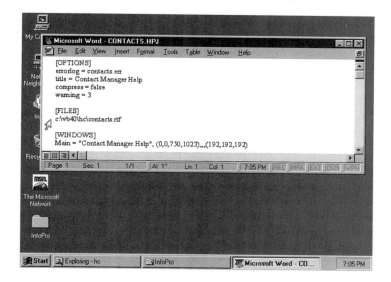

All you're doing in the [OPTIONS] section is setting the Help System's title bar and indicating that no special file compression should take place. You're also specifying an error log for any Help Compiler errors that may be generated; and you're setting an associated warning level, level 3 in this case. There are three warning levels: (1) where only the most severe errors are reported; (2) which results in the display of intermediate and severe errors; and (3) where all errors and warnings are reported. (Warnings indicate that something is wrong, but not wrong enough to prevent the creation of your Help file. Fatal errors are always reported, as they result in a failed compilation.)

The [FILES] section contains the fully qualified path to your Help Text file. If you're working along with the book, provide your own path here. The last section, [WINDOWS], contains a single line that sets the Help Window's size, position, and color.

That's it for Step 2. Save the file as Contacts.HPJ. Now it's compile time.

Compiling the Help File: Contacts.HLP

The third step is the easiest. To create your Contacts.HLP file, you use the Windows Help Compiler, a copy of which is included with Visual Basic's Professional Edition. The Help Compiler is located in the HC subdirectory of your Visual Basic installation directory. Open a DOS window and locate the HC directory. At the prompt type

How

```
HC Contacts.HPJ
```

and press Enter. (Be sure to pass the correct name and location of your Help Project file. This example assumes the file is in the HC directory.) You may get some error messages and/or warnings during the compile process. If so, they will most likely be due to problems with your

RTF file, such as improperly hidden or referenced tags. There's no penalty for compiling more than once, so fix the RTF source and try again.

Tip It's not a bad idea to keep your help-related files in the same directory, at least during the development phase. In fact, the HC directory of the VB40 directory is a good place to keep them, since you'll need to run the Help Compiler (HC.EXE) located there. Another tip is to create a batch file containing the call to the compiler, HC Contacts.HPJ, in this case. It's then a simple matter to compile (and recompile, as necessary) by running the batch file from the File Manager or the Windows 95 Explorer.

The fourth and final step in setting up your own Custom Help System is to attach Contacts.HLP to your Visual Basic application, in this case, the Contact Manager program.

Attaching the Help File to the Contact Manager Program

How This last step is where the rubber meets the road. If you're working along with the book, go to your EVB_BOOK project and open frmContacts. The first place to attach your new Help file is in the Project's Options dialog box. Locate the Help File text box and enter the full path to Contacts.HLP. This will allow the user to get Help by pressing F1, in addition to accessing it through the Help menu. (While you're here, you might want to make sure that frmContacts is the Startup Form.)

Next you need to add one DECLARE (for the API WinHelp() function) and a few helpful constants to your EVB_CODE module's general declarations section. Feel free to use the API Text Viewer if you find it easier than typing. Here's what must be added to EVB_CODE's general declarations section:

```
'   Help engine declaration — All on one line.
Declare Function WinHelp Lib "user32" Alias "WinHelpA" (ByVal hwnd As Long,
➥ByVal lpHelpFile As String, ByVal wCommand As Long, ByVal dwData As Long) As Long

'   Useful Constants which may be passed to WinHelp()
Global Const HELP_CONTEXT = &H1        'Display topic identified by number in dwData
Global Const HELP_QUIT = &H2           ' Terminate help
Global Const HELP_INDEX = &H3          ' Display index
Global Const HELP_HELPONHELP = &H4     ' Display help on using help
Global Const HELP_SETINDEX = &H5       ' Set an alternate Index, if needed
Global Const HELP_KEY = &H101          ' Display topic for keyword in dwData
Global Const HELP_MULTIKEY = &H201     ' Lookup keyword in alternate table
```

Now use the Menu Editor to add a Help menu to the Contact Manager form. The Help menu will contain just two items, as seen in Table 40.2.

Table 40.2. Design-time settings—Help menu for Contact Manager.

Visual Basic Object	Property	Design-Time Setting
Form	Name	frmContacts
Menu Control	Name	mnuHelp
	Caption	&Help
Sub-Menu Item	Name	mnuContents
	Caption	&Contents
Sub-Menu Item	Name	mnuAbout
	Caption	&About Contact Manager...

Now here's the code to be added to mnuContent's Click event; it consists of a call to the API function WinHelp():

```
Private Sub mnuContents_Click()
RV = WinHelp(frmContacts.hWnd,"c:\vb40\hc\contacts.hlp", HELP_INDEX,CLng(0))
End Sub
```

Here the first argument is the main form's Windows handle, which is just frmContact's hWnd property. The second argument points to the precise location of the compiled Help file, which for now is found in the HC directory (the final version of the Help file would most likely be stored in the same directory as the application). The third argument indicates that the Help contents (or Index) screen is to be displayed; and the fourth may be used to provide context-sensitive Help Compiler based on which program object the user was focused on when F1 was pressed (context-sensitive Help Compiler is covered next, in Chapter 41).

That's all there is to it. Now when you run your Contact Manager program and select Contents from the Help menu (or Press F1), this is what you'll see, as shown in Figure 40.5.

Then when you click on the green, single underlined keyword <u>Program Setup</u> and click on the dotted underlined keyword, you'll see this (see Figure 40.6).

Once you're in the Help System, you may use all the features you're familiar with, such as searching, stepping back, printing, or jumping to the top-level Contents screen. When you're done with Help, exit in any of the usual ways.

In your testing, you may have noticed that it's possible to quit your program and still leave the Help System on the screen. This is because the WinHelp application is a stand-alone, shared resource available to all Windows programs. As a result, your program's Help System has limited control over the WinHelp application. You may, however, force WinHelp to quit at the same time your own program is shut down. To do this, add the following line to frmContact's Unload event procedure:

```
Private Sub Form_Unload(Cancel As Integer)
RetVal = WinHelp(hWnd, dummy$, HELP_QUIT, 0)
End Sub
```

Figure 40.5.
The Help file in action:
Help Contents.

Figure 40.6.
The Help file in action:
Program Setup jump
screen.

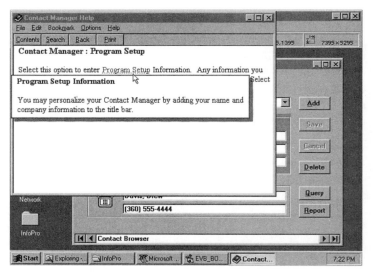

Here you make another call to WinHelp, except this time, the third argument is a constant which politely informs WinHelp that its services are no longer needed (the second argument is just a "dummy" placeholder).

That's it. You've now got the beginnings of a full-blown Custom Help System. More importantly, you've acquired the skills to add simple Custom Help to all of your Visual Basic applications. In the next chapter, you'll see how to enhance your Help System by adding context-sensitivity and a secondary window.

Essential Summary

In this chapter, you learned how to create a simple custom Help System for your Visual Basic application. You saw that it isn't necessary to write a Help program of your own, that you may instead compile a Windows compatible HLP file containing Help text (including hypertext "jumps") specific to your application. The information in this file is then presented to the user through Windows' own WinHelp application. **What**

Because users have come to expect at least some online Help Compiler in their Windows applications, it is important to develop at least the minimal help-writing skills presented in this chapter. Learning to create Windows compatible Help files, rather than developing complete Help Systems from scratch, allows you to spend more time on application-specific Help information and other special features that make your program unique. **Why**

You created the first version of a custom Help System for your Contact Manager program. This version exhibits both of the main Help features covered in this chapter: hypertext topic jumping and pop-up definition windows. In the following chapters, you'll explore some of the more advanced Help System features, and learn the techniques required to implement them. **How**

Creating Context-Sensitive Help

In this chapter, you'll add context-sensitive Help to your Contact Manager program. You'll also see how to redirect Help information to a second window, one that operates independently of the main Help screen. In the process, you'll learn how to work with the [MAP] and [WINDOWS] sections of the Help project file.

What Is Context-Sensitive Help?

What You're probably already familiar with the notion of *context-sensitive Help*. If you've ever selected a Windows application object and then pressed F1 to find out more about it, you've used the application's context-sensitive Help feature. The application is smart enough to determine which object has the focus, read the object's context reference (see the next section), and send it to WinHelp, which in turn displays the appropriate Help topic.

Creating Context References

In developing context-sensitive Help, you're required to establish a set of *context references* so that WinHelp and your application pass the correct information back and forth. In Visual Basic applications, the *context reference* is a unique number, stored in the `HelpContextID` property, which corresponds to a particular object; for example, to a menu item, form, control, or screen region. You can assign `HelpContextIDs` arbitrarily, but they must be unique for each object, and you should not change them afterward.

You then use these `HelpContextIDs` (or context numbers) to create links between your application and the corresponding Help topics. This is done by listing your topic file's jump tags, along with the associated object's `HelpContextID`, in the [MAP] section of the Help project file (HPJ). When writing the [MAP] section, you can use either decimal or hexadecimal numbers to specify context numbers, but be sure to separate jump tags and context numbers by an arbitrary amount of white space, using either space characters or tabs.

The following example illustrates two formats you can use in your project file's [MAP] section.

```
[MAP]

dcmb_scr        30      ; Jump tags and decimal numbers representing
dmxi_scr        31      ; unique HelpContextIDs...
dmni_scr        32
dri_scr         33
dtb_scr         34

Edit_Window     0x0001  ; Or work a little harder and use Hex,
Control_Menu    0x0002  ; if there's a good reason...
Maximize_Icon   0x0003
Minimize_Icon   0x0004
Split_Bar       0x0005
Scroll_Bar      0x0006
Title_Bar       0x0007
Window_Border   0x0008
```

> **Caution**   Be sure to assign a unique context number to each jump tag. Assigning the same context number to more than one jump tag generates a compiler error. The Help Compiler also generates a warning message if a context string appearing in the [MAP] section is not defined in the RTF topic file or files.

What   A secondary Help window is one that operates independently of the main Help screen. It may be sized, moved, scrolled through, or closed at the user's discretion. Secondary windows may display any Help topic defined in the RTF Topic file, and are often used to show a list, such as a Help glossary, or examples of code, or any other topic the user might like to view simultaneously with the main Help text.

As you saw in the previous chapter, the [WINDOWS] section of the Help project file defines the size, location, and colors for the primary Help window. It's also where you may specify the dimensions and other attributes of any secondary window types you might want to use.

Window characteristics are defined by using the following syntax:

```
typename = "caption", (hpos, vpos, width, height), sizing, (rgb), (ns_rgb), top
```

Following is a list describing each parameter:

typename	Specifies the type of window that uses the defined attributes. For the primary Help window, this parameter is main. For a secondary window type, this parameter can be any unique name up to eight characters other than main. Any jumps that display a topic in a secondary window give this unique type name as part of the jump.
caption	The caption that appears on the title bar of different types of secondary windows. For the main Help window, this caption is given by the Help TITLE option in the [OPTIONS] section of the Help project file.
hpos, vpos	Horizontal and vertical position, respectively, of the window's upper-left corner. WinHelp uses a 1024 × 1024 coordinate system (starting at 0,0) and maps this coordinate system onto the resolution of the video card displaying the Help file.
width, height	Gives the default width and height of a secondary window. The width and height, like the x and y positions, are based on the resolution of the video adapter (as indicated for the hpos and vpos parameters in the preceding description).
sizing	Specifies how a secondary window is sized when WinHelp first opens it. This parameter is 0 for normal size and 1 for maximized. If the value is 1, WinHelp ignores the hpos, vpos, width, and height parameters given in the type definition.
rgb, ns_rgb	Three comma-delimited, three-digit values giving the background colors for the window and nonscrolling region (if any) in the window. The three digits represent the red, green, and blue (RGB) components of the color. If these colors are not given, the scrolling and nonscrolling areas are displayed with the normal system colors in the background.
top	Specifies whether a secondary window always remains on top of all other windows. This parameter is optional. If not specified, the secondary window normally moves behind other windows. If the value is 1, WinHelp keeps the secondary window on top of other windows.

The following example shows the format of the [WINDOWS] section in a sample Help project file:

```
[WINDOWS]
main = "Sample Help System", (0,0,1023,1023),,, (192,192,192)
glossary = "Sample Glossary", (222,206,725,486),,, (192,192,192), 1
```

This section sets the color of the nonscrolling region of the main Help window to gray. It also defines a type of secondary window named `glossary` with the following characteristics:

- Caption `"Sample Glossary"` in the title bar.
- Upper-left corner at `(222, 206)`.
- Length of 725 and width of 486 (in WinHelp coordinates).
- Displayed in normal size (`0`).
- Gray background (`192, 192, 192`) for the nonscrolling region.
- Appears on top of all other windows.

In the following section, you'll set up a secondary Help window for your Contact Manager program and see how to send information to it.

How to Add Context-Sensitive Help to an Application

How

The first step in adding context-sensitive Help to your Visual Basic application is to open your project's Options dialog box (select **O**ptions from the **T**ools menu and click the Project tab). Enter the name of your Help file in the Help File text box or click the ellipsis to browse for it. This setting can be a filename or a full path and filename; it indicates the file to be started when the user presses F1 from within your Visual Basic application. For now, during the development phase, use the full path. Figure 41.1 shows how the project Options dialog box might look.

Figure 41.1.
*Adding context-sensitive
Help to your Visual
Basic project.*

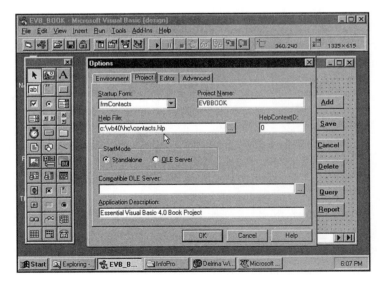

> **Tip** For best results after delivery, put the Help file in the same directory as your application and specify only the name of the Help file in the Help File text box. That way, you can keep the same setting for the Help File text box for each site using your application, and allow users to install the application in the directory of their choice.

The next step is to set the `HelpContextID` property for any forms and/or controls you want to be context-sensitive. This property is available for Visual Basic forms and for controls that can get focus; for example, text boxes, option groups, combo boxes, and frames. It is not available for controls that can't get focus, such as lines, labels, and graphs. The `HelpContextID` property sets the identifying number for a topic in the custom Help file specified in the project's Help File option. The setting for the `HelpContextID` property must be a `Long` integer between 0 and 2,147,483,647.

How

Table 41.1 displays the `HelpContextID` settings for significant controls on your Contact Manager's main form.

Table 41.1. `HelpContextID` settings—the Contact Manager form.

Visual Basic Object	Property	Design-Time Setting
Form	Name	frmContacts
	HelpContextID	0
Menu Item	Name	mnuImport
	HelpContextID	1
Menu Item	Name	mnuExport
	HelpContextID	2
Menu Item	Name	mnuSetup
	HelpContextID	3
TextBox	Name	txtCode
	HelpContextID	4
DBCombo	Name	dbcContacts
	HelpContextID	5
Frame Control	Name	fraCompany
	HelpContextID	6
Frame Control	Name	fraContact
	HelpContextID	7

continues

Table 41.1. continued

Visual Basic Object	Property	Design-Time Setting
Command Button	Name	cmdAdd
	HelpContextID	8
Command Button	Name	cmdSave
	HelpContextID	9
Command Button	Name	cmdCancel
	HelpContextID	10
Command Button	Name	cmdDelete
	HelpContextID	11
Command Button	Name	cmdQuery
	HelpContextID	12
Command Button	Name	cmdReport
	HelpContextID	13

Notice that you're giving a HelpContextID to the frames surrounding the company and contact information fields, rather than to each field individually. The idea is to have a single Help Topic for each of the field groups. The containership hierarchy comes into play here: When a user presses F1 for Help, Visual Basic checks to see if the current object has a HelpContextID; if it doesn't, Visual Basic looks for a HelpContextID in the object's container, and so on, back to form level. In this way, a user may be focused on any field within the company frame, for example, and the proper Help topic will be displayed when he or she presses F1.

Note If users press F1 while in a form, control, or group for which there is no context-sensitive Help, the default topic for the Help file specified in the project Options dialog box is displayed. If no Help file has been assigned for the project, the default topic for the Help file specified in your application's INI file is displayed.

 You must now modify your Help project's HPJ file. Here's how it should look at this point:

```
[OPTIONS]
errorlog = contacts.err
title = Contact Manager Help
compress = false
warning = 3
```

```
[FILES]
c:\vb40\hc\contacts.rtf

[WINDOWS]
Main = "Contact Manager Help", (0,0,750,1023),,,(192,192,192)
Second = "Secondary Window", (512,512,511,511),,,(192,192,192),1

[MAP]
FILE_IMPORT        1
FILE_EXPORT        2
PROG_SETUP         3
CODE_FIELD         4
CONTACTS_DD        5
COMPANY_FRAME      6
CONTACT_FRAME      7
ADD_BTN            8
SAVE_BTN           9
CANCEL_BTN        10
DELETE_BTN        11
QUERY_BTN         12
REPORT_BTN        13
```

You must also add the new topics shown in Figures 41.2 and 41.3 to your Contacts.RTF file; each new topic must be appropriately #footnoted to link it with the corresponding jump tag. Remember that in the RTF topic file, each topic must appear on a separate page. The jump tag is shown in parentheses. Figure 41.4 shows the results for comparison.

How

Figure 41.2.
Help Topics to add to Contacts.RTF.

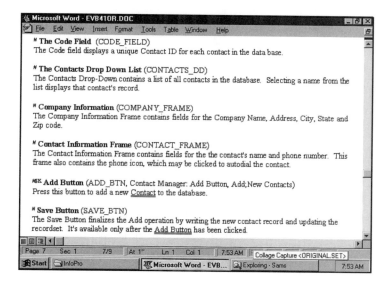

Figure 41.3.
Help Topics to add to
Contacts.RTF (contin-
ued).

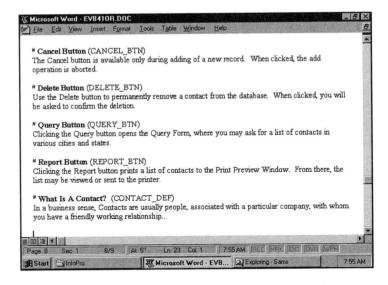

Figure 41.4.
Contact Manager
context-sensitive Help
Topics.

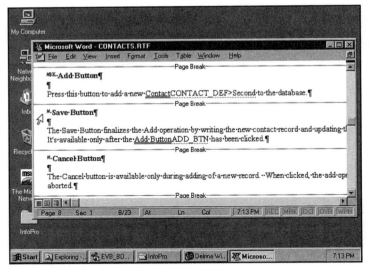

Notice the double-underlining in the Add and Save button topics. In the Add topic, the word
`Contact` is double-underlined, as is `Add Button` in the Save topic. In both cases, topic jumps are
indicated, but remember that the jump tags associated with these hypertext phrases are formatted as hidden, so you don't see them in the topics listed in Figure 41.4. Here, in Figure
41.5, is how they'll look when formatting codes are revealed in Microsoft Word.

Figure 41.5.
More hidden jump tags.

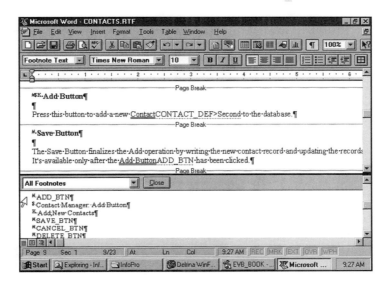

Jumps to a Secondary Window

When you create a jump to another topic, the WinHelp application assumes you want to display the topic in the main Help window. But you can code the jump to display the new topic in a secondary window. Use this syntax to code a jump that displays a topic in a secondary window:

```
JumpTag>windowname
```

Immediately following the jump tag of the new topic is a greater than (>) symbol followed by the name of the secondary window.

Now look again at Figure 41.5. The jump to the ADD_BTN topic is nothing new, but notice the jump tag for the double-underlined phrase Contact in the Add topic. Here, you're jumping to a new topic, CONTACT_DEF, but you're displaying it in your secondary window, rather than the main Help screen.

Now it's time to recompile your Help file, then run the Contact Manager program. You should thoroughly test your new context-sensitive Help feature. Notice that you may click on a field and press F1 to get related Help information. Rather than clicking command buttons (thereby executing their code), it might be better to test their context-sensitivity by using the Tab key to cycle through them, pressing F1 as you go. Be sure to see your secondary window in action by clicking the Contact hypertext in the Add Button topic. Here, in Figure 41.6, is a sample session.

Figure 41.6.
The secondary Help window in action.

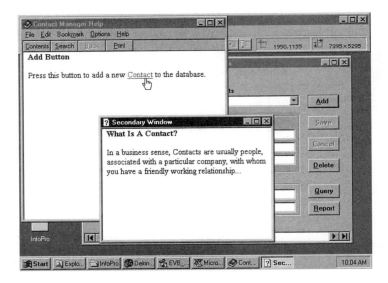

Essential Summary

What

In this chapter, you acquired an understanding of context-sensitive Help and saw how it may be added to your Visual Basic applications. You also learned how to redirect Help text to a secondary window, one that operates independently of the main Help screen and that may be used to display glossaries, lists, sample code, or any other information the user may want to view concurrently with the main Help text.

Why

Using context-sensitive help is another way of getting your user to feel more comfortable, or more at home, with your application. It's friendly and convenient to be able to get help on your current operation or control by pressing a single key, without having to navigate the help system's contents or search features.

How

By adding context-sensitive Help and a secondary Help window to your Contact Manager program, you increased its value by making it more user-friendly. In the process, you saw how to set your objects' HelpContextID property and how to manipulate the [MAP] and [WINDOWS] sections of the Help project file, thereby increasing your own value as a Windows applications programmer.

Help Graphics and Hypergraphics

You can increase clarity and add interest to a Help system by using graphics. In this chapter, you'll learn some easy ways to add graphics images to your Help files. You'll receive a brief review of graphics types, and you'll be introduced to a special kind of graphics called *hypergraphics*, which may be used like hypertext to jump between help topics.

What Are Help File Graphics?

What You can include four types of graphics in your Help system, two of which you've already worked with in Chapters 11 and 12, where you created your Image Manager program. Table 42.1 describes each of the four types.

Table 42.1. Help file graphics types.

Graphic Type	Description
Bitmap	A *bitmap* defines an image as a pattern of dots (pixels). A bitmap has the extensions .BMP or .DIB. Also called *paint-type* or *raster graphics.*
Metafile	A *metafile* defines an image as coded lines and shapes. A metafile has the extension .WMF. Only files that are compatible with Microsoft Windows version 3.0 or later can be included in the Help file. Also called *draw-type* or *vector graphics.*
Hypergraphic	A bitmap or metafile that contains at least one *hot spot.* Hot spots are areas on the graphic that may be used to jump to Help topics or execute Help macros (see Chapter 43), just like hypertext. An entire graphic may be used as a single hot spot. If a hypergraphic is to contain more than one hot spot, or if only part of the graphic is to be "hot," you must edit it using the Hotspot Editor (SHED.EXE). A hypergraphic usually has the extension .SHG.
MRB	A *multiple-resolution-bitmap* (MRB) is compiled from several bitmaps with different screen resolutions by the Multiple-Resolution Bitmap Compiler (MRBC.EXE). A multiple-resolution bitmap has the extension .MRB.

Note In this chapter, you'll work with three bitmap files: EMDASH.BMP, PHONE.BMP, and SMOKES.BMP. The first, EMDASH.BMP, is located in the Visual Basic Help Compiler directory, \VB40\HC. It's recommended that you copy the other two bitmap files to that location, as well. PHONE.BMP and SMOKES.BMP are found in the \VB40\BITMAPS\ASSORTED directory.

What
There are two methods for including graphics in a Help file. You may place the bitmap or metafile directly in the topic file, or you may place a bitmap or metafile *reference* in the topic file. In this section, you'll explore the advantages and disadvantages of each method.

Placing a Graphic Directly

The easiest way to place a graphic into a Help topic file is to import the graphic or metafile directly from the Windows Clipboard into Word for Windows. You then simply paste the graphic where you want it to appear in the Help topic file. You may format your text so it's positioned below or alongside the graphic. When you save the Help topic file in rich-text format (RTF) and recompile your Help file, the pasted bitmaps and metafiles are automatically included.

There are a few advantages to this method: it's simple, requiring only basic word processing skills; you're able to see the graphic whenever you work in the Help topic file; and you don't have to enter the graphic's location in the Help project file.

The disadvantages of this method are many in comparison. Following is a list:

- You can use only Word for Windows in creating your topic files.

- You can use only *inline graphics*, which are treated the same as a character and therefore limit the ways you can display text and graphics. For example, it's not possible to wrap text *around* an inline graphic.

- Graphics pasted directly into a Word document increase the time needed to scroll or save the topic file.

- You can't change the graphic inside Word for Windows. Instead, you must modify it in your graphics application and then re-import it.

- You can't paste hypergraphics (graphics created with the Hotspot Editor) in topic files.

- Including the same graphic directly at multiple locations in the topic file adds multiple copies of the graphic to the compiled Help file, increasing its size.

Inserting a Graphic by Reference

To insert a graphic into a Help topic by reference, you include special "embraced" text that tells the WinHelp application the name of the bitmap file or metafile and how to position it with respect to related Help topic text. There are many advantages to including Help file graphics by reference:

- You can create your Help file with any text editor that produces RTF files.

- You have the widest range of options for displaying text and graphics. For example, you can treat the graphic as a character, or you can wrap text around the graphic's left or right edge.

- You can change the graphic without having to re-import it into the Help topic file. The references are pointers to the graphics files. The Help Compiler inserts the actual graphics only when you compile the Help file.

- Graphic references are the only way you can include hypergraphics (created with the Hotspot Editor) in your topic files. You cannot paste hypergraphics directly into your RTF file.

- Including the same graphic by reference at multiple locations in a topic file adds only one copy of the graphic in the compiled Help file, thereby keeping the size of the file to a minimum.

There are really only two slight disadvantages to the reference method of including graphics in your Help files: You can't see the graphic when you work in the topic file, and you have to enter the locations of the graphics files in the Help project file. Although entering graphic locations in the Help project file is a simple task, any mistakes will cause errors at compile time.

Since the advantages of the "reference" method far outweigh those of the "direct paste" method, and since importing and pasting is more a word processing issue than a programming one, the rest of this chapter will focus on including graphics by reference.

How to Include Graphics by Reference

How

Placing a graphic by reference is a two-step process. First you enter the reference text in the topic file where you want the graphic to appear. Then you enter the location of the graphic file in the Help project (.HPJ) file. One advantage to moving all your Help graphics files to the same directory (as was suggested in a note at the beginning of this chapter) is that you may inform the compiler of their location by adding but a single line to your Help project file. This line identifies the directory where bitmaps and other help-related graphics will be stored. Here's the listing of CONTACTS.HPJ, with the new line formatted in bold:

```
[OPTIONS]
errorlog = contacts.err
title = Contact Manager Help
compress = false
warning = 3
BMROOT = C:\VB40\HC

[FILES]
c:\vb40\hc\contacts.rtf

[WINDOWS]
Main = "Contact Manager Help", (0,0,750,1023),,,(192,192,192)
Second = "Secondary Window", (512,512,511,511),,,,(192,192,192),1

[MAP]
FILE_IMPORT      1
FILE_EXPORT      2
PROG_SETUP       3
CODE_FIELD       4
CONTACTS_DD      5
COMPANY_FRAME    6
CONTACT_FRAME    7
ADD_BTN          8
SAVE_BTN         9
CANCEL_BTN      10
DELETE_BTN      11
QUERY_BTN       12
REPORT_BTN      13
```

Now, here's the syntax for creating references to graphics not directly included in a topic file:

```
{Command FileName}
```

Notice the "squiggly" braces {}; they are required. `FileName` is the name of the graphics file, and you *do not* include a path. The following table (see Table 42.2) lists the three `Commands` you can use in creating a graphic reference.

Table 42.2. Graphic reference commands.

Command	Description
bmc	Aligns the graphic as a character. This command is used when you'd like the graphic to appear as a single character in a line of text, as a bullet or an em-dash, for example.
bml	Aligns the graphic at the left margin and allows text to wrap or flow along the graphic's right edge.
bmr	Aligns the graphic at the right margin; text wraps along the graphic's left edge.

With all three Commands, the compiled Help file contains a single copy of the graphic data separate from any related text. The FileName given in the graphic reference includes only the file name, not the file's full path. The Help project (.HPJ) file contains all the path information for graphics included by reference.

Aligning Graphics as Characters

The Help Compiler treats a graphic inserted with a bmc reference as a character. After compiling the Help file, graphics aligned as characters appear on the type baseline at the location of the reference command. The graphic actually becomes part of the paragraph, so any formatting applied to the paragraph also applies to the graphic. Text appearing above and below doesn't wrap around the graphic, but the size of the graphic may increase the line space between the line containing the graphic and the preceding line in the text.

> **Caution** Don't specify negative line spacing for a paragraph that has a bmc graphic reference. If you do, the graphic might appear on top of the paragraph when the WinHelp displays the topic.

A bullet or other special symbol is a good use of a graphic as a character. Here is how a bmc reference might appear in a Help topic file, using a small bitmap, BULLET.BMP, as the bullet in a bulleted list:

```
{bmc bullet.bmp}     The Add button is used to add a new contact.
{bmc bullet.bmp}     The Cancel button aborts the Add operation.
```

Aligning Graphics at the Left Margin

The Help Compiler places a bml graphic along the left margin. Text wraps automatically along the right edge of the image. Text is aligned with the graphic's upper-right corner, so any white space saved at the top of the image affects the way text appears in relation to the graphic.

Normally, a bml reference appears at the beginning of a paragraph, which ensures proper wrapping of text around the graphic's right edge. The following example shows a typical bml reference:

```
{bml bozo.bmp}This paragraph text follows the bitmap reference...
```

Unless you want the first line of text to appear indented, do not put any space characters between the bml reference and the paragraph text.

You can also put a bml reference at the end of a paragraph. When you code a bml reference this way, WinHelp wraps the text up to the end of the paragraph, and then displays the graphic. After you compile the Help file, the image appears under the text and to the left. Here's an example usage:

```
This paragraph text precedes the bitmap reference.{bml bozo.bmp}
```

Aligning Graphics at the Right Margin

The Help Compiler places a bmr graphic along the right margin. Text automatically wraps along the image's left edge. Under normal circumstances, you would place bmr references at the beginning of a paragraph. This ensures proper wrapping of text around the images' left edge. Here's an example of a valid bmr graphic reference:

```
{bmr smokes.shg}Click the part of the cigarette you want to know more about.
```

Here, in Figure 42.1, is how such a graphic reference might look in your Help system.

Figure 42.1.
A right-aligned graphic and text.

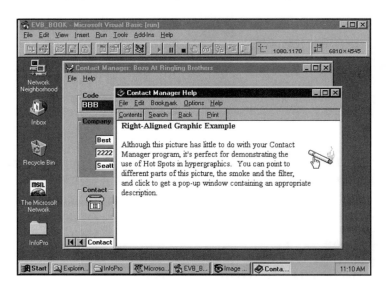

You can also place a bmr reference at the end of a paragraph. In this case, the text is wrapped up to the end of the paragraph, and then the graphic is displayed beneath the text and to the right. Here's an example of such a reference:

```
This paragraph text precedes the right-aligned bitmap.{bmr name.bmp}
```

You can do much more with graphics in your Help file than simply display them. The WinHelp application allows you to use graphics as hot spots. This means that you can use graphics, such as icons or buttons, as jumps to particular topics or as hot spots for pop-up windows or to execute Help macros.

It's time to make some enhancements to your Contact Manager's Help system. You'll edit the first page of your CONTACTS.RTF file to include a list of command buttons, each preceded by an em-dash bitmap graphic. The em-dash and the accompanying text will become a hot spot for jumping to the appropriate Help topic.

Figure 42.2 is a screen-shot of your modified Help topic file's first page, with the arrow pointing to the new hot spots.

Figure 42.2.
Using graphics as hot spots.

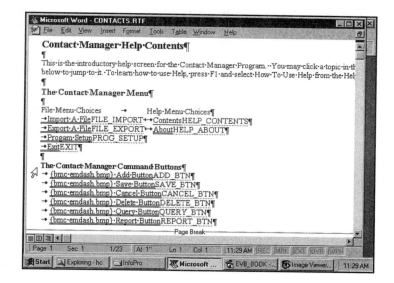

Notice the double-underlining, which indicates that you're creating hot spots for jumping to a new topic page, rather than opening a pop-up window. Here are the steps to follow in coding a graphic reference as a jump-topic (or pop-up window) hot spot:

1. Enter the graphic reference (bmc, bml, or bmr) in the topic file where you want the jump. Be sure you've already created the topic text (and set its jump tag).

2. Select the entire graphic reference, including the file name and opening and closing braces.

3. Format the graphic reference as double-underlined text to create a jump. (Or format the graphic reference as single-underlined text to create a hot spot for a pop-up window.)

Part VIII

4. Type the jump tag of the destination topic immediately following the graphic reference.

5. Format the jump tag as hidden text.

Now follow the preceding steps in adding a hot spot graphic to your Contact Information topic, which you created in the last chapter. Locate that topic in CONTACTS.RTF. Here, in Figure 42.3, is how it will look once you've added the Phone.BMP reference as a hot spot.

Figure 42.3.
The Phone bitmap hot spot.

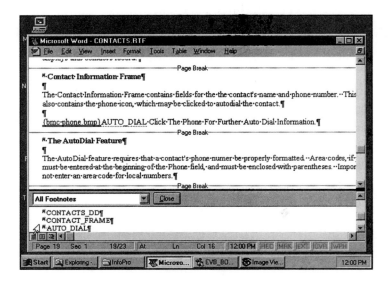

In Figure 42.3, you can see how the phone bitmap reference is double-underlined, and you can see the hidden jump tag AUTO_DIAL. You'll need to create the AutoDial topic page, which is also visible in Figure 42.3, and be sure to register its jump tag as a # symbol footnote. (See the arrow in the footnote pane of Figure 42.3 for reference.)

Once you have your new hot spots properly coded, recompile your Help file and try it out. You should be able to jump to each button's Help topic by clicking either the em-dash bitmap or the associated hypertext. You'll also be able to click the phone graphic in the Contact Information topic, and be transported to the AutoDial Help page.

Hot Spots and Hypergraphics

The preceding section showed you how to create a single hot spot in a graphic. Multiple hot spots can make the graphics in your Help file even more useful. To create more than one hot spot within a single graphic, you must create a hypergraphic.

A *hypergraphic* is a graphic (bitmap or metafile) with embedded hot spots that users can click to do the following:

- Jump to another Help topic.
- Display a pop-up window.
- Activate a Help macro.
- Activate routines in external dynamic-link libraries (DLLs).

You create hypergraphics with the Hotspot Editor (SHED.EXE). This tool is conveniently located in the \VB40\HC directory, where the rest of your help-related files are currently stored. You can use the Hotspot Editor to open a bitmap (.BMP), a device-independent bitmap (.DIB), or a Windows metafile (.WMF), and add hot spots to the existing graphic image. You may then save the graphic as a hypergraphic (.SHG) file.

Caution Because the Hotspot Editor is not a drawing or painting program, you must create the actual graphic outside the Hotspot Editor. Once you save a graphic as a hypergraphic, you can't open it again with a drawing or painting program. Therefore, it's a good idea to make copies of graphics files you intend to convert to hypergraphics.

Follow these general steps to create a hypergraphic:

1. Open a bitmap or metafile in the Hotspot Editor.
2. Draw hot-spot locations in the graphic.
3. Define attributes for each hot spot in the graphic.
4. Save the graphic as a hypergraphic.

Once you define the hot spots, the graphic is ready to be included by reference in any RTF topic file, from where it may be compiled into your Help file.

You'll work with the Hotspot Editor in this section, but first you will add three new topic pages to your CONTACTS.RTF. One topic will have a jump tag of HOT_SPOTS and be titled "Hot Spots and Hypergraphics"; it will have a title $ footnote, as well as a keyword K footnote containing the search words Hot spots;Hypergraphics. The other two topic pages will have only jump tag footnotes, SMOKE_ONLY and FILTER_ONLY, which will allow them to be displayed, when called upon, in a pop-up window. Here, in Figure 42.4, is what they'll look like in your RTF topic file.

There are a couple of new things to notice here. First, your left-aligned bitmap reference is to SMOKES.SHG, which indicates that you're using a hypergraphic file (you haven't created it yet, but you will soon). The second thing to note is that there is no double- or single-underlining and no hidden jump tags. This is because all of the jumping will be handled by setting hot spot attributes in the Hotspot Editor, which is what you'll do next.

Figure 42.4.
The Hot Spot and
Hypergraphics topics.

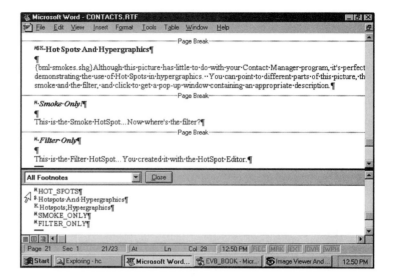

Using the Hotspot Editor

Before you can add hot spots to a graphic, you must open the graphic in the Hotspot Editor.

After opening a graphic in the Hotspot Editor, you can create hot spots that link to topics, pop-up windows, or macros. When you compile with the Help Compiler, the hot spots you define become part of the completed Help file.

A hot spot can be any rectangular area within the graphic. You draw hot spots on the graphic as you would a rectangle in any Windows drawing or painting program.

Following are the general steps to follow in creating a hot spot:

1. Click the location on the graphic where you want to anchor one corner of the hot spot.

2. Drag the mouse until the rectangle encloses the area you want to define as the hot spot. The box stretches from the anchor point to the position of the mouse, and expands and contracts as you move the mouse.

3. When the hot-spot rectangle is the desired size, release the mouse button.

   After you release the mouse button, the hot-spot rectangle displays eight sizing handles, indicating the currently selected hot spot. You can use the sizing handles to resize the rectangle.

   After creating a hot spot, you must define the attributes that determine what happens when a user clicks the hot spot. To define these attributes, you use the Attributes dialog box, which is discussed next.

Defining Hot Spot Attributes

Follow these general steps in defining hot spot attributes:

1. Select the hot spot or create a new one.

2. Click the hot spot with the right mouse button to display the Attributes dialog box.

3. For a jump or pop-up window, enter the jump tag for the destination jump or pop-up window topic in the Context String box. For a Help macro, enter the macro in the Context String box (Help macros are covered in Chapter 43).

4. Choose the type of hot spot you want to create from the Type list. Valid types are Jump, Pop-up, and Macro.

5. Choose Visible or Invisible for the display attribute. If you want to make the hot-spot region visible to users (it will appear with a bounding rectangle), choose Visible from the Attribute list.

6. If you want to change the default name assigned to the hot spot, edit the hot-spot identifier.

7. If you want to change the size or location of the hot spot, edit the bounding box coordinates.

8. Choose OK.

The attributes defined for the hot spot now appear in the Hotspot Editor status bar.

The Attributes dialog box allows you to maintain important binding information about each hot spot you create. Table 43.3 contains a summary of the information contained in the Attributes dialog box.

Table 42.3. Hot spot attributes.

Field	Description
Context string	Specifies binding information for the hot spot. Can be either a jump tag (context string) or a macro.
Type	Indicates the type of action taken when the user selects the hot spot. You can jump to another topic, display a topic in a pop-up window, or run a Help macro.
Attribute	Specifies whether the hot spot is visible or invisible in the Help window. Hot spots are always visible in the Hotspot Editor.
Hotspot ID	Specifies a unique identifier for the hot spot. The hot-spot name is used internally by the Hotspot Editor and helps you identify hot spots in the Select dialog box. The Hotspot Editor automatically assigns an incremental number to the hot-spot name; however, you can type in a unique name.

continues

Table 42.3. continued

Field	Description
Bounding Box	Displays the coordinates for the hot-spot rectangle: left, right, top, and bottom. The coordinates are measured in pixels and are restricted to the size of the graphic image.

Now it's time to create your first hypergraphic. Open the Hotspot Editor (SHED.EXE in \VB40\HC). Select **F**ile **O**pen from the menu, then locate SMOKES.BMP, which should be in the same directory. Follow the previous steps to define two hot spots, as you see them in Figure 42.5.

Figure 42.5.
Defining hot spots with the Hotspot Editor.

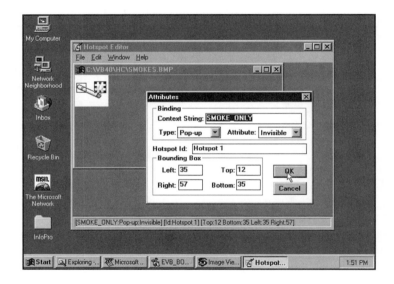

Figure 42.5 shows the bounding rectangles for Hotspot 1 and Hotspot 2. It also shows the Attribute dialog box for Hotspot 1, which is the rectangle surrounding the smoke from the cigarette. The attributes for Hotspot 2, the cigarette filter, will be very similar. Obviously, the Bounding Box coordinates will be different, and the jump tag or (context string) will be FILTER_ONLY, rather than SMOKE_ONLY.

Once the hot spots are drawn and their proper attributes are defined, save the bitmap as SMOKES.SHG, to indicate that it's a hypergraphic containing multiple hot spots. (You'll also want to be sure to name it SMOKES.SHG because that's the file name you use as your topic file reference.

That's it for hypergraphics. Close the Hotspot Editor, if you like, to clear the decks a little. You'll now need to recompile your Help file. When that's done, fire up your Contact Manager program and thoroughly test your new, improved, custom Help system. Since you added keywords for the Hot spot and Hypergraphics topic, you'll be able to locate it easily by using WinHelp's search feature. You'll be able to click on your hypergraphic's smoke, or filter, and get a nice pop-up window, like that seen in Figure 42.6.

Figure 42.6.
Hypergraphic hot spots in action.

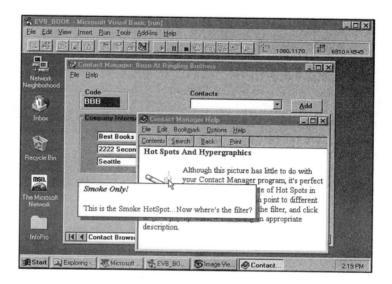

Essential Summary

In this chapter, you learned some different ways to add graphic images to your Help files. You saw that you may set up references to your images so that they may be used as hot spots for jumping between related Help topics. Finally, you were introduced to a special kind of graphics called hypergraphics, which may contain multiple hot spots, each of which may be used to jump between topics, or pop-up windows, or execute Help macros.

What

Standard graphics alone can add clarity and interest to your custom Help System. Graphical hot spots and hypergraphics add a whole new level of sophistication and ease-of-use to your Help system, a level that Windows application users are coming to expect.

Why

You added several graphics to your Contact Manager's Help system. You referenced some simple em-dashes as part of a neatly bulleted list of command button topics; you included a telephone bitmap, which became a hot spot to your AutoDial topic; and you used the Hotspot Editor to create your first hypergraphic containing two separate hot spots, each of which popped open its own distinct definition window.

How

Using Help Macros

In this chapter, you'll add still more functionality to your Contact Manager Help system by calling on the Windows Help macros, which you can use to customize the way the WinHelp application works with your Help files. You'll receive an overview of the more than 50 available macros and get a chance to see several of them in action.

What Are Help Macros?

Help macros are routines built into the WinHelp application that allow you to further customize your own Help systems. Using macros, you can add and remove custom buttons and menus, change the function of buttons and menu items, execute applications from within Help, and even execute functions from external dynamic link libraries (DLLs).

The following series of tables constitute a categorized list of WinHelp macros and their descriptions. If a particular macro may be called by using an abbreviated form, the abbreviation is given in parentheses at the end of the description.

Use the following macros (see Table 43.1) to access standard Help buttons, to create new buttons, or to modify button functionality and appearance.

Table 43.1. Button Manipulation macros.

Macro	Description
Back	Displays the previous topic in the Back list.
ChangeButtonBinding	Changes the current function of a Help button. (CBB)
Contents	Displays the Contents topic of the current Help file.
CreateButton	Creates a new button and adds it to the Toolbar. (CB)
DestroyButton	Removes a button from the Toolbar.
DisableButton	Disables a button on the Toolbar. (DB)
EnableButton	Enables a disabled button. (EB)
History	Displays the history list.
Next	Moves to the next topic in a browse sequence.
Prev	Displays the previous topic in a browse sequence.
Search	Opens the Search dialog box.
SetContents	Designates a specific topic as the Contents topic.

The following macros may be used to access standard Help menu items, to create new menus, or to modify the performance of existing menus and menu items (see Table 43.2).

Table 43.2. Menu Manipulation macros.

Macro	Description
About	Shows the About dialog box.
Annotate	Displays the Annotate dialog box.
AppendItem	Appends a menu item to the end of a custom menu.
BookmarkDefine	Displays the Bookmark Define dialog box.
BookmarkMore	Displays the Bookmark dialog box.
ChangeItemBinding	Changes the assigned function of a menu item. (CIB)
CheckItem	Displays a check mark next to a menu item. (CI)
CopyDialog	Opens the Copy dialog box.
CopyTopic	Copies the current topic to the Clipboard.
DeleteItem	Removes a menu item from a menu.

Macro	*Description*
DisableItem	Disables a menu item. (DI)
EnableItem	Enables a disabled menu item. (EI)
Exit	Exits the WinHelp application.
FileOpen	Displays the Open dialog box.
HelpOn	Displays the How To Use Help file.
InsertItem	Inserts a menu item at a given position on a menu.
InsertMenu	Adds a new menu to the Help menu bar.
Print	Sends the current topic to the printer.
PrinterSetup	Displays the Print Setup dialog box.
SetHelpOnFile	Specifies a custom How To Use Help file.
UncheckItem	Removes a check mark from a menu item. (UI)

It's often convenient to use macros in creating links between Help topics. You might, for example, decide to create a button which, when clicked, jumps to a Glossary of terms or example code. You may use the following macros to create hypertext links to specific Help topics (see Table 43.3).

Table 43.3. Hypertext Link macros.

Macro	*Description*
JumpContents	Jumps to the Contents topic of a specific Help file.
JumpContext	Jumps to the topic with a specific context number. (JC)
JumpHelpOn	Jumps to the Contents of the How To Use Help file.
JumpId	Jumps to the topic with a specific jump tag. (JI)
JumpKeyword	Jumps to the first topic containing a specified keyword.
PopupContext	Displays the topic with a specific number in a pop-up window. (PC)
PopupId	Displays the topic with a specific jump tag in a pop-up window. (PI)

The remaining auxiliary macros are used to control or modify the behavior and appearance of the Help windows, to add or remove keyboard accelerators, to run external applications, and to manage and manipulate bookmarks (see Table 43.4).

Table 43.4. WinHelp Auxiliary macros.

Macro	Description
CloseWindow	Closes the main or secondary Help window.
FocusWindow	Changes the focus to a specific Help window.
HelpOnTop	Places all Help windows on top of other windows.
PositionWindow	Sets the size and position of a Help window.
AddAccelerator	Assigns an accelerator key to a Help macro. (AA)
RemoveAccelerator	Removes an accelerator key from a Help macro. (RA)
ExecProgram	Starts an application. (EP)
RegisterRoutine	Registers a function within a DLL as a Help macro. (RR)
DeleteMark	Removes a marker added by SaveMark.
GotoMark	Jumps to a marker set by SaveMark.
IfThen	Executes a Help macro if a given marker exists.
IfThenElse	Executes one of two macros if a given marker exists.
IsMark	Tests whether a marker set by SaveMark exists.
Not	Reverses the result returned by IsMark.
SaveMark	Saves a marker for the current topic and Help file.

A Closer Look

In this section, you'll get a closer look at several of the macros listed in the preceding tables, many of which you'll be using in the "How to Run Help Macros" section of this chapter. The discussion will include complete definitions, parameters, and usage examples.

CreateButton

The CreateButton macro (or CB) is used to define a new button and display it in your Help system's button or Toolbar. Here's how it's used:

```
CreateButton("ButtonId", "Caption", "Macro")
```

The *ButtonId* argument is a name that WinHelp uses to identify the button. This name must appear in quotation marks, and may be referred to in the DisableButton or DestroyButton macro, if you want to remove or disable the button, or in the ChangeButtonBinding macro, if you want to change the macro that the button runs in certain topics.

The second argument, *Caption*, is the text that appears on the button. This name must appear in quotation marks. To designate a letter for Alt Key access, place an ampersand (&) before it.

The *Macro* argument is the Help macro or macro string that is run when the user chooses the button. The macro must appear in quotation marks. Multiple macros in a macro string must be separated by semicolons (;).

Here's an example of the CreateButton macro. This call creates a new button labeled Clowns that jumps to a topic with the jump tag LIST_CLOWNS in the CIRCUS.HLP file when the button is chosen:

```
CreateButton("CLOWNS_BTN", "&Clowns", "JumpId('circus.hlp', 'LIST_CLOWNS')")
```

Notice the use of single quotes within double-quoted strings here. The third argument is a double-quoted string representing another macro. In fact, you're calling one macro from within another. This is perfectly legal as long as you don't mismatch quotes and double-quotes.

> **Caution** When using single quotes in your macros, remember that there's a difference between a left single quote ('), which appears below the tilde (~) on your keyboard, and a right single quote, which is the apostrophe ('). These quotes must be properly matched and balanced, or the Help Compiler will squawk.

DisableButton

The DisableButton macro (or DB) is used to dim or "gray out" a particular button when it is unavailable to the user. The syntax is simple; here it is:

```
DisableButton("ButtonId")
```

The `ButtonId` is the identifier assigned to the button in the CreateButton macro. The button identifier must appear in quotation marks. A button disabled by the DisableButton macro cannot be used in the topic until an EnableButton macro is run.

EnableButton

This macro, abbreviated EB, re-enables a button disabled with the DisableButton macro.

Here's its simple syntax:

```
EnableButton("ButtonId")
```

Here, as with all button-manipulation macros, `ButtonId` is the identifier assigned to the button in the CreateButton macro. Again `ButtonId` must appear in quotation marks.

DestroyButton

This macro removes a button added with the CreateButton macro, causing it to disappear from your Help system's button bar. Here's how you call it:

```
DestroyButton("ButtonId")
```

Again, `ButtonId` is the identifier assigned to the button in the CreateButton macro. The button identifier must appear in quotation marks. The button identifier cannot duplicate an identifier used for one of the standard Help buttons.

InsertMenu

The InsertMenu macro adds a new menu to the Windows Help menu bar. Here's its syntax:

```
InsertMenu("MenuId", "Caption", MenuPosition)
```

MenuId is the name that WinHelp uses to identify the menu; it must be enclosed in quotation marks. You'll use this identifier in the AppendItem macro (see next section) to add menu items (commands) to the menu.

The *Caption* argument is the name for the menu that WinHelp displays on the menu bar. This name is case-sensitive and must be enclosed in quotation marks. Within the quotation marks, place an ampersand (&) before the character you want to use for the menu's accelerator key.

MenuPosition is a number specifying the position on the menu bar that the new menu name will have. This number must be an integer. Positions are numbered from left to right, with position 0 being the leftmost menu. WinHelp's default menu contains File, Edit, Bookmark, Options, and Help, numbered 0 through 4, respectively.

The following example uses the InsertMenu macro to add a menu named Utilities to WinHelp's default menu:

```
InsertMenu("Menu_Utils", "&Utilities", 3)
```

Now Utilities will appear as the fourth menu on the Windows Help menu bar, between the Bookmark and Options menus. In this case, the user may press Alt+U to access the menu.

Caution Be sure that the accelerator key you assign to a menu is unique. If you assign a key that conflicts with another menu accelerator key, WinHelp displays an `Unable to add menu` error message and ignores the macro.

AppendItem

This macro is used to add menu items to the end of a menu created with the InsertMenu macro. Here's how it looks:

```
AppendItem("MenuId", "ItemId", "Caption", "Macro")
```

MenuId is the name used in the InsertMenu macro to create the menu. This name must be enclosed in quotation marks. The new item is added to the end of this menu.

ItemId is the name that WinHelp uses to identify the menu item. This name is case-sensitive and must be enclosed in quotation marks.

Caption is the name that is displayed on the menu for the item. This name is case-sensitive and must be enclosed in quotation marks. As usual, you may use an ampersand (&) before the letter you want to use for the item's accelerator key.

Macro is the Help macro or macro string that executes when the user chooses the menu item. The macro must be enclosed in quotation marks. Separate multiple macros in a string with semicolons (;).

Here's an example of how the AppendItem macro might be used to add an item to the Utilities menu created in the previous example:

```
AppendItem("Menu_Utils", "New_Item", "E&xample", "JI('sample.hlp','eg_012_topic')")
```

Choosing the menu item causes a jump to a topic with the eg_012_topic jump tag in the SAMPLE.HLP file. Note that the letter *x* serves as the accelerator key for this menu item.

JumpId

This macro jumps to the topic with the specified jump tag in the specified Help file. Here's how it's used:

```
JumpId("FileName", "JumpTag")
```

FileName is the name of the Help file (.HLP) containing the jump tag. The file name must appear in quotation marks. If WinHelp does not find this file, it displays an error message and does not perform the jump.

JumpTag is the jump tag of the topic in the destination file. The jump tag must appear in quotation marks. If the tag does not exist, WinHelp jumps to the contents topic for that file instead.

The following example is the JumpId macro to jump to a topic with GLOSSARY as its jump tag in the Help file named CONTACTS.HLP:

```
JumpId("CONTACTS.HLP", "GLOSSARY")
```

> **Tip** You can use the JumpId macro to display topics in secondary windows by adding the window name to the FileName parameter, as in this example:
>
> ```
> JumpId("Circus.hlp>BigTop", "Lion_List")
> ```
>
> The topic identified by the Lion_List jump tag would appear in the BigTop secondary window.

ExecProgram

This macro, abbreviated EP, launches a Windows-based application from within your custom Help system. Here's the syntax:

```
ExecProgram("CommandLine", DisplayState)
```

Here *CommandLine* is the command line for the application to be executed. The command line must appear in quotation marks. WinHelp searches for this application in the current directory, followed by the Windows directory, the user's path, and the directory of the currently displayed Help file.

The *DisplayState* argument is a value indicating how the application is displayed when executed. A value of 0 indicates normal, 1 indicates minimized, and 2 indicates maximized.

Here's an example of the ExecProgram macro in action; it runs the Windows NotePad program in its normal window size:

```
ExecProgram("notepad.exe", 0)
```

CloseWindow

This macro closes the specified window, which is either the main WinHelp window or a secondary window. Its syntax is simple:

```
CloseWindow("WinName")
```

Here *WinName* is the name of the window to close. The name "main" is reserved for the primary Help window. For secondary windows, the window name is defined in the [WINDOWS] section of the .HPJ file. This name must appear in quotation marks.

The following macro closes the secondary window named Glossary:

```
CloseWindow("Glossary")
```

HelpOn

This simple macro displays the Using Help file for the WinHelp application (same as the Using Help command on the Help menu). It requires no arguments and is called directly, like this:

```
HelpOn()
```

How to Run Help Macros

Help macros can be run when WinHelp first opens a Help file; when the user selects a particular topic in the Help file; and when the user chooses a button, menu item, or hot spot containing a macro. In this section, you'll explore all three ways to run macros while adding extra functionality to your Contact Manager's Help system.

If a macro appears in the [CONFIG] section of your Help project file (.HPJ), WinHelp runs that macro when it first opens the Help file. If more than one macro is listed in the [CONFIG] section, they are executed in their listed order.

Open CONTACTS.HPJ and add the following lines at the bottom of the file, beneath the [MAP] section:

```
[CONFIG]
InsertMenu("Menu_Tools", "&Tools", 4)
```

```
AppendItem("Menu_Tools","Calc_Item","&Calculator", "EP('calc.exe',0)")
AppendItem("Menu_Tools","Note_Item","&NotePad","EP('notepad.exe',0)")

CB("Glos_Btn","&Glossary","JumpId('Contacts.hlp>Second','GLOSSARY')")
CB("Help_Btn","&Help","HelpOn()")
CB("Exit_Btn","E&xit","Exit()")
```

You're accomplishing a lot here in a very few lines. The first macro creates a new menu called Tools in the fifth position of the default Help menu; that is, after Options but before Help. The next two macros add items to the new Tools menu and specify what should happen when the items are selected. In this case, you'll run the Windows calculator or notebook programs by calling the ExecProgram macros, shortened to EP here. (Again, pay close attention when entering the single quotes.)

The next three macros add buttons to WinHelp's default button bar. The first CB macro (remember, CB is short for CreateButton) creates a Glossary button which, when chosen, will cause a jump to the topic tagged GLOSSARY (which you'll define in the next section) in your Help file named CONTACTS.HLP. But that's not all that happens here. Notice that the first argument contains a > symbol, which redirects the topic output to your secondary help window. This way the user will have the Glossary displayed in its own independent window.

The last two macros are much simpler. You're creating a button that will launch WinHelp's own Help On Help search window, and you're giving the user a button that will provide an alternate way of exiting your Help system. Macros that control Help buttons, menus, or menu items remain in effect until the user quits WinHelp or opens a new Help file.

If a Help macro is called in a topic footnote, WinHelp runs that macro automatically whenever the user jumps to the topic. A user can jump to a topic by clicking a hypertext label or graphic hot spot, by clicking the Back button or a browse button, and by selecting the topic from the history list or keyword search list.

How

To call a macro from a topic footnote, you use the special footnote symbol (!), an exclamation mark. Now open CONTACTS.RTF and add a new page at the bottom. This is where you'll define your Glossary topic. Refer to Figure 43.1 for the topic text (which is obviously not a complete glossary at this point) and for the associated footnotes.

Almost everything here will be familiar to you (you've worked with such displays many times in the last three chapters). But there is something new to notice: the topics' last footnote, indicated by the arrow, is set with the ! symbol and identifies the macro to run when this GLOSSARY topic is first displayed. In this case, you've anticipated that the user might appreciate having a place to jot down notes, so you'll open the Windows NotePad automatically.

Help macros can also be run from hot spots within a topic. WinHelp runs a hot-spot macro whenever the user chooses the hot spot containing that macro. A hot spot containing a macro is formatted like any other hot spot. The text or bitmap reference used for the macro is double-underlined, and the macro (preceded by an exclamation mark) is formatted as hidden text.

How

Figure 43.1.
*The Glossary topic and
footnotes.*

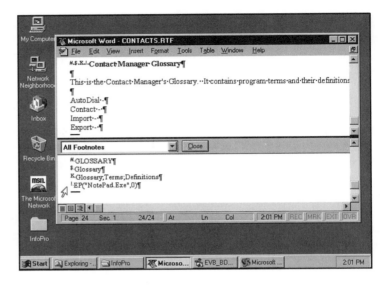

In CONTACTS.RTF, move to the first page, the Help Contents. What you'll do here is add a new bit of hypertext that, instead of jumping to a topic, will execute the About() macro, which simply displays your Help system's own About dialog box. Here, in Figure 43.2, is how the Contents page will look.

Figure 43.2.
*Running the About
macro from hypertext.*

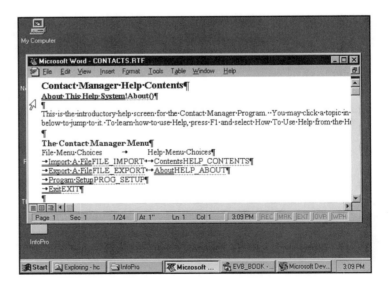

Notice the arrow pointing to the new hot spot, in this case a hypertext label. The text is double-underlined, and the About() macro is called immediately after it. Don't forget to precede the macro with an exclamation mark and format the call as hidden text.

That's it for running Help macros from your custom Help system. You should now recompile and start up the Contact Manager program for testing. Be sure to admire and test all your new buttons and menu items, and notice that the NotePad starts up whenever you switch to the Glossary topic. Figure 43.3 shows your enhanced Help system in action.

Figure 43.3.
The macro-enhanced
Help system.

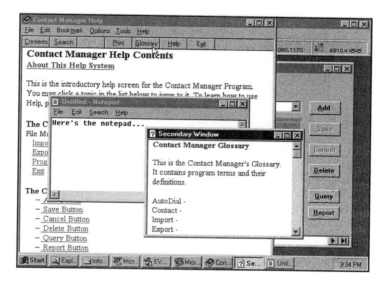

Essential Summary

In this chapter, you received a brief introduction to the more than 50 Help macros available in the WinHelp application. You received a detailed look at several of the more commonly used macros, and saw how they may be invoked to customize the way WinHelp works in conjunction with your own Help files.

What

WinHelp macros are a simple way to further customize and enhance your own Help systems. By using these macros, you are able to go beyond the default limits of the WinHelp engine and sort of dip into the power of C itself. If you require (or simply want) a Help system interface that sports its own unique menus, buttons, and specialized functionality, then you'll find these macros indispensable.

Why

You added new functionality to your Contact Manager Help system by calling upon the services of several Help macros. In the [CONFIG] section of your Help project file, you used InsertMenu() and AppendItem() to create a new Tools menu; and you used the CB() macro to add three custom buttons to the default button bar. You invoked other macros by referencing them in your RTF Help topic file. One macro, the About() macro, was attached to a text hot spot on your Help system's Contents page; another macro was footnoted in your Glossary topic so that it executed any time the topic was displayed.

How

Windows 95 Program Design Philosophy

One of the many ways in which Windows programs differ from DOS programs is that Windows programs provide a common and familiar user interface. This appendix is about the design conventions that Windows users will expect your programs to follow.

The people who use your Windows applications will have a set of design expectations they'll expect you to meet. Indeed, this has always been part of the attraction of Windows: If you know how to use one application, say a word processor, you can often learn to use others with little or no additional instruction. You should attempt to make your programs as intuitive as possible. A simple set of Windows skills—say clicking, selecting, dragging, and menu selection—should be sufficient to allow a new user to settle into your application and be at home. (In larger, specialized programs, this may be more idealism than reality.)

Another important aspect of good Windows design is that the user should be the one controlling the flow of the program, not the other way around.

You should try to give the user a complete visual representation of salient program choices whenever possible—a column of command buttons, for example, or a frame full of check boxes or option buttons. Be careful not to overwhelm the screen with objects, however; if your window is becoming crowded with buttons, put some options into menus. A good rule of thumb is that you should continually display only those options that will be in continual use.

Also, a well-designed Windows program will provide feedback to the user, keeping him or her informed as to the progress and status of operations. Do not allow your program to just "freeze" when a long process is under way; you should at least switch to the Hourglass cursor, or better, use a gauge or SSPanel control to graphically display the progress of the operation.

Finally, you should try to make your program robust. Your users should be confident that they have a useful tool that will perform efficiently and predictably. A *robust* program must be able to perform under a wide and sometimes unforeseen variety of conditions and inputs, *and must not fail!* If some kind of trappable error occurs, your program should handle it gracefully, using recovery code of some sort, and not simply halt with either a whimper *or* a bang.

Coming up is a look at a few of the accepted mouse, keyboard, and menu standards employed in most Windows applications.

Mouse Conventions

This section is not about large gatherings of tiny rodents. Rather, it focuses on the mouse actions that have become somewhat standardized in Windows applications. Of course, there's the familiar single-click, which makes a selection or activates a control; and the double-click, which is used to open an application or confirm a selection. As you know, most clicking is done with the left mouse button (although left-handed users can use the Control Panel to switch the buttons); but lately, more and more applications, including Windows 95 and Visual Basic 4.0 itself, are making use of a right mouse-click to activate pop-up menus associated with whatever object received the click. This right-click action may not yet qualify as a Windows convention, but it's well on its way to becoming one.

Here, in Table A.1, is a summary of common mouse actions and their descriptions.

Table A.1. Windows 95 mouse conventions.

Action	Description
Left-Click	Activates a control; makes a selection; or positions the insertion point within a block of text.
Right-Click	Opens a pop-up menu of action items related to the clicked object.
Double-Click	Activates a control; opens an application; or confirms a selection.

Action	Description
Ctrl-Click	In the selection process, toggles the current selection.
Shift-Click	In the selection process, extends the selection to the mouse pointer location.
Dragging	Moves a draggable control; encloses an area for selection; moves the selection.

Keyboard Conventions

Windows users almost always expect to have keyboard equivalents for everything that can be done with a mouse, the idea being that they should be able to use your application even if the mouse takes a holiday. With today's very sophisticated Windows applications, this expectation is not entirely realistic. For example, imagine trying to work efficiently, without a mouse, in Visual Basic. Still, you should try to provide as much keyboard functionality as possible. There are many standard keyboard operations in Windows; some of the most common are seen in Table A.2.

Table A.2. Windows 95 keyboard conventions.

Key	Standard Operation
Alt	Used with letters to create quick access keys.
Alt+F4	Closes current application.
Ctrl	Used with letters to create shortcut keys.
Ctrl+F4	Closes current window.
Ctrl+X	Shortcut: Quits an application.
End	Navigation: Moves to rightmost position of row.
Enter	Activates currently selected control.
Esc	Closes dialog box; exits current mode; cancels current selection.
F1	Activated Help System.
F10	Toggles menu bar.
Home	Navigation: Moves to leftmost position of row.
Tab	In text block, inserts Tab character; in dialog box, moves to next field or control in the tab order.
Shift+Tab	Reverses operation of Tab.

Menu Conventions

Windows applications usually employ a few standard menus, in addition to whatever menu choices may be unique to a particular program. In general, this is the expected order of standard menu names in the horizontal menu bar, at the top of the main window: File, Edit, View, Tools, Window, Help. Here's one last table, Table A.3, which lists the common menu items found in the File, Edit, Window, and Help menus:

Table A.3. Windows 95 menu conventions.

Menu	Menu Item	Description
File	New	Creates a new document.
	Open...	Displays an Open dialog box for selecting a document.
	Save	Saves the currently opened document.
	Save As...	Opens the Save As dialog box, for setting name, file type, and so on.
	Print...	Opens a Print dialog box, for setting Print options and Printing.
	Exit	Exits the application. (Every program should have this, at least.)
Edit	Undo	Reverses (undoes) the last operation.
	Cut	Cuts selection to the Clipboard.
	Copy	Copies selection to the Clipboard.
	Paste	Pastes from Clipboard to selection or current location.
	Find...	Opens a Find dialog box, for locating text or filenames.
	Replace...	Opens a Replace dialog box, for searching and replacing.
Window	Cascade	Arranges open MDI child windows in a cascading format, like a fanned deck of cards, or slices of ham on a deli platter.
	Tile	Arranges open MDI child windows so that each is visible and of the same size.
	Split	Splits current window into two or more panes, either horizontally or vertically, depending on selection.
Help	Contents	Displays a list of your program's available Help topics.

Menu	*Menu Item*	*Description*
	Search	Opens Search dialog box, to locate a particular Help topic.
	Index	Displays an Index of your program's Help topics.
	About...	Displays About dialog box, providing author, copyright, and licensing information for your application.

ndex

Add to Your Sams Library Today with the Best Books for Programming, Operating Systems, and New Technologies

The easiest way to order is to pick up the phone and call

1-800-428-5331

between 9:00 a.m. and 5:00 p.m. EST.

For faster service please have your credit card available.

ISBN	Quantity	Description of Item	Unit Cost	Total Cost
0-672-30602-6		Programming Windows 95 Unleashed (Book/CD)	$49.99	
0-672-30474-0		Windows 95 Unleashed (Book/CD)	$35.00	
0-672-30611-5		Your Windows 95 Consultant, Pre-Release Edition	$19.99	
0-672-30685-9		Windows NT 3.5 Unleashed, Second Edition	$39.99	
0-672-30765-0		Navigating the Internet with Windows 95	$25.00	
0-672-30568-2		Teach Yourself OLE Programming in 21 Days (Book/CD)	$39.99	
0-672-30619-0		Real-World Programming with Visual Basic (Book/CD)	$45.00	
0-672-30594-1		Programming WinSock (Book/Disk)	$35.00	
0-672-30655-7		Developing Your Own 32-Bit Operating System (Book/CD)	$49.99	
0-672-30596-8		Develop a Professional Visual Basic Application in 21 Days (Book/CD)	$35.00	
0-672-30737-5		World Wide Web Unleashed, Second Edition	$35.00	
❏ 3 ½" Disk		Shipping and Handling: See information below.		
❏ 5 ¼" Disk		TOTAL		

Shipping and Handling: $4.00 for the first book, and $1.75 for each additional book. Floppy disk: add $1.75 for shipping and handling. If you need to have it NOW, we can ship product to you in 24 hours for an additional charge of approximately $18.00, and you will receive your item overnight or in two days. Overseas shipping and handling adds $2.00 per book and $8.00 for up to three disks. Prices subject to change. Call for availability and pricing information on latest editions.

201 W. 103rd Street, Indianapolis, Indiana 46290

1-800-428-5331 — Orders   **1-800-835-3202 — FAX**   **1-800-858-7674 — Customer Service**

Book ISBN 0-672-30771-5

PLUG YOURSELF INTO...

THE MACMILLAN INFORMATION SUPERLIBRARY™

Free information and vast computer resources from the world's leading computer book publisher—online!

FIND THE BOOKS THAT ARE RIGHT FOR YOU!

A complete online catalog, plus sample chapters and tables of contents give you an in-depth look at *all* of our books, including hard-to-find titles. It's the best way to find the books you need!

● STAY INFORMED with the latest computer industry news through our online newsletter, press releases, and customized Information SuperLibrary Reports.

● GET FAST ANSWERS to your questions about MCP books and software.

● VISIT our online bookstore for the latest information and editions!

● COMMUNICATE with our expert authors through e-mail and conferences.

● DOWNLOAD SOFTWARE from the immense MCP library:
   - Source code and files from MCP books
   - The best shareware, freeware, and demos

● DISCOVER HOT SPOTS on other parts of the Internet.

● WIN BOOKS in ongoing contests and giveaways!

TO PLUG INTO MCP: ➜ WORLD WIDE WEB: **http://www.mcp.com**

GOPHER: gopher.mcp.com

FTP: ftp.mcp.com